W9-AWN-572

Fodor's 05

CAPE COD

Where to Stay and Eat
for All Budgets

Must-See Sights
and Local Secrets

Ratings You Can Trust

Fodor's Travel Publications   New York, Toronto, London, Sydney, Auckland
www.fodors.com

CAPE COD 2005
Editor: Jessica E. Lee

Editorial Production: Jenna L. Bagnini
Editorial Contributors: Andrew Collins, Lori A. Nolin, James Rohlf
Maps: David Lindroth, *cartographer;* Bob Blake and Rebecca Baer, *map editors*
Design: Fabrizio La Rocca, *creative director;* Moon Sun Kim, *cover design;* Guido Caroti, *art director;* Melanie Marin, *senior photo editor*
Cover Photo (Boys catching marine life with net, Cape Cod): Jeff Greenberg/Index Stock Imagery
Production/Manufacturing: Robert B. Shields

ISBN 1–4000–1453–0

ISSN 1542–3476

SPECIAL SALES
This book is available for special discounts for bulk purchases for sales promotions or premiums. Special editions, including personalized covers, excerpts of existing books, and corporate imprints, can be created in large quantities for special needs. For more information, write to Special Markets/Premium Sales, 1745 Broadway, MD 6-2, New York, New York 10019, or e-mail specialmarkets@randomhouse.com.

AN IMPORTANT TIP & AN INVITATION
Although all prices, opening times, and other details in this book are based on information supplied to us at press time, changes occur all the time in the travel world, and Fodor's cannot accept responsibility for facts that become outdated or for inadvertent errors or omissions. So **always confirm information when it matters,** especially if you're making a detour to visit a specific place. Your experiences—positive and negative—matter to us. If we have missed or misstated something, **please write to us.** We follow up on all suggestions. Contact the Cape Cod editor at editors@fodors.com or c/o Fodor's at 1745 Broadway, New York, New York 10019.

PRINTED IN THE UNITED STATES OF AMERICA

10 9 8 7 6 5 4 3 2 1

CONTENTS

CloseUps

ON THE ROAD WITH FODOR'S

At Fodor's we make sure that you know all your options, so that you don't miss something that's around the next bend just because you didn't know it was there. Because the best memories of your trip might well have nothing to do with what you came to Cape Cod to see, we guide you to sights large and small all over the region. You might set out to see Cape Cod's most fascinating small museum, but back at home you find yourself unable to forget that quirky crafts gallery or cozy clam shack. With Fodor's at your side, serendipitous discoveries are never far away.

Our success in showing you every corner of Cape Cod is a credit to our extraordinary writers. Although there's no substitute for travel advice from a good friend who knows your style, our contributors are the next best thing.

Former Fodor's staff editor Andrew Collins grew up in New England and has visited and written about the Outer Cape for many years in *Fodor's Gay Guide to the USA* and several newspapers and magazines. He contributes regularly to *Travel & Leisure, Sunset, Frommer's Budget Travel,* and *New Mexico Magazine,* and he teaches a course on travel writing for New York City's Gotham Writers' Workshop.

Just weeks old, from the comfort of a car seat, Lori A. Nolin waited and wailed through the weekend traffic from Rhode Island to make it over the bridge to North Truro. Unable to shake the sand from her shoes, she moved to Cape Cod eight years ago to work as a news reporter. She is now a freelance writer and editor living in West Harwich. Her writing has appeared in the *Cape Cod Community Newspapers, Barnstable Patriot, Primetime Magazine,* and the *Cape Cod Times.* She still wails in Cape traffic.

An experimental high-energy physicist and professor of physics at Boston University, James W. Rohlf lived and worked in Europe for more than a decade before migrating to Cape Cod, where he's indulged his passions for sailing, lobstering, and his family for 13 years and counting. He has written about travel for *Cape Cod Life* and his work has also appeared in the *Cape Cod Times.*

Our thanks to Glenn M. Faria and Bill DeSousa of Michael Patrick Destinations & Communications, Ltd., for their assistance.

ABOUT THIS BOOK

The best source for travel advice is a like-minded friend who's just been where you're headed. But with or without that friend, you'll be in great shape to find your way around your destination once you learn to find your way around your Fodor's guide.

SELECTION
Our goal is to cover the best properties, sights, and activities in their category, as well as the most interesting communities to visit. We make a point of including local food-lovers' hot spots as well as neighborhood options, and we avoid all that's touristy unless it's really worth your time. You can go on the assumption that everything in this book is recommended wholeheartedly by our writers and editors. Flip to On the Road with Fodor's to learn more about who they are. It goes without saying that no property pays to be included.

RATINGS
Orange stars ★ denote sights and properties that our editors and writers consider the very best in the area covered by the entire book. These, the best of the best, are listed in the Fodor's Choice section in the front of the book. Black stars ★ highlight the sights and properties we deem Highly Recommended, the don't-miss sights within any region. Use the index to find complete descriptions. In cities, sights pinpointed with numbered map bullets ❶ in the margins tend to be more important than those without bullets.

SPECIAL SPOTS
Pleasures & Pastimes and text on chapter title pages focus on experiences that reveal the spirit of the destination. Also watch for Off the Beaten Path sights. Some are out of the way, some are quirky, and all are worthwhile. When the munchies hit, look for Need a Break? suggestions.

TIME IT RIGHT
Wondering when to go? Check On the Calendar up front.

SEE IT ALL
Use Fodor's exclusive Great Itineraries, at the beginning of each chapter, as a model for your trip. In cities, Good Walks guide you to important sights in each neighborhood; ⌐ indicates the starting points of walks and itineraries in the text and on the map.

BUDGET WELL
Hotel and restaurant price categories from ¢ to $$$$ are defined in the opening pages of each chapter. For attractions, we always give standard adult admission fees; reductions are usually available for children, students, and senior citizens. Look in Discounts & Deals in Smart Travel Tips for information on destination-wide ticket schemes. Want to pay with plastic? AE, D, DC, MC, V following restaurant and hotel listings indicate whether American Express, Discover, Diner's Club, MasterCard, or Visa are accepted.

BASIC INFO
Smart Travel Tips lists travel essentials for the entire area covered by the book; city- and region-specific basics end each chapter. To find the best way to get around, see the transportation section; see indi-

vidual modes of travel ("Car Travel," "Train Travel") for details. We assume you'll check Web sites or call for particulars.

ON THE MAPS	Maps throughout the book show you what's where and help you find your way around. Black and orange numbered bullets ❶ ① in the text correlate to bullets on maps.
BACKGROUND	In general, we give background information within the chapters as well as in CloseUp boxes and in Understanding Cape Cod.
FIND IT FAST	Within the book, chapters are arranged regionally. Chapters are divided into smaller regions, within which towns are covered in logical geographical order; attractive routes and interesting places between towns are flagged as En Route.
DON'T FORGET	Restaurants are open for lunch and dinner daily unless we state otherwise; we mention dress only when there's a requirement and reservations only when they're essential or not accepted—it's always best to book ahead. Hotels have private baths, phones, TVs, and air-conditioning and operate on the European Plan (aka EP, meaning without meals) unless we state otherwise. We always list facilities but not extra charges for them, so find out what's included.

SYMBOLS

Many Listings

★ Fodor's Choice
★ Highly recommended
⊠ Physical address
✛ Directions
⊄ℙ Mailing address
☎ Telephone
🖷 Fax
⊕ On the Web
✉ E-mail
☜ Admission fee
◷ Open/closed times
► Start of walk/itinerary
Ⓜ Metro stations
▭ Credit cards

Outdoors

🏌 Golf
⛺ Camping

Hotels & Restaurants

🏨 Hotel
🛏 Number of rooms
♿ Facilities
🍽 Meal plans
✕ Restaurant
🍸 Reservations
🎩 Dress code
☒ Smoking
🍷 BYOB
✕🏨 Hotel with restaurant that warrants a visit

Other

☺ Family-friendly
🎯 Contact information
⇨ See also
✉ Branch address
☞ Take note

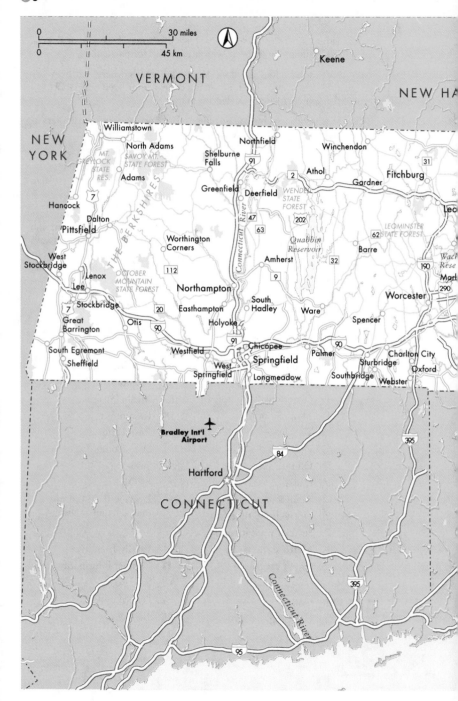

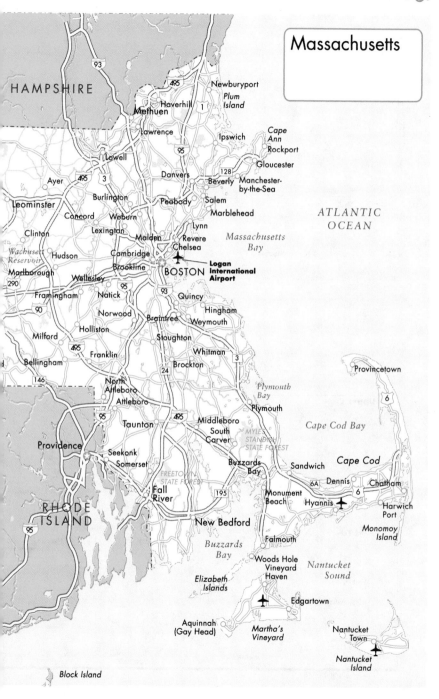

Massachusetts

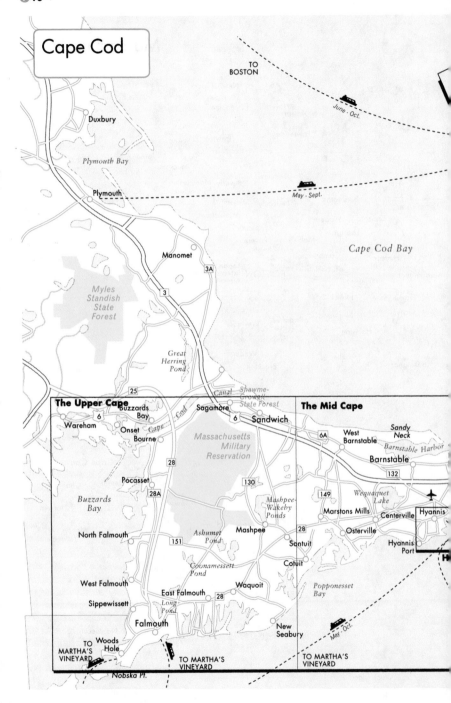

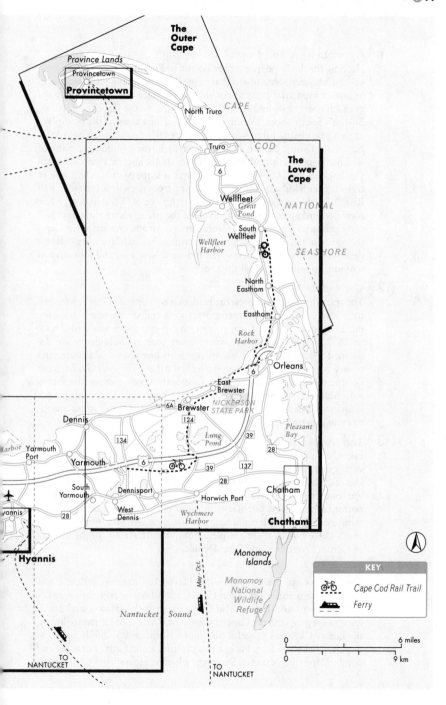

The Outer Cape

Province Lands
Provincetown
Provincetown

North Truro

CAPE

Truro

6

COD

The Lower Cape

Wellfleet
Great Pond

NATIONAL

South Wellfleet

Wellfleet Harbor

SEASHORE

North Eastham

Eastham

Rock Harbor

Orleans

6

East Brewster

6A   Brewster
124

NICKERSON STATE PARK

Dennis

134

Long Pond

Pleasant Bay

39

28

Harbor   Yarmouth Port

Yarmouth   6

39

137

South Yarmouth

Dennisport

Harwich Port

28

annis

28

West Dennis

Wychmere Harbor

Chatham

Chatham

Hyannis

Monomoy Islands

Monomoy National Wildlife Refuge

Nantucket Sound

May.-Oct.

KEY

Cape Cod Rail Trail

Ferry

0   6 miles
0   9 km

TO NANTUCKET

TO NANTUCKET

WHAT'S WHERE

① Approaching the Cape

Heading for the Cape from either Boston or Providence, you pass south-eastern Massachusetts towns that range from intriguing historic villages to former industrial cities to bucolic seaside communities with perhaps as much charm as—and far fewer crowds than—the Cape itself. Along Boston's South Shore, the city of Quincy claims fame as the birthplace of two presidents, John Adams and John Quincy Adams. The Adams National Historic Park is composed of 11 historic buildings, many of which are open to the public. A bit farther south, historic Plymouth takes you back to the 1600s and is well worth a stop, particularly if you're traveling with kids. If you're approaching from the south and west, Fall River's Battleship Cove provides a floating piece of WWII history, while New Bedford gives a powerful image of the country's whaling days and early industrial era. Along the southeastern coast and onward to the Cape, the communities of Westport, South Dartmouth, and Marion are seafront destinations that hark back to the old-time New England pleasures of seafood, summertime, and the shore.

② The Upper Cape

The sprawling region nearest the bridges is perhaps the Cape's most historic area and its most contemporary area rolled into one. Along the northern bay side lie the Cape's oldest towns—Sandwich was settled back in 1637. Nearby Mashpee, where more than 600 residents are descended from the original Wampanoags, is one of two Massachusetts towns with Native American–governed areas. The west coast from Bourne through North and West Falmouth mixes residential suburbs with hidden coves and beaches lining the bay, while Falmouth proper is an established year-round community with all the suburban amenities you'd expect.

③ The Mid Cape

Like the Upper Cape, the Mid Cape region has a northern shore lined with quiet, historic villages, in this case Barnstable, Yarmouth, and Dennis. There's more hubbub, traffic, taffy, and all that's tacky along the southern coast. Hyannis, the Cape's geographic center and transportation nucleus, is popular with those who like to be in the thick of things; dining and entertainment options are many. Still, even amid the south-shore bustle, there are plenty of quiet attractions in the villages of Cotuit, Osterville, and West Dennis.

④ The Lower Cape

The Lower Cape towns of Brewster, Harwich, Chatham, Orleans, and Eastham are reminiscent of old Cape Cod. While the population swells in these towns as it has on Mid Cape, the growth is slower and building is in keeping with the Cape of yesteryear. A fine area for nature lovers, the Lower Cape has peaceful Monomoy National Wildlife Refuge, the popular Nickerson State Park, and a plentiful assortment of beaches and ponds. Cape Cod National Seashore, which stretches from Chatham to

Provincetown, begins here; Salt Pond Visitor Center is in Eastham. The area also has plenty of fine restaurants and attractive shops.

(5) The Outer Cape

The narrow "forearm" of the Cape—less than 2 mi wide between Cape Cod Bay and the Atlantic Ocean in some spots—includes two of the Cape's least-developed areas, Wellfleet and Truro. This is the Cape of dunes and beach grasses, of crashing surf and scrubby pines—the Cape that most attracts creative minds and seekers of solitude. But there's action here, too, at the Cape's "fist," in bohemian Provincetown, where the dunes give way to a summer scene packed with nightlife, art, food, and fun.

WHEN TO GO

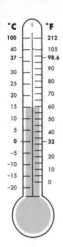

°C		°F
100		212
40		105
37		98.6
30		90
25		80
20		70
15		60
10		50
5		40
0		32
-5		20
-10		10
-15		0
-20		

Memorial Day through Labor Day (or, in some cases, Columbus Day) is high season on Cape Cod. This is summer with a capital *S*, a time for barbecues, beach bumming, swimming, and water sports. In summer everything is open for business on the Cape, but you can also expect high-season evils: high prices, crowds, and traffic.

The Cape, however, is increasingly a year-round destination. *See* The Cape's Six Seasons *in* Chapter 7 for some highlights of the off-season.

Climate

The following are average daily maximum and minimum temperatures for Hyannis.

🎿 Forecasts **Weather Channel** ⊕ www.weather.com.

For local Cape weather, coastal marine forecasts, and today's tide times, call the weather line of **WQRC** ☎ 508/771-5522 in Hyannis.

HYANNIS

Jan.	40F	4C	May	62F	17C	Sept.	70F	21C
	25	-4		48	9		56	13
Feb.	41F	5C	June	71F	22C	Oct.	59F	15C
	26	-3		56	13		47	8
Mar.	42F	6C	July	78F	26C	Nov.	49F	9C
	28	-2		63	17		37	3
Apr.	53F	12C	Aug.	76F	24C	Dec.	40F	4C
	40	4		61	16		26	-3

The Massachusetts Office of Travel & Tourism offers events listings and a whale-watch guide for the entire state. Also see the events calendar in "CapeWeek," an arts-and-entertainment supplement published every Friday in the *Cape Cod Times*; it's available online at ⊕ www.capeweek.com

WINTER

Early December

Many Cape towns do up the Christmas season in grand style. To take in the best-known celebration, plan an excursion to the nearby island of Nantucket for the annual Christmas Stroll (☎ 508/228–1700 ⊕ www.nantucket-stroll.com), which takes place the first weekend of the month. Carolers and musicians entertain strollers as they walk the festive cobblestone streets and sample shops' wares and seasonal refreshments. Activities include theatrical performances, art exhibitions, crafts sales, and a tour of historic homes. To avoid the throngs, visit on one of the surrounding weekends (festivities begin the day after Thanksgiving and last through New Year's Eve).

Various Cape towns also have holiday strolls; call the Cape Cod Chamber of Commerce (☎ 508/862–0700) for a free brochure.

Falmouth's Christmas by the Sea (☎ 508/548–8500 or 800/526–8532), the first full weekend of December, includes lighting ceremonies at the Village Green, caroling at Nobska Light in Woods Hole, a house tour, church fairs, and a parade.

December

Chatham's Christmas by the Sea weekend (☎ 508/945–5199), generally the first weekend of the month, includes caroling and other special events. The events are part of a monthlong celebration beginning just after Thanksgiving and ending with a lavish First Night celebration, with fireworks over Oyster Pond on New Year's Eve.

SPRING

Late April

The weekend-long Brewster in Bloom (☎ 508/896–3500 ⊕ www.brewsterinbloom.com) greets the spring season with a daffodil fest each year during the last weekend in April. Geared to promote small-town life, the festival includes arts-and-crafts shows, a parade, tours of historic homes and inns, a golf tournament, and a giant antiques and collectibles market.

Mid-May

The Green Briar Nature Center and Jam Kitchen in Sandwich holds its annual Green Briar Herb Festival (☎ 508/888–6870), where you can pick up perennials, wildflowers, and dozens of herb varieties.

During Cape Cod Maritime Week (☎ 508/362–3828 ⊕ www.capecodcommission.org/hdn) lighthouse tours, guided shorefront walks, and special exhibits Cape-wide help celebrate the Cape's maritime history.

SUMMER	
June–August	Summer theater, town-band concerts, and arts-and-crafts fairs enliven most every Cape town.
Early June	The Cape Cod Antique Dealers Association Annual Antiques Show (☎ 508/888–3300) at Sandwich's Heritage Plantation is attended by 50 dealers of fine 18th- and 19th-century English and American furniture, folk art, Sandwich glass, jewelry, paintings, and quilts.
Mid- to late June	The Portuguese Festival (☎ 508/487–3424) honors Provincetown's Portuguese heritage with a lively weekend of ethnic foods and crafts, bands playing in the streets, a children's fishing derby, traditional dances, fireworks, and other events.
	The Blessing of the Fleet in Provincetown concludes the Portuguese Festival weekend. On Sunday, a parade ends at the wharf, where anglers and their families and friends pile onto boats and form a procession. The bishop stands on the dock and blesses the boats with holy water as they pass by.
	Falmouth welcomes the Soundfest Chamber Music Festival (☎ 508/548–2290 ⊕ www.coloradoquartet.com), including the Colorado Quartet and guest artists. Daily events during the two-week festival include student performances, concerts, master classes, and lectures.
July 4 weekend	The Mashpee Powwow (☎ 508/477–0208) brings together Wampanoags from North and South America for three days of dance contests, drumming, a fireball game, and a clambake, plus the crowning of the Mashpee Wampanoag Indian princess on the final night.
	Fireworks displays are a part of July 4 celebrations in several Cape towns.
Mid-July	The Barnstable County Fair (☎ 508/563–3200 ⊕ www.barnstablecountyfair.org) in East Falmouth, begun in 1844, is Cape Cod's biggest event. The nine-day affair includes livestock and food judging; horse, pony, and oxen pulls and shows; arts-and-crafts demonstrations; carnival rides; lots of food; and appearances by the formerly famous bent on comebacks.
Late July	The Cape Cod Symphony Orchestra sets up at the Mashpee Commons for the first of two annual Sounds of Summer Pops Concerts (☎ 508/362–1111).
August	The Cape & Islands Chamber Music Festival (☎ 508/945–8060 or 800/818–0608 ⊕ www.capecodchambermusic.org) is three weeks of top-caliber performances, including a jazz night, at various locations in August. The festival also sponsors an off-season concert series; call or check the Web site for the schedule.
Early August	The Boston Pops Esplanade Orchestra wows the crowds with its annual Pops by the Sea concert (☎ 508/362–0066 ⊕ www.

artsfoundationcapecod.org), held at the Hyannis Village Green at 5 PM. Each year a guest conductor strikes up the band.

New Bedford's Feast of the Blessed Sacrament (☎ 508/979–1745 or 800/508-5353 ⊕ www.portuguesefeast.com) is one of the largest celebrations of Portuguese culture in the country. Music, dance, a parade, carnival rides, and traditional foods—particularly the giant *carne de espeto* outdoor barbecue—are all part of the four-day event.

Mid-August	The Falmouth Road Race (🖂 Box 732, Falmouth 02541 ☎ 508/ 540–7000 ⊕ www.falmouthroadrace.com) is a world-class race covering the coast from Woods Hole to Falmouth Heights; to participate, apply by mail the fall or winter prior to the race.
Late August	The Cape Cod Symphony Orchestra comes to Eldridge Field Park in Orleans for its Sounds of Summer Pops Concert (☎ 508/362–1111).
	The annual New England Jazz Festival (☎ 508/477–2580 ⊕ www. bochcenterarts.com), produced by the Boch Center for the Performing Arts, takes place at Mashpee Commons.
	The Osterville Historical Society holds its annual antiques show (☎ 508/428–5861) on the third or fourth Thursday in August.

FALL

September	The Annual Bourne Scallop Fest (☎ 508/759–6000) attracts thousands of people to Buzzards Bay for three days of music, parades, carnival rides, and, of course, fried scallops.
	The Harwich Cranberry Festival (☎ 508/430–2811 ⊕ www. harwichcranberryfestival.com) includes an arts-and-crafts show, a carnival, fireworks, pancake breakfasts, an antique-car show, and much more.
Mid-October	During Seafest (☎ 508/945–5199) an annual tribute to the maritime industry, Chatham Light is open to the public.
Late October	Fall foliage. The leaf season usually peaks around the end of October. Colors might flame a few weeks earlier or later, however, depending on the weather the preceding months.
	Thanksgiving Eve The Lighting of the Monument festivities ☎ 508/ 487–1310 commemorate the Pilgrims' landing, with the lighting of 5,000 white and gold bulbs draped over the Pilgrim Monument. The lighting occurs each night until just after the New Year. A musical performance accompanies the lighting, and the monument museum holds an open house and tours. Other events include dramatic readings of the Mayflower Compact (which was signed in Provincetown Harbor), fireworks, and numerous Thanksgiving dinner celebrations. Various arts-and-crafts events kick off around the same time and continue through the holiday season.

PLEASURES & PASTIMES

Beaches Cape Cod has more than 150 ocean and freshwater beaches, with something for just about every taste. Bay-side beaches generally have more temperate waters and gentle waves. South-side beaches, on Nantucket Sound, have rolling surf and, though still on the chilly side, are moderated by the Gulf Stream. The inland areas of the Cape are dotted with numerous freshwater ponds, many with warm water and sandy beaches that are ideal for young children. Ocean beaches on the Cape Cod National Seashore have cold water and serious surf, and are, by and large, superior—wide, long, sandy, and dune backed, with great views. They're also contiguous: you can walk from Eastham to Provincetown practically without leaving sand. This almost always ensures privacy, if you stroll far enough away from crowds. From late July through August, Outer Cape beaches are sometimes troubled with red algae in the water, which, while harmless, can be annoying; check with the Cape Cod National Seashore about conditions. To mitigate the crowd factor, arrive either early in the morning or later in the afternoon. Parking lots tend to fill up by 10 AM in summer.

In season you have to pay for parking at public beaches; parking at restricted beaches is open to residents and visitors with permits (⇨ Beaches *in* Smart Travel Tips A to Z). Walkers and bicyclists can enter these restricted beaches without permits, however. From the last June weekend ending before July 1 through Labor Day is the latest official take on what constitutes the season's boundaries. Although parking is usually free in the off-season, you'll probably also find snack bars closed and lifeguards nowhere to be found.

Biking Biking on the Cape will satisfy avid and occasional cyclists alike. There are plenty of flat back roads, as well as a number of well-developed bike trails. The Cape's top bike path, the Cape Cod Rail Trail, offers a scenic ride through the area. Following the paved right-of-way of the old Penn Central Railroad, it's about 25-mi long, stretching from South Dennis to South Wellfleet. The Cape Cod National Seashore maintains three bicycle trails. The head of the Meadow Trail is 2 mi of easy cycling between dunes and salt marshes from High Head Road, off Route 6A in North Truro, to the Head of the Meadow Beach parking lot. Province Lands Trail is a 5¼-mi loop off the Beech Forest parking lot on Race Point Road in Provincetown, with spurs to the Herring Cove and Race Point beaches and to Bennett Pond. The paths wind up and down hills amid dunes, marshes, woods, and ponds and offer spectacular views—on an exceptionally clear day, you can see the Boston skyline. There's a picnic grove at Pilgrim Spring. Nickerson State Park in Brewster has 8 mi of trails through forest.

Conservation Areas Bustle and noise may seem unavoidable on a Cape vacation, but you can find a surefire escape at one of the numerous nature refuges. There you can delight in seeing an osprey nest, the slow-motion stalking of a great blue heron, the head of a river otter coursing through the water, great shorebird colonies, a meadow in late summer, or that stray berry-studded blueberry bush. This is simply the best way to experience the vitality and diversity of the region.

Flora and fauna of local interest are beach-plum bushes, which bloom in late May and bear fruit in fall; the spring-blooming, white-flower shadbush and its red-purple June berries; shade- and moisture-loving cinnamon ferns; June-blooming pasture roses and the lovely rugosa roses, which bloom throughout the summer; the brilliant orange butterfly weed, so named for the affinity monarch butterflies have for the nectar of its summer flowers; the fragrant midsummer blooms of the sweet pepper bush; blueberry and huckleberry bushes; the low-slung, waxy-leaf, dark-green teaberry, with its early fall red berries; fall-flowering seaside goldenrod and sea lavender; caribou moss, also near the sea; the plentiful beach grass (which you should avoid treading on in order to keep it plentiful); oval-leaf bayberry bushes, whose scent is a wintertime household delight; and tupelo, sassafras, pygmy beech, cottonwood, Norway spruce, red cedar, pitch pine, tamarack, and numerous other trees. Unfortunately, you need to watch out for poison ivy, that invasive spoiler of human comfort (its berries are a great boon to birds, however).

As for wildlife, there are hawks and harriers, ospreys, pheasants, quail, numerous ducks and geese, terns, bobwhites, meadowlarks, catbirds, towhees, swallows, orioles, goldfinches, yellowthroats, warblers, and more spring and fall migrants than can be mentioned; a kingdom of mollusks and sea creatures—horseshoe, hermit, fiddler, and blue crabs; oysters; scallops; quahogs; and so on; and rabbits, raccoons, otter, muskrats, mice, and deer. From beach to marsh to meadow to salt-sprayed sand plains, the number of habitats is tremendous.

Note: Along with the poison ivy alert, check yourself for deer ticks after a day's walk or hike in the outdoors.

Where to Eat Cape Cod received its name from the thickness of the schools of cod that early explorers found around its shores. These days the ominous local joke is that the peninsula should be renamed, except there is no alternative species certain to be around for the next few generations. But don't give up hope and expect to eat steaks. Plenty of great seafood can still be had, and here's one encouraging little secret: largely because of strict federal regulations, codfish have been making a quiet but remarkable comeback in the past few years. You'll see more and more cod on the menus, and it will be fresh.

Many Cape fisherfolk took a look at the offshore problems and decided to become less hunter and more farmer. Some have moved into aquaculture, staking grants along the tidal flats of Cape Cod Bay and planting quahogs or oysters. These shellfish are not fed any artificial food, and they aren't laced with any chemicals. They are simply planted in one area, protected from predators, and harvested when they reach market size. As a result, fresh shellfish is a great bet at restaurants and markets. If you buy some littlenecks or quahogs, turn the shell over and see if there are little rays or lines of lighter color radiating from the base of the shell. If so, you've gotten a cultured clam, known by scientists as a "notata." They're as sweet to eat as their wild cousins.

Traditionally, Cape restaurants have not favored fancy sauces or sophisticated cooking techniques. Now there's a younger generation of Cape Cod chefs who aren't afraid to bring more ingredients and international influence to the table, who know that if they keep everything else on the plate as fresh as the fish, the results can be truly memorable. This approach has tended to drive the price of dinner ever higher. Prices have not reached chic New York levels by a long shot, but good Cape restaurants are charging as much as many good Boston restaurants—and delivering equally impressive quality.

The other emerging trend at many Cape restaurants is toward a menu that runs up and down the price ladder. Except for at the most elegant spots, it's common to find both expensive full dinners and fancy burgers and eclectic pizzas side by side. This can help hold down the price of an evening out.

That said, there's a—you name it—Lobster Pot/Trap/Claw/Bowl/Net in every town. These restaurants are still authentic and great to go to with a family, although there's no place left where good seafood could be called inexpensive. And if you order lobster, you're likely to find its price to be easily the highest on the menu. You don't need to be a stodgy traditionalist to agree that the fry-o-lators in many home-style seafood restaurants and clam shacks impart the real lusciousness to classic Cape Cod cooking. For a quintessential summertime Cape experience, nothing beats simple standbys. The standard summer lunch is a lobster roll—a very light lobster salad with practically no mayonnaise on a plain white frankfurter roll.

At dinnertime dress is largely casual. According to legend, one older Cape Codder takes this edict so seriously that he chops off any ties he sees and adorns his cabin in Chatham with the remains. But in certain dining rooms—such as Chillingsworth or the Dan'l Webster Inn or Chatham Bars Inn—a sports coat is virtually mandatory.

Increasingly, onetime seasonal restaurants are remaining open year-round, even if they scale back in winter. Finally, note that many towns on the Cape do not allow smoking inside any restaurant, and a few have also banned lighting up in bars; Provincetown recently prohibited smoking in both venues. Such bans are strictly enforced, so if you see some people standing outside your restaurant of choice in one of these towns, they may not be in line for a table but may be taking a puff in the open air.

Where to Stay
With a tourism-based economy, the Cape naturally abounds in lodgings, including self-contained luxury resorts, grand old oceanfront hotels, chain hotels, mom-and-pop motels, antiques-filled bed-and-breakfasts, cottages, condominiums, and apartments. If you're planning to stay a week or longer, renting a house is another popular option.

Choosing where you want to stay will depend on the kind of vacation you have in mind. If you love the beach, think about whether you'd rather stay near the dune-backed National Seashore, where waters are coldest, or near the somewhat warmer south-shore waters. The National Seashore is less developed and great for walking, while the Mid Cape and Falmouth beaches most often are more circumscribed and more crowded with families.

Sandwich and other towns along the north-shore Route 6A Historic District have quiet, traditional villages with old-Cape touches and charming B&Bs. If you want more action, head for the Mid Cape. Hyannis is the center of it all, with a busy Main Street, active nightlife, and some fine beaches.

For the austere Cape of dunes and sea, try the beach cottages of the sparsely developed Lower Cape between Wellfleet and Provincetown. P-town itself is something completely different: in summer a frantic wall-to-wall jumble of shops and houses bursting with a large contingent of lesbians and gay men, along with a hopping nighttime scene. Staying in town makes getting to everything by foot or bike possible.

FODOR'S CHOICE

The sights, restaurants, hotels, and other travel experiences on these pages are our editors' top picks—our Fodor's Choices. They're the best of their type in the area covered by the book—not to be missed and always worth your time. In the destination chapters that follow, you can find all the details.

LODGING

$$$$	**Scallop Shell Inn, Falmouth.** Breakfast is a feast at this swank inn that's just one block from the sea.
$$$$	**Wequassett Inn Resort & Golf Club, Chatham.** Great restaurants, attentive service, and expansive facilities are the attraction at this elegant, upscale resort.
$$$–$$$$	**Augustus Snow House, Harwich Port.** This elegant Victorian inn takes you back to another era, with a tearoom where you can savor afternoon tea on weekends.
$$$–$$$$	**Capt. Farris House, South Yarmouth.** Large rooms and suites have either antique or canopied beds at this imposing 1845 Greek Revival home.
$$$–$$$$	**Captain's House Inn, Chatham.** Friendly and professional service, colonial feel, and wonderful old buildings make this one of the Cape's most pleasant B&Bs.
$$$–$$$$	**Crowne Pointe Historic Inn, Provincetown.** One of the top small luxury hotels on the Cape, the Crowne Pointe furthered its sterling image in 2004 with the addition of a supremely sumptuous day spa. It's one of the few centrally located properties in town with a pool, and the rooms contain every cushy amenity you could want.
$$$–$$$$	**Pelham House, Dennisport.** For its striking views, spacious rooms, and prime location, Pelham House is worth the splurge.
$$–$$$$	**Martin House, Provincetown.** Set inside a diminutive 18th-century cottage, Martin House serves fine contemporary American food that's right out of the 21st century. The New England seafood paella with lobster, littlenecks, chorizo, corn, peas, and blood orange-tomato nage on saffron rice is legendary.
$$–$$$$	**Surf Side Colony Cottages, Wellfleet.** Few accommodations on the Outer Cape afford better ocean views than these dapper cottages, many of them designed in hip retro-Florida style with pastel shingles and flat roofs, some with decks on top of them. Available only on a weekly basis, they're ideal for families or friends traveling together.
$$$	**Moses Nickerson House, Chatham.** Luxurious amenities and well-landscaped grounds set this inn apart.

$$-$$$ | **Isaiah Hall B&B Inn, Dennis.** Lilacs and pink roses trail along the white picket fence outside this historic and romantic 1857 Greek Revival farmhouse.

$$-$$$ | **Seadar Inn, Harwich.** The beachside location and views of Nantucket Sound are the draw at the Seadar Inn.

$-$$$ | **Christopher's by the Bay, Provincetown.** The four shared-bath units at this classy guesthouse are among the best summer bargains on the Outer Cape. And even the five rooms with private bath are a relatively good value, many of them offering a glimpse of Cape Cod Bay.

BUDGET LODGING

¢-$$$ | **Old Sea Pines Inn, Brewster.** Relax on the wraparound veranda or in the enclosed sunporch at this charming B&B.

RESTAURANTS

$$$-$$$$ | **Chillingsworth, Brewster.** Generally regarded as the crown jewel of Cape restaurants, Chillingsworth has a formal presentation, excellent French menu, and diverse wine cellar.

$$-$$$$ | **Abba, Orleans.** Come to this sophisticated restaurant or visit its café next door for fine cuisine with touches of exotic flavor.

$$-$$$$ | **The Paddock, Hyannis.** Synonymous with excellent formal dining on the Cape, the Paddock has sumptuous upholstery in its main dining room and, for a change of pace, old-style wicker on its breezy summer porch.

$$-$$$$ | **Red Pheasant, Dennis.** This is one of the Cape's best cozy country inns, with a consistently good kitchen, where hearty American food is prepared with elaborate sauces and herb combinations.

$$-$$$ | **The Back Eddy, Westport.** On your way to the Cape, stop by for superb seafood—from classic preparations to sophisticated contemporary variations—at this casual harborside treasure.

$$-$$$ | **Bleu, Mashpee.** Chef Frederic Feufeu, a native of the Loire Valley, brings a little bit of France to Cape Cod.

$$-$$$ | **Brewster Fish House, Brewster.** Long overshadowed by its pricier neighbors, the Fish House finally has carved a niche for itself with such Cape Cod standards as classic scrod and New England boiled dinner.

$$-$$$ | **Inaho, Yarmouth Port.** The careful presentation, informed service, and serene surroundings create an ideal backdrop for first-rate sushi and sashimi and other artfully prepared Japanese dishes.

$$-$$$ | **Roadhouse Café, Hyannis.** Candlelight flickers off the white-linen tablecloths and dark-wood wainscoting at this smart choice for a night out.

$$–$$$	**Vining's Bistro, Chatham.** Creative global cuisine shines at this tiny Cape standby that more than lives up to its reputation.
$–$$$	**OceAnna, New Bedford.** Towering arched windows line the dining room of this former bank, where seafood and steaks dominate.
$$	**Finely JP's, Wellfleet.** An Outer Cape institution among discerning diners, this simple roadhouse restaurant can be counted on for fresh and innovative Mediterranean and regional American fare, including a knockout warm spinach-and-scallop salad.
$–$$	**Brazilian Grill, Hyannis.** The Cape has a large Brazilian population, and you can find many of these residents, plus plenty of satisfied visitors, at this all-you-can-eat *churrascaria.*
$–$$	**Cap'n Frosty's, Dennis.** With back-to-back fried seafood shacks, it's hard to discern the good from the greasy; this is the place the locals turn to year after year.
$–$$	**La Cucina Sul Mare, Falmouth.** The Northern Italian and Mediterranean specialties here are worth the inevitable wait for a table.

BUDGET RESTAURANTS

¢–$	**Clem & Ursie's, Provincetown.** This fabulous short-order seafood café and market, although a slightly long haul from downtown, serves simply superb treats from the sea, including a hot lobster roll that'll bring tears of joy to your eyes.
¢–$	**Stir Crazy, Bourne.** Savor fresh ingredients with lively Cambodian, Thai, and Vietnamese flavors.
¢–$	**Tofu A Go-Go, Provincetown.** Vegetarian food has rarely been rendered so deliciously and creatively than at this cozy spot set amid the many art galleries along Commercial Street. The tofu breakfast burritos are a favorite.
¢	**Red Cottage Restaurant, Dennis.** This breakfast spot is consistently tasty, reasonable, and friendly.

BEACHES & CONSERVATION AREAS

The **Massachusetts Audubon Wellfleet Bay Wildlife Sanctuary** in South Wellfleet, with its numerous adult and children's programs and its beautiful salt-marsh surroundings, is a favorite migration stop for Cape vacationers year-round.
Nauset Light, Coast Guard, Marconi, and Race Point beaches stretch majestically along the length of the Cape Cod National Seashore. Backed by dunes, they are *the* classic Cape beaches.
Walking along the beach, any beach, particularly in the peaceful early morning or late afternoon, even if it's overcast or rainy, is a great reminder of what the Cape is all about.

CHILDREN'S ACTIVITIES

Sandwich has the Thornton W. Burgess Museum, namesake of the creator of Peter Cottontail and a great place for children; Heritage Museums and Gardens, with superb old cars, a working 1912 carousel, and grounds perfect for running around; and the Green Briar Nature Center and Jam Kitchen, with walking trails, the Smiling Pool pond, natural-history exhibits, and Peter Rabbit's great-great-grandchildren.

The Cape Cod Museum of Natural History in Brewster offers a great selection of bay, marsh, and estuary cruises with naturalists who haul up traps so children can observe aquatic creatures up close. There are also field walks, exhibits, and a pond- and sea-life room with live specimens.

The popular summertime greeters at National Marine Fisheries Service Aquarium in Woods Hole are two harbor seals swimming out front; inside, kids can get their hands wet touching starfish, lobsters, and other sea creatures.

Whale watches out of Provincetown can be a tremendous thrill—genuinely exciting and pleasantly educational.

NATURAL PHENOMENA

Art's Dune Tours affords visitors a rare glimpse into the mysterious and pristine beauty of Province Land's dunes. The 1- to 1½-hour tours also offer a look at the fascinating colony of dune shacks and point out the myriad bird- and plant life that inhabit the dunes.

From Chatham Light, looking out at the Chatham Break in the sandbar is a reminder of the power of the sea and a fascinating display of the process of geological change.

The Giving Tree Gallery's nature trail in East Sandwich is a haven of peace and tranquillity. The trail winds through a bamboo stand, across a footbridge, and along a suspension bridge through a salt marsh.

Seeing harbor seals off Race Point in Provincetown in winter is one of the pleasures of the seaside Cape at a time when you feel like you have the place to yourself.

Sunset over Cape Cod Bay on any bay beach from Eastham to Provincetown is an unforgettable delight at any time of year.

Whales breaching alongside your whale-watch boat will fill you with a sense of wonder unlike any you've ever felt. It's also quite a treat to see dolphins jumping in and out of the boat's bow waves or in its wake.

QUINTESSENTIAL CAPE

For Broadway-style dramas, comedies, and musicals, as well as kids' plays, you can attend a production at the oldest professional summer theater in the country, Cape Playhouse, in Dennis.

In the midst of a massive expansion and renovation, the Provincetown Art Association and Museum already ranks among the Cape's leading cultural institutions, preserving Provincetown's rich arts tradition.

Bright crimson cranberries floating on flooded bogs just before the fall harvest are a perfect reminder of the handwork that was one of the joys of the seasonal roundup.

En route to the Cape, Plimoth Plantation, a living-history museum that takes you back to the Pilgrims' 1627 settlement, makes a fascinating detour to the New England of centuries past.

SHOPPING

Farm stands (often roadside) throughout the Cape provide one of the best ways to get close to the land and the rhythm of rural life.

It's been more than 50 years since Harry Holl founded Scargo Pottery in a wooded knoll adjacent to Scargo Lake in Dennis. His studio and kiln have evolved over the years into a fanciful sculpture garden with the work of some of the Cape's finest artisans.

The weekly flea market (Wednesday, Thursday, and weekends in summer; weekends all other seasons) at the Wellfleet Drive-In Theater is one big browse, whether or not you take anything home with you.

SMART TRAVEL TIPS

AIR TRAVEL

BOOKING

When you book **look for nonstop flights** and **remember that "direct" flights stop at least once.** Try to avoid connecting flights, which require a change of plane. Two airlines may operate a connecting flight jointly, so ask if your airline operates every segment of the trip; you may find that the carrier you prefer flies you only part of the way. To find more booking tips and to check prices and make on-line flight reservations, log on to ⊕ www.fodors.com

CARRIERS

The major U.S. airlines provide service to Boston, the nearest gateway city to Cape Cod. Providence, Rhode Island—also served by the major carriers—is an easy drive from the Cape. Airline service to Cape Cod itself is extremely unpredictable, however, because of the seasonal nature of travel; carriers come and go, while others juggle their routes. Barnstable Municipal Airport will always know which carriers are currently operating.

For charters, note that Direct Flight is based on Martha's Vineyard and provides charter service off-island. Jet Equity serves Cape Cod (and Martha's Vineyard and Nantucket) from White Plains, New York.

🛪 Major Airlines : **American** ☎ 800/433-7300 ⊕ **www.aa.com. Continental** ☎ 800/525-0280 ⊕ **www.continental.com. Delta** ☎ 800/221-1212 ⊕ **www.delta.com. Northwest** ☎ 800/225-2525 ⊕ **www.nwa.com. United** ☎ 800/241-6522 ⊕ **www.ual.com. US Airways** ☎ 800/428-4322 ⊕ **www.usairways.com.**

🛪 Smaller Airlines : **Cape Air** ☎ 508/771-6944 or 800/352-0714 ⊕ www.flycapeair.com flies between Boston and Hyannis. **Island Airlines** ☎ 508/775-6606 or 800/248-7779 ⊕ www.nantucket.net/trans/islandair flies between Hyannis and Nantucket. **Nantucket Airlines** ☎ 508/790-0300 or 800/635-8787 ⊕ www.nantucketairlines.com, run by Cape Air, has frequent flights between Hyannis and Nantucket. **US Airways Express** ☎ 800/428-4322 ⊕ www.usair.com flies to Hyannis from Boston and New York (La Guardia Airport).

🛪 Charters : **Direct Flight** ☎ 508/693-6688. **Jet Equity** ☎ 800/759-2929 ⊕ www.jetequity.com.

CHECK-IN & BOARDING

Always **ask your carrier about its check-in policy.** Plan to arrive at the airport about 2 hours before your scheduled departure time for domestic flights and 2½ to 3 hours before international flights. Assuming that not everyone with a ticket will show up, airlines routinely overbook planes. When everyone does, airlines ask for volunteers to give up their seats. In return, these volunteers usually get a certificate for a free flight and are rebooked on the next flight out. If there are not enough volunteers, the airline must choose who will be denied boarding. The first to get bumped are passengers who checked in late and those flying on discounted tickets, so **get to the gate and check in as early as possible,** especially during peak periods.

Always **bring a government-issued photo ID to the airport;** even when it's not required, a passport is best.

CUTTING COSTS

The least expensive airfares to Cape Cod are priced for round-trip travel and must usually be purchased in advance. Airlines generally allow you to change your return date for a fee; most low-fare tickets, however, are nonrefundable. It's smart to **call a number of airlines,** and when you are quoted a good price, **book it on the spot**—the same fare may not be available the next day. Always **check different routings** and look into using alternate airports. Also, price off-peak flights, which may be significantly less expensive than others. Travel agents, especially low-fare specialists (⇨ Discounts & Deals, *below*), are helpful.

Consolidators are another good source. They buy tickets for scheduled international flights at reduced rates from the airlines, then sell them at prices that beat the best fare available directly from the airlines. Sometimes you can even get your money back if you need to return the ticket. Carefully read the fine print detailing penalties for changes and cancellations, purchase the ticket with a credit card, and **confirm your consolidator reservation with the airline.**

⁊ Consolidators **AirlineConsolidator.com** ☎ 888/468-5385 ⊕ www.airlineconsolidator.com; for international tickets. **Best Fares** ☎ 800/880-1234 or 800/576-8255 ⊕ www.bestfares.com; $59.90 annual membership. **Cheap Tickets** ☎ 800/377-1000 or 800/652-4327 ⊕ www.cheaptickets.com. **Expedia** ☎ 800/397-3342 or 404/728-8787 ⊕ www.expedia.com. **Hotwire** ☎ 866/468-9473 or 920/330-9418 ⊕ www.hotwire.com. **Now Voyager Travel** ✉ 45 W. 21st St., Suite 5A New York, NY 10010 ☎ 212/459-1616 ⬛ 212/243-2711 ⊕ www.nowvoyagertravel.com. **Onetravel.com** ⊕ www.onetravel.com. **Orbitz** ☎ 888/656-4546 ⊕ www.orbitz.com. **Priceline.com** ⊕ www.priceline.com. **Travelocity** ☎ 888/709-5983, 877/282-2925 in Canada, 0870/876-3876 in the U.K. ⊕ www.travelocity.com.

⁊ Courier Resources **Air Courier Association/Cheaptrips.com** ☎ 800/280-5973 or 800/282-1202 ⊕ www.aircourier.org or www.cheaptrips.com; $34 annual membership. **International Association of Air Travel Couriers** ☎ 308/632-3273 ⊕ www.courier.org; $45 annual membership.

ENJOYING THE FLIGHT

State your seat preference when purchasing your ticket, and then repeat it when you confirm and when you check in. For more legroom, you can request one of the few emergency-aisle seats at check-in, if you are capable of lifting at least 50 pounds—a Federal Aviation Administration requirement of passengers in these seats. Seats behind a bulkhead also offer more legroom, but they don't have under-seat storage. Don't sit in the row in front of the emergency aisle or in front of a bulkhead, where seats may not recline.

Ask the airline whether a snack or meal is served on the flight. If you have dietary concerns, **request special meals when booking.** These can be vegetarian, low-cholesterol, or kosher, for example. It's a good idea to pack some healthy snacks and a small (plastic) bottle of water in your carry-on bag. On long flights, try to maintain a normal routine, to help fight jet lag. At night, **get some sleep.** By day, **eat light meals, drink water** (not alcohol), and **move around the cabin** to stretch your legs. For additional jet-lag tips consult *Fodor's FYI: Travel Fit & Healthy* (available at bookstores everywhere).

Smoking policies vary from carrier to carrier. Many airlines prohibit smoking on all of their international flights; others allow smoking only on certain routes or certain departures. Ask your carrier about its policy.

FLYING TIMES

Flying time to Boston is 1 hour from New York, 2½ hours from Chicago, 6 hours from Los Angeles, and 3½ hours from Dallas.

HOW TO COMPLAIN

If your baggage goes astray or your flight goes awry, complain right away. Most carriers require that you **file a claim immediately.** The Aviation Consumer Protection Division of the Department of Transportation publishes *Fly-Rights,* which discusses airlines and consumer issues and is available on-line. At PassengerRights.com, a Web site, you can compose a letter of complaint and distribute it electronically.

🛂 Airline Complaints **Aviation Consumer Protection Division** ✉ U.S. Department of Transportation, Office of Aviation Enforcement and Proceedings, C-75, Room 4107, 400 7th St. SW, Washington, DC 20590 ☎ 202/366-2220 ⊕ airconsumer.ost.dot.gov. **Federal Aviation Administration Consumer Hotline** ✉ for inquiries: FAA, 800 Independence Ave. SW, Washington, DC 20591 ☎ 800/322-7873 ⊕ www.faa.gov.

RECONFIRMING

Check the status of your flight before you leave for the airport. You can do this on your carrier's Web site, by linking to a flight-status checker (many Web booking services offer these), or by calling your carrier or travel agent.

AIRPORTS

The major gateway to Cape Cod is Boston's Logan International Airport (BOS). The T. F. Green Airport (PVD) in Providence, Rhode Island, served by the low-cost carrier Southwest Airlines and other major carriers, is an alternative. Smaller airports include the Barnstable and Provincetown municipal airports.

🛂 Airport Information : Boston: **Logan International Airport** ☎ 617/561-1806 or 800/235-6426 ⊕ www.massport.com/logan. Providence: **T. F.**

Green Airport ☎ 401/737-8222 or 888/268-7222 ⊕ www.pvd-ri.com. Hyannis: **Barnstable Municipal Airport** ☎ 508/775-2020. Provincetown: **Provincetown Airport** ☎ 508/487-0241.

BEACHES

In season you have to pay for parking at public beaches. Parking at "restricted" beaches is available only to residents and to visitors with permits. If you're renting a house, you can purchase a weekly beach permit; contact the local town hall for details (⇨ Visitor Information *in* the A to Z sections of the appropriate chapters). Walkers and cyclists do not need permits to use restricted beaches. The official season generally begins the last weekend in June and ends on Labor Day. Note that even at resident beaches in season, the lots are often open to all early in the morning (before 8) and late in the afternoon (after 4 or 5).

BIKE TRAVEL

Biking is very popular on Cape Cod—some trails are as busy as the roads in summer. Note that Massachusetts law requires children under 13 to wear protective helmets while riding a bike, even as a passenger. For information on trails, maps, and rentals in your area, *see* listings for specific towns.

🛂 Bike Maps : **Rubel Bike Maps** ⎁ Box 401035, Cambridge, MA 02140 ⊕ www.bikemaps.com.

BIKES IN FLIGHT

Most airlines accommodate bikes as luggage, provided they are dismantled and boxed; check with individual airlines about packing requirements. Some airlines sell bike boxes, which are often free at bike shops, for about $20 (bike bags can be considerably more expensive). International travelers often can substitute a bike for a piece of checked luggage at no charge; otherwise, the cost is about $100. Most U.S. and Canadian airlines charge $40–$80 each way.

BOAT & FERRY TRAVEL

In season, ferries connect Boston and Plymouth with Provincetown. Ferries are also a convenient way to get to Martha's Vineyard and Nantucket, two islands south of

Cape Cod that have attractive, historic towns and lovely beaches well worth a day trip or a longer stay. For further information, *see* Close-Up: A Day on Martha's Vineyard *in* Chapter 3 and Close-Up: A Visit to the Gray Lady *in* Chapter 4; also *see* Guidebooks.

Ferries to Martha's Vineyard leave Woods Hole year-round. In summer you can also catch Vineyard ferries in Falmouth and Hyannis. All provide parking lots where you can leave your car overnight ($6–$10 per night). A number of parking lots in Falmouth hold the overflow of cars when the Woods Hole lot is filled, and free shuttle buses take passengers to the ferry, about 15 minutes away. Signs along Route 28 heading south from the Bourne Bridge direct you to open parking lots, as does AM radio station 1610, which you can pick up within 5 mi of Falmouth.

Ferries to Nantucket leave Hyannis year-round. In season, a passenger ferry connects Nantucket with Martha's Vineyard, and a cruise from Hyannis makes a day trip with stops at both islands. From New Bedford you can take a ferry to Martha's Vineyard from mid-May to mid-October and to Cuttyhunk Island year-round (although between mid-October and mid-April, service is very limited).

FERRIES TO PROVINCETOWN

For details on ferries from Boston to Provincetown, *see* The Outer Cape A to Z *in* Chapter 6. For service from Plymouth to Provincetown, *see* Approaching the Cape A to Z *in* Chapter 2.

FERRIES TO MARTHA'S VINEYARD

The Steamship Authority runs the only car ferries, which make the 45-minute trip from Woods Hole to Vineyard Haven year-round and to Oak Bluffs from late May through mid-October. In summer and on autumn weekends, you *must* have a reservation if you want to bring your car (passenger reservations are never necessary). You should **make car reservations as far ahead as possible**; in season the reservations office is open daily 7 AM–9 PM. You can also make car reservations online at the Steamship Authority's Web

site (⊕ www.islandferry.com). Standby car reservations to the Vineyard are only available Tuesday–Thursday. Those with confirmed car reservations must be at the terminal 30 minutes (45 minutes in season) before sailing time. One-way passenger fare year-round is $6.00, bicycles $3. Cost for a car traveling one-way in season (May–October) is $57 (not including passengers). Call or see the Web site for off-season rates.

July through Labor Day, the Steamship Authority also offers a "Vineyard Express" bus and ferry service. Buses depart from the Route 128 Amtrak station in the Boston suburb of Westwood and connect with the ferry in Woods Hole. One-way bus-ferry fare is $15.50.

Hy-Line makes the 1¾-hour run from Hyannis to Oak Bluffs May–October. The parking lot fills up in summer, so **call to reserve a parking space** in high season. One-way fare is $14; bicycles cost $5. From June to mid-September, Hy-Line's Around the Sound cruise makes a one-day round-trip from Hyannis with stops at Nantucket and Martha's Vineyard ($42).

The *Island Queen* makes the 35-minute trip from Falmouth to Oak Bluffs from late May through mid-October. Ferries run multiple times a day from mid-June through early September, with less frequent service in the spring and fall; call for schedule. Round-trip fare is $12, bicycles $6; one-way $6, bicycles $3. Only cash and traveler's checks are accepted for payment.

Patriot Boats runs a Falmouth Harbor to Oak Bluffs ferry year-round, with several trips Monday through Saturday; there's no service on Sunday or national holidays. The company also operates a year-round 24-hour water taxi and offers boat charters. The ferry costs $7 one-way.

The New England Fast Ferry Company makes the hour-long trip by catamaran from New Bedford to Oak Bluffs from early July to mid-September. The company runs on a scaled-back schedule to Vineyard Haven the remainder of the year. One way is $20, bicycles $5.

F Boat & Ferry Information : **Hy-Line** ✉ Ocean St. dock ☎ 508/778-2600 or 888/778-1132, 508/778-2602 reservations, 508/693-0112 in Oak Bluffs ⊕ www.hy-linecruises.com. *Island Queen* ✉ Falmouth Harbor ☎ 508/548-4800 ⊕ www.islandqueen.com. **Patriot Boats** ✉ 227 Clinton Ave., Falmouth Harbor ☎ 508/548-2626, 800/734-0088 in Massachusetts ⊕ www.patriotpartyboats.com. **Steamship Authority** ✉ 508/477-8600 information and car reservations, 508/693-9130 on the Vineyard, 508/540-1394 TTY information and car reservations, 508/548-3788 day-of-sailing information ⊕ www.steamshipauthority.com. **The New England Fast Ferry Company** ✉ State Pier Ferry Terminal ☎ 866/453-6800 ⊕ www.nefastferry.com.

FERRIES TO NANTUCKET

For details on ferries from Harwich Port, *see* The Lower Cape A to Z *in* Chapter 5.

The Steamship Authority runs car-and-passenger ferries from Hyannis to Nantucket year-round, a 2¼-hour trip. A faster passenger ferry only takes an hour. All of the ferries have snack bars. For policies *see* Ferries to Martha's Vineyard. Note that there are no standby car reservations on ferries to Nantucket. One-way passenger fare is $14, bicycles $6. Cost for a car traveling one-way May through October is $175; November through April, $115. One-way high-speed passenger ferry fare is $27.50, bicycles $6.

Hy-Line's high-end, high-speed *Grey Lady II* ferries between Hyannis and Nantucket year-round in an hour. Such speed has its downside in rough seas—lots of bucking and rolling that some find literally nauseating. Seating ranges from benches on the upper deck to airlinelike seats in side rows of the cabin to café-style tables and chairs in the cabin front. There's a snack bar on board. Make reservations in advance, particularly during the summer months or for holiday travel. One-way fare is $34, bicycles $5.

Hy-Line's slower ferry makes the roughly two-hour trip from Hyannis between early May and late October. The M/V *Great Point* offers a first-class section ($23 one-way) with a private lounge, restrooms, upholstered seats, carpeting, complimentary continental breakfast or afternoon cheese and crackers, a bar, and a snack bar. Standard one-way fare is $14, bicycles $5.

F Boat & Ferry Information : **Hy-Line** ✉ Ocean St. dock ☎ 508/778-0404 or 888/778-1132 Grey Lady II, 508/778-2602 Great Point ferry reservations, 508/778-2600 general ferry information, 508/228-3949 on Nantucket ⊕ www.hy-linecruises.com. **Steamship Authority** ✉ South St. dock ☎ 508/477-8600, 508/228-3274 on Nantucket for reservations, 508/228-0262 information, 508/540-1394 TTD ⊕ www.steamshipauthority.com.

FERRIES TO CUTTYHUNK ISLAND

The M/V *Alert II* runs about one-hour-long ferries between New Bedford and Cuttyhunk Island, daily mid-June through mid-September, several times a week from mid-April to mid-June and from mid-September to mid-October, and once a week the rest of the year. Same-day round-trip fare is $20, one-way $13, bicycles $3.50.

F Boat & Ferry Information : *M/V Alert II* ✉ Fisherman's Wharf/Pier 3, New Bedford ☎ 508/992-1432 ⊕ www.cuttyhunk.com.

BUSINESS HOURS

MUSEUMS & SIGHTS

Hours for sights on the Cape vary widely from place to place and from season to season. Some places are staffed by volunteers and have limited hours (open just a few hours a day several days a week), even in summer, although major museums and attractions will be open daily in summer. Always check the hours of a place you plan to visit, and if you'll be traveling some distance to a sight, call ahead to confirm that it will be open.

PHARMACIES

Many pharmacies on the Cape are open from 8 or 9 AM until 8 or 9 PM; several are now open 24 hours or stay open later in summer. *See* chapter A to Z sections for specific listings.

SHOPS

Shop hours are generally from 9 or 10 to 5, though in high season many tourist-oriented stores stay open until 9 PM or later. Except in the main tourist areas, shops are often closed on Sunday.

BUS TRAVEL

Greyhound serves Boston from all over the United States; from there you can connect to a local carrier, such as Bonanza Bus Lines, which serves Bourne, Falmouth, and Woods Hole on the Cape, plus nearby Fall River and New Bedford. The Plymouth & Brockton Street Railway buses travel all the way to Provincetown from Boston and Logan Airport, with stops en route.

The Cape Cod Regional Transit Authority operates several "Breeze" buses within the Cape, all of them wheelchair-accessible and equipped with bike racks. The SeaLine runs along Route 28 Monday through Saturday between Hyannis and Woods Hole (one-way fare $3.50, from Hyannis to Woods Hole; shorter trips are less), with stops including Mashpee Commons, Falmouth, and the Woods Hole Steamship Authority docks. The SeaLine connects in Hyannis with the Plymouth & Brockton line as well as the Villager, another bus line that runs along Route 132 between Hyannis and Barnstable Harbor, serving the Cape Cod Mall. The driver will stop when signaled along the route.

The H2O Line offers daily regularly scheduled service year-round between Hyannis and Orleans along Route 28. The Hyannis–Orleans fare is $3.50; shorter trips are less. Buses connect in Hyannis with the SeaLine, the Villager, and Plymouth & Brockton lines.

The b-bus is composed of a fleet of minivans that will transport passengers door to door between any towns on the Cape. You must register in advance to use the b-bus service; phone the Cape Cod Regional Transit Authority between 1 and 4 PM on weekdays to sign up. You must also make advance reservations when you want to ride the b-bus. After you are enrolled, call for reservations between 8 AM and 4 PM on weekdays; reservations may be made up to a week in advance. Service runs seven days a week, year-round. The cost is $2 per ride plus 10¢ per mile.

The Yarmouth Shuttle runs from the Hyannis Transportation Center in downtown Hyannis along Route 28 to several Yarmouth beaches and the Yarmouth Municipal Lot on the Yarmouth–Dennis town line.

The Provincetown Shuttle runs through September 1 between North Truro, Provincetown, the Provincetown Inn and Herring Cove Beach.

🚌 Bus Information **Bonanza** ☎ 508/548-7588 or 888/751-8800 ⊕ www.bonanzabus.com. **Cape Cod Regional Transit Authority** ☎ 508/385-8326, 800/352-7155 in Massachusetts ⊕ www.capecodtransit.org. **Greyhound** ☎ 800/229-9424 ⊕ www.greyhound.com. **Plymouth & Brockton Street Railway** ☎ 508/746-0378 ⊕ www.p-b.com.

CAMERAS & PHOTOGRAPHY

Early-morning or early-evening fog can present a photographic challenge on the Cape, but when it's not foggy, these are great times for pictures—beaches are less crowded and the light is especially magical. Shots of lighthouses or sand dunes are classics, as are photos of your dinner of lobster or fried clams.

The *Kodak Guide to Shooting Great Travel Pictures* (available at bookstores everywhere) is loaded with tips.

🚌 Photo Help : **Kodak Information Center** ☎ 800/242-2424 ⊕ www.kodak.com.

EQUIPMENT PRECAUTIONS

Don't pack film or equipment in checked luggage, where it is much more susceptible to damage. X-ray machines used to view checked luggage are extremely powerful and therefore are likely to ruin your film. Try to ask for hand inspection of film, which becomes clouded after repeated exposure to airport X-ray machines, and keep videotapes and computer disks away from metal detectors. Always keep film, tape, and computer disks out of the sun. Carry an extra supply of batteries, and be prepared to turn on your camera, camcorder, or laptop to prove to airport security personnel that the device is real.

CAR RENTAL

Rates in Boston begin at $30–$40 a day and $170–$205 a week for an economy car with air-conditioning, an automatic transmission, and unlimited mileage. Rates in Hyannis range from $30 to $45 a day and from $159 to $259 a week. These rates do not include tax on car rentals, which is 5%.

Major Agencies Alamo ☎ 800/327-9633 ⊕ www.alamo.com. **Avis** ☎ 800/331-1212, 800/879-2847 or 800/272-5871 in Canada, 0870/606-0100 in the U.K., 02/9353-9000 in Australia, 09/526-2847 in New Zealand ⊕ www.avis.com. **Budget** ☎ 800/527-0700, 0870/156-5656 in the U.K. ⊕ www.budget.com. **Dollar** ☎ 800/800-4000, 0800/085-4578 in the U.K. ⊕ www.dollar.com. **Hertz** ☎ 800/654-3131, 800/263-0600 in Canada, 0870/844-8844 in the U.K., 02/9669-2444 in Australia, 09/256-8690 in New Zealand ⊕ www.hertz.com. **National Car Rental** ☎ 800/227-7368, 0870/600-6666 in the U.K. ⊕ www.nationalcar.com.

Limousine Agencies Aristocrat Limousine ☎ 508/420-5466 or 800/992-6163 for service from the Boston or Providence airport to the Cape. **King's Coach** ☎ 508/771-1000 ⊕ www.kingscoach.com for service to Boston or Providence airports to and from the Cape.

CUTTING COSTS

For a good deal, book through a travel agent who will shop around. Also, price local car-rental companies—whose prices may be lower still, although their service and maintenance may not be as good as those of major rental agencies—and research rates on the Internet. Consolidators that specialize in air travel can offer good rates on cars as well (⇨ Air Travel). Remember to ask about required deposits, cancellation penalties, and drop-off charges if you're planning to pick up the car in one city and leave it in another. If you're traveling during a holiday period, also make sure that a confirmed reservation guarantees you a car.

INSURANCE

When driving a rented car you are generally responsible for any damage to or loss of the vehicle. You may also be liable for any property damage or personal injury that you may cause while driving. Before you rent, see what coverage you already have under the terms of your personal auto-insurance policy and credit cards.

For about $15 to $20 a day, rental companies sell protection, known as a collision- or loss-damage waiver (CDW or LDW), that eliminates your liability for damage to the car; it's always optional and should never be automatically added to your bill. In Massachusetts the car-rental agency's insurance is primary; therefore, the company must pay for damage to third parties up to a preset legal limit, beyond which your own liability insurance kicks in. However, **make sure you have enough coverage to pay for the car.** If you do not have auto insurance or an umbrella policy that covers damage to third parties, purchasing liability insurance and a CDW or LDW is highly recommended.

REQUIREMENTS & RESTRICTIONS

In Massachusetts you must be 21 to rent a car, and rates may be higher if you're under 25. When picking up a car, non-U.S. residents will need a reservation voucher (for prepaid reservations made in the traveler's home country), a passport, a driver's license, and a travel policy that covers each driver.

SURCHARGES

Before you pick up a car in one city and leave it in another, ask about drop-off charges or one-way service fees, which can be substantial. Also inquire about early-return policies; some rental agencies charge extra if you return the car before the time specified in your contract while others give you a refund for the days not used. To avoid a hefty refueling fee, fill the tank just before you turn in the car, but be aware that gas stations near the rental outlet may overcharge. It's almost never a deal to buy the tank of gas that's in the car when you rent it; the understanding is that you'll return it empty, but some fuel usually remains. Surcharges may apply if you're under 25 or if you take the car outside the area approved by the rental agency. You'll pay extra for child seats (about $8 a day), which are compulsory for children under five, and usually for additional drivers (up to $25 a day, depending on location).

CAR TRAVEL

Your driver's license may not be recognized outside your home country. International driving permits (IDPs) are available from the American and Canadian automobile associations and, in the United Kingdom, from the Automobile Association and Royal Automobile Club. These international permits, valid only in conjunction with your regular driver's license, are universally recognized; having one may save you a problem with local authorities.

To reach Cape Cod from Boston (60 mi), take Route I–93 south, then Route 3 south, and cross the Sagamore Bridge. After finding your way out of a rotary, you'll be on U.S. 6, the Cape's main artery, leading toward Hyannis and Provincetown. From western Massachusetts, northern Connecticut, and northern New York State, take I–84 East to the Massachusetts Turnpike (I–90E) and take I–495 to the Bourne Bridge. From New York City, New Jersey, Philadelphia, Washington, D.C., and all other points south and west, take I–95 north toward Providence, where you'll pick up I–195 east (toward Fall River–New Bedford) to Route 25 east to the Bourne Bridge. From the Bourne Bridge you can take Route 28 south to Falmouth and Woods Hole (about 15 mi), or follow signs to U.S. 6 if you're headed east.

Driving times can vary widely depending on traffic. In good driving conditions you can reach the Sagamore Bridge from Boston in about 1½ hours, the Bourne Bridge from New York City in about 5 hours.

On summer weekends, when more than 100,000 cars a day cross each bridge, **make every effort to avoid arriving in late afternoon**, especially on holidays. U.S. 6 and Route 28 are heavily congested eastbound on Friday evening, westbound on Sunday afternoon, and in both directions on Saturday (when rental homes change hands). On the north shore, the Old King's Highway—Route 6A—parallels U.S. 6 and is a scenic country road passing through occasional towns. When you're in no hurry, use back roads—you won't get there any faster, but they're less frustrating and much more rewarding.

RULES OF THE ROAD

In Massachusetts, highway speed limits are 55 mph near urban areas, 60 or 65 mph elsewhere. Speed limits on U.S. 6 on the Cape vary as it changes from four lanes to two lanes. Radar detectors are legal in Massachusetts.

Massachusetts permits a right turn on a red light (*after* a full stop) unless a sign says otherwise. Also, when you approach one of the Cape's numerous rotaries (traffic circles), note that the vehicles already in the rotary have the right of way and that those vehicles entering the rotary must yield. Be careful: some drivers forget (or ignore) this principle.

On Route I–93, a high-occupancy vehicle (HOV) lane—for cars with two or more occupants—is available between downtown Boston and Route 3 southbound during the afternoon rush hour and northbound during the morning rush hour.

Always **strap children under age five into approved child-safety seats.**

CHILDREN ON CAPE COD

Cape Cod, which has everything from miniature golf to beaches, is extremely family-oriented. Every imaginable diversion is available for children, including lodgings and restaurants that cater specifically to them and that are affordable for families on a budget. Cottages and condominiums are popular with families, offering privacy, room, kitchens, and sometimes laundry facilities. Often cottage or condo communities have play yards and pools, sometimes even a selection of children's programs. For some child-friendly events, *see* Festivals and Seasonal Events.

If you are renting a car, don't forget to **arrange for a car seat** when you reserve. For general advice about traveling with children, consult *Fodor's FYI: Travel with Your Baby* (available in bookstores everywhere).

⊞ Local Information : **The Cape Cod Chamber of Commerce** ⊠ Junction Rte. 6 and Rte. 132 ⬚ Box 790, Hyannis, MA 02601 ☎ 508/362–3225 or 888/332–2732 ⊕ www.capecodchamber.org.

FLYING

If your children are two or older, ask about children's airfares. As a general rule, infants under two not occupying a seat fly at greatly reduced fares or even for free. But if you want to guarantee a seat for an infant, you have to pay full fare. Consider flying during off-peak days and times; most airlines will grant an infant a seat without a ticket if there are available seats.Experts agree that it's a good idea to use safety seats aloft for children weighing less than 40 pounds. Airlines set their own policies: if you use a safety seat, U.S. carriers usually require that the child be ticketed, even if he or she is young enough to ride free, because the seats must be strapped into regular seats. And even if you pay the full adult fare for the seat, it may be worth it, especially on longer trips. Do **check your airline's policy about using safety seats during takeoff and landing.** Safety seats are not allowed everywhere in the plane, so get your seat assignments as early as possible.

When reserving, request children's meals or a freestanding bassinet (not available at all airlines) if you need them. But note that bulkhead seats, where you must sit to use the bassinet, may lack an overhead bin or storage space on the floor.

WHERE TO STAY

Most hotels on Cape Cod allow children under a certain age to stay in their parents' room at no extra charge, but others will charge children as extra adults; be sure to **find out the cutoff age for children's discounts.**

If you're planning to stay at a bed-and-breakfast, be sure to **ask the owners in advance** whether the B&B welcomes children. Some establishments are filled with fragile antiques, and owners may not accept families with children below a certain age.

SIGHTS & ATTRACTIONS

Places that are especially appealing to children are indicated by a rubber-duckie icon (🐥) in the margin.

CONSUMER PROTECTION

Whether you're shopping for gifts or purchasing travel services, **pay with a major credit card** whenever possible, so you can cancel payment or get reimbursed if there's a problem (and you can provide documentation). If you're doing business with a particular company for the first time, contact your local Better Business Bureau and the attorney general's offices in your state and (for U.S. businesses) the company's home state as well. Have any complaints been filed? Finally, if you're buying a package or tour, always consider travel insurance that includes default coverage (⇨ Insurance).

🔳 BBBs : **Council of Better Business Bureaus** ✉ 4200 Wilson Blvd., Suite 800, Arlington, VA 22203 ☎ 703/276-0100 🖷 703/525-8277 ⊕ www.bbb.org.

CUSTOMS & DUTIES

IN AUSTRALIA

Australian residents who are 18 or older may bring home A$400 worth of souvenirs and gifts (including jewelry), 250 cigarettes or 250 grams of cigars or other tobacco products, and 1,125 ml of alcohol (including wine, beer, and spirits). Residents under 18 may bring back A$200 worth of goods. Members of the same family traveling together may pool their allowances. Prohibited items include meat products. Seeds, plants, and fruits need to be declared upon arrival.

🔳 **Australian Customs Service** ⌖ Regional Director, Box 8, Sydney, NSW 2001 ☎ 02/9213-2000 or 1300/363263, 02/9364-7222 or 1800/020-504 quarantine-inquiry line 🖷 02/9213-4043 ⊕ www.customs.gov.au.

IN CANADA

Canadian residents who have been out of Canada for at least seven days may bring in C$750 worth of goods duty-free. If you've been away fewer than seven days but more than 48 hours, the duty-free allowance drops to C$200. If your trip lasts 24 to 48 hours, the allowance is C$50. You may not pool allowances with family members. Goods claimed under the C$750 exemption may follow you by mail; those claimed under the lesser exemptions must accompany you. Alcohol and tobacco products may be included in the seven-day and 48-hour exemptions but not in the 24-

hour exemption. If you meet the age requirements of the province or territory through which you reenter Canada, you may bring in, duty-free, 1.5 liters of wine *or* 1.14 liters (40 imperial ounces) of liquor *or* 24 12-ounce cans or bottles of beer or ale. Also, if you meet the local age requirement for tobacco products, you may bring in, duty-free, 200 cigarettes and 50 cigars. Check ahead of time with the Canada Customs and Revenue Agency or the Department of Agriculture for policies regarding meat products, seeds, plants, and fruits.

You may send an unlimited number of gifts (only one gift per recipient, however) worth up to C$60 each duty-free to Canada. Label the package UNSOLICITED GIFT—VALUE UNDER $60. Alcohol and tobacco are excluded.

🚹 **Canada Customs and Revenue Agency** ✉ 2265 St. Laurent Blvd., Ottawa, Ontario K1G 4K3 ☎ 800/461-9999 in Canada, 204/983-3500, 506/636-5064 ⊕ www.ccra.gc.ca.

IN NEW ZEALAND

All homeward-bound residents may bring back NZ$700 worth of souvenirs and gifts; passengers may not pool their allowances, and children can claim only the concession on goods intended for their own use. For those 17 or older, the duty-free allowance also includes 4.5 liters of wine or beer; one 1,125-ml bottle of spirits; and either 200 cigarettes, 250 grams of tobacco, 50 cigars, *or* a combination of the three up to 250 grams. Meat products, seeds, plants, and fruits must be declared upon arrival to the Agricultural Services Department.

🚹 **New Zealand Customs** ✉ Head office: The Customhouse, 17–21 Whitmore St., Box 2218, Wellington ☎ 09/300-5399 or 0800/428-786 ⊕ www.customs.govt.nz.

IN THE U.K.

From countries outside the European Union, including the United States, you may bring home, duty-free, 200 cigarettes, 50 cigars, 100 cigarillos, or 250 grams of tobacco; 1 liter of spirits or 2 liters of fortified or sparkling wine or liqueurs; 2 liters of still table wine; 60 ml of perfume; 250

ml of toilet water; plus £145 worth of other goods, including gifts and souvenirs. Prohibited items include meat and dairy products, seeds, plants, and fruits.

🚹 **HM Customs and Excise** ✉ Portcullis House, 21 Cowbridge Rd. E, Cardiff CF11 9SS ☎ 0845/010-9000 or 0208/929-0152 advice service, 0208/929-6731 or 0208/910-3602 complaints ⊕ www.hmce.gov.uk.

DINING

For additional dining information, *see* Pleasures & Pastimes *in* Chapter 1. There's a 5% sales tax on restaurant meals. The restaurants we list are the cream of the crop in each price category. Note that ordering a lobster dinner, which can be far more expensive than other menu items, may push your meal into a higher price category than the restaurant's price range shows. Properties indicated by a ✕⌗ are lodging establishments whose restaurant warrants a special trip.

CATEGORY	COST*
$$$$	over $30
$$$	$20–$30
$$	$15–$20
$	$10–$15
¢	under $10

*per person for a main course at dinner

CUTTING COSTS

Even the best Cape restaurants offer slightly scaled-down portions of pricier dinner menus during lunchtime. Any time of day, you can indulge in fresh local seafood and clambakes at **seat yourself shanties** for a much lower price than their fine-dining counterparts. Often the tackier the decor (plastic fish on the walls), the better the seafood. These laid-back local haunts usually operate a fish market on the premises and are in every town on the Cape.

RESERVATIONS & DRESS

Reservations are always a good idea; we mention them only when they're essential or not accepted. Book as far ahead as you can, and reconfirm as soon as you arrive. (Large parties should always call ahead to check the reservations policy.) We mention dress only when men are required to wear a jacket or a jacket and tie.

WINE, BEER & SPIRITS

Massachusetts is not a major wine-growing area, but Westport Rivers Winery in Westport and the Cape Cod Winery in East Falmouth produce respectable vintages. The family that owns Westport Rivers also runs the local Buzzards Bay Brewing Co. Wines from Truro Vineyards of Cape Cod are local favorites.

In Massachusetts, you can generally buy alcoholic beverages (wine, beer, and spirits) in liquor stores, known locally as package stores. A few exceptions allow some grocery stores to sell wine and beer.

DISABILITIES & ACCESSIBILITY

The Cape Cod Disability Access Directory includes access information about ATMs, beaches, health-care facilities, theaters, and other places on the Cape. It's available online, or you can request a copy from the Cape Cod Chamber of Commerce (⇨ Visitor Information). The Cape Cod National Seashore visitor centers can provide information about accessible facilities at the park. The Cape Organization for Rights of the Disabled (CORD) will supply information on accessibility of restaurants, hotels, beaches, and other tourist facilities on Cape Cod. Sight Loss Services provides information on accessibility and other needs and referrals for people with vision impairments. For information about accessibility in Massachusetts state parks and beaches, contact the Massachusetts Department of Environmental Management.

Local Resources : **Cape Cod Disability Access Directory** ⊕ www.capecoddisability.org. **Cape Cod National Seashore** ⊠ South Wellfleet 02663 ☎ 508/349-3785 ⊕ www.nps.gov/caco. **Cape Cod National Seashore visitor centers** ☎ 508/255-3421 in Eastham, 508/487-1256 in Provincetown ⊕ www.nps.gov/caco. **Cape Organization for Rights of the Disabled** (CORD) ☎ 508/775-8300, 800/541-0282 in Massachusetts ⊕ www.cordonline.org. **Massachusetts Department of Environmental Management** (⇨ Visitor Information). **Sight Loss Services** ☎ 508/394-3904, 800/427-6842 in Massachusetts ⊕ www.sightloss.org.

LODGING

Despite the Americans with Disabilities Act, the definition of accessibility seems to differ from hotel to hotel. Some properties may be accessible by ADA standards for people with mobility problems but not for people with hearing or vision impairments, for example.

If you have mobility problems, ask for the lowest floor on which accessible services are offered. If you have a hearing impairment, check whether the hotel has devices to alert you visually to the ring of the telephone, knock at the door, and a fire/emergency alarm. Some hotels provide these devices without charge. Discuss your needs with hotel personnel if this equipment isn't available, so that a staff member can personally alert you in the event of an emergency.

If you're bringing a guide dog, get authorization ahead of time and write down the name of the person you spoke with.

Best Choices : **Brass Key** ⊠ 67 Bradford St., Provincetown 02657 ☎ 508/487-9005 or 800/842-9858 ⊟ 508/487-9020 ⊕ www.brasskey.com. **Cape Codder Resort** ⊠ 1225 Iyanough Rd., Hyannis 02601 ☎ 508/771-3000 or 888/297-2200 ⊟ 508/771-6564 ⊕ www.capecodderresort.com. **Chatham Wayside Inn** ⊠ 512 Main St., Chatham 02633 ☎ 508/945-5550 or 800/391-5734 ⊟ 508/945-3407 ⊕ www.waysideinn.com. **Dan'l Webster Inn** ⊠ 149 Main St., Sandwich 02563 ☎ 508/888-3622 or 800/444-3566 ⊟ 508/888-5156 ⊕ www.danlwebsterinn.com. **English Garden B&B** ⊠ 32 Inman Rd., Dennisport 02639 ☎ 508/398-2915 or 888/788-1908 ⊟ 508/398-2852 ⊕ www.theenglishgardenbandb.com. **Scallop Shell Inn** ⊠ 16 Massachusetts Ave., Falmouth Heights 02540 ☎ 508/495-4900 or 800/249-4587 ⊟ 508/495-4600 ⊕ www.scallopshellinn.com.

RESERVATIONS

When discussing accessibility with an operator or reservations agent, ask hard questions. Are there any stairs, inside *or* out? Are there grab bars next to the toilet *and* in the shower/tub? How wide is the doorway to the room? To the bathroom? For the most extensive facilities meeting the latest legal specifications, opt for newer accommodations. If you reserve through a toll-free number, consider also calling the hotel's local number to confirm the information from the central reservations office. Get confirmation in writing when you can.

TRANSPORTATION

🔲 Complaints : **Aviation Consumer Protection Division** (⇨ Air Travel) for airline-related problems. **Departmental Office of Civil Rights** ✉ for general inquiries, U.S. Department of Transportation, S-30, 400 7th St. SW, Room 10215, Washington, DC 20590 ☎ 202/366-4648 📠 202/366-9371 ⊕ www.dotcr. ost.dot.gov. **Disability Rights Section** ✉ NYAV, U.S. Department of Justice, Civil Rights Division, 950 Pennsylvania Ave. NW, Washington, DC 20530 ☎ ADA information line 202/514-0301, 800/514-0301, 202/514-0383 TTY, 800/514-0383 TTY ⊕ www. ada.gov. **U.S. Department of Transportation Hotline** ☎ for disability-related air-travel problems, 800/778-4838 or 800/455-9880 TTY.

TRAVEL AGENCIES

In the United States, the Americans with Disabilities Act requires that travel firms serve the needs of all travelers. Some agencies specialize in working with people with disabilities.

🔲 Travelers with Mobility Problems **Access Adventures/B. Roberts Travel** ✉ 206 Chestnut Ridge Rd., Scottsville, NY 14624 ☎ 585/889-9096 ⊕ www.brobertstravel.com ✍ dltravel@prodigy. net, run by a former physical-rehabilitation counselor. **Accessible Vans of America** ✉ 9 Spielman Rd., Fairfield, NJ 07004 ☎ 877/282-8267, 888/282-8267 reservations 📠 973/808-9713 ⊕ www. accessiblevans.com. **CareVacations** ✉ No. 5, 5110-50 Ave., Leduc, Alberta T9E 6V4, Canada ☎ 780/986-6404 or 877/478-7827 📠 780/986-8332 ⊕ www.carevacations.com, for group tours and cruise vacations. **Flying Wheels Travel** ✉ 143 W. Bridge St. ✍ Box 382, Owatonna, MN 55060 ☎ 507/451-5005 📠 507/451-1685 ⊕ www. flyingwheelstravel.com.

🔲 Travelers with Developmental Disabilities **Sprout** ✉ 893 Amsterdam Ave., New York, NY 10025 ☎ 212/222-9575 or 888/222-9575 📠 212/222-9768 ⊕ www.gosprout.org.

DISCOUNTS & DEALS

You can sometimes pick up discount coupons for various attractions at local chamber of commerce offices. Some places, from restaurants to amusement centers, also post discount coupons on their Web sites.

Be a smart shopper and compare all your options before making decisions. A plane ticket bought with a promotional coupon from travel clubs, coupon books, and direct-mail offers or purchased on the Internet may not be cheaper than the least expensive fare from a discount ticket agency. And always keep in mind that what you get is just as important as what you save.

For Cape antiques and nautical finds at a discount, **visit the flea markets** in Wellfleet and Dennis. **Crafts and artisan fairs** bound in the spring and summer where up-and-coming artists show their stuff and sell at prices way below those in galleries. If you can visit in late fall you will find considerable sales as many shop owners prepare to close their doors for the winter months.

DISCOUNT RESERVATIONS

To save money, look into discount reservations services with Web sites and toll-free numbers, which use their buying power to get a better price on hotels, airline tickets (⇨ Air Travel), even car rentals. When booking a room, always **call the hotel's local toll-free number** (if one is available) rather than the central reservations number—you'll often get a better price. Always ask about special packages or corporate rates.

🔲 Airline Tickets **Air 4 Less** ☎ 800/AIR4LESS; low-fare specialist.

🔲 Hotel Rooms **Accommodations Express** ☎ 800/444-7666 or 800/277-1064 ⊕ www.acex. net.**Hotels.com** ☎ 800/246-8357 ⊕ www.hotels. com. **Quikbook** ☎ 800/789-9887 ⊕ www. quikbook.com.**Turbotrip.com** ☎ 800/473-7829 ⊕ www.turbotrip.com.

PACKAGE DEALS

Don't confuse packages and guided tours. When you buy a package, you travel on your own, just as though you had planned the trip yourself. Fly-drive packages, which combine airfare and car rental, are often a good deal.

ECOTOURISM

Throughout the Cape, including the Monomoy Islands, Sandy Neck in Barnstable, and the Cape Cod National Seashore, signs indicate (in season) the nesting areas of the endangered piping plover. Warning signs around the Cape urge you to protect fragile sand dunes by not walking or climbing on them.

Most towns have recycling protocols; if you're renting a house, ask your agent for information.

GAY & LESBIAN TRAVEL

Provincetown, at the tip of the Cape, is one of the East Coast's leading lesbian and gay seaside destinations and also has a large year-round lesbian and gay community. Dozens of P-town establishments, from B&Bs to bars, cater specifically to lesbian and gay visitors, and all of the town's restaurants are gay-friendly; many are gay-owned and -operated. Hyannis has Cape Cod's sole gay bar outside P-town.

For details about the gay and lesbian scene, consult *Fodor's Gay Guide to the USA* (available in bookstores everywhere). ⚑ Gay- & Lesbian-Friendly Travel Agencies **Different Roads Travel** ⊠ 8383 Wilshire Blvd., Suite 520, Beverly Hills, CA 90211 ☎ 323/651–5557 or 800/429–8747 (Ext. 14 for both) 🖷 323/651–5454 ✉ lgernert@tzell.com. **Kennedy Travel** ⊠ 130 W. 42nd St., Suite 401, New York, NY 10036 ☎ 212/840–8659, 800/237–7433 🖷 212/730–2269 ⊕ www. kennedytravel.com. **Now, Voyager** ⊠ 4406 18th St., San Francisco, CA 94114 ☎ 415/626–1169 or 800/255–6951 🖷 415/626–8626 ⊕ www.nowvoyager. com. **Skylink Travel and Tour/Flying Dutchmen Travel** ⊠ 1455 N. Dutton Ave., Suite A, Santa Rosa, CA 95401 ☎ 707/546–9888 or 800/225–5759 🖷 707/636–0951; serving lesbian travelers.

HEALTH

Most Cape Cod pharmacies will refill an out-of-town prescription if you provide the prescribing doctor's phone number for verification. Most pharmacies post emergency numbers on their doors.

A common problem on the East Coast is Lyme disease (named after Lyme, Connecticut, where it was first diagnosed). This bacterial infection is transmitted by deer ticks and can be very serious, leading to chronic arthritis and worse if left untreated. Pregnant women are advised to **avoid areas of possible deer tick infestation**; if contracted during early pregnancy, Lyme disease can harm a fetus.

Deer ticks are most prevalent April–October but can be found year-round. They are about the size of a pinhead. Wear light-color clothing, which makes it easier

to spot any ticks that might have attached themselves to you. Anyone planning to explore wooded areas or places with tall grasses (including dunes) should **wear long pants, socks drawn up over pant cuffs, and a long-sleeve shirt with a close-fitting collar**; boots are also recommended. The National Centers for Disease Control recommends that DEET repellent be applied to skin (not face!) and that permethrin be applied to clothing directly before entering infested areas; **use repellents very carefully** and conservatively with small children. Ticks also attach themselves to pets.

Recent research suggests that if ticks are removed within 12 hours of attachment to the body, the infectious bacteria is not likely to enter the bloodstream. That makes evenings a good opportunity to check yourself for ticks—look at the warm spots and hairlines on the body that attract ticks.

To remove a tick, apply tweezers to where it's attached to the skin and pull on the mouth parts. Try not to squeeze the body of the tick, which can send the body fluids containing the bacteria into the bloodstream. (Heating the tip of the tweezers before grasping the tick will cause the bug to release its bite, allowing for removal of the entire tick, including the sometimes-embedded head.) Disinfect the bite with alcohol and save the tick in a closed jar in case symptoms of the disease develop.

The first symptom of Lyme disease may be a ringlike rash or flulike symptoms, such as general feelings of malaise, fever, chills, and joint or facial pains. If diagnosed early, it can be treated with antibiotics. If you suspect your symptoms may be due to a tick bite, inform your doctor and ask to be tested.

Poison ivy is a pervasive vinelike plant, recognizable by its leaf pattern: three shiny green leaves together. In spring new poison ivy leaves are red; likewise, they can take on a reddish tint as fall approaches. The oil from these leaves produces an itchy skin rash that spreads with scratching. If you think you may have touched some leaves, **wash as soon as you can** with soap and cool water.

⑦ Lyme Disease Info **Massachusetts Department of Public Health** ✉ Southeast Office, 109 Rhode Island Rd., Lakeville, MA 02347 ☎ 508/947-1231 ⊕ www.state.ma.us/dph. **National Centers for Disease Control and Prevention** CDC; National Center for Infectious Diseases, Division of Quarantine, Traveler's Health Section ✉ 1600 Clifton Rd. NE, M/S E-03, Atlanta, GA 30333 ☎ 888/232-3228 general information, 877/394-8747 travelers' health line, 800/311-3435 public inquiries 🖷 888/232-3299 ⊕ www.cdc.gov.

HOLIDAYS

Major national holidays include New Year's Day; Martin Luther King Jr. Day (3rd Mon. in Jan.); President's Day (3rd Mon. in Feb.); Memorial Day (last Mon. in May); Independence Day; Labor Day (1st Mon. in Sept.); Thanksgiving Day (4th Thurs. in Nov.); Christmas Eve and Christmas Day; and New Year's Eve.

INSURANCE

The most useful travel-insurance plan is a comprehensive policy that includes coverage for trip cancellation and interruption, default, trip delay, and medical expenses (with a waiver for pre-existing conditions).

Without insurance you will lose all or most of your money if you cancel your trip, regardless of the reason. Default insurance covers you if your tour operator, airline, or cruise line goes out of business. Trip-delay covers expenses that arise because of bad weather or mechanical delays. Study the fine print when comparing policies.

U.K. residents can buy a travel-insurance policy valid for most vacations taken during the year in which it's purchased (but check preexisting-condition coverage).

Always **buy travel policies directly from the insurance company**; if you buy them from a cruise line, airline, or tour operator that goes out of business you probably won't be covered for the agency or operator's default, a major risk. Before making any purchase, review your existing health and home-owner's policies to find what they cover away from home.

⑦ Travel Insurers In the U.S.: **Access America** ✉ 2805 N. Parham Rd., Richmond, VA 23294 ☎ 800/284-8300 🖷 804/673-1491 or 800/346-9265 ⊕ www.accessamerica.com. **Travel Guard International** ✉ 1145 Clark St., Stevens Point, WI 54481 ☎ 715/345-0505 or 800/826-1300 🖷 800/955-8785 ⊕ www.travelguard.com.

FOR INTERNATIONAL TRAVELERS

For information on customs restrictions, *see* Customs and Duties, *above.*

CAR RENTAL

When picking up a rental car, non-U.S. residents need a reservation voucher for any prepaid reservations that were made in the traveler's home country, a passport, a driver's license, and a travel policy that covers each driver.

CAR TRAVEL

Gas stations on the Cape are plentiful. Most stay open late (24 hours along large highways and in big cities), except in rural areas, where Sunday hours are limited and where you may drive long stretches without an opportunity to refuel. Interstate highways—limited-access, multilane highways whose numbers are prefixed by "I–"—are the fastest routes. Interstates with three-digit numbers encircle urban areas, which may have other limited-access expressways, freeways, and parkways as well. Tolls may be levied on limited-access highways. So-called U.S. highways and state highways are not necessarily limited-access but may have several lanes.

Along larger highways, roadside stops with rest rooms, fast-food restaurants, and sundries stores are well spaced. State police and tow trucks patrol major highways and lend assistance. If your car breaks down on an interstate, pull onto the shoulder and wait for help, or have your passengers wait while you walk to an emergency phone. If you carry a cell phone, dial *55, noting your location on the small green roadside mileage markers.

Driving in the United States is on the right. Do **obey speed limits** posted along roads and highways. Watch for lower limits in small towns and on back roads. Massachusetts state law requires drivers and all passengers to **wear seat belts.** On weekdays between 6 and 10 AM and again between 4 and 7 PM **expect heavy traffic.** To encourage carpooling, some freeways have special lanes for so-called high-occupancy vehicles (HOV)—cars carrying more than one passenger (⇨ *above*).

Bookstores, gas stations, convenience stores, and rest stops sell maps (about $3) and multiregion road atlases (about $10).

CONSULATES & EMBASSIES

The nearest consulates are in Boston. New Zealand doesn't have a consulate in Boston. 🉐 Australia ✉ 15 School St., Boston ☎ 617/227-3131.
🉐 Canada ✉ 3 Copley Pl., Boston ☎ 617/262-3760.
🉐 United Kingdom ✉ 600 Atlantic Ave., Boston ☎ 617/248-9555.

CURRENCY

The dollar is the basic unit of U.S. currency. It has 100 cents. Coins include the copper penny (1¢); the silvery nickel (5¢), dime (10¢), quarter (25¢), and half-dollar (50¢); and the golden $1 coin, replacing a now-rare silver dollar. Bills are denominated $1, $5, $10, $20, $50, and $100, all green and identical in size; designs vary. Check exchange rates while planning your trip, keeping in mind that they can fluctuate many times before you depart.

ELECTRICITY

The U.S. standard is AC, 110 volts/60 cycles. Plugs have two flat pins set parallel to each other.

EMERGENCIES

For police, fire, or ambulance, **dial 911** (0 in rural areas).

INSURANCE

Britons and Australians need extra medical coverage when traveling overseas.
🉐 Insurance Information In the U.K.: **Association of British Insurers** ✉ 51 Gresham St., London EC2V 7HQ ☎ 020/7600-3333 🖶 020/7696-8999 ⊕ www.abi.org.uk. In Australia: **Insurance Council of Australia** ✉ Insurance Enquiries and Complaints, Level 12, Box 561, Collins St. W, Melbourne, VIC 8007 ☎ 1300/780808 or 03/9629-4109 🖶 03/9621-2060 ⊕ www.iecltd.com.au. In Canada: **RBC Insurance** ✉ 6880 Financial Dr., Mississauga, Ontario L5N 7Y5 ☎ 800/668-4342 or 905/816-2400 🖶 905/813-4704 ⊕ www.rbcinsurance.com. In New Zealand: **Insurance Council of New Zealand** ✉ Level 7, 111-115 Customhouse Quay, Box 474, Wellington ☎ 04/472-5230 🖶 04/473-3011 ⊕ www.icnz.org.nz.

MAIL & SHIPPING

You can buy stamps and aerograms and send letters and parcels in post offices. Stamp-dispensing machines can occasionally be found in airports, bus and train stations, office buildings, drugstores, and the like. You can also deposit mail in the stout, dark blue, steel bins at strategic locations everywhere and in the mail chutes of large buildings; pickup schedules are posted. You can deposit packages at public collection boxes as long as the parcels are affixed with proper postage and weigh less than one pound. Packages weighing one or more pounds must be taken to a post office or handed to a postal carrier.

For mail sent within the United States, you need a 37¢ stamp for first-class letters weighing up to 1 ounce (23¢ for each additional ounce) and 23¢ for postcards. You pay 80¢ for 1-ounce airmail letters and 70¢ for airmail postcards to most other countries; to Canada and Mexico, you need a 60¢ stamp for a 1-ounce letter and 50¢ for a postcard. An aerogram—a single sheet of lightweight blue paper that folds into its own envelope, stamped for overseas airmail—costs 70¢.

To receive mail on the road, have it sent c/o General Delivery at your destination's main post office (use the correct five-digit ZIP code). You must pick up mail in person within 30 days and show a driver's license or passport.

PASSPORTS & VISAS

When traveling internationally, carry your passport even if you don't need one (it's always the best form of I.D.) and **make two photocopies of the data page** (one for someone at home and another for you, carried separately from your passport). If you lose your passport, promptly call the nearest embassy or consulate and the local police.

Visitor visas aren't necessary for Canadian or European Union citizens, or for citizens of Australia who are staying fewer than 90 days.
🉐 Australian Citizens **Passports Australia** ☎ 131-232 ⊕ www.passports.gov.au. **United States Consulate General** ✉ MLC Centre, Level 59, 19-29 Martin Pl., Sydney, NSW 2000 ☎ 02/9373-9200,

1902/941–641 fee-based visa-inquiry line ⊕ usembassy-australia.state.gov/sydney.

🔲 Canadian Citizens **Passport Office** ✉ to mail in applications: 200 Promenade du Portage, Hull, Québec J8X 4B7 ☎ 819/994–3500, 800/567–6868, 866/255–7655 TTY ⊕ www.ppt.gc.ca.

🔲 New Zealand Citizens **New Zealand Passports Office** ✉ for applications and information, Level 3, Boulcott House, 47 Boulcott St., Wellington ☎ 0800/22–5050 or 04/474–8100 ⊕ www.passports.govt.nz. **Embassy of the United States** ✉ 29 Fitzherbert Terr., Thorndon, Wellington ☎ 04/462–6000 ⊕ usembassy.org.nz. **U.S. Consulate General** ✉ Citibank Bldg., 3rd floor, 23 Customs St. E, Auckland ☎ 09/303–2724 ⊕ usembassy.org.nz.

🔲 U.K. Citizens **U.K. Passport Service** ☎ 0870/521–0410 ⊕ www.passport.gov.uk. **American Consulate General** ✉ Danesfort House, 223 Stranmillis Rd., Belfast, Northern Ireland BT9 5GR ☎ 028/9032–8239 🖨 028/9024–8482 ⊕ usembassy.org.uk. **American Embassy** ✉ for visa and immigration information or to submit a visa application via mail (enclose an SASE), Consular Information Unit, 24 Grosvenor Sq., London W1 1AE ☎ 09055/444–546 for visa information (per-minute charges), 0207/499–9000 main switchboard ⊕ usembassy.org.uk.

TELEPHONES

All U.S. telephone numbers consist of a three-digit area code and a seven-digit local number. In eastern Massachusetts, including Boston and Cape Cod, you must dial the full 10-digit phone number (the area code plus the local number) when making a local call. To call between area-code regions, dial "1" then all 10 digits; the same goes for calls to numbers prefixed by "800," "888," "866," and "877"—all toll free. For calls to numbers preceded by "900" you must pay—usually dearly.

For international calls, dial "011" followed by the country code and the local number. For help, dial "0" and ask for an overseas operator. The country code is 61 for Australia, 64 for New Zealand, 44 for the United Kingdom. Calling Canada is the same as calling within the United States. Most local phone books list country codes and U.S. area codes. The country code for the United States is 1.

For operator assistance, dial "0." To obtain someone's phone number, call directory assistance at 555–1212 or occasionally 411 (free at many public phones). To have the person you're calling foot the bill, phone collect; dial "0" instead of "1" before the 10-digit number.

At pay phones, instructions often are posted. Usually you insert coins in a slot (usually 25¢–50¢ for local calls) and wait for a steady tone before dialing. When you call long-distance, the operator tells you how much to insert; prepaid phone cards, widely available in various denominations, are easier. Call the number on the back, punch in the card's personal identification number when prompted, then dial your number.

LODGING

Accommodations on the Cape range from campsites to B&Bs to luxurious self-contained resorts offering all kinds of sporting facilities, restaurants, entertainment, services (including business services and children's programs), and all the assistance you'll ever need in making vacation arrangements.

Single-night lodgings for those just passing through can be found at countless tacky but cheap and conveniently located little roadside motels, as well as at others that are spotless and cheery yet still inexpensive, or at chain hotels at all price levels; these places often have a pool, TVs, or other amenities to keep children entertained in the evening.

Families may want to **consider condominiums, cottages, and efficiencies**, which offer more space; living areas; kitchens; and sometimes laundry facilities, children's play areas, or children's programs.

The lodgings we list are the cream of the crop in each price category. We always list the facilities that are available—but we don't specify whether they cost extra: when pricing accommodations, always ask what's included and what costs extra. Properties indicated by a ✕▣ are lodging establishments whose restaurant warrants a special trip even if you are not staying at that establishment.

CATEGORY	COST*
$$$$	over $220
$$$	$140–$220
$$	$100–$140
$	$80–$100
¢	under $80

*All prices are for a standard double room in high season, excluding 5.7% state tax and gratuities. Some inns add a 15% service charge.

*Assume that hotels operate on the **European Plan** (EP, with no meals included) unless we specify that they use the **Continental Plan** (CP, with a continental breakfast), **Breakfast Plan** (BP, with a full breakfast), **Modified American Plan** (MAP, with breakfast and dinner), or the **Full American Plan** (FAP, with all meals).*

CONDO & HOUSE RENTALS

If you want a home base that's roomy enough for a family and comes with cooking facilities, consider a furnished rental. These can save you money, especially if you're traveling with a group. Home-exchange directories sometimes list rentals as well as exchanges.

Many travelers to the Cape rent a house if they're going to stay for a week or longer rather than stay at a B&B or hotel. These can save you money; however, some rentals are luxury properties, economical only when your party is large. Many local real-estate agencies deal with rentals, and most specialize in a specific area. If you do decide to rent, be sure to book a property well in advance of your trip, as many properties are rented out to the same families or groups year after year. Rental choices are often greater in the smaller, quieter towns, such as Yarmouth, Chatham, Wellfleet, and Truro. For the names of regional agencies, *see* the A to Z section of the appropriate chapter in this book, consult the local chamber of commerce guide, and if you can, get hold of the local yellow pages. *See* the Home, Sweet Rental Home *section for tips on arranging a rental.*

📋 International Agent **Hideaways International** ✉ 767 Islington St., Portsmouth, NH 03801 ☎ 603/430–4433 or 800/843–4433 🖷 603/430–4444 ⊕ www.hideaways.com, annual membership $145. 📋 Local Agent **Waterfront Rentals** ✉ 20 Pilgrim Rd., West Yarmouth 02673 ☎ 508/778–1818 🖷 508/

771–3563 ⊕ www.waterfrontrentalsinc.com covers Bourne to Truro.

BED-AND-BREAKFASTS

Bed-and-breakfast inns have long been very popular on Cape Cod. Many are in interesting old sea captains' homes and other 17th-, 18th-, and 19th-century buildings; others are in newer homes in which a few rooms and bathrooms have been set aside for rent. In many cases, B&Bs are not appropriate for families—noise travels easily, rooms are often small, and the furnishings are often fragile; so be sure to ask. Most B&Bs do not provide phones or TVs in guest rooms, some are not air-conditioned, and more and more prohibit smoking.

In summer you must reserve lodgings as far in advance as possible—several months for the most popular inns. Assistance with last-minute reservations is available at the Cape Cod Chamber of Commerce information booths and through the chamber of commerce's Web site (⇨ Web Sites). Off-season, rates are much reduced, and service may be more personalized.

Numerous B&B reservation agencies can aid you in choosing an inn. One company, DestINNations (part of the TOURCO company), handles a limited number of upscale inns, resorts, and B&Bs on the Cape. For more information get a free B&B guide from the Massachusetts Office of Travel & Tourism (⇨ Visitor Information). The Cape Cod Chamber of Commerce (⇨ Visitor Information) also publishes a free B&B guide.

📋 Reservation Services **Bed and Breakfast Cape Cod** 🏠 Box 1312, Orleans 02653 ☎ 508/255–3824 or 800/541–6226 🖷 508/240–0599 ⊕ www.bedandbreakfastcapecod.com. **DestINNations** ✉ 29 Bassett La., Hyannis 02601 ☎ 508/771–5165 or 800/333–4667 🖷 508/790–1115 ⊕ www.destinnations.com.

CAMPING

There are many private and state-park camping areas on Cape Cod. Write to the Massachusetts Office of Travel & Tourism and the Cape Cod Chamber of Commerce (⇨ Visitor Information). For details on camping in specific areas, look for the

⚠ icon in that area's Dining and Lodging section and consult the A to Z section of that chapter.

HOME EXCHANGES

If you would like to exchange your home for someone else's, join a home-exchange organization, which will send you its updated listings of available exchanges for a year and will include your own listing in at least one of them. It's up to you to make specific arrangements.

📧 Exchange Clubs **HomeLink International** 🖂 Box 47747, Tampa, FL 33647 ☎ 813/975–9825 or 800/638–3841 🖷 813/910–8144 ⊕ www.homelink. org; $110 yearly for a listing, online access, and catalog; $70 without catalog. **Intervac U.S.** 🖂 30 Corte San Fernando, Tiburon, CA 94920 ☎ 800/756–4663 🖷 415/435–7440 ⊕ www.intervacus.com; $125 yearly for a listing, online access, and a catalog; $65 without catalog.

HOSTELS

No matter what your age, you can **save on lodging costs by staying at hostels.** In some 4,500 locations in more than 70 countries around the world, Hostelling International (HI), the umbrella group for a number of national youth-hostel associations, offers single-sex, dorm-style beds and, at many hostels, rooms for couples and family accommodations. Membership in any HI national hostel association, open to travelers of all ages, allows you to stay in HI-affiliated hostels at member rates; one-year membership is about $25 for adults (C$35 for a two-year minimum membership in Canada, £13 in the United Kingdom, A$52 in Australia, and NZ$40 in New Zealand); hostels run about $10–$30 per night. Members have priority if the hostel is full; they're also eligible for discounts around the world, even on rail and bus travel in some countries.

Cape Cod has some excellent hostels. In season, when all other rates are jacked up beyond belief, hostels are often the only budget-accommodation option, but you must plan ahead to reserve space. The hostel in Eastham has eight cabins that each sleep six to eight; two can be used as family cabins. In the Truro hostel, accommo-dations are dormitory-style. You may luck out on last-minute cancellations, but it would be unwise to rely on them. See the lodging listings in the appropriate chapters for specific information.

📧 Organizations **Hostelling International–USA** 🖂 8401 Colesville Rd., Suite 600, Silver Spring, MD 20910 ☎ 301/495–1240 🖷 301/495–6697 ⊕ www. hiusa.org. **Hostelling International–Canada** 🖂 205 Catherine St., Suite 400, Ottawa, Ontario K2P 1C3 ☎ 613/237–7884 or 800/663–5777 🖷 613/237–7868 ⊕ www.hihostels.ca. **YHA England and Wales** 🖂 Trevelyan House, Dimple Rd., Matlock, Derbyshire DE4 3YH, U.K. ☎ 0870/870–8808, 0870/770–8868, 0162/959–2600 🖷 0870/770–6127 ⊕ www.yha.org.uk. **YHA Australia** 🖂 422 Kent St., Sydney, NSW 2001 ☎ 02/9261–1111 🖷 02/9261–1969 ⊕ www.yha.com.au. **YHA New Zealand** 🖂 Level 1, Moorhouse City, 166 Moorhouse Ave., Box 436, Christchurch ☎ 03/379–9970 or 0800/278–299 🖷 03/365–4476 ⊕ www.yha.org.nz.

HOTELS

All hotels listed have private bath unless otherwise noted.

📧 Toll-Free Numbers **Best Western** ☎ 800/528–1234 ⊕ www.bestwestern.com. **Choice** ☎ 800/424–6423 ⊕ www.choicehotels.com. **Comfort Inn** ☎ 800/424–6423 ⊕ www.choicehotels.com. **Days Inn** ☎ 800/325–2525 ⊕ www.daysinn.com. **Doubletree and Red Lion Hotels** ☎ 800/222–8733 ⊕ www.hilton.com. **Embassy Suites** ☎ 800/362–2779 ⊕ www.embassysuites.com. **Fairfield Inn** ☎ 800/228–2800 ⊕ www.marriott.com. **Hilton** ☎ 800/445–8667 ⊕ www.hilton.com. **Holiday Inn** ☎ 800/465–4329 ⊕ www.sixcontinentshotels.com. **Howard John-son** ☎ 800/654–4656 ⊕ www.hojo.com. **Hyatt Ho-tels & Resorts** ☎ 800/233–1234 ⊕ www.hyatt.com. **La Quinta** ☎ 800/531–5900 ⊕ www.laquinta.com. **Marriott** ☎ 800/228–9290 ⊕ www.marriott.com. **Quality Inn** ☎ 800/424–6423 ⊕ www.choicehotels. com. **Radisson** ☎ 800/333–3333 ⊕ www.radisson. com. **Ramada** ☎ 800/228–2828, 800/854–7854 in-ternational reservations ⊕ www.ramada.com. **Shera-ton** ☎ 800/325–3535 ⊕ www.starwood.com/ sheraton. **Sleep Inn** ☎ 800/424–6423 ⊕ www. choicehotels.com. **Westin Hotels & Resorts** ☎ 800/228–3000 ⊕ www.starwood.com/westin.

MEDIA

NEWSPAPERS & MAGAZINES

Glossy regional magazines include *Cape Cod Life* and *Cape Cod Magazine*, which both have articles about Cape people and places; *Provincetown Arts,* which focuses on Provincetown artists, performers, and writers, and also publishes essays, fiction, interviews, and poetry; and *Cape Women,* with profiles of Cape-based women and other articles that address issues of interest to women.

The *Cape Cod Times* (⊕ www. capecodonline.com/cctimes) is a daily newspaper with news from around the Cape and elsewhere. In Provincetown look for the *Banner* and *Provincetown Magazine,* both weeklies, for art and entertainment listings.

RADIO & TELEVISION
You can generally get Boston and Providence TV stations on the Cape. Boston stations include PBS WGBH (2), CBS WBZ (4), ABC WCVB (5), NBC WHDH (7), FOX WFXT (25), and WB WLVI (56). From Providence, stations include ABC WLNE (6), NBC WJAR (10), CBS WPRI (12), PBS WSBE (36), and FOX WNAC (64). There is also a Cape community station, C3TV.

WBUR, a Boston-based National Public Radio station, broadcasts on the Cape with different frequencies in different towns: 1240 AM in West Yarmouth, WSDH 91.5 FM in Sandwich, and WCCT 90.3 FM in Harwich. A second public radio station operates at WCAI 90.1 FM from Woods Hole, with support from WGBH in Boston.

MONEY MATTERS
Prices throughout this guide are given for adults. Substantially reduced fees are almost always available for children, students, and senior citizens. For information on taxes, *see* Taxes, *below.*

ATMS
Cape Cod has many ATM machines in all the towns.

CREDIT CARDS
Throughout this guide, the following abbreviations are used: **AE,** American Express; **D,** Discover; **DC,** Diners Club; **MC,** MasterCard; and **V,** Visa.

🔳 Reporting Lost Cards **American Express** ☎ 800/441-0519. **Diners Club** ☎ 800/234-6377.

Discover ☎ 800/347-2683. **MasterCard** ☎ 800/622-7747. **Visa** ☎ 800/847-2911.

NATIONAL PARKS
Look into discount passes to save money on park entrance fees. For $50, the National Parks Pass admits you (and any passengers in your private vehicle) to all national parks, monuments, and recreation areas, as well as other sites run by the National Park Service, for a year. (In parks that charge per person, the pass admits you, your spouse and children, and your parents, when you arrive together.) Camping and parking are extra. The $15 Golden Eagle Pass, a hologram you affix to your National Parks Pass, functions as an upgrade, granting entry to all sites run by the NPS, the U.S. Fish and Wildlife Service, the U.S. Forest Service, and the Bureau of Land Management. The upgrade, which expires with the parks pass, is sold by most national-park, Fish-and-Wildlife, and BLM fee stations. A major percentage of the proceeds from pass sales funds National Parks projects.

Both the Golden Age Passport ($10), for U.S. citizens or permanent residents who are 62 and older, and the Golden Access Passport (free), for persons with disabilities, entitle holders (and any passengers in their private vehicles) to lifetime free entry to all national parks, plus 50% off fees for the use of many park facilities and services. (The discount doesn't always apply to companions.) To obtain them, you must show proof of age and of U.S. citizenship or permanent residency—such as a U.S. passport, driver's license, or birth certificate—and, if requesting Golden Access, proof of disability. The Golden Age and Golden Access passes are available only at NPS-run sites that charge an entrance fee. The National Parks Pass is also available by mail and via the Internet.

🔳 **National Park Foundation** ✉ 11 Dupont Circle NW, 6th floor, Washington, DC 20036 ☎ 202/238-4200 ⊕ www.nationalparks.org. **National Park Service** ✉ National Park Service/Department of Interior, 1849 C St. NW, Washington, DC 20240 ☎ 202/208-6843 ⊕ www.nps.gov. **National Parks Conser-**

vation Association ✉ 1300 19th St. NW, Suite 300, Washington, DC 20036 ☎ 202/223-6722 ⊕ www. npca.org.

▣ Passes by Mail & Online **National Park Foundation** ⊕ www.nationalparks.org. **National Parks Pass** National Park Foundation ✆ Box 34108, Washington, DC 20043 ☎ 888/467-2757 ⊕ www. nationalparks.org; include a check or money order payable to the National Park Service, plus $3.95 for shipping and handling (allow 8 to 13 business days from date of receipt for pass delivery), or call for passes.

PACKING

Only a few Cape Cod restaurants require formal dress, as do some dinner cruises. The area prides itself on informality. Do **pack a sweater or jacket, even in summer,** for nights can be cool. For suggested clothing to minimize bites from deer ticks and to prevent Lyme disease, *see* Health. Perhaps most important of all, **don't forget a swimsuit** (or two).

In your carry-on luggage, pack an extra pair of eyeglasses or contact lenses and enough of any medication you take to last a few days longer than the entire trip. You may also ask your doctor to write a spare prescription using the drug's generic name, as brand names may vary from country to country. In luggage to be checked, **never pack prescription drugs, valuables, or undeveloped film.** And don't forget to carry with you the addresses of offices that handle refunds of lost traveler's checks. Check *Fodor's How to Pack* (available at online retailers and bookstores everywhere) for more tips.

To avoid customs and security delays, carry medications in their original packaging. Don't pack any sharp objects in your carry-on luggage, including knives of any size or material, scissors, nail clippers, and corkscrews, or anything else that might arouse suspicion.

To avoid having your checked luggage chosen for hand inspection, don't cram bags full. The U.S. Transportation Security Administration suggests packing shoes on top and placing personal items you don't want touched in clear plastic bags.

CHECKING LUGGAGE

You're allowed to carry aboard one bag and one personal article, such as a purse or a laptop computer. Make sure what you carry on fits under your seat or in the overhead bin. Get to the gate early, so you can board as soon as possible, before the overhead bins fill up.

Baggage allowances vary by carrier, destination, and ticket class. On international flights, you're usually allowed to check two bags weighing up to 70 pounds (32 kilograms) each, although a few airlines allow checked bags of up to 88 pounds (40 kilograms) in first class. Some international carriers don't allow more than 66 pounds (30 kilograms) per bag in business class and 44 pounds (20 kilograms) in economy. On domestic flights, the limit is usually 50 to 70 pounds (23 to 32 kilograms) per bag. In general, carry-on bags shouldn't exceed 40 pounds (18 kilograms). Most airlines won't accept bags that weigh more than 100 pounds (45 kilograms) on domestic or international flights. Expect to pay a fee for baggage that exceeds weight limits. Check baggage restrictions with your carrier before you pack.

Airline liability for baggage is limited to $2,500 per person on flights within the United States. On international flights it amounts to $9.07 per pound or $20 per kilogram for checked baggage (roughly $640 per 70-pound bag), with a maximum of $634.90 per piece, and $400 per passenger for unchecked baggage. You can buy additional coverage at check-in for about $10 per $1,000 of coverage, but it often excludes a rather extensive list of items, shown on your airline ticket.

Before departure, itemize your bags' contents and their worth, and label the bags with your name, address, and phone number. (If you use your home address, cover it so potential thieves can't see it readily.) Include a label inside each bag and **pack a copy of your itinerary.** At check-in, make sure each bag is correctly tagged with the destination airport's three-letter code. Because some checked bags will be opened for hand inspection, the U.S. Transportation Security Administration recommends that you leave luggage unlocked or use the plastic locks offered at check-in. TSA screeners place an inspection notice inside searched bags, which are re-sealed with a special lock.

If your bag has been searched and contents are missing or damaged, file a claim with the TSA Consumer Response Center as soon as possible. If your bags arrive damaged or fail to arrive at all, file a written report with the airline before leaving the airport.

▓ Complaints **U.S. Transportation Security Administration Contact Center** ☎ 866/289-9673 ⊕ www.tsa.gov.

RESTROOMS

In each Cape town, the tourist information office or chamber of commerce office (⇨ Visitor Information) either has a restroom or can refer you to the nearest facilities. Gas stations usually have restrooms as well. If you're driving between Boston and the Cape on Route 3, there are restrooms in the Tourist Information Center at Exit 5; if you're taking Route 24 south from Boston, there's a rest stop with a gas station, minimarket, and fast food at the intersection of Route 495.

SENIOR-CITIZEN TRAVEL

Many museums and attractions on the Cape have discounted rates for senior citizens. Ask about discounts when you're purchasing your ticket.

To qualify for age-related discounts, **mention your senior-citizen status up front** when booking hotel reservations (not when checking out) and before you're seated in restaurants (not when paying the bill). Be sure to have identification on hand. When renting a car, ask about promotional car-rental discounts, which can be cheaper than senior-citizen rates.

▓ Educational Programs **Elderhostel** ✉ 11 Ave. de Lafayette, Boston, MA 02111-1746 ☎ 877/426-8056, 978/323-4141 international callers, 877/426-2167 TTY ☐ 877/426-2166 ⊕ www.elderhostel.org.

SHOPPING

For an overview of some of the local specialties, *see the* Pleasures & Pastimes *section.* Because of the Cape's large

year-round population, shops tend to remain open, though many Provincetown and Wellfleet shops and galleries do close in winter. Throughout the Cape, shop owners respond to both the flow of tourists and their own inclinations. Especially off-season, it's best to **phone a shop before going out of your way to visit.**

Cape Cod Arts, published by *Cape Cod Life,* lists galleries Cape-wide. Provincetown and Wellfleet are the main centers for art, and their gallery associations have pamphlets on local galleries. For a directory of area antiques dealers and auctions, contact the Cape Cod Antique Dealers Association. For a listing of crafts shops on the Cape, write to the Artisans' Guild of Cape Cod, Cape Cod Potters, or the Society of Cape Cod Craftsmen.

▓ Local Resources **Artisans' Guild of Cape Cod** Send business-size SASE to 🖅 46 Debs Hill Rd., Yarmouth 02675. **Cape Cod Antique Dealers Association** Send business-size SASE to 🖅 Box 191, Yarmouth Port 02675 ⊕ www.ccada.com. **Cape Cod Arts** 🖅 Box 1385, Pocasset 02559 ⊕ www.capecodlife.com. **Cape Cod Potters** 🖅 Box 76, Chatham 02633 ⊕ www.capecodpotters.com. **Provincetown Gallery Guild** 🖅 Box 242, Provincetown 02657. **Society of Cape Cod Craftsmen** 🖅 Box 1709, Wellfleet 02667-1709. **Wellfleet Art Galleries Association** 🖅 Box 916, Wellfleet 02667.

SMART SOUVENIRS

Local crafts, cranberry glass or a Pairpoint Crystal cup plate, and special-interest books about the Cape (purchased at one of the many fine bookstores) can be satisfying reminders of a visit.

SPORTS & THE OUTDOORS

For details on enjoying the outdoors in your chosen vacation spot, including water sports, *see* the appropriate regional chapter.

BASEBALL

The Cape Cod Baseball League, considered the country's best summer league, is scouted by all the major-league teams. Ten teams play a 44-game season from mid-June to mid-August; admission is free to games at all 10 fields, although donations are accepted. The teams also conduct baseball clinics for children and teens.

F Cape Cod Baseball League ☎ 508/432-6909 ⊕ www.capecodbaseball.org.

BIKING

The Travel Center at the American Youth Hostels' Boston hostel sells a "Cape Ann & North Shore/Cape Cod & Islands" bike map that includes information on the Claire Saltonstall Bikeway between Boston and Provincetown (135 mi) or between Boston and Woods Hole (85 mi). Brochures about the bikeway, as well as other bike trails on the Cape, may also be available from the Cape Cod Chamber of Commerce (⇨ Visitor Information).

F : **Travel Center at the American Youth Hostels' Boston hostel** ⊠ 12 Hemenway St., Boston 02115 ☎ 617/531-3523 ⊕ www.usahostels.org.

FISHING

Charter boats and party boats (per-head fees, rather than the charters' group rates) fish in season for bluefish, tuna, marlin, and mako and blue sharks. Throughout the year there's bottom fishing for flounder, tautog, scup, fluke, cod, and pollack.

The Cape Cod Chamber of Commerce's *Sportsman's Guide* provides fishing regulations, surf-fishing access locations, a map of boat-launching facilities, and more. The state Division of Fisheries and Wildlife has a book with dozens of maps of Cape ponds; the maps are also available on the Division's Web site. Remember, you'll need a license for freshwater fishing, available for a nominal fee at bait-and-tackle shops. Molly Benjamin's fishing column in the Friday *Cape Cod Times* gives the latest information about fishing on the Cape—what's being caught and where.

GOLF

The Cape Cod Chamber of Commerce has a "Golf Map of Cape Cod," locating dozens of courses on the Cape. Summer greens fees range from $25 to $50.

STUDENTS ON CAPE COD

Some Cape attractions have discounted prices for students; it always pays to ask.

F **I.D.s & Services STA Travel** ⊠ 10 Downing St., New York, NY 10014 ☎ 212/627-3111, 800/777-0112 24-hr service center ⊟ 212/627-3387 ⊕ www.sta.

com. **Travel Cuts** ⊠ 187 College St., Toronto, Ontario M5T 1P7, Canada ☎ 800/592-2887 in the U.S., 416/979-2406 or 866/246-9762 in Canada ⊟ 416/979-8167 ⊕ www.travelcuts.com.

TAXES

The state hotel tax rate is 5.7%.

SALES TAX

Massachusetts state sales tax is 5%.

TELEPHONES

Eastern Massachusetts has a 10-digit dialing system. You have to **dial the area code plus the seven-digit number for all local calls.** To call another region, as always, dial "1," then all 10 digits; the same goes for calls to numbers prefixed by 800, 888, 866, and 877.

TIME

Cape Cod is in the Eastern Standard time zone.

TIPPING

At restaurants a 15% tip is standard for waiters; up to 20% may be expected at more expensive establishments. The same goes for taxi drivers, bartenders, and hairdressers. Coat-check operators usually expect $1 per coat; bellhops and porters should get $1 to $2 per bag; hotel chambermaids should get $1 to $3 per night of your stay, and up to $5 per night at upscale hotels. On package tours, conductors and drivers usually get $10–$15 per day from the group as a whole; check whether this has already been figured into your cost. For local sightseeing tours you may individually tip the driver-guide $1–$5, depending on the length of the tour and the number of people in your party, if he or she has been helpful or informative. Ushers in theaters do not expect tips.

TOURS & PACKAGES

Because everything is prearranged on a prepackaged tour or independent vacation, you spend less time planning—and often get it all at a good price.

BOOKING WITH AN AGENT

Travel agents are excellent resources. But it's a good idea to collect brochures from several agencies, as some agents' suggestions may be influenced by relationships with tour and package firms that reward them for volume sales. If you have a special interest, **find an agent with expertise in that area**; the American Society of Travel Agents (ASTA; ⇨ Travel Agencies, *below*) has a database of specialists worldwide.

Make sure your travel agent knows the accommodations and other services of the place being recommended. Ask about the hotel's location, room size, beds, and whether it has a pool, room service, or programs for children, if you care about these. Has your agent been there in person or sent others whom you can contact?

Do some homework on your own, too: local tourism boards can provide information about lesser-known and small-niche operators, some of which may sell only direct.

BUYER BEWARE

Each year consumers are stranded or lose their money when tour operators—even large ones with excellent reputations—go out of business. So check out the operator. Ask several travel agents about its reputation, and try to **book with a company that has a consumer-protection program.** (Look for information in the company's brochure.) In the United States, members of the United States Tour Operators Association are required to set aside funds ($1 million) to help eligible customers cover payments and travel arrangements in the event that the company defaults. It's also a good idea to choose a company that participates in the American Society of Travel Agents' Tour Operator Program; ASTA will act as mediator in any disputes between you and your tour operator.

Remember that the more your package or tour includes, the better you can predict the ultimate cost of your vacation. Make sure you know exactly what is covered, and **beware of hidden costs.** Are taxes, tips, and transfers included? Entertainment and excursions? These can add up.

🖪 Tour-Operator Recommendations **American Society of Travel Agents** (⇨ Travel Agencies). **National Tour Association (NTA)** ⊠ 546 E. Main St., Lexington, KY 40508 ☎ 859/226-4444 or 800/682-8886 🖷 859/226-4404 ⊕ www.ntaonline.com. **United**

States Tour Operators Association (USTOA) ⊠ 275 Madison Ave., Suite 2014, New York, NY 10016 ☎ 212/599-6599 🖷 212/599-6744 ⊕ www.ustoa.com.

TRAIN TRAVEL

Because of continuing financial difficulties, Amtrak service to the Cape was suspended in 1998; it is not currently scheduled to resume, but call 800/USA-RAIL (800/872-7245) for an update.

TRANSPORTATION AROUND CAPE COD

A car is by far the most practical way to get around the Cape. There's limited bus service. A good general resource for information about getting around the Cape is the free Smart Guide, published by the Cape Cod Chamber of Commerce. It includes bus, ferry, train, trolley, and flight services; bicycling and walking information; and sources for traffic reports. It's available from the chamber (⇨ Visitor Information) or online at ⊕ www. smartguide.org Also refer to the A to Z sections of the regional chapters for more transportation information.

TRAVEL AGENCIES

A good travel agent puts your needs first. Look for an agency that has been in business at least five years, emphasizes customer service, and has someone on staff who specializes in your destination. In addition, **make sure the agency belongs to a professional trade organization.** The American Society of Travel Agents (ASTA)—the largest and most influential in the field with more than 20,000 members in some 140 countries—maintains and enforces a strict code of ethics and will step in to help mediate any agent-client disputes involving ASTA members if necessary. ASTA (whose motto is "Without a travel agent, you're on your own") also maintains a Web site that includes a directory of agents. (If a travel agency is also acting as your tour operator, *see* Buyer Beware *in* Tours & Packages.)

🖪 Local Agent Referrals **American Society of Travel Agents (ASTA)** ⊠ 1101 King St., Suite 200, Alexandria, VA 22314 ☎ 703/739-2782 or 800/965-2782 24-hr hotline 🖷 703/684-8319 ⊕ www. astanet.com. **Association of British Travel Agents**

✉ 68–71 Newman St., London W1T 3AH ☎ 020/
7637–2444 🖷 020/7637–0713 ⊕ www.abta.com. **Association of Canadian Travel Agencies** ✉ 130 Albert St., Suite 1705, Ottawa, Ontario K1P 5G4 ☎ 613/
237–3657 🖷 613/237–7052 ⊕ www.acta.ca. **Australian Federation of Travel Agents** ✉ Level 3, 309 Pitt St., Sydney, NSW 2000 ☎ 02/9264–3299 or 1300/363–416 🖷 02/9264–1085 ⊕ www.afta.com. au. **Travel Agents' Association of New Zealand** ✉ Level 5, Tourism and Travel House, 79 Boulcott St., Box 1888, Wellington 6001 ☎ 04/499–0104 🖷 04/499–0786 ⊕ www.taanz.org.nz.

VISITOR INFORMATION

Before you go, contact the state's office of tourism and the area's chambers of commerce for general information, seasonal events, and brochures. For specific information on Cape Cod's state forests and parks, the area's farmers' markets and fairs, or wildlife, contact the special-interest government offices below. You can also check Web sites on the Internet (⇨ Web Sites). When you arrive, you can pay a visit to the local chamber of commerce for additional information. For a list of local Cape Cod and nearby chambers of commerce that can also provide information, *see* Visitor Information *in* the A to Z sections of the appropriate chapters.

The Army Corps of Engineers has a 24-hour recreation hotline for canal-area events, weather, and tidal and fishing information.

🗹 Local Contacts : **Bristol County Convention & Visitors Bureau** ✉ 70 N. 2nd St. 🕮 Box 976, New Bedford, MA 02741 ☎ 508/997–1250 or 800/
288–6263 ⊕ www.southofboston.org. **Cape Cod Chamber of Commerce** ✉ Junction of Rtes. 6 and 132, Hyannis 02601 ☎ 508/862–0700 or 888/332–2732 🖷 508/862–0727 ⊕ www.capecodchamber. org. **Cape Cod National Seashore** ✉ South Wellfleet 02663 ☎ 508/349–3785 ⊕ www.nps. gov/caco. **Destination Plymouth** ⊕ www.visitplymouth.com.

🗹 State : **Massachusetts Office of Travel & Tourism** ✉ 10 Park Plaza, Suite 4510, Boston 02116 ☎ 800/227–6277, 800/447–6277 brochures 🖷 617/
973–8525 ⊕ www.massvacation.com.

🗹 Special Interests : **Army Corps of Engineers** ☎ 508/759–5991. **Department of Environmental Management** ✉ Division of Forests and Parks, 251 Causeway St., Suite 600, Boston 02114 ☎ 617/626–1250 ⊕ www.massparks.org. **Department of Food**

and Agriculture ✉ 251 Causeway St., Suite 500, Boston 02114 ☎ 617/626–1700 🖷 617/626–1850 ⊕ www.state.ma.us/dfa. **Division of Fisheries and Wildlife** ✉ Field Headquarters, 1 Rabbit Hill Rd., Westborough 01581 ☎ 508/792–7270 🖷 508/792–7275 ⊕ www.state.ma.us/dfwele.

WEB SITES

Do check out the World Wide Web when planning your trip. You'll find everything from weather forecasts to virtual tours of famous cities. Be sure to visit Fodors.com (⊕ www.fodors.com), a complete travel-planning site. You can research prices and book plane tickets, hotel rooms, rental cars, vacation packages, and more. In addition, you can post your pressing questions in the Travel Talk section. Other planning tools include a currency converter and weather reports, and there are loads of links to travel resources.

GENERAL INFORMATION

For general information, visit the Cape Cod Chamber of Commerce online at ⊕ www.capecodchamber.org. Other resources include Cape Cod Information Center (⊕ www.allcapecod.com) or Cape Cod Online (⊕ www.capecodonline.com); also *see* Visitor Information.

TRANSPORTATION

Smart Traveler (⊕ www.smartraveler.com) provides real-time updates on traffic conditions on Cape Cod. You can look at live Web cam pictures of the Bourne and Sagamore bridges at the Cape Cod USA site (⊕ www.capecodlivecam.com).

For Cape Cod bus and trolley schedules, check with the Cape Cod Regional Transit Authority (⊕ www.capecodtransit.org). The transportation information site of the Cape Cod Commission (⊕ www. gocapecod.org) has links to transportation providers, updates on transportation-related construction projects, and information on bicycling and walking, including updates on the Cape Cod Rail Trail. The Massachusetts Bicycle Coalition (⊕ www. massbike.org) has information for bicyclists. Rails-to-Trails Conservancy (⊕ www.railtrails.org) provides general information about rail trails, such as the Cape Cod Rail Trail.

Island ferry information and schedules are available online from the Steamship Authority (⊕ www.islandferry.com) and from Hy-Line (⊕ www.hy-linecruises.com). From New Bedford you can travel to Vineyard Haven on the ferry *Schamonchi* (⊕ www.mvferry.com) and to Cuttyhunk Island on the M/V *Alert II* (⊕ www. cuttyhunk.com).

DISABILITY ACCESS

Directory of Accessible Facilities lists accessible recreational facilities in Massachusetts (⊕ www.state.ma.us/dem/access. htm). Cape Cod Disability Access Directory (⊕ www.capecoddisability.org) has useful information about facilities on Cape Cod.

APPROACHING THE CAPE

PLYMOUTH, FALL RIVER, WESTPORT,
SOUTH DARTMOUTH,
NEW BEDFORD & MARION

1

Revised by
James W. Rohlf **MANY LESSER-KNOWN SITES** in southeastern Massachusetts make enjoyable stops en route to Cape Cod. If you're a history buff or want to give your kids an educational experience they won't soon forget, don't miss Plymouth, the community locals proudly call America's Hometown: here you can see that monument you've heard about since childhood, Plymouth Rock, and walk the decks of the *Mayflower II*. A few miles down the road is Plimoth Plantation, a re-created 17th-century Puritan village where trained staff members vividly dramatize the everyday lives of the first English settlers. Watch them make cheese, forge nails, and explain where and when they bathe (hint: not often).

If you're coming from the south or west, consider stopping in the seafaring towns of New Bedford and Fall River. In Fall River, history took a macabre turn with the Trial of the Century—the 19th century, that is. Fall River was the hometown of Lizzie Borden, who was accused, and acquitted, of dispatching her parents with "40 whacks" of an axe. Borden history has become a cottage industry here, but there's more to Fall River than just the Borden saga; if you're interested in nautical history, plan a stop at Battleship Cove, a floating museum complex.

Nearby New Bedford was a major whaling port in the 19th century and now holds the nation's largest museum on the history of whaling. Exhibits include the world's largest model ship and a rare skeleton of a 66-foot blue whale.

Along the coves of Buzzards Bay, southeastern Massachusetts is dotted with seaside towns and sandy beaches, the best known of which is Horseneck Beach in Westport. The pretty villages of South Dartmouth are also worth a stop. Last but not least, a sustained roll through this part of the state reveals some high-quality restaurants and charming bed-and-breakfasts.

Exploring the Approach to the Cape

The relationship between man and the sea in our nation's history is perhaps no more apparent than in the region approaching the Cape. Located on what is referred to as the South Shore (relative to Boston), the town of Plymouth occupies the site of the Pilgrims 1620 landing. Fall River, home to battleship cove (as well as the infamous Lizzie Borden), is the gateway to Southeastern Massachusetts, the region between Rhode Island and Cape Cod. Located here are a variety of interesting seaside communities, both large and small, lining the shores of Buzzards Bay: Westport, South Dartmouth, the whaling city of New Bedford, and Marion.

Numbers in the margin correspond to points of interest on the Approaching the Cape map.

About the Restaurants

Like other Massachusetts shorefront towns, the communities approaching the Cape have plenty of seafood restaurants, where you

Numbers in the text correspond to numbers in the margin and on the Approaching the Cape map.

Approaching the Cape from the Southwest on I–195, the mile-long Braga Bridge has a great view of Mt. Hope Bay and the Taunton River upon entering **Fall River** ②. Directly under the bridge is **Battleship Cove,** home to the 35,000-ton USS Massachusetts and several other WWII ships. The **Marine Museum at Fall River** with its large Titanic exhibit is within walking distance. The nearby town of **Westport** ③ is a pleasant community with much open space including **Horseneck Beach State Reservation** with its sweeping views of Buzzards Bay and the nearby Elizabeth Islands, including remote **Cuttyhunk Island.** The role of **New Bedford** ⑤ in the world's whaling industry is documented at the **New Bedford Whaling Museum** located in an historic district of cobblestone streets near the waterfront. The picturesque town of **Marion** ⑥ is located on Sippican Harbor, home to hundreds of sailboats including the schooner SSV Tabor Boy, a 92-foot floating classroom for Tabor Academy.

Approaching from the North on Route 3, Exit 6 leads to downtown **Plymouth** ①. A replica of the historic *Mayflower II* is docked in the expansive harbor, near the famous **Plymouth Rock.** Established in 1824, making it one of the nation's oldest public repositories, **Pilgrim Hall Museum** contains many interesting artifacts from the Pilgrims' 1620 landing. South of downtown on the Atlantic Ocean is **Plimoth Plantation,** an authentic re-creation of how people lived here in 1627. Nearby are **Plymouth Beach** with restrooms and showers and the expansive **White Horse Beach.** To the East of Route 3 (take Exit 5), lies the 16,000 acre **Myles Standish State Forest** providing numerous opportunities for biking, swimming, picnicking, and canoeing on numerous streams and ponds.

1

---

find everything from clam shacks to more upscale dining options. In New Bedford and Fall River, which have large Portuguese populations, you can sample dishes made with spicy *linguica* (sausage) or *bacalau* (salt cod), and pick up some soft, doughy Portuguese sweet bread to sustain you as you explore.

About the Hotels

Plymouth's numerous lodgings include quaint B&Bs and large motels. Choices on the coast are more limited, although the area does have several recommendable small inns and B&Bs. If you're traveling with kids, be sure to ask whether they are welcome at smaller properties; some are not set up for youngsters.

WHAT IT COSTS				
$$$$	$$$	$$	$	¢
RESTAURANTS over $30	$20–$30	$15–$20	$10–15	under $10
HOTELS over $220	$140–$220	$100–$140	$80–$100	under $80

Restaurant prices are per person for a main course at dinner. Hotel prices are for a standard double room in high season, excluding 5.7% state tax and gratuities. Some inns add a 15% service charge.

Timing

The fair-weather days of autumn make a good time to visit Plymouth and the surrounding area. The Thanksgiving holiday is filled with special events at Plimouth Plantation, the site of the first permanent European settlement in Southern New England in 1620. Heavy traffic is the norm on weekends and holidays on all major routes approaching the Sagamore and Bourne bridges.

Plymouth

❶ *40 mi southeast of Boston.*

On December 26, 1620, 102 weary British men, women, and children disembarked from the *Mayflower* to found the first permanent European settlement north of Virginia. (Virginia was their intended destination, but storms pushed the ship off course.) Of the settlers, now known as the Pilgrims, a third were members of a Puritan sect of religious reformers known as the Separatists, so called because they wanted to establish their own church separate from the national Church of England. This separation was considered treasonous, so the group first fled to the city of Leiden in the Netherlands seeking religious freedom. After more than 10 years there, the group joined with other emigrants to start a new life in the New World.

Before coming ashore, the expedition's leaders drew up the Mayflower Compact, a historic agreement binding the group to the law of the majority. This compact became the basis for the colony's government. After a rough start (half the original settlers died during the first winter), the colony stabilized and grew under the leadership of Governor William Bradford. Two other founding fathers—military leader Myles Standish and John Alden—acquired mythical status via a poem by Longfellow, *The Courtship of Miles Standish.*

Forty miles south of Boston, Plymouth today is characterized by narrow streets, clapboard mansions, shops, and antiques stores. Some commercial names would make the Pilgrims shudder: the John Alden Gift Shop, Mayflower Seafoods, and, incongruously, Pocahontas Gifts, Sportswear and Sundries (Pocahontas lived in Virginia). But it's easy to overlook these and admire the picturesque waterfront. The town also holds a parade, historic-house tours, and other activities to mark Thanksgiving.

Beaches

With a coastline that meanders in and out of Buzzards Bay, southeastern Massachusetts has plenty of choice seaside areas. Westport's Horseneck Beach is a long stretch of sand that's hugely popular on weekends. Plymouth, too, has several popular beaches, from Plymouth Beach near town to the long crescent of sand at White Horse Beach to the south. But there are smaller beaches and coves where you can enjoy the shore in relative quiet—in Fairhaven, South Dartmouth, Mattapoisett, Marion, and other small towns that dot the area.

If you're more interested in being on the water than in it, try a cruise from Onset Harbor or take a whale-watching trip. Whale-watch excursions run from Plymouth daily between June and September and on a more limited basis in April, May, and October; they usually last three to four hours.

Outdoor Activities

The approach to the Cape provides numerous possibilities to get close to nature. The 16,000-acre Myles Standish State Forest in Plymouth is great for hiking, as is the Freetown-Fall River State Forest. The numerous rivers and inlets on Buzzards Bay—for example, the Westport, Mattapoisett, Paskamanset, Agawam, and Weweantic Rivers—are excellent for canoeing and kayaking.

The Arts

A variety of wonderful musical and theatrical events are staged in a classic setting at the Zieterion Theater in New Bedford. On the second Thursday evening of every month, New Bedford hosts AHA! Nights, a program that highlights the city's art, history, and architecture. Various performing arts events are also held regularly in Plymouth.

Touring & Shopping

Route 6 from New Bedford to Buzzards Bay contains numerous specialty, antiques, and honky-tonk shops both inside and outside of the villages. The same is true, perhaps to a lesser extent, of Route 3A from Plymouth to Sagamore. It is in any case a pleasant drive to get off the main highway for a stretch.

Museums

For rainy- and sunny-day activities alike, the area approaching the Cape is rich in interesting, unique museums including Plymouth's Mayflower II and Plimoth Plantation, Fall River's Battleship Cove and adjacent Maritime Museum, and New Bedford's Whaling Museum.

Plymouth is dotted with historic statues, including depictions of William Bradford on Water Street, a Pilgrim maiden in Brewster Gardens, and Massasoit (chief of the local Wampanoag tribe) on Carver Street. The largest freestanding granite statue in the country, the **National Monument to the Forefathers,** stands high on a grassy hill. Designed by Hammet Billings of Boston in 1854 and dedicated in 1889, it de-

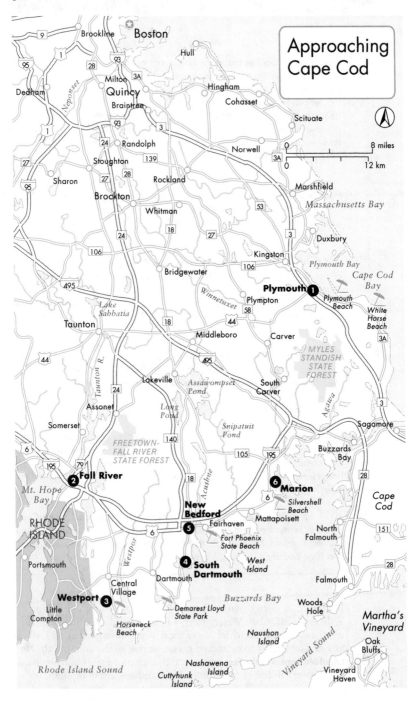

Approaching Cape Cod

picts Faith surrounded by Liberty, Morality, Justice, Law, and Education, and includes scenes from the Pilgrims' early days in Plymouth. ⊠ *Allerton St.*

Several historic houes are open for visits, including the 1640 **Sparrow House,** Plymouth's oldest structure. You can peek into several rooms furnished in the spartan style of the Pilgrims' era. A contemporary crafts gallery also on the premises seems somewhat incongruous, but the works on view are high-quality. ⊠ *42 Summer St.* ☎ *508/747–1240* ✉ *$2; gallery free* ☉ *Apr.–late Nov., Thurs.–Tues. 10–5.*

The 1749 **Spooner House,** home to the same family for 200 years, has guided tours and a garden. ⊠ *27 North St.* ☎ *508/746–0012* ✉ *$4* ☉ *June–early Oct., Thurs.–Sat. 10–4.*

☾ Like Plimoth Plantation, the **Mayflower II,** a replica of the 1620 *Mayflower,* is manned by staff in period dress. The ship was built in England through research and a bit of guesswork, and then it sailed across the Atlantic in 1957. ⊠ *State Pier* ☎ *508/746–1622* ⊕ *www.plimoth.org* ✉ *$8; free with Plimoth Plantation combination ticket* ☉ *Apr.–Nov., daily 9–5.*

A few dozen yards from the *Mayflower II* is **Plymouth Rock,** popularly believed to have been the Pilgrims' stepping-stone when they left the ship. Given the stone's unimpressive appearance—it's little more than a boulder—and dubious authenticity (as explained on a nearby plaque), the grand canopy overhead seems a trifle ostentatious.

Across the street from Plymouth Rock is **Cole's Hill,** where the company buried its dead—at night, so the local Native Americans could not count the dwindling numbers of survivors. Just past the hill, on what was once called 1st Street, is the site of the original settlement; in 1834 the street was renamed Leyden Street in honor of the Dutch city that sheltered the Pilgrims. Look for plaques designating the locations of the original lots.

☾ For a traditional view of the Pilgrims, visit the **Plymouth National Wax Museum,** on top of Cole's Hill. It contains 26 scenes with 180 life-size models that tell the settlers' story. ⊠ *16 Carver St.* ☎ *508/746–6468* ✉ *$7* ☉ *Mar.–May and Nov., daily 9–5; June, Sept., and Oct., daily 9–7; July and Aug., daily 9–9.*

From the waterfront sights it's a short walk to one of the country's oldest public museums. The **Pilgrim Hall Museum,** established in 1824, transports you back to the time just before the Pilgrims' landing with its exhibition of items carried by those weary travelers to the New World. Included are a carved chest, a remarkably well preserved wicker cradle, Myles Standish's sword, John Alden's Bible, Native American artifacts, and the remains of the *Sparrow Hawk,* a sailing ship that was wrecked in 1626. ⊠ *75 Court St. (Rte. 3A)* ☎ *508/746–1620* ⊕ *www.pilgrimhall. org* ✉ *$6* ☉ *Feb.–Dec., daily 9:30–4:30.*

need a break? Sample some cranberry wine—it's oddly refreshing, and free—at the **Plymouth Bay Winery** (⊠ 114 Water St. ☎ 508/746–2100), open March–December, Monday–Saturday 10–5, Sunday noon–5.

★ ☺ Above the entrance of the **Plimoth Plantation** is the caution: you are now entering 1627. Believe it. Against the backdrop of the Atlantic Ocean, a Pilgrim village has been painstakingly re-created, from the thatch roofs, cramped quarters, and open fireplaces to the long-horned livestock. Throw away your preconceptions of white collars and funny hats; through ongoing research, the Plimoth staff has developed a portrait of the Pilgrims that's more complex than the dour folk pictured in elementary-school textbooks. Listen to the accents of the "residents," who never break character. You might see them plucking ducks, cooking rabbit stew, or tending garden. Feel free to engage them in conversation about their life, but expect only curious looks if you ask about anything that happened later than 1627.

Elsewhere on the plantation is **Hobbamock's Homestead,** where descendants of the Wampanoag Indians re-create the life of a Native American who chose to live near the newcomers. In the **Carriage House Craft Center** you'll see earthenware, candles, clothing, and other items created using the techniques of 17th-century English craftsmanship— that is, replicas of what the Pilgrims might have imported (you can also buy samples). At the **Nye Barn** you can see descendants of 17th-century goats, cows, pigs, and chickens, bred to resemble animals raised in the original plantation. The visitor center has gift shops, a cafeteria, and multimedia presentations. Dress for the weather, since many exhibits are outdoors. Admission tickets are good for two consecutive days; if you have time, you may want to spread out your plantation visit to take in all the sights. ⊠ *Warren Ave. (Rte. 3A)* ☎ *508/746–1622* ⊕ *www.plimoth.org* ⊠ *$20; $22, including entry to Mayflower II* ☉ *Apr.–Nov., daily 9–5.*

| off the beaten path | **JOHN ALDEN HOUSE MUSEUM –** The only standing structure in which original Pilgrims are known to have lived is about 10 mi north of Plymouth in the town of Duxbury, settled in 1628 by Pilgrim colonists Myles Standish and John Alden, among others. Alden, who served as assistant governor of Plymouth colony, occupied this house, which was built in 1653, along with his wife Priscilla and eight or nine of their children. One bedroom has a "seven-day dresser" with a drawer for each day of the week; the Sunday drawer, which held formal church wear, is the largest. ⊠ *105 Alden St., Duxbury* ☎ *781/934–9092* 🖷 *508/934–9149* ⊕ *www.alden.org* ⊠ *Guided tours $5* ☉ *Mid-May–mid-Oct., Mon.–Sat. noon–5.* |

Where to Stay & Eat

$–$$$ ✕ **Martha's Galley.** In an unlikely spot—a nondescript strip mall about ½ mi from Plymouth's historic district—this tiny trattoria serves up Italian-inspired fare. Chef Martha Stone's menu starts with the classics, such as linguine with fresh clams or chicken piccata, but you might find pork tenderloin with cranberry or even cassoulet. ⊠ *179 Court St., Benny's Plaza* ☎ *508/747–9200* ⊟ *AE, D, DC, MC, V* ☉ *Closed Sun. and Mon. No lunch.*

¢–$$ ✕ **Lobster Hut.** This casual, cafeteria-style eatery at the waterfront offers seafood in the classic breaded-and-fried style, plus sandwiches and luncheon specials. The interior is Formica-basic, but the fish is tasty, and the water views are excellent. You can eat inside or outdoors on the patio under a tent. ⊠ *Town Wharf* ☎ *508/746–2270* ⊟ *MC, V* ☉ *Closed Jan.*

¢–$$ ✕ **Wood's Seafood.** Furnished with a simple counter for ordering fish and a handful of plastic tables and chairs, this harborside seafood shack doesn't look like much upon first glance. Still, if you're looking for reasonably priced seafood (fried clams, lobster rolls, and assorted fish plates), with a water view, it's a good choice. You can also buy live lobsters to take with you or to ship. ⊠ *Town Wharf* ☎ *508/746–0261* ⊟ *AE, MC, V.*

¢ ✕ **The All-American Diner.** The look is nostalgia—red, white, and blue with movie posters. The specialty is beloved American foods—omelets and pancakes for breakfast, burgers, sandwiches, soups, and a variety of entrées such as Yankee pot roast for lunch. ⊠ *60 Court St.* ☎ *508/ 747–4763* ⊟ *AE, DC, MC, V* ☉ *No dinner.*

$$$–$$$$ ✕▥ **John Carver Inn.** This three-story colonial-style redbrick building is steps from Plymouth's main attractions. The public rooms are lavish, with period furnishings and stylish drapes. The guest rooms are more matter-of-fact, but the six environmentally sensitive rooms have filtered air and water and four-poster beds. The two-room suites have fireplaces and whirlpool baths. The indoor pool has a *Mayflower* ship theme and a water slide. At its Hearth 'n Kettle Restaurant, staff in colonial attire serve a huge selection of American favorites, including seafood and hearty sandwiches. ⊠ *25 Summer St., 02360* ☎ *508/746–7100 or 800/274–1620* ⊞ *508/746–8299* ⊕ *www.johncarverinn.com* ⤳ *79 rooms, 6 suites* ⌂ *Restaurant, pool, gym, bar, meeting rooms* ⊟ *AE, D, DC, MC, V.*

$$$ ▥ **Cold Spring Harbor Motel.** This neat-as-a-pin motel, about ½ mi from Plymouth's downtown historic district, is a good choice for families. Several buildings cluster around the parking areas and a lush green lawn, while inside, the rooms are nicely maintained, if nondescript, with floral bedspreads and sturdy wooden furnishings. The newer "deluxe" rooms are a tad more spacious than the standard ones, and a few second-floor rooms look out toward the harbor. Coffee, juices, and pastries are set out for guests in the mornings from late May through mid-October. ⊠ *188 Court St., 02360* ☎ *508/746–2222 or 800/678–8667* ⊞ *508/746–2744* ⊕ *www.coldspringmotel.com* ⤳ *55 rooms, 3 suites, 2 cottages* ⌂ *No-smoking rooms* ⊟ *AE, D, MC, V* ☉ *Closed Jan.–Mar.*

★ $$–$$$ ▥ **Beach House Oceanfront B&B.** At the end of a long dirt road, this contemporary gray-shingle home overlooking the Atlantic makes a perfect hideaway. Although only about 10 minutes south of Plymouth center, the house feels a world away. The deck, screened porch, and living room–dining room with floor-to-ceiling windows all face the wide expanse of the ocean, and steps lead down the cliff to a small private beach. Inside, the theme is white—from the leather sofas in the living room to the lace curtains and quilts in the bedrooms. ⊠ *45 Black Pond La.* ⌖ *429 Center Hill Rd., 02360* ☎ *508/224–3517 or 888/262–2543* ⊕ *www. beachhouseplymouth.com* ⤳ *2 rooms, 1 suite* ⌂ *Beach; no smoking* ⊟ *MC, V* ▦ *BP.*

$$–$$$ 🏨 **Governor Bradford on the Harbour.** The waterfront location here (directly across from the *Mayflower II*) is a big plus. Rooms are motel-basic, each with two double beds, a small refrigerator, and free HBO. ✉ *98 Water St., 02360* ☎ *508/746–6200 or 800/332–1620* 🖷 *508/747–3032* ⊕ *www.governorbradford.com* 🛏 *94 rooms* ⚘ *Refrigerators, pool, no-smoking rooms* 🖃 *AE, D, DC, MC, V.*

Sports & the Outdoors

BEACHES **Plymouth Beach** (✉ Warren Ave. [Rte. 3A]), south of town, has restrooms, showers, and lifeguards (in season). Daily parking fees are $7 weekdays, $10 weekends.

White Horse Beach (✉ Taylor Ave.) is a popular long, sandy beach in a neighborhood of summer cottages, off Route 3A south of Plimoth Plantation. Parking is very limited.

STATE PARKS **Myles Standish State Forest** (✉ Cranberry Rd., South Carver, Exit 5 off Rte. 3 ☎ 508/866–2526 ⊕ www.state.ma.us/dem/parks/mssf.htm) has more than 16,000 acres for hiking, biking, swimming, picnicking, and canoeing.

Fall River

❷ *54 mi southeast of Boston.*

It's a famous rhyme of woe: "Lizzie Borden took an axe / And gave her mother forty whacks. / When she saw what she had done, / She gave her father forty-one." And yet Lizzie, the maiden daughter of the town's prominent banker, was found innocent of the 1892 bludgeoning deaths of her father and stepmother in the most sensational trial of its time. She went on to spend the rest of her life quietly in Fall River, today a fading port and factory town.

In the 1800s Fall River became a major textile milling area, but by the 1920s much of the textile industry had moved to southern states. Many former mills housed factory outlets that attracted bargain hunters, although many of the outlets, too, have shut down or moved on. It's primarily the Borden tragedy—and the city's nautical attractions—that draws visitors today. The town's most famous contemporary native son is celebrity chef Emeril Lagasse, who often recalls his Portuguese roots and other Fall River memories for his fans.

The best place to learn about the Borden case is the **Fall River Historical Society,** which has the world's largest collection of Borden artifacts, including courtroom evidence, photographs, and the handleless hatchet suspected of being the murder weapon. The 1835 Greek Revival–style mansion also has a wealth of information about the region, displaying memorabilia from the Fall River steamship line and artifacts related to Fall River's days as home of the world's largest cotton cloth manufacturer. Another exhibit illustrates 19th-century mourning practices, including elaborate decorations woven from human hair. One-hour tours are available on the hour (weekdays 9–11 and 1–3, weekends 1–4). ✉ *451 Rock St., at Maple St.* ☎ *508/679–1071* ⊕ *www.lizzieborden.org*

🖾 *Guided tours $5* ⊙ *Apr., May, Oct., and Nov., Tues.–Fri. 9–4:30; June–Sept. and Dec., Tues.–Fri. 9–4:30, weekends 1–5.*

If you're strong of heart and stomach, you may want to take in the **Lizzie Borden Bed & Breakfast Museum,** in the Borden's former home, the site of the murders, which has been transformed into a B&B. Even if you don't spend the night here, you can stop in to see the display of Lizzie-related items. ⊠ *92 2nd St.* ☎ *508/675–7333* ⊕ *www.lizzie-borden. com* 🖾 *Guided tours $7.50* ⊙ *July–early Sept., daily 11–2:30; late May–June and early Sept.–Oct., weekends 11–2:30; tours every ½ hr; last tour at 2:30.*

Another Lizzie highlight is the **Borden burial plot** in the Oak Grove Cemetery on Prospect Street. Lizzie's home after her acquittal was at **306 French Street** (a private residence), where she lived until her death in 1927.

A visit to Fall River can skirt Lizzie Borden's sad saga entirely. The town's industrial docks and enormous factories recall the city's past as a major textile center in the 19th and early 20th centuries. In the past, Fall River served as a port; today the most interesting nautical site is **Battleship Cove,** a "floating" museum complex docked on the Taunton River. You can go aboard the 35,000-ton battleship USS *Massachusetts*; the destroyer USS *Joseph P. Kennedy, Jr.*; a World War II attack sub, the USS *Lionfish*; two PT boats from World War II; and a Cold War–era Russian-built warship. ⊠ *5 Water St., at Davol St., off Rte. 79* ☎ *508/678–1100 or 800/533–3194* ⊕ *www.battleshipcove. org* 🖾 *$10* ⊙ *Apr.–June, daily 9–5; July–early Sept., daily 9–5:30; early Sept.–Mar., daily 9–4:30.*

🔅 The **Fall River Carousel,** built in the 1920s, was rescued from the defunct Lincoln Amusement Park and moved to Battleship Cove. The glorious restoration is housed dockside. ⊠ *Battleship Cove* ☎ *508/324–4300* 🖾 *Rides 50¢* ⊙ *Generally late May–early Sept., daily 11–7.*

The riverside **Fall River Heritage State Park** tells the story of Fall River's industrial past, focusing on the city's textile mills and their workers. The park has a visitor center, exhibits, and a summer concert series. ⊠ *200 Davol St.* Ⓦ ☎ *508/675–5759* ⊕ *www.state.ma.us/dem/parks/frhp. htm* 🖾 *Free* ⊙ *Daily 10–4.*

Two blocks from Battleship Cove, the **Marine Museum at Fall River** celebrates the age of sail and steamship travel, especially the lavishly fitted ships of the Old Fall River Line, which operated until 1937 between New England and New York City. The museum also contains the 28-foot-long, 1-ton model of the *Titanic* used in the 1952 movie. ⊠ *70 Water St.* ☎ *508/674–3533* ⊕ *www.marinemuseum.org* 🖾 *$5* ⊙ *Weekdays 9–5, Sat. noon–5, Sun. noon–4.*

Where to Stay & Eat

$–$$$ ✕ **Abbey Grille.** Is it a school? A church? A restaurant? Well, yes. This striking, high-ceiling space in a former church, complete with stained-glass windows and elaborate woodwork, is a restaurant run by students at the International Institute of Culinary Arts, a local culinary school. The menu changes, depending on what the students are learning, but typical selections range from brick-oven pizzas to baked stuffed swordfish, rack of lamb, or seafood risotto. A brunch buffet is served the first Sunday of each month from 10:30 to 2:00. ⊠ *100 Rock St.* ☎ *508/679–9108* 🖃 *AE, D, MC, V* ☉ *Closed Sun., except the first in the month. No lunch Sat., no dinner Mon.*

$–$$$ ✕ **Waterstreet Café.** This casually sophisticated café, with exposed brick and sponge-painted walls, serves hummus and tabbouleh roll-ups, falafel, and other Middle Eastern–inspired salads and sandwiches together with live music. Other specialties are "something fresh in a shell over linguine" (pasta with clams or mussels) and Greek Island Shrimp, sautéed with artichoke hearts and feta cheese. It's across the street from the Marine Museum and walking distance from Battleship Cove. A special brunch menu is served on Sunday. ⊠ *36 Water St.* ☎ *508/672–8748* ⊕ *www.waterstreetcafe.com* 🖃 *AE, D, MC, V* ☉ *Closed Mon. and Tues.*

¢–$$ ✕ **T.A. Restaurant.** Fall River has a substantial Portuguese community, and this modest but popular eatery is one place to sample the local fare. *Alentejana* (marinated pork with clams and potatoes), garlicky shrimp Mozambique, and baked cod with onions and tomatoes are among the specialties. There s an all-you-can-eat lunch buffet Monday--Saturday. ⊠ *408 S. Main St.* ☎ *508/673--5890* 🖃 *AE, D, MC, V.*

$$$ 🏠 **Lizzie Borden Bed & Breakfast Museum.** Could you stand to sleep in the same house where Lizzie Borden's father and stepmother met a bloody end? Choose from one of the four original bedrooms, two of which are suites, or two rooms converted from attic space. A full breakfast and a house tour are included, as well as a map of the "Lizzie Trail" (related sites in the Fall River area). You can also watch videos about the Borden case. Nonguests may tour the place between 11 and 2:30, from late May through October. Overnight guests must be 12 or older. ⊠ *92 2nd St., 02721* ☎🖷 *508/675–7333* ⊕ *www.lizzie-borden.com* 🛏 *4 rooms, 2 suites* ⚹ *No smoking* 🖃 *AE, D, MC, V* ⦿ *BP.*

Westport

❸ *12 mi southeast of Fall River.*

As you venture south and east of Fall River, the urban landscape gives way to farm country. You'll pass rows of corn, old stone walls, and pastures of cows and horses. About 12 mi from Fall River, Westport has a mix of farmland and summer homes in a small village and scattered throughout the countryside, as well as one of the area's nicest beaches.

Although grapes may not come immediately to mind as a Massachusetts crop, the **Westport Rivers Vineyard and Winery** grows grapes and has been selling its wines since 1991. Its sparkling wines are particularly well regarded. You can sample the wines, and there's a small art gallery above the store with changing exhibits. Free winery tours are offered on weekends. The winery also holds special food-and-wine events and festivals throughout the year; call or check the Web site for details. ✉ *417 Hixbridge Rd., off Rte. 88* ☎ *508/636–3423* ⊕ *www. westportrivers.com* ☽ *Tasting room, shop, and gallery daily 11–5; tours weekends at 1 and 3.*

For more than 25 years, Chris and Alex Kogler have carried on the home-made traditional baking techniques at **Butler's Colonial Donut House.** Specialties include cream puffs, Long Johns, and a variety of old-time favorites all hand made with real cream. Up to 400 dozen donuts are made on a busy day. ✉ *459 Sanford Rd.* ☎ *508/672–4600* ☽ *Fri. 6–1, weekends 7–5.*

Where to Stay & Eat

$$–$$$ ✕ **The Back Eddy.** Fresh fish such as fennel-crusted yellowfin tuna, pan-
FodorsChoice seared Atlantic salmon, and crispy fried native cod is the specialty at
★ this casual waterfront restaurant where many diners arrive by boat. The casual, wood-floor dining room is boisterous, with a lively bar scene, and most of the large windows overlook the busy harbor, ideal at sunset. Expect to wait for a table; reservations are accepted only for parties of six or more. ✉ *1 Bridge Rd.* ☎ *508/636–6500* ⊕ *www. thebackeddy.com* ▭ *AE, D, MC, V* ☽ *No lunch Mon.–Wed. late May–early Sept.; early Sept.–late May, hrs vary, call ahead.*

¢–$ ✕ **Marguerite's.** The scene is pure country kitchen inside this gray-shingle house—from the wooden tables to the cheerful waitresses who circulate with ever-full coffee pots. Diner-style breakfasts and old-time New England specialties, from stuffed quahogs (clams) and chowder to broiled scrod, liver and onions, and chicken pie, make up most of the menu; the daily specials offer some contemporary flourishes, such as scallops sauced with pesto cream. It's all fresh and homemade, which has earned this little house a devoted local following. Note that dinner is served only until 8 PM weeknights and until 8:30 on Friday and Saturday. ✉ *778 Main Rd., Village Commons shopping center* ☎ *508/636– 3040* ⊕ *www.hometown.aol.com/margueritesrest* ▭ *No credit cards* ☽ *Closed Sun.*

$$$ 🏠 **Paquachuck Inn.** Built in 1827 as a supply house for whaling ships, this wood-shingle building on Westport Point is now a modest, comfortable inn. The wood-floor rooms with exposed beams aren't large, but several have four-poster beds, and all offer at least a glimpse of the water. Unfortunately, none have a private bath (the nine rooms share four baths), although one shared bath does have a whirlpool tub, and there's an outdoor shower, too. The large, sunny breakfast room with comfy couches leads to a patio and yard—note the three whale vertebrae that are now a garden sculpture. ✉ *2056 Main Rd., 02791* ☎🏠 *508/636–4398* ⊕ *www.paquachuck.com* ⇥ *9 rooms* ⚬ *Coffee shop, dock; no a/c, no room phones, no room TVs, no smoking* ▭ *MC, V* ⦿ *CP.*

Sports & the Outdoors

BEACHES One of the nicest beaches in this part of the state, **Horseneck Beach State Reservation** (✉ Rte. 88 ☎ 508/636–8816 ⊕ www.state.ma.us/dem/ parks/hbch.htm) draws summer crowds to its 2 mi of sand with access to kayaking and boating on the Westport River. There are restrooms with showers, and lifeguards in season. Parking is $7 a day from May through early September.

South Dartmouth

4 *4 mi east of Westport.*

As in nearby Westport, the South Dartmouth countryside is dotted with farms and summer homes, but since it's only a few miles south of New Bedford, residents who work in the New Bedford area also make their homes here year-round. One of the prettiest spots is Padanarum Village, where Gulf Road and Dartmouth Road meet—built around the sailboat-filled harbor, Padanarum is a little oasis of shops, galleries, and cafés. Nearby, the village of Russells Mills houses one of the region's oldest general stores and a pottery studio.

Where to Stay

$$–$$$ Residence Inn. This comfortable inn is conveniently located near shopping and golf, and is 12 mi from Horseneck Beach. All rooms are spacious suites with full kitchens, high-speed Internet, and separate sleeping and living areas; some units have fireplaces. Amenities include a gym, hot tub, and indoor pool. There's a complimentary full breakfast, and you can order in from local restaurants through a dinner delivery service. ⊠ *181 Faunce Corner Rd., North Dartmouth 02747* ☎ *508/954–5858* 🖷 *508/747–3032* 📠 *96 suites* 🖶 *In-room data ports, kitchens, pool (indoors), hot tub, gym, laundry facilities, laundry service, concierge, Internet, free parking, some pets allowed (fee)* 🖃 *AE, D, DC, MC, V.*

$$ Saltworks Bed & Breakfast. This large 1840 Greek Revival house on the edge of Padanarum Village has only two guest suites, but they're lovely. Each suite has a large bedroom with a fireplace, plus a smaller sitting room or second bedroom. The walls are decorated with artwork by owner Sandra Hall, who runs the inn with her husband, David. Downstairs is a comfortable common room with a TV, and outside is a wraparound porch with views out to the harbor, as well as an English garden. Internet access and fax services are available. ⊠ *115 Elm St., Padanarum Village 02748* ☎ *508/991–5491* 🖷 *508/979–8470* 📠 *2 suites* 🖶 *No room phones, no room TVs, no smoking* 🖃 *AE, MC, V* ☉ *Closed Nov.–May* 🍽 *BP.*

Sports & the Outdoors

BEACHES **Demarest Lloyd State Park** (⊠ Barney's Joy Rd. ☎ 508/636–8816 ⊕ www.state.ma.us/dem/parks/deml.htm) may be hard to find, but it's worth seeking out for its long beach of soft, white sand on a sheltered Buzzards Bay cove. Behind the beach is a wooded area with picnic tables and barbecue grills. The bathhouse has restrooms and showers. In season (late May–early September) there are lifeguards, and parking is $7 a day.

Shopping

Davoll's General Store (⊠ 1228 Russells Mills Rd. ☎ 508/636–4530), established in 1793, sells antiques and collectibles, as well as clothing, deli sandwiches, and a small selection of groceries.

Salt Marsh Pottery (⊠ 1167 Russells Mills Rd. ☏ 508/636–4813 or 800/
859–5028 ⊕ www.saltmarsh.com) makes platters, bowls, and other
unique ceramic pieces decorated with wildflowers.

New Bedford

❺ *15 mi east of Fall River, 50 mi south of Boston.*

In 1652 colonists from Plymouth settled in the area that now includes
the city of New Bedford. The city has a long maritime tradition, beginning
as a shipbuilding center and small whaling port in the late 1700s. By
the mid-1800s the city had developed into a center of North American
whaling.

Today New Bedford still has the largest fishing fleet on the East Coast,
and although much of the town is industrial, the restored historic district near the water is a pleasant stop. It was here that Herman Melville
set some of the opening sections of his masterpiece, *Moby-Dick*. New
Bedford's whaling tradition is commemorated in the **New Bedford Whaling National Historical Park,** encompassing 13 blocks of the waterfront
historic district. The park visitor center, in an 1853 Greek Revival former bank, provides maps and information about whaling-related sites.
Free walking tours of the park leave from the visitor center at 10 AM
and noon in July and August. You can also view an orientation film about
American whaling and the New Bedford historic sites; the film is free
and is shown on the hour, daily 10–3, at the nearby New Bedford Whaling Museum. ⊠ *33 William St., Downtown* ☏ *508/996–4095* ⊕ *www.
nps.gov/nebe* ۞ *Daily 9–5.*

★ ☾ The **New Bedford Whaling Museum,** established in 1903, is the world's
largest museum devoted to the history of whaling. A highlight is the skeleton of a 66-foot blue whale, one of only three on view anywhere in the
world. An interactive exhibit lets you listen to the underwater sounds
of whales, dolphins, and other sea life, plus the sounds of a thunder-
storm and a whale-watching boat—all as a whale might hear them. You
can also peruse the collection of scrimshaw, visit exhibits on regional
history, and climb aboard an 89-foot half-scale model of the 1826 whaling ship *Lagoda*—the world's largest ship model. ⊠ *18 Johnny Cake
Hill, Downtown* ☏ *508/997–0046* ⊕ *www.whalingmuseum.org* 🎫 *$10*
۞ *Daily 9–5; late May–early Sept. until 9 on Thurs.*

Seaman's Bethel, the small chapel described in *Moby-Dick*, is across the
street from the whaling museum. ⊠ *15 Johnny Cake Hill, Downtown*
☏ *508/992–3295* ۞ *Weekdays 10–5.*

The **New Bedford Art Museum,** a compact gallery space in the 1918 Vault
Building (a former bank), showcases the work of area artists. Included
are paintings by 19th- and early-20th-century New Bedford artists Albert Bierstadt, William Bradford, and Charles Henry Gifford. ⊠ *608
Pleasant St., Downtown* ☏ *508/961–3072* ⊕ *www.
newbedfordartmuseum.org* 🎫 *$3* ۞ *Late May–early Sept., Mon.–Wed.
and Fri.–Sun. 10–5, Thurs. 10–7; early Sept.–late May, Wed. and
Fri.–Sun. noon–5, Thurs. noon–7.*

For a glimpse of upper-class life during New Bedford's whaling heyday, head ½ mi south of downtown to the **Rotch-Jones-Duff House and Garden Museum.** This 1834 Greek Revival mansion, set amid a full city block of gardens, housed three prominent families in the 1800s and is filled with elegant furnishings from the era, including a mahogany piano, a massive marble-top sideboard, and portraits of the house's occupants. A self-guided audio tour is available. ⊠ *396 County St.* ☏ *508/997–1401* ⊕ *www.rjdmuseum.org* 🎫 *$4* ⊗ *Mon.–Sat. 10–4, Sun. noon–4.*

Where to Stay & Eat

$–$$$ ╳ **OceAnna.** Towering arched windows line the dining room of this for-
FodorsChoice mer bank, and chandeliers are suspended from the high ceilings. Seafood
★ and steaks figure prominently among the offerings here, and many dishes have Greek influences. At lunch, the menu is fairly all-American, with burgers, sandwiches, pastas, and fish, but in the evening, the food has a Mediterranean flair. The restaurant's name is pronounced O-kay-*anna.* ⊠ *95 William St., Downtown* ☏ *508/997–8465* ▤ *AE, D, MC, V* ⊗ *Closed Sun. No lunch Sat.*

¢–$$$ ╳ **Antonio's.** If you'd like to sample the traditional fare of New Bedford's large Portuguese population, friendly, unadorned Antonio's serves up hearty portions of pork and shellfish stew, *bacalau* (salt cod), and grilled sardines, often on plates piled high with crispy fried potatoes and rice. ⊠ *267 Coggeshall St., near intersection of I–195 and Rte. 18* ☏ *508/990–3636* ▤ *No credit cards.*

★ $$ ╳ **Freestone's City Grill.** In an 1877 former bank in the historic district, Freestone's serves soups and chowders, sandwiches and salads, plus fish, steaks, and vegetarian dishes. Traditional details—mahogany paneling, marble floors, brass rails—blend with contemporary art. ⊠ *41 William St., Downtown* ☏ *508/993–7477* ⊕ *www.freestones.com* ▤ *AE, DC, MC, V.*

$–$$ ╳ **Davy's Locker.** A huge seafood menu is the main draw at this spot overlooking Buzzards Bay. Choose from more than a dozen shrimp preparations or a Healthy Choice entrée—dishes prepared with olive oil, vegetables, garlic, and herbs. For landlubbers, chicken, steak, ribs, and the like are also served. ⊠ *1480 E. Rodney French Blvd.* ☏ *508/992–7359* ▤ *AE, D, MC, V.*

$–$$ 🛏 **Edgewater Bed & Breakfast.** One of New Bedford's most pleasant places to stay is just across the Acushnet River in Fairhaven, a residential suburb. The Edgewater's slogan is "So close to the water, you'll think you're on a boat," and it's true—this house, built in 1760 and expanded in the 1880s, has water views from three sides. All the rooms are simply and traditionally furnished; the window-lined Captain's Suite, with a working fireplace and a king-size bed, has the best views. Owner Kathy Reed, who has run the B&B since the early 1980s, has plenty of ideas for things to see and do. ⊠ *2 Oxford St., Fairhaven 02719* ☏ *508/997–5512* 🖷 *508/997–5784* ⊕ *www.rixsan.com/edgewater* ⤴ *3 rooms, 3 suites* ⚅ *No room phones, no kids under 5, no smoking* ▤ *AE, D, MC, V* ⑩ *CP.*

CUTTYHUNK ISLAND

FOR A TASTE of old New England island magic without the development or crowds of Cape Cod, Martha's Vineyard, or Nantucket, visit bucolic Cuttyhunk Island, which is accessible only by boat or a small plane with water skis that lands in the harbor. Cuttyhunk is the Southwestern end of the Elizabeth Islands, an isolated 16-mi chain extending from Woods Hole and separating Vineyard Sound from Buzzards Bay. The rest of these lovely islands (Noamesset, Uncatena, Naushon, Nashawena, and Pasque) are privately owned and inaccessible to the public. Cuttyhunk was first explored by Bartholomew Gosnold in 1602 and was settled in 1641. In the days of sail, Cuttyhunk served as home to the pilots who guided the whaling ships safely into New Bedford harbor. Today's year-round population is under 100 as living testament to the island's reputation for isolation. In summer, the population swells to several hundred. You'll see very few cars here—golf carts tend to be the vehicle of choice for residents—but there's little need for one. At just 2½ mi long and less than 1 mi wide, Cuttyhunk is easily navigable on foot.

Upon arrival at the dock, you will be surrounded by many boats both large and small. You need not bother to bring much pocket money as there's little to buy except perhaps some fresh oysters and maybe an ice cream. Outdoor toilets are available nearby for public use. A short uphill walk brings you to the center of the island where you will be treated to majestic views of Vineyard Sound. Here you will find a small general store, a one-room schoolhouse, a church, a library, a seasonal café, and a B&B. An unpaved dirt road leads to the far end of the island where you can find a pond amongst bucolic natural surroundings.

If you want to stay overnight, contact the **Cuttyhunk Fishing Club B&B** (☎ 508/992–5585 ⊕ www.cuttyhunkfishingclub.com), which rents rooms, apartments and houses from mid-May–mid-October. **Pete's Place Rentals** (☎ 508/992–5131 ⊕ www.cuttyhunk.com/rental.html) has a small number of waterview properties available for weekly rentals from late May to mid-October.

The **M/V Alert II ferry** (☎ 508/992–1432 ⊕ www.cuttyhunk.com) makes the one-hour trip from New Bedford's Fisherman's Wharf (Pier 3) to Cuttyhunk daily mid-June to mid-September. The ferry departs New Bedford at 10 AM and returns from Cuttyhunk at 3 PM (with additional trips on Friday, Saturday, and Sunday); same-day round-trip fares are $21.

Bayside Air (☎ 508/992–1645) provides service to Cuttyhunk from the New Bedford regional Airport.

— By James W. Rohlf

Nightlife & the Arts

On the second Thursday of every month from 5 to 9 PM, New Bedford hosts **AHA! nights** (☎ 508/264–8859 ⊕ www.ahanewbedford.org), a downtown gallery night program to highlight the city's art, history, and architecture. Museums and galleries, including the Whaling Museum and the New Bedford Art Museum, have extended hours and offer free admission. Concerts, crafts demonstrations, and other special events are often on the programs.

A variety of musical and artistic events are held at the **Zeiterion Theater** (☎ 508/994–2900 ⊕ www.zeiterion.org) a wonderful old building in New Bedford's historic district.

Sports & the Outdoors

BEACHES **Fort Phoenix State Beach Reservation** (✉ Green St., Fairhaven, off Rte. 6 ☎ 508/992–4524 ⊕ www.state.ma.us/dem/parks/ftph.htm), the site of the Revolutionary War's first naval battle, has a small sandy beach. Parking is free, and there are restrooms with showers.

> en route   As you head east toward Cape Cod, a wet and wild adventure for the kids awaits at the **Water Wizz Water Park,** with a 50-foot-high water slide complete with tunnels and dips, a wave pool, a river ride, three tube rides, two enclosed water-mat slides, a children's slide, a pool, miniature golf, and food. The enclosed Black Wizard water slide descends 75 feet in darkness. ✉ *U.S. 6 and Rte. 28, Wareham, 2 mi west of Bourne Bridge* ☎ *508/295-3255* ⊕ *www.waterwizz. com* ✐ *$27* ⊙ *Mid-June–mid-Aug., daily 10–6:30; mid-Aug.–early Sept., daily 10–6.*

Marion

❻ *20 mi east of Fall River; 50 mi south of Boston.*

Small-town charm and a sense of history pervade the modest village center of Marion, a town that has tried to preserve its historic buildings and landmarks. Nineteenth-century and even some earlier homes, many with white picket fences and well-tended flower gardens, line the narrow streets. The present home of the **Sippican Historical Society,** which is very active and is an integral part of the Town of Marion, was built in 1834 by Dr. Walton Nathan Ellis. The **Marion Art Center** was once the Universalist Church, which was built in 1833 by a group of people who wanted to start a "new religion" in Sippican Village. **Handy's Tavern,** built in 1812, was a popular place for the sea-faring men who gathered there soon after their ships docked at the foot of Main Street. What is now the **Marion General Store** was a place of worship from 1799 to 1841.

During the early and mid-1800s, Marion was mainly a home for sea captains and sailors who went everywhere, carrying cotton to Europe, cargoes to the Orient, and returning with products from the East. Many of them became wealthy and some built magnificent homes in Marion. Marion was also a small shipbuilding community. Today, the year-round community of about 6,000 is tenacious about preserving its historic character and private to the point of not encouraging publicity, and shunning tourism. The majority of out-of-towners come to visit children boarding at **Tabor Academy,** a private school for grades 9–12 whose campus stretches along a half mile of Sippican Harbor, or to attend a high-end antiques show every August. Still, Marion is worth a stop to view the spectacle of more than 700 boats moored in picturesque **Sippican Harbor** and soak up the historical beauty of this hidden treasure of a town.

need a
break?

Maggie's Homemade Ice Cream offers more than 25 flavors of homemade ice cream, Maggie's own hot fudge, homemade Danish waffle cones as well as custom-made ice cream cakes and pies, and freshly baked cookies. ⊠ *Spring St. at Rte. 6* ☎ *508/748–9711.*

Where to Eat

¢–$$ ✕ **Sippican Café.** Marion has historically been a one-restaurant town, and when Kathleen and Bob Bost bought and renovated a local breakfast joint, this became the place to go for dinner. Chef Loretta Imbriglio, an alumna of the Meridien and the Chatham Bars Inn, delights locals with her lighthanded inventive twists on fresh seafood, beef, chicken, and pasta. Like the place itself, which has limited seating, the menu is small but enticing, with three or four specials nightly and even a cheese course. Liquor policy is BYOB. Breakfast, lunch, and Sunday brunch draw the locals as well. ⊠ *167 Spring St.* ☎ *508/748–0176* ▭ *AE, MC, V.*

¢ ✕ **Uncle John's Café & Cookies.** Known around town as the local version of Starbuck's, this eatery for breakfast and lunch makes a controversial contemporary statement, at least designwise, in this historically inclined community. Coffee, specialty drinks, scones, muffins, bagels, sandwiches, soups, and salads may be consumed at tables or the counter. Despite its name, the cookie selection is small. ⊠ *356 Front St.* ☎ *508/748–0063.*

Sports & the Outdoors

BEACHES **Silvershell Beach,** at the south end of Front Street, is open to the public. Facilities include lifeguards and a playground.

Shopping

Firefly Outfitters (⊠ 155 Front St. ☎ 508/748–2777) in Marion Center, a recent offshoot of the Boston store, specializes in fly-fishing equipment, outdoor clothing and accessories, and gift items. They also organize hosted fishing adventures to Cuttyhunk Island for beginner and seasoned anglers. Closed Monday.

Look for the treasures outside on the front lawn of the **Hobby Horse** (⊠ 339 Front St. ☎ 508/748–0763), an eclectic antiques store. Owner Robert Mower buys daily from local southeastern Massachusetts estates, which accounts for his constantly changing stock. Open weekends 11–4, or by appointment or chance.

Marion Sports Shop (⊠ 290 Front St. ☎ 508/748–1318) is one of the oldest tennis specialty shops in New England, but the impressive selection of tennis gear at the back of the store is not all it has to offer. Owner Frank Fletcher, a former tennis instructor, also stocks hip clothing lines for both men and women by up-and-coming designers and unusual jewelry and accessories, items procured during his regular buying trips to Manhattan.

Nightlife & the Arts

The **Marion Art Center** (⊠ 80 Pleasant St. ☎ 508/748–1266 ⊕ www.marionartcenter.org), comprised of two galleries, a small, intimate theater, and a studio, offers classes in art, music, dance, and theater arts year-round to both children and adults. Local artists have shows year-round, and four major theatrical productions are performed each year. In the late 19th century, during Marion's "Gilded Age," many famous writers and artists—including Henry James, Charles Dana Gibson, Sanford White, and the Barrymores—came to the area to share ideas and each other's company.

APPROACHING THE CAPE A TO Z

To research prices, get advice from other travelers, and book travel arrangements, visit www.fodors.com.

AIR TRAVEL

Boston and Providence are the major air gateways for the region approaching Cape Cod (⇨ Air Travel *and* Airports *in* Smart Travel Tips A to Z).

BIKE TRAVEL

In the Plymouth area, the Myles Standish State Forest (⇨ Sports & the Outdoors *in* Plymouth, *above*) has 15 mi of bike trails.

Fall River and New Bedford are predominately urban areas that are not well suited for cyclists, but nearby, many local roads in Westport and South Dartmouth are pleasant biking spots. In the New Bedford suburb of Fairhaven, the Phoenix bike trail is a 3.3-mi rail trail that begins at the intersection of Ferry and Main streets. It runs east to the Mattapoisett town line.

🚲 Bike Rentals **Martha's Cyclery** ⊠ 300 Court St., Plymouth ☎ 508/746–2109.

BOAT & FERRY TRAVEL

Capt. John Boats runs a seasonal ferry between Plymouth and Provincetown, with daily service from mid-June through early September and less-frequent service in spring and fall. The boat departs from State Pier (near the *Mayflower II*) in Plymouth and docks at MacMillan Wharf in Provincetown. The trip takes approximately 90 minutes. A round-trip ticket costs $30, the one-way fare is $18 (no one-way in July and August), and bicycles can be transported for an additional $3. Ferry service is available late May–September.

🚢 Boat & Ferry Lines **Capt. John Boats** ☎ 508/747–2400 or 800/242–2469 ⊕ www.provincetownferry.com.

BUS TRAVEL

American Eagle Motorcoach Inc. offers service from Boston to New Bedford. Bonanza Bus Lines runs frequent direct service between Boston and Fall River, as well as service to both Fall River and New Bedford from Providence. From Fall River and New Bedford to the Cape, Bonanza provides service to Bourne, Falmouth, Woods Hole, and Hyannis. Plymouth & Brockton Street Railway buses stop in Plymouth en route to the Cape from Boston. From the Plymouth stop take the Plymouth Area Link buses to the town center or to Plimoth Plantation.

🚏 Bus Depots **American Eagle New Bedford station** ✉ Southeastern Regional Transit Authority Terminal, 134 Elm St., New Bedford ☎ 800/453-5040. **Bonanza Bus Fall River terminal** ✉ Depot Ave., Fall River ☎ 508/548-7588. **Bonanza Bus New Bedford terminal** ✉ Southeastern Regional Transit Authority Terminal, 134 Elm St., New Bedford ☎ 508/990-3366. **Plymouth & Brockton Plymouth depot** ✉ Visitor's Center Park/Ride lot, Rte. 3, Exit 5, Plymouth ☎ 508/746-4795.

🚏 Bus Lines **American Eagle Motorcoach Inc.** ☎ 800/453-5040. **Bonanza Bus Lines** ☎ 508/548-7588 or 800/556-3815 ⊕ www.bonanzabus.com. **Plymouth & Brockton Street Railway** ☎ 508/746-0378 ⊕ www.p-b.com. **Plymouth Area Link** ☎ 508/746-0378 ⊕ www.gatra.org/pal.htm.

CAR TRAVEL

To get to Plymouth from Boston, take the Southeast Expressway (I–93) south to Route 3 toward Cape Cod; Exits 6 and 4 lead to downtown Plymouth and Plimoth Plantation, respectively. To reach Fall River from Boston, take I–93 to Route 24 south; then take Route 79 south to reach the Battleship Cove area. From Providence to Fall River, follow I–195 east. To get to New Bedford from Fall River, go east on I–195, or, if you're coming from Boston, follow I–93 to Route 24 south to Route 140 south, and continue to I–195 east; exit at Route 18 south for the historic district. Allow about one hour from Boston to Plymouth, Fall River, or New Bedford; about one hour from Plymouth to either Fall River or New Bedford; and about 15–20 minutes between New Bedford and Fall River. From Providence you can reach Fall River in about 20–25 minutes. To reach Westport from Fall River, take I–195 east to Route 88 south, and continue on Route 88. For South Dartmouth take I–195 east to the Faunce Corner Mall Road exit, or take Dartmouth Road south from New Bedford, toward Padanarum Village.

PARKING Metered street parking is available throughout the downtown Plymouth historic district; meters take quarters. There's also a large metered parking lot behind the Visitor Information Center on Water Street. In Fall River, free parking is available in a large lot at Battleship Cove. Metered street parking is available in the New Bedford historic district, where there are also two public parking lots: one on William Street (between North 2nd Street and Acushnet Avenue) and one on Elm Street at North 2nd.

TRAFFIC Plymouth, Fall River, and New Bedford do have small morning and afternoon rush hours, but the major traffic problems are leaving and entering Boston or in continuing to or returning from the Cape. In Boston, morning traffic is heaviest between 7 and 9 AM; the afternoon rush hour can extend from 3 to 7 PM, particularly in summer months. Traffic to the Cape is heaviest on Friday afternoon and evening and all day Saturday. Traffic from the Cape is at its worst on Saturday and on Sunday afternoon.

DISABILITIES & ACCESSIBILITY

At Plimoth Plantation, the paths through the village and the floors of the village buildings are dirt or straw and may be difficult to navigate for visitors in wheelchairs; users of electric wheelchairs will find it easier to manage. In New Bedford, most of the Whaling Museum is accessible to travelers with disabilities. Horseneck Beach in Westport has two types of beach wheelchairs available, at no charge; the beach also has wheelchair-accessible picnic facilities.

EMERGENCIES

🔳 Emergency Services **Ambulance, fire, police** ☎ 911 or dial township station.
🔳 Hospitals **Jordan Hospital** ✉ 275 Sandwich St., Plymouth ☎ 508/746-2000 ⊕ www.jordan.org. **St. Luke's Hospital** ✉ 101 Page St., New Bedford ☎ 508/997-1515.
🔳 24-Hour Pharmacies **CVS Pharmacy** ✉ 1145 Kempton St. [Rte. 6, near Rte. 140], New Bedford ☎ 508/999-3241 ✉ 8 Pilgrim Hill Rd. [off Rte. 44], Plymouth ☎ 508/747-1465 ⊕ www.cvs.com.

MEDIA

The *Standard-Times* is a daily newspaper, published in New Bedford, that covers the southeastern Massachusetts communities. Much of the paper's content is available online at ⊕ www.s-t.com. The *Boston Globe* publishes a "South Weekly" supplement on Sunday that covers Plymouth and other South Shore towns; it's available online at ⊕ www.bostonglobe.com

RADIO & TELEVISION The Boston area has two National Public Radio stations: WGBH 89.7 FM and WBUR 90.9 FM (which also broadcasts from Cape Cod at WSDH 91.5 FM, Sandwich; WCCT 90.3 FM, Harwich; and WBUR-AM 1240, Yarmouth).

Boston television stations are accessible throughout much of southeastern Massachusetts. Stations include PBS WGBH (2), CBS WBZ (4), ABC WCVB (5), NBC WHDH (7), FOX WFXT (25), and WB WLVI (56). In the New Bedford area, the local ABC station is WLNE (6).

TAXIS

🔳 Taxi Companies **Central Transportation** ✉ Plymouth ☎ 508/746-0018. **Yellow Cab** ✉ Fall River ☎ 508/674-4633. **Yellow Cab** ✉ New Bedford ☎ 508/999-5213.

TOURS

Cape Cod Canal Cruises (two or three hours, narrated) leave from Onset, just northwest of the Bourne Bridge. A Sunday jazz cruise, sunset cocktail cruises, and Friday and Saturday dance cruises are also available. Children 12 and under cruise free on Family Discount Cruises, Monday–Saturday at 4. Cruises cost between $10 and $15.

Colonial Lantern Tours offers guided evening walking tours April through November of the original Plymouth plantation site and historic district, as well as the nightly "Ghostly Haunts and Legends" tour highlighting Plymouth's more macabre history.

Plymouth Amphibious Tours are one-hour tours of Plymouth and its waterfront, half on land and half in the water, in restored World War II amphibious "duck boats." The tours are in late May–September for $17.

WHALE-
WATCHING
TOURS

Capt. John Boats offers several daily whale-watch cruises from Plymouth Town Wharf, June–early September, and on a more limited schedule April, May, and early September and October. Andy Lynn Boats, at Plymouth Town Wharf, runs whale-watch trips June–September; call for schedule.

⛴Fees & Schedules **Andy Lynn Boats** ☎508/746-7776. **Cape Cod Canal Cruises** ✉Onset Bay Town Pier, Onset ☎ 508/295-3883 ⊕ www.hy-linecruises.com/canal.htm. **Capt. John Boats** ☎ 508/746-2643 or 800/242-2469 ⊕ www.whalewatchingplymouth.com. **Colonial Lantern Tours** ✉ 5 North St., Plymouth ☎ 508/747-4161 or 800/698-5636 ⊕ www. plimouth.com. **Splashdown Amphibious Duckboat Tours** ✉ Harbor Pl. off Water St., Plymouth ☎ 508/747-7658 or 800/225-4000 ⊕ www.ducktoursplymouth.com.

TRAIN TRAVEL

With the exception of Plymouth, southeastern Massachusetts is not well served by trains. MBTA commuter rail service is available from Boston to Plymouth. Travel time is about one hour. From the station take the Plymouth Area Link buses (⇨ Bus Travel) to the historic attractions.

🚆 Train Information **MBTA** ☎ 617/222-3200 ⊕ www.mbta.com.

VISITOR INFORMATION

Plymouth Waterfront Visitor Information Center is generally open between April and November.

🚩 Tourist Information **Bristol County Convention and Visitors Bureau** ✉ 70 N. 2nd St. ⬛ Box 976, New Bedford 02741 ☎ 508/997-1250 or 800/288-6263 ⊕ www.bristol-county.org. **Destination Plymouth** ✉ 170 Water St., Suite 10C, Plymouth 02360 ☎ 508/747-7533 ⊕ www.visit-plymouth.com. **Fall River Chamber of Commerce** ✉ 200 Pocasset St., Fall River 02721 ☎ 508/676-8226 ⊕ www.fallriverchamber.com. **New Bedford Office of Tourism** ✉ Waterfront Visitors Center, Pier 3, New Bedford 02740 ☎ 508/979-1745 or 800/508-5353. **Plymouth Waterfront Visitor Information Center** ✉ 130 Water St. [at Rte. 44], Plymouth 02360 ☎ 508/747-7525.

THE UPPER CAPE

2

Revised by
James W. Rohlf

THE CLOSEST PART OF THE CAPE to the mainland, the Upper Cape has none of the briny, otherworldly breeziness of the Outer Cape and little of the resort feel of some Lower Cape towns such as Chatham. Instead, its year-round population is substantial, its beaches are intimate, and more of its attractions—freshwater ponds, conservation areas, and small museums—are inland. You'll discover plenty of history here: Sandwich is the oldest town on the Cape, and Bourne was the Pilgrims' first Cape Cod settlement and an important trading area. The first Native American reservation in the United States was established in Mashpee, which still has a large Wampanoag population and a tribal-council governing body.

Being able to find peace and quiet so close to the mainland and the traffic-clogged bridges is an unexpected and much-appreciated characteristic of the Upper Cape. Sandwich, its village streets lined with historic houses and museums, is remarkably well preserved. Heading east, Route 6A meanders past antiques shops, bed-and-breakfasts, and salt marshes. Falmouth, to the south, is an active year-round community, more suburban than seaside, though its easy-to-reach beaches are popular with families. In the villages of North and West Falmouth, along Buzzards Bay, tree-lined country lanes lead to sandy coves, while in East Falmouth and Waquoit, narrow spits of land jut into marshy inlets, and plenty of secluded sites for hiking and walking are yours for the taking. Woods Hole, a small but bustling village on the Cape's southwestern tip, is a center for international marine research; it's also the departure point for ferries to Martha's Vineyard.

To make the most of the Upper Cape, take an early-morning hike through a nature reserve or sit on a beach overlooking the sound and Martha's Vineyard. Pack a picnic, with fresh-from-the-farm-stand fruits or home-baked breads, and eat on the banks of a freshwater pond. Ride your bike along a shaded country road, or stretch out in the sand to watch the sailboats bobbing in the harbor and the sun sinking low over Buzzards Bay. You'll still have time to head back into town for that perfect lobster roll or plate of fried clams.

Exploring the Upper Cape

On the north shore, Sandwich, gracious and lovely, is the Cape's oldest town. Centered inland, Mashpee is a long-standing Native American township in which Native American–owned land is governed by local Wampanoags. Falmouth, the Cape's second-most populous town, is still green and historic, if seemingly overrun with strip malls. Woods Hole, the major port for ferries to Martha's Vineyard, is world-renowned for its biological research institutions. Along the west coast, in parts of Bourne and West and North Falmouth, you can find wooded areas ending in secluded coves; the south coast has long-established resort communities.

About the Restaurants

Much like the rest of Cape Cod, the Upper Cape's dining scene ranges from basic seafood shacks to contemporary restaurants that draw inspiration from the far corners of the globe—plus everything in between. Overall, the restaurant options tend toward the traditional, with fried clams, baked scrod, and boiled lobster gracing the most popular menus. Restaurants are more widely scattered in the Upper Cape towns—there are few "restaurant rows"—but if you like to wander and check out your dining options, try Main Street in Falmouth Center or Water Street in Woods Hole.

About the Hotels

Sandwich and other towns along the north-shore Route 6A Historic District have quiet, traditional villages with an old-Cape feel and charming B&Bs. Along Route 6A you can also find family-friendly motels, ranging from the modest to the better equipped. Historic B&Bs fill the center of Falmouth, while other small inns line the shore and the neighboring streets of Falmouth Heights. Lodging options are fewer in Bourne and West and North Falmouth, but a few B&Bs hidden away on country lanes provide glimpses of old New England. In Mashpee's New Seabury community you can rent modern town houses and condominiums with extensive resort amenities.

WHAT IT COSTS				
$$$$	**$$$**	**$$**	**$**	**¢**
RESTAURANTS over $30	$20–$30	$15–$20	$10–15	under $10
HOTELS over $220	$140–$220	$100–$140	$80–$100	under $80

Restaurant prices are per person for a main course at dinner. Hotel prices are for a standard double room in high season, excluding 5.7% state tax and gratuities. Some inns add a 15% service charge.

Timing

Although summer on the Upper Cape is the quintessential New England vacation experience, perhaps the ideal time of the year to visit is in early autumn, between mid-September and late October, when the summer crowds have left but the weather is still mild. Enjoy the beaches and water activities on Cape Cod Bay, Buzzards Bay, and Nantucket Sound in tranquility. The Bourne Scallop Festival takes place in mid-September for three days.

Sagamore

60 mi southeast of Boston; 30 mi northeast of New Bedford.

The village of Sagamore straddles the Cape Cod Canal and is perhaps best known for the bridge, completed in 1935, that bears its name. Primarily a small suburban community, the town has several stores for those interested in bargain hunting or gift shopping.

At **Pairpoint Glass Company,** watch richly colored lead crystal being hand-blown in America's oldest glass factory, founded in 1837. The shop sells candlesticks, vases, stemware, sun catchers, cup plates, lamps, per-

2

Numbers in the text correspond to numbers in the margin and on the Upper Cape map.

It's astonishing that the lovely old town of **Sandwich** ❶, so close to the busy mainland, stands as one of the best examples of the Cape of yesteryear. Visit the Hoxie House, the Sandwich Glass Museum, or the beautiful grounds and collection of old cars at **Heritage Museums and Gardens** ❷; picnic on the banks of Shawme Pond; or spend the afternoon at the old-timey Green Briar Nature Center and Jam Kitchen walking the nature trails and picking out home-made jam to take with you. Here and all along the bay shore you can explore salt marshes, so full of sea and bird life. If history's your thing, take a step back and start your Upper Cape trip at **Plimoth Plantation,** about 22 mi northwest of the Sagamore Bridge on Route 3A. The reconstructed settlement, where actors dress in period clothing and carry out the activities typical of earlier days, conveys a very tangible sense of the Cape's history.

To reach the Upper Cape's south shore, take Route 28A south through some lovely little towns, with detours to beautiful white-sand beaches. This is a pretty alternative to Route 28 if you're going to Falmouth and to **Woods Hole** ❻, the center for international marine research and the year-round ferry port for Martha's Vineyard. A small aquarium in town has regional sea-life exhibits, and there are several shops and museums. On the way out of town, the view from Nobska Light is breathtaking. In **Falmouth** ❹ stroll around the village green, look into some of the historic houses, and stop at the Waquoit Bay National Estuarine Research Reserve for a walk along the estuary and barrier beach. Inland, on the eastern extent of the Upper Cape, the Wampanoag township of **Mashpee** ❽ is one of the best places to learn about the Cape's Native American heritage.

---

fume bottles, witchballs, and reproductions of original Boston and Sandwich glass pieces. ⊠ *851 Sandwich Rd. (Rte. 6A), 02561 ☎ 508/888–2344 or 800/899–0953 ⊕ www.pairpoint.com ✉ Free ☾ Show-room May–Dec., weekdays 9–6, Sat. 10–6, Sun. 11–6; Jan.–Apr., Mon.–Sat. 10–5, Sun. noon–5. Demonstrations May–Dec., weekdays 9–4; Jan.–Apr., call before visiting; demonstration hrs are limited.*

Where to Stay & Eat

¢–$$$ ✕ **Sagamore Inn.** Old Cape Cod traditions with an Italian twist can be found at this local favorite, owned by the Pagliarani family since 1963. Pressed-tin walls and ceilings, fans, old wooden booths and tables, lace curtains, and white linen add up to a dining room so casual you almost overlook its elegance. The seafood platter is a knockout, the chicken potpie and the prime rib substantial. Luncheon specials attract regulars from all over town, and the service is friendly. A cozy, handsome old bar is under the same roof. Reservations accepted only for parties of eight or more. ⊠ *1131 Rte. 6A, 02561* ☎ *508/888–9707* ⊟ *AE, MC, V* ⊘ *Closed Tues. and Nov.–Mar.*

$ ⚠ **Scusset Beach State Reservation.** Encompassing 300 acres adjacent to the Cape Cod Canal, the park has a beach on Cape Cod Bay and 98 RV sites plus five tent sites, some wooded. There are cold showers on the beach and hot showers in the campground. ᴖ *Beach* ⤔ *103 sites* ⊠ *140 Scusset Beach Rd., off Rte. 3 at Sagamore Bridge rotary, 02532* ☎ *877/422–6762 campsite reservations, 508/888–0859 general information* ⊕ *www.reserveamerica.com* ⊠ *Full hookups $15 (MA res.) $18 (nonresident), tent sites $12* ⊟ *MC, V.*

Sports & the Outdoors

The **Scusset Beach State Reservation** is a pleasant place for a swim, walk, or bike ride near the mainland side of the Sagamore Bridge. The beach sweeps along Cape Cod Bay, and its pier and canal breakwater are popular for fishing and viewing boat traffic; other activities include hiking, picnicking, and camping. There's a parking fee from mid-April to mid-October. ⊠ *140 Scusset Beach Rd., off Rte. 3 at Sagamore Bridge rotary, 02532* ☎ *508/888–0859* ⊠ *Mid-Apr.–mid-Oct., parking $7* ⊘ *Daily 8–8.*

Shopping

Cape Cod Factory Outlet Mall (⊠ Factory Outlet Rd., Exit 1 off Rte. 6 ☎ 508/888–8417) has more than 20 outlet stores, including Corning–Revere, Carter's, Van Heusen, Izod, Bass, and Reebok.

ChocoLatte (⊠ 11 Cranberry Hwy. [Rte. 6A] ☎ 508/888–7065), just over the Sagamore Bridge on the Cape side, specializes in classic fudge and exotic truffles, made on the premises, and rich coffees brewed from Arabica beans.

Christmas Tree Shops (⊠ Cranberry Hwy. [Rte. 6A], Exit 1 off Rte. 6 ☎ 508/888–7010 ⊕ www.christmastreeshops.com) sell a wide variety of household goods at bargain prices. There are other locations at Falmouth, Hyannis, Yarmouthport, West Yarmouth, West Dennis, and Orleans.

Sandwich

★ ❶ *3 mi east of Sagamore Bridge; 11 mi west of Barnstable.*

A well-preserved, quintessential New England village, Sandwich wears its history proudly. The oldest town on Cape Cod, Sandwich was established in 1637 by some of the Plymouth Pilgrims and incorporated on March 6, 1638. Driving through town past the white-column town hall, the gristmill on Shawme Pond, the First Church of Christ with its spindlelike spire, and the 18th- and 19th-century homes that line the streets is like driving back in time—you may feel as if you should be holding a horse's reins rather than the steering wheel of a car. When you reach Main Street, park the car and get out for a stroll. Look at old houses on Main Street, stop at a museum or two, and work your way to the delightful Shawme Pond. While you walk, look for etched

2

Beaches   Water surrounds the Upper Cape on three sides, giving beach lovers plenty of options. The south-side beaches, on Nantucket Sound, have rolling surf and are warmed by the Gulf Stream. Along Buzzards Bay, many small coves have sandy stretches (although most restrict parking to residents or permit holders in season). To the north, on Cape Cod Bay, the beaches generally have more temperate waters and gentle waves, but watch out for pebbles mixed in with the sand, particularly in the Sandwich area. Remember that you can also swim inland—the Upper Cape has many child-friendly freshwater ponds with sandy beaches and calm waters.

Biking   Several short bike trails, including the Shining Sea Trail between Falmouth and Woods Hole and the Cape Cod Canal Trail, which follows both sides of the canal, make the Upper Cape a good place for easy day rides. Many of the less-traveled roads in Bourne, West and North Falmouth, and in the interior between Sandwich and Falmouth are also good biking areas. The beaches of Buzzards Bay, their parking restricted to those with resident stickers, make excellent destinations for bike rides.

Nightlife & the Arts   There's plenty of entertainment on the Upper Cape, especially in season; choices range from the summer concerts at Sandwich's Heritage Museums and Gardens to the staged readings at the Cape Cod Theatre Project (in Falmouth and Woods Hole) to the year-round concerts sponsored by Mashpee's Boch Center for the Performing Arts. Bourne, Sandwich, and Falmouth all host summer town-band concerts, and festivals with entertainment take place throughout the year. If you're looking for art galleries and crafts shows, explore the Falmouth downtown area, Route 6A in East Sandwich, and Mashpee Commons.

Sports & the Outdoors   Hikers and walkers will find plenty of places to wander on the Upper Cape. Several recreation areas line the Cape Cod Canal, and trails crisscross the region's wildlife sanctuaries and nature reserves, including the Ashumet Holly sanctuary, Waquoit Bay National Estuarine Research Reserve, and the Mashpee River Woodlands. Canoeing and kayaking are great around the marshy inlets of both Cape Cod Bay and Buzzards Bay and on the Upper Cape's many freshwater ponds. Also, the ponds, as well as the banks of the canal, are popular fishing sites.

Shopping   With its large year-round population, the Upper Cape has many of the same shops you find anywhere in the suburban United States. Strip malls line Route 28 in Falmouth, although by far the nicest mall in this part of the Cape is the villagelike Mashpee Commons. Like any other good tourist destination, the Upper Cape has plenty of T-shirt and souvenir shops almost everywhere you turn, and just over the bridges several outlet malls, including the Cape Cod Factory Outlet Mall and the Tanger Outlet Center, draw shoppers. The real charms of this part of the Cape are in its small boutiques and tucked-away galleries, where you can find that one-of-a-kind sweater or a watercolor inspired by the sun setting over the bay.

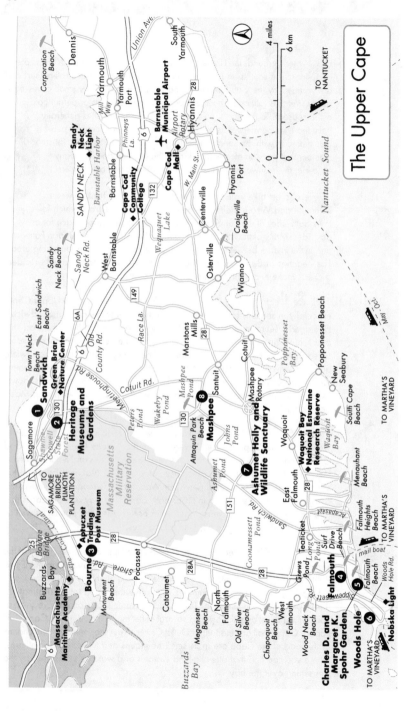

The Upper Cape

TO NANTUCKET

Nantucket Sound

4 miles
6 km

South Yarmouth

Dennis

Union Ave.

Yarmouth

Yarmouth Port

Mill Way

Phinneys La.

Barnstable Municipal Airport

Airport Rotary

Sandy Neck Light ◆

SANDY NECK

Barnstable Harbor

Cape Cod Community College ◆

Hyannis

Cape Cod Mall ◆

W Main St.

Hyannis Port

Corporation Beach

Town Neck Beach

1 Sandwich

Sagamore

Shawme Crowell State Forest

2 Green Briar Nature Center ◆

Heritage Museums and Gardens ◆

6A

East Sandwich Beach

Sandy Neck Beach

Sandy Neck Rd.

West Barnstable

Barnstable

132

Wequaquet Lake

Centerville

Craigville Beach

Osterville

Wianno

TO MARTHA'S VINEYARD

May – Oct.

Popponesset Beach

New Seabury

Popponesset Bay

South Cape Beach

Old County Rd.

6

Meetinghouse Rd.

149

Race La.

Marstons Mills

28

Cotuit

Santuit

Mashpee Rotary

8 Mashpee

130

Mashpee Pond

Attaquin Park Beach

Wakeby Pond

Peters Pond

Cotuit Rd.

Massachusetts Military Reservation

Johns Pond

Waquoit

Waquoit Bay National Estuarine Research Reserve ◆

Waquoit Bay

Menauhant Beach

7 Ashumet Holly and Wildlife Sanctuary ◆

Ashumet Pond

Coonamessett Pond

151

Sandwich Rd.

East Falmouth

28

Aptucxet Trading Post Museum ◆ **3**

TO SAGAMORE BRIDGE, PLIMOTH PLANTATION

Bourne Bridge

25

Bourne

28

Shore Rd.

Cape Cod Canal

Buzzards Bay

Massachusetts Maritime Academy ◆ **6**

Monument Beach

Pocasset

28A

Cataumet

North Falmouth

Old Silver Beach

Megansett Beach

Chapoquoit Beach

West Falmouth

Wood Neck Beach

Buzzards Bay

Charles D. and Margaret K. Spohr Garden ◆

Woods Hole

TO MARTHA'S VINEYARD

Nobska Light ◆ **6**

Woods Hole Rd.

Falmouth Beach

5

Surf Drive Beach

Falmouth 4

Teaticket

Long Pond

Giews Pond

Acapasket

Falmouth Heights Beach

TO MARTHA'S VINEYARD

mail boat

Sandwich glass from the old factory on front doors. There probably aren't two identical glass panels in town. Unlike other Cape towns, whose deep-water ports opened the doors to prosperity in the whaling days, Sandwich was an industrial town for much of the 19th century. The main industry was the production of vividly colored glass, called Sandwich glass, which is now sought by collectors. The Boston and Sandwich Glass Company's factory here produced the glass from 1825 until 1888, when competition with glassmakers in the Midwest—and finally a union strike—closed it.

The **Sandwich Glass Museum,** with its 9,000 square feet of exhibits, has information about the history of the company, including a diorama showing how the factory looked in its heyday, an "ingredient room" showcasing a wide spectrum of glass colors along with the minerals added to the sand to obtain them, and an outstanding collection of blown and pressed glass in many shapes and shimmering hues. Large glass lamps, vases, and pitchers are impressive, as are the hundreds of candlesticks and small saucers on display. Glassmaking demonstrations are held in summer. A few galleries contain relics of the town's early history (the museum is also the Sandwich Historical Society). The extensive, ornate gift shop sells some handsome reproductions, including some made by local and national artisans. ⊠ *129 Main St., Sandwich Center* ☎ *508/888–0251* ⊕ *www.sandwichglassmuseum. org* ☑ *$4.50* ⊙ *Apr.–Dec., daily 9:30–5; Feb. and Mar., Wed.–Sun. 9:30–4.*

🐄 A lovely place for a stroll or a picnic is the park around **Shawme Pond** (⊠ Water and Grove Sts., Sandwich Center), a favorite fishing site for children. The ducks and swans love to be fed, though posted signs warn you not to indulge them. Across the way—a perfect backdrop for this setting—stands the spired, white 1848 First Church of Christ, inspired by a design by British architect Christopher Wren.

Where Shawme Pond drains over its dam, a little wooden bridge leads over a watercourse to the waterwheel-powered **Dexter Gristmill,** built in 1654. In season the miller demonstrates and talks about the mill's operation and also sells its ground corn. ⊠ *Water and Grove Sts., Sandwich Center* ☎ *508/888–4910* ☑ *$2; combination ticket with Hoxie House $3* ⊙ *Late May and early Sept.–late Sept., Sat. 10–4:45; June–early Sept., Mon.–Sat. 10–4:45.*

need a break? The delightful **Dunbar Tea Shop** (⊠ 1 Water St. [Rte. 130], Sandwich Center ☎ 508/833–2485) is in a former billiards room–carriage house, now converted into a country cottage with paneled walls and assorted antiques and kitschy doodads. Lunch (from a smoked-fish platter with salad to quiche or a salmon tart), English cream tea, and tasty sweets are served from 11 to 5 daily, July through October ('til 4:30 the rest of the year). A gift shop sells British tea, specialty foods, and home-decorating items.

The **Thornton W. Burgess Museum** is dedicated to the Sandwich native whose tales of Peter Cottontail, Reddy Fox, and a host of other creatures of the Old Briar Patch have been part of children's bedtimes for decades. Thornton Burgess (1874–1965), an avid conservationist, made his characters behave true to their species to educate children as he entertained them. Storytelling sessions, often including the live animal that the Burgess story is about, take place regularly in July and August. On display are some of Burgess's 170 books (although children are welcome, the exhibits are of the don't-touch variety). The small gift shop carries puppets, Burgess books, and Pairpoint Crystal cup plates decorated with Burgess characters. ⊠ *4 Water St. (Rte. 130), Sandwich Center* ☎ *508/888–4668* ⊕ *www.thorntonburgess.org* ⚑ *$2 suggested donation* ☉ *Apr.–Oct., Mon.–Sat. 10–4, Sun. 1–4; weekends in Dec., Sat. 10–4, Sun. 1–4.*

Overlooking Shawme Pond is the **Hoxie House,** a remarkable old saltbox virtually unaltered since it was built in 1675. Even though people lived in it until the 1950s, the house was never modernized with electricity or plumbing. Furnishings reflect daily life in the colonial period, with some pieces on loan from the Museum of Fine Arts in Boston. Highlights are diamond-shape lead-glass windows and a collection of antique textile machines. ⊠ *18 Water St. (Rte. 130), Sandwich Center* ☎ *508/888–1173* ⚑ *$2; combination ticket with Dexter Gristmill $3* ☉ *Late May–mid-June, Sat. 10–5, Sun. 1–5; mid-June–mid-Oct., Mon.–Sat. 10–5, Sun. 1–5.*

The **Old Town Cemetery** (⊠ Grove St., Sandwich Center), on the opposite side of Shawme Pond from Hoxie House, is a classic, undulating New England graveyard. You can stop in for a peaceful moment and trace the genealogy of old Sandwich.

❷ Heritage Museums and Gardens, 100 beautifully landscaped acres overlooking the upper end of Shawme Pond, includes gardens and a café as well as an impressive complex of museum buildings with specialty collections ranging from cars to toys. In 1967 pharmaceuticals magnate Josiah K. Lilly III purchased the estate and turned it into a nonprofit museum. A highlight is the Shaker Round Barn, which showcases classic and historic cars—including a 1930 yellow-and-green Duesenberg built for Gary Cooper, a 1919 Pierce-Arrow, and a 1911 Stanley Steamer—as well as art exhibitions. The American History museum has antique firearms, a collection of 2,000 hand-painted miniature soldiers, military uniforms, and Native American arts. The art museum has an extensive Currier & Ives collection, Americana (including a mechanical-bank collection), antique toys such as a 1920 Hubley Royal Circus, and a working 1912 Coney Island–style carousel that both adults and little ones can ride as often as they like. A shuttle bus—equipped with a wheelchair lift and space to stow baby strollers—transports visitors every few minutes from the car museum to other exhibit sites.

Paths crisscross the grounds, which include gardens planted with daylily, hosta, heather, herb, and fruit trees. Rhododendron enthusiasts will recognize the name of onetime estate owner and hybridizer Charles O. Dexter; the rhododendrons are in full glory from mid-May through mid-June. Daylilies reach their peak from mid-July through early August. Families visiting with youngsters should ask at the ticket office for the Family Funpacks with children's activities, or the Clue tours, scavenger-hunt games for exploring the grounds. In summer, concerts are held in the gardens, often on Wednesday or Saturday evening or Sunday afternoon. The center of the complex is about ¾ mi on foot from the in-town end of Shawme Pond. ⊠ *67 Grove St.* ☎ *508/888–3300* ⊕ *www.heritagemuseumsandgardens.org* 🎟 *$12* ⊙ *May–Oct., Mon., Tues., and Thurs.–Sat. 9–6, Wed. 9–8, Sun. noon–6; Nov.–Apr., Wed.–Sat. 10–4, Sun. noon–4.*

At the **Cape Cod Canal Visitor Center,** run by the Army Corps of Engineers, exhibits and video presentations describe the canal's history, area wildflowers, and local "critters." Among the special ranger-led programs are beach and dune walks, as well as evening star watches. The visitor center is opposite the Coast Guard Station, near Joe's Fish Market. From late June through late September, the center is generally open Wednesday–Sunday; call for hours the rest of the year. ⊠ *Ed Moffitt Dr.* ☎ *508/833–9678 or 508/759–4431* 🎟 *Free* ⊙ *Call for seasonal hrs.*

For a view of the bay, you can walk to Town Neck Beach on the **Sandwich Boardwalk,** built over a salt marsh, creek, and low dunes. In 1991 Hurricane Bob and an October nor'easter destroyed the previous boardwalk. Individuals and businesses donated planks to rebuild it, which volunteers then installed. The donors' names, jokes (GET OFF OUR BOARD), thoughts (SIMPLIFY/THOREAU), and memorials to lovers, grandparents, and boats are inscribed on the planks. The long sweep of Cape Cod Bay stretches out around the beach at the end of the walk, where a platform provides fine views, especially at sunset. Stone jetties, dunes, and waving grasses, and the entrance to the canal are in the foreground, and you can look out toward Sandy Neck, Wellfleet, and Provincetown or toward the white cliffs beyond Sagamore. The sandy strip on this mostly rocky beach is near the rugosa rose–patch dunes; the flowers have a delicious fragrance, and it's a good place for birding. The creeks running through the salt marsh make for great canoeing. From the town center it's about a mile to the boardwalk; cross Route 6A on Jarves Street and at its end turn left, then right, and continue to the boardwalk parking lot.

🌞 At the **Sandwich Fish Hatchery** you can see more than 200,000 brook, brown, and rainbow trout at various stages of development; they are raised to stock the state's ponds. The mesh over the raceways keeps kingfishers and herons from a free lunch. You can buy feed for 25¢ and watch the fish jump for it. ⊠ *164 Rte. 6A* ☎ *508/888–0008* 🎟 *Free* ⊙ *Daily 9–3.*

| off the beaten path | **GREEN BRIAR NATURE CENTER AND JAM KITCHEN** – Is it the soothing pond-side location or its simple earthiness—who's to say? Whatever the reason, Green Briar Nature Center and Jam Kitchen, owned and operated by the Thornton Burgess Society, is a solid |

symbol of the old Cape. You pass a wildflower garden on your way in, and the Smiling Pool sparkles out back. Birds flit about the grounds, and great smells waft from vintage stoves in the Jam Kitchen, where you can watch as jams and pickles are made according to Ida Putnam's recipes, used here since 1903 (sun-cooked fruit preserves are especially superb). Come weekdays mid-April through mid-December to see jam being made in the Jam Kitchen; you can even take a jam-making class some evenings or Saturday. The nature center has classes for adults and children, as well as walks, lectures, and a May herb festival, where herbs, wildflowers, and perennials are for sale. The Briar Patch Conservation Area behind the building has nature trails—take a walk and visit the real live animals that inspired Peter Cottontail, Grandfather Frog, and other beloved Thornton Burgess characters. ⊠ *6 Discovery Hill Rd., off Rte. 6A, East Sandwich* ☎ *508/888–6870* ⊕ *www.thorntonburgess.org* ✉ *$2 suggested donation* ☉ *Apr.–Dec., Mon.–Sat. 10–4, Sun. 1–4; Jan.–Mar., Tues.–Sat. 10–4.*

Where to Stay & Eat

★ **$–$$** ✕ **Aqua Grille.** At this smart-casual bistro by the marina, offerings range from Cape basics (clam chowder, fried seafood, boiled lobsters) to more creative contemporary fare. The excellent lobster salad, for example, is a hearty serving of greens, tomatoes, avocados, baby green beans, and big, meaty lobster chunks. Sandwiches (salmon burgers, turkey wraps), grilled seafood, pastas, and steaks are also available. ⊠ *14 Gallo Rd., 02563* ☎ *508/888–8889* ⊕ *www.aquagrille.com* ⊟ *AE, DC, MC, V* ☉ *Closed late Oct.–Mar.*

$–$$ ✕ **Bee-Hive Tavern.** This informal and friendly colonial-style tavern hasn't been here since Revolutionary times (it opened in 1992), but the cozy dark-wood booths and wide-board floors look the part. The food is solid American fare such as burgers and sandwiches, fried seafood, Yankee pot roast, ribs, and steaks. Dinner-size salads are also available. ⊠ *406 Rte. 6A, East Sandwich 02537* ☎ *508/833–1184* ⊟ *MC, V.*

¢–$ ✕ **Marshland Restaurant and Bakery.** Sandwich's version of down-home is this tiny coffee shop tucked onto a parking lot. For breakfast try an Italian omelet, a rich mix of Italian sausage, fresh vegetables, and cheese. The lunch specials—a grilled chicken club sandwich, lobster salad, a turkey Reuben, a daily quiche, and the like—are the best choices midday, and for dinner the prime rib does not disappoint. ⊠ *109 Rte. 6A, 02563* ☎ *508/888–9824* ⊟ *No credit cards* ☉ *No dinner Mon.*

¢–$ ✕ **Seafood Sam's.** Fried seafood reigns supreme at Sam's, across from the Coast Guard station and a stone's throw from the Cape Cod Canal. Order from the counter, take a number, and sit in an airy dining room where the munch of fried clams accompanies the sound of lobsters cracking open. Sam's also has branches in Harwichport, Falmouth, and South Yarmouth. ⊠ *6 Coast Guard Rd., 02563* ☎ *508/888–4629* ⊕ *www.seafoodsams.com* ⊟ *D, MC, V* ☉ *Closed early Nov.–early Mar.*

$$$–$$$$ ✕🏠 **Dan'l Webster Inn.** Built on the site of a 17th-century inn, the Dan'l Webster is a contemporary hotel with old New England friendliness. Contemporary dishes, such as Tuscan shrimp with white beans or horseradish-crusted salmon, take their places beside veal Oscar, broiled scrod, and other classics. A casual tavern serves pizzas, burgers, and salads. Guest rooms have fine reproduction mahogany and cherry furnishings. ⌂ *149 Main St., 02563* ☎ *508/888–3622 or 800/444–3566* 🖷 *508/888–5156* ⊕ *www.danlwebsterinn.com* ⊲ *45 rooms, 9 suites* ♨ *2 restaurants, room service, some in-room hot tubs, cable TV, pool, no-smoking rooms* 🟰 *AE, D, DC, MC, V.*

$$–$$$ ✕🏠 **Belfry Inne & Bistro.** This one-of-a-kind inn comprises a 1902 former church, an authentic Victorian "painted lady," and an 1830 Federal-style house clustered on a main campus, plus a fourth building—a 1638 former parish house, the oldest standing structure in Sandwich—just a short walk down the road. Room themes in each building nod to their respective histories—the Drew House's charmingly appointed rooms, for example, are named after former inhabitants. The luxurious rooms in the Abbey, named for the six days of creation, have whirlpool tubs and gas fireplaces, and are set along a corridor overlooking the restaurant below. The Bistro serves creative interpretations of popular foods in a striking setting—look up at the church's original arches and stained glass as you dine. Guests of the inn also eat breakfast here. ⌂ *8 Jarves St., 02563* ☎ *508/888–8550 or 800/844–4542* 🖷 *508/888–3922* ⊕ *www.belfryinn.com* ⊲ *28 rooms* ♨ *Restaurant, some in-room hot tubs, bar; no kids under 10, no smoking* 🟰 *AE, D, DC, MC, V* ⊗ *No dinner Sun. and Mon., no lunch* ⍾⊙ *CP.*

$$$$ 🏠 **Bay Beach.** Waterfront accommodations are few in this part of the Cape, but you can wake to broad vistas of the bay at this B&B in a contemporary bay-side house. Guest rooms are appointed like a well-turned-out suburban home, with lots of wicker, floral comforters, CD players, refrigerators, and, best of all, panoramic windows facing the ocean and adjacent marshes. All have whirlpool tubs, gas fireplaces, and decks. Breakfast is a buffet in the casual dining room, with floor-to-ceiling windows for still more bay views; a boardwalk leads to a private beach. ⌂ *3 Bay Beach La., 02563* ☎ *508/888–8813 or 800/475–6398* 🖷 *508/888–5416* ⊕ *www.baybeach.com* ⊲ *3 rooms* ♨ *Dining room, in-room hot tubs, refrigerators, cable TV, beach; no kids under 16, no smoking* 🟰 *MC, V* ⊗ *Closed Nov.–Apr.* ⍾⊙ *BP.*

★
ⓒ $$$–$$$$ 🏠 **Wingscorton Farm.** This is perhaps the Upper Cape's best-kept secret: an enchanting working farm with chickens, goats, horses, and other animals. Built in 1763, the main house, once a stop on the Underground Railroad, has a dining room with a fireplace with a 9-foot-long hearth, as well as two suites, each with a fireplace, wide-plank floors, and a smaller adjoining bedroom with twin beds. The property also includes a detached cottage with a kitchen, which rents by the week in season. A stone carriage house has a fully equipped kitchen, a living room with a pullout sofa, and a wood-burning stove; a spiral staircase leads to a loft with a bed and an oversize sundeck. A private bay beach is a five-minute walk. ⌂ *11 Wing Blvd., off Rte. 6A, about 4½ mi east of Sandwich Center,*

East Sandwich 02537 ☎ *508/888–0534* 📠 *508/888–0545* 🛏 *2 suites, 1 carriage house, 1 2-bedroom cottage* ⚒ *Dining room, some kitchens, refrigerators, beach, library, some pets allowed (fee); no room phones, no room TVs* 🍴 *AE, MC, V* 🍽 *BP.*

$$$ 🏨 **Inn at Sandwich Center.** Across from the Sandwich Glass Museum, this 18th-century house with Victorian-style rooms is listed on the National Register of Historic Places. The pretty Lottie Chipman Room has an antique four-poster bed and a rocker, while the spacious Robert Morse Room has a private deck overlooking the gardens. A gazebo on a nearby hill houses a secluded spa where a professional massage may be arranged. A hearty breakfast is served in the keeping room, which contains a fireplace, the house's original 1750 beehive oven, and an antique table (older than the inn) that seats ten. There's a small gift shop and concierge service provided by the gracious owners. ⊠ *118 Tupper Rd., 02563* ☎ *508/ 888–6958 or 800/249–6949* 📠 *508/888–2746* ⊕ *www.innatsandwich. com* 🛏 *5 rooms* ⚒ *No room phones, no room TVs, no kids under 10, no smoking* 🍴 *MC, V* 🍽 *BP.*

$$–$$$ 🏨 **Earl of Sandwich Motor Manor.** Single-story Tudor-style buildings form a "U" around a duck pond and wooded lawn set with lawn chairs. Rooms are sparsely furnished with dark pine headboards and doors but are of good size and have large windows. A continental breakfast is provided from April through November. ⊠ *378 Rte. 6A, East Sandwich 02537* ☎ *508/888–1415 or 800/442–3275* 📠 *508/833–1039* ⊕ *www. earlofsandwich.com* 🛏 *24 rooms* ⚒ *Refrigerators, cable TV, pool, some pets allowed; no smoking* 🍴 *AE, D, DC, MC, V.*

$$–$$$ 🏨 **Sandwich Lodge & Resort.** This glorified motel—emphasis on glorified— on 10 rolling acres has several different types of accommodations. Suites and efficiencies have kitchens with refrigerators and two-burner stoves or microwave ovens; some even have two-person whirlpool tubs. The modern indoor pool is a highlight, and is conveniently accessed from many of the rooms. The homey on-site restaurant serves lunch and dinner (ample portions, great prices). ⊠ *54 Rte. 6A* 🏷 *Box 1038, 02563* ☎ *508/888–2275 or 800/282–5353* 📠 *508/888–8102* ⊕ *www. sandwichlodge.com* 🛏 *24 rooms, 36 suites, 4 efficiencies* ⚒ *Restaurant, some in-room hot tubs, some kitchens, some microwaves, some refrigerators, cable TV, 2 pools (1 indoor), hot tub, Ping-Pong, shuffleboard, bar, laundry facilities, some pets allowed (fee), no-smoking rooms* 🍴 *AE, D, MC, V* 🍽 *CP.*

¢ 🏕 **Shawme-Crowell State Forest.** Less than a mile from the Cape Cod Canal, this 742-acre state forest is a good base for local biking and hiking, and campers get free day use of Scusset Beach. Open-air campfires are allowed at the wooded tent and RV (no hookups) campsites. Heated bathroom and shower facilities are a blessing on chilly mornings. The campground is generally open year-round, but if you're planning a winter trip, call to confirm before visiting. 🛏 *285 sites* ⊠ *Rte. 130, 02563* ☎ *508/888–0351, 877/422–6762 reservations* ⊕ *www.reserveamerica. com* 🛏 *Basic sites $10* 🍴 *MC, V.*

Nightlife & the Arts

THE ARTS **Heritage Museums and Gardens** (⊠ 67 Grove St. ☎ 508/888–3300) sponsors summer jazz and other concerts in its gardens from June to mid-

September; bring chairs or blankets. Most concerts are free with admission to the complex. **Town-band concerts** (✉ Bandstand, Henry T. Wing Elementary School, Rte. 130 and Beale Ave., Sandwich Center ☎ 508/888–5144) are held Thursday evening from July through late August starting at 7:30.

NIGHTLIFE **Bobby Byrne's Pub** (✉ 65 Rte. 6A ☎ 508/888–6088), with other locations in Hyannis and Mashpee, is a comfortable pub, with a jukebox, and good light and full menus.

British Beer Company (✉ 46 Rte. 6A ☎ 508/833–9590 ⊕ www.britishbeer.com), with other locations in Cedarville, Falmouth, and Plymouth, has a traditional British "public house" atmosphere with a great menu including fish, ribs and pizza.

Sports & the Outdoors

BEACHES **East Sandwich Beach,** on North Shore Road, lies behind the grass-covered dunes beyond a row of gray-shingle beach cottages. It's a long stretch of sand, but nearby parking is very limited (and restricted to residents between 8 AM and 4 PM in season). From Route 6A follow Ploughed Neck Road to North Shore Road.

Town Neck Beach, off Town Neck Road, is a long, dune-backed bay beach with a mix of sand and pebbles. You need a resident parking sticker to leave your car in the large parking area between 8 AM and 4 PM in season. There are restrooms and a snack bar.

GOLF **Sandwich Hollows Golf Club** (✉ 1 Round Hill Rd., East Sandwich 02537 ☎ 508/888–3384 ⊕ www.sandwichhollows.com) has an 18-hole, par-71 course that's open to the public.

Shopping

Fodor'sChoice The **Giving Tree** (✉ 550 Rte. 6A, East Sandwich ☎ 508/888–5446 or
★ 888/246–3551 ⊕ www.givingtreegallery.com), an art gallery and sculpture garden, sells contemporary crafts, jewelry, ceramics, and prints. It has walking paths through a peaceful bamboo grove, along the marsh, and over a narrow wooden suspension bridge.

Joe's Lobster Mart (✉ Cape Cod Canal ☎ 508/888–2971), opposite Seafood Sam's and the Coast Guard station, sells fresh-from-the-tank lobsters. Call ahead, and they'll boil your crustaceans to order—a great idea for an easy dinner at your cottage or hotel or for a picnic overlooking the canal. Joe's also sells many varieties of fresh fish.

Sandwich Auction House (✉ 15 Tupper Rd., 02563 ☎ 508/888–1926 ⊕ www.sandwichauction.com), which auctions antiques, general merchandise, and Oriental rugs, is a great place to spend part of a Wednesday night (Saturday in the off-season); come after 2 to preview the items for sale. This local institution has weekly sales; in addition, specialty sales every six to eight weeks feature upscale antiques received in that period. Sales are also held for antique and modern rugs.

Titcomb's Bookshop (✉ 432 Rte. 6A, East Sandwich ☎ 508/888–2331) stocks used, rare, and new books, including a large collection of Cape and nautical titles and Americana, as well as an extensive selection of children's books.

en route   **Route 6A** heads East from Sandwich, passing through the oldest settlements on the Cape. Part of the Old King's Highway historic district, the route is protected from development. Classic inns and enticing antiques shops alternate with traditional gray-shingle homes on this tree-lined road, and the woods periodically give way to broad vistas across the marshes. In autumn the foliage along the way is bright; maples with their feet wet in ponds and marshes put on a good display. Along Route 6A just east of Sandwich Center, you can stop to watch cranberries being harvested in flooded bogs. If you're heading down-Cape and you're not in a hurry, this is a lovely route to take.

Bourne

❸ *6 mi southwest of Sandwich.*

The town of Bourne includes nine villages—Bourne Village, Bournedale, Buzzards Bay, Cataumet, Gray Gables, Monument Beach, Pocasset, Sagamore, and Sagamore Beach—along Buzzards Bay and both sides of the Cape Cod Canal. The villages range from honky-tonk commercial districts to bucolic waterfront suburbs. With a mix of year-round and summer residents, the area includes places for learning about the region's marine life and early commercial history, as well as several attractive recreation areas, established and maintained by the Army Corps of Engineers, for biking, hiking, and fishing along the canal.

The Pilgrims established their first Cape Cod settlement in Bourne in 1627, but back then it was still part of Sandwich; Bourne didn't become a separate town until 1884. By that time it had grown into a popular summer colony whose part-time residents included President Grover Cleveland and *Boston Globe* publisher Charles Taylor. Present-day Bourne's maritime orientation was created by the Cape Cod Canal, which opened in 1914. The 17½-mi canal cut the distance for shipping traffic between Boston and New York by 75 mi and eliminated the often-treacherous journey around the Cape. The Army Corps of Engineers took over the canal's operation in the late 1920s and embarked on a project to widen it; the current Bourne and Sagamore bridges were built in the 1930s as part of this project.

The **National Marine Life Center,** on the mainland near the Chamber of Commerce office, has a small exhibit area devoted to whales, dolphins, seals, and other marine life. In summer there are marine-life educational programs for children and evening lectures about the ocean environment for adults. The center hopes to break ground on an expanded facility for rehabilitating stranded marine animals that will include a marine animal hospital and nursery, rehabilitation pools, and additional exhibit space. ⊠ *120 Main St., Buzzards Bay* ☎ *508/759–8722* ⊕ *www.nmlc. org* ✆ *Free, donations accepted* ☉ *Late May–early Sept., Mon.–Sat. 10–6, Sun. noon–6.*

On the mainland side, the **Massachusetts Maritime Academy,** founded in 1891, is the oldest such academy in the country. Future members of the Merchant Marines receive their training at its 55-acre campus in Buzzards Bay. The library has nautical paintings and scale models of ships from the 18th century to the present and is open to the public at no charge (hours are extensive but vary widely depending on whether school is in session; call ahead). For a 30- to 60-minute tour of the academy (weekdays only; times vary), call 48 hours in advance. The tours are designed for prospective students and their families but are open to all. ⊠ *Taylor's Point, Buzzards Bay* ☎ *508/830–5000* ⊕ *www. mma.mass.edu.*

A monument to the birth of commerce in the New World, the **Aptucxet Trading Post Museum** was erected on the foundation of the original post archaeologically excavated in the 1920s. Here, in 1627, Plimoth Plantation leaders established a way station between the Native American encampment at Great Herring Pond 3 mi to the northeast, Dutch colonists in New Amsterdam (New York), to the south, and English colonists on Cape Cod Bay. Before the canal was built, the Manomet River connected Herring Pond with Buzzards Bay (no, scavengers don't frequent it—it was misnamed for the migrating osprey that do), and a short portage connected the pond to Scusset River, which met Cape Cod Bay. The Native Americans traded furs; the Dutch traded linen cloth, metal tools, glass beads, sugar, and other staples; and the Pilgrims traded wool cloth, clay beads, sassafras, and tobacco (which they imported from Virginia). Wampum was the medium of exchange.

Inside the post, 17th-century cooking utensils hang from the original brick hearth; beaver and otter skins, furniture, and other artifacts such as arrowheads, tools, and tomahawks are displayed throughout. Also on the grounds are a gift shop in a Dutch-style windmill, a saltworks, herb and wildflower gardens, a picnic area overlooking the canal, and a small Victorian railroad station built for the sole use of President Grover Cleveland, who had a summer home in Bourne. To get here, cross the Bourne Bridge; then take the first right from the Bourne Bridge rotary onto Trowbridge Road and follow the signs. Note that the site is also open on holiday Mondays in season. ⊠ *24 Aptucxet Rd.* ☎ *508/759– 9487* ⊕ *www.bournehistoricalsoc.org* ⊠ *$4* ⊙ *May, June, and Sept.–mid-Oct., Tues.–Sat. 10–5, Sun. 2–5; July and Aug., Mon.–Sat. 10–5, Sun. 2–5.*

Ⓒ A break for energetic children pent up in a car for too many miles, **Adventure Isle** has a go-kart track, bumper boat lagoon, 18 holes of miniature golf, 25-foot Super Slide, batting cages, kiddie rides, laser tag, and an arcade with snack bar. Check the Web site for discount coupons. ⊠ *Rte. 28, 2 mi south of Bourne Bridge* ☎ *508/759–2636 or 800/535–2787* ⊕ *www.adventureisle.com* ⊠ *$1.75–$4 per ride or $11.95 per day for unlimited rides* ⊙ *Apr.–Oct., call for off-season hrs, July–early Sept., daily 10 AM–11 PM.*

Where to Stay & Eat

$–$$$ ✕ **Chart Room.** Harborside at the marina in a former cargo barge, this traditional watering hole has been serving up seafood classics since 1966. Clam chowder, lobster rolls, broiled scrod, seafood Newburg, baked stuffed shrimp—they're all here, as are sirloin steak, broiled lamb chops, and even grilled cheese-and-tomato sandwiches. ✉ *1 Shipyard La., at Kingman Yacht Center, Cataumet* ☎ *508/563–5350* ⊕ *www.kingmanyachtcenter.com* ▭ *AE, DC, MC, V* ☉ *Closed mid-Oct.–late May and weekdays late May–late June and early Sept.–mid-Oct.*

¢–$ ✕ **Stir Crazy.** Fresh ingredients with lively Cambodian, Thai, and Vietnamese flavors dominate every dish that graces the menu (owner Bopha Samms hails from Cambodia). Try the *nhem shross* (an appetizer of vegetables and shrimp) and the refreshing *bar bong* (chilled noodles topped with pork, egg rolls, and coconut-peanut sauce). ✉ *570 MacArthur Blvd. (Rte. 28 S), Pocasset* ☎ *508/564–6464* ⚑ *Reservations not accepted* ▭ *MC, V* ♿ *No smoking* ☉ *Closed Mon. No lunch Sat.–Thurs.*

FodorsChoice ★

$$–$$$ 🏨 **Wood Duck Inn.** Behind this cozy B&B, a working cranberry bog and acres of conservation land spread out as far as you can see. The small but comfy Cottage Room has lace curtains and a brass bed with a floral comforter, and both suites have a bedroom plus a sitting room that doubles as extra sleeping space. The Garden Suite is done in romantic florals, and the family-friendly Treetops Suite resembles a contemporary apartment in forest green and white; it has a tiny but fully equipped kitchen and sweeping views. The innkeepers deliver breakfast to your door. ✉ *1050 County Rd., Cataumet 02534* ☎ *508/564–6404* ⊕ *www.woodduckinnbb.com* ⤴ *1 room, 2 suites* ⚒ *Kitchen, microwaves, refrigerator, cable TV, in-room VCRs; no a/c in some rooms, no smoking* ▭ *No credit cards* ¶⊘¶ *CP.*

Nightlife & the Arts

The **Army Corps of Engineers** (☎ 508/759–4431), which maintains the Cape Cod Canal via a field office in Buzzards Bay, offers free daily programs in summer, including evening campfire programs on Canal-related topics (with marshmallow roasting). Call for program details and locations. In Bourne, Thursday evening **town-band concerts** (✉ Main St. ☎ 508/759–6000) in July and August start at 7 in Buzzards Bay Park.

Sports & the Outdoors

The **Army Corps of Engineers** (☎ 508/759–4431) sponsors guided walks, bike trips, and hikes, including canal and area natural-history walks.

BASEBALL The **Bourne Braves** of the collegiate Cape Cod Baseball League play home games at **Coady School** (✉ Trowbridge Rd., Bourne 02532 ☎ 508/432–6909 ⊕ www.bournebraves.org) from mid-June to mid-August.

BEACHES **Monument Beach,** off Shore Road, a small but pretty crescent of sand adjacent to the town dock, faces Buzzards Bay just south of Bourne Bridge. The beach has a snack bar, restrooms, and a parking lot, restricted in season to those with resident permits. From Shore Road, turn right onto Emmons Road just past the old train depot.

BIKING   An easy, straight trail stretches on either side of the **Cape Cod Canal**, 6½ mi on the south side, 7 mi on the north, with views of the bridges and ship traffic on the canal. Contact the Army Corps of Engineers **Herring Run Visitor Center** (☎ 508/759–4431) for information about Canal trail access and parking. Directly across the street from the canal bike path on the mainland (near the Massachusetts Maritime Academy), **P&M Cycles** (✉ 29 Main St., Buzzards Bay ☎ 508/759–2830) rents mountain and hybrid bikes at reasonable rates.

FISHING   The Cape Cod Canal is a great place to fish—from the service road on either side—for the big blues and striped bass making their way through the passage seasonally (April–November).

HIKING &   Run by the Army Corps of Engineers, the **Herring Run Visitor Center** (✉ U.S.
WALKING   6, Bournedale ☎ 508/759–4431, 508/759–5991 tides, weather, and special events), on a bank of the canal with an excellent view, has picnic tables (close to noisy U.S. 6), access to the canal bike path, a herring run through which the fish travel on their spawning run in May, and short self-guided walking trails through woodland. The visitor center is on the mainland side of the canal, between the bridges.

On the Cape side of the canal, the Army Corps of Engineers manages the **Tidal Flats Recreation Area** (✉ Shore Rd. ☎ 508/759–4431), a small but peaceful canal-side park near the Cape railroad bridge. It's a pleasant site for picnicking or fishing, with a great view of the canal's ship traffic. There's access to the canal bike path, too. In the late afternoon, between 5 and 7, you can watch the bridge lower to allow a service train to cross the canal; these times are approximate and can vary widely due to traffic and bridge work. To reach the recreation area, cross the Bourne Bridge and follow Trowbridge Road to Shore Road.

ICE-SKATING   **John Gallo Ice Arena** (✉ 231 Sandwich Rd. ☎ 508/759–8904) is the place to go for ice-skating year-round (except May). Lessons are offered and skate rental is available. Admission is $2.

SCUBA DIVING   Rentals, instruction, group dives, and information are available through **Aquarius Diving Center** (✉ 3239 Cranberry Hwy., Buzzards Bay ☎ 508/759–3483 ⊕ www.aquariusdivingctr.com), across the Bourne Bridge on the mainland.

North & West Falmouth

9 mi south of Bourne.

With their wooded country lanes that lead to secluded coves, small harbors dotted with sailboats, and farm stands selling sweet corn and fresh berries, the villages along Route 28 between Bourne and Falmouth proper offer up a glimpse of the old Cape Cod. Native American names serve as reminders of the true first settlers here, and houses that date from the 18th century (as well as more modern summer retreats) line the roads. Although Route 28 from the Bourne Bridge south to Falmouth is overly commercial in many areas, Route 28A between Pocasset and West Falmouth is more scenic, with side roads leading to attractive beaches, particularly Old Silver Beach, and small harbors. If you've brought your bicycle, the less-traveled lanes here make for good biking; many of the beaches along the bay restrict parking to residents, but bicyclists and walkers are free to explore.

> **need a break?**
>
> **Peach Tree Circle Farm** (⊠ 881 Old Palmer Ave., West Falmouth ☎ 508/548–4006) includes a bakery, a farm stand, and a cheery tearoom. Inexpensive lunches of soups, sandwiches, salads, and a few entrées such as quiche and chicken potpie are served April–December amid the smells of baking bread and herbs hung to dry.

Where to Stay & Eat

$–$$$ ✕ **Chapoquoit Grill.** Comfortable and bustling, this unassuming local favorite has an Italian slant, starting with the creative pizzas and pastas. The long list of daily specials might include grilled salmon over greens with a lemon-basil vinaigrette or sirloin with a tamarind-mango glaze. A fireplace and coral-color walls make the front room intimate, while the larger rear dining room seems vaguely tropical (with a palm tree in the middle). Expect daunting waits for a table on summer weekends; come early or late. ⊠ *410 W. Falmouth Hwy. (Rte. 28A), West Falmouth* ☎ *508/540–7794* ⊄ *Reservations not accepted* ⊟ *MC, V* ⊘ *No lunch.*

$$$$ ⊡ **Inn at West Falmouth.** This luxurious 1898 estate-house inn is in a secluded area of an exclusive village. A combination of contemporary and antique furnishings and polished hardwood floors sets an elegant but relaxed mood. Guest rooms have king- or queen-size beds (some with canopies), Italian marble bathrooms with whirlpool tubs, phones, hair dryers, and wall safes; some have fireplaces and private decks. Beyond the French doors, off the pale pink-and-green breakfast room, a patio spilling over with potted plants and trees overlooks woods, gardens, and a tennis court and leads to the small pool and deck. Leave the kids at home; this inn is best suited for an adults-only escape. ⊠ *66 Frazar Rd.* ⊄ *Box 1208, West Falmouth 02574* ☎ *508/540–7696 or 800/397–7696* ⊟ *508/540–9977* ⊕ *www.innatwestfalmouth.com* ⇄ *6 rooms* ⊘ *Tennis court, pool; no smoking* ⊟ *MC, V* ⊙⊨ *CP.*

$$$–$$$$ ⊡ **Sea Crest Resort.** Location and amenities are strong draws at this modern conference center and resort, whose eight buildings sprawl along one end of beautiful Old Silver Beach. Rooms, done in dark blues and pastels, are crisp and clean; many have ocean views, and some have gas-log fireplaces. A number of lodging packages are available. ⊠ *350 Quaker Rd., North Falmouth 02556* ☎ *508/540–9400 or 800/225–3110* ⊟ *508/548–0556* ⊕ *www.seacrest-resort.com* ⇄ *258 rooms, 8 suites* ⊘ *Restaurant, room service, in-room data ports, refrigerators, cable TV with movies and video games, putting green, 2 tennis courts, 2 pools (1 indoor), health club, hot tub, sauna, shuffleboard, piano bar, children's programs (ages 3–12), meeting rooms* ⊟ *AE, D, DC, MC, V.*

$$–$$$$ ⊡ **Chapoquoit Inn.** Four-poster beds, pastel quilts, and garden views fill the rooms at this cozy B&B in a former Quaker homestead built in 1739. Owners Kim and Tim McIntyre (she's a former marketing exec, he's a landscape designer) have furnished their inn with antiques and other family heirlooms. In the sunny breakfast room, which opens to the deck, you might find lemon pancakes or crème brûlée French toast. In season, the inn cannot accommodate kids under 12 in the main house, but families are welcome in two spacious rooms that are housed in a separate cottage. ☒ *495 Rte. 28A, West Falmouth 02574* ☎ *508/540–7232 or 800/842–8994* ⊕ *www.chapoquoit.com* ➲ *6 rooms, 2 suites* ⚹ *No room phones, no room TVs, no kids under 12 in season (except in cottage), no smoking* ▤ *MC, V* ⦶ *BP.*

$$$–$$$$ 🏠 **Beach Rose Inn.** In 2002, new owners David and Donna McIlrath rehabbed this rambling 1863 farmhouse on a quiet lane to create a comfortable country-style B&B. The rooms—some in the main inn, some in the adjacent carriage house—are furnished with quilts and a mix of antiques and reproductions. The Falmouth suite has an airy, private sunporch; this room, and those in the adjacent carriage house, have whirlpool tubs. A three-bedroom apartment on the second floor of the carriage house (without a full kitchen, though it does have a refrigerator, microwave, coffeemaker, and toaster) and a separate, tiny two-bedroom cottage both rent by the week. One room is reserved for guests with a pet. ☒ *17 Chase Rd., off Rte. 28A, West Falmouth 02574* ☎ *508/540–5706 or 800/498–5706* 🖷 *508/540–4880* ⊕ *www. thebeachroseinn.com* ➲ *7 rooms, 1 suite, 1 apartment, 1 cottage* ⚹ *Some in-room hot tubs, some kitchenettes, some microwaves, some refrigerators; no room phones, no room TVs, no kids under 10 (except in cottage), no smoking* ▤ *MC, V* ⦶ *BP.*

$$ 🏠 **Ideal Spot Motel.** Neat-as-a-pin, quiet, and a bit old-fashioned, this gray-shingle motel has simple, family-friendly rooms that are all of good size. Efficiencies have a queen-size bed or two doubles, plus a kitchen and a sitting area with a sofa bed; the large motel rooms have refrigerators. There's no pool, but it's only a mile to Chapoquoit Beach. ☒ *Rte. 28A at Old Dock Rd.* ⓘ *Box 465, West Falmouth 02574* ☎ *508/548–2257 or 800/269–6910* ➲ *12 efficiencies, 2 rooms* ⚹ *Some kitchens, some refrigerators, cable TV; no smoking* ▤ *D, MC, V* ⦶ *Closed Jan.–Mar.*

Nightlife & the Arts

Sea Crest Resort (☒ 350 Quaker Rd., North Falmouth ☎ 508/540–9400) has a summer and holiday-weekend schedule of nightly entertainment on the outdoor terrace, including dancing to country, Top 40, reggae, and jazz bands and a big-band DJ.

Sports & the Outdoors

BEACHES **Chapoquoit Beach** (☒ Chapoquoit Rd., West Falmouth), a narrow stretch of white sand, lines a peninsula that juts dramatically into the bay. Resident parking stickers are required at the beach lot in season, but the surrounding roads are popular with bicyclists. The beach has lifeguards and portable toilets.

Megansett Beach (☒ County Rd., North Falmouth), hidden in a residential neighborhood, is a small, family-friendly location. Weathered gray-shingle homes line the cove, while boats moored at the adjacent yacht club bob in the bay. The beach has lifeguards and a portable toilet but no other services. Resident parking stickers are required at the beach lot in season.

Old Silver Beach (⊠ Off Quaker Rd., North Falmouth) is a long, beautiful crescent of soft white sand bordered by the Sea Crest Resort at one end. It's especially good for small children because a sandbar keeps it shallow at the southern end and creates tide pools full of crabs and minnows. The beach has lifeguards, restrooms, showers, and a snack bar. There's a $20 fee for parking in summer.

Wood Neck Beach (⊠ Wood Neck Rd., West Falmouth), in the Sippewisset area, is a sandy bay-side beach backed by grass-covered dunes. At high tide the beach is very narrow, but sandbars and shallow tide pools make this a good place for children when the tide is out. Resident parking stickers are required in season.

HORSEBACK **Haland Stables** (⊠ 878 Rte. 28A, West Falmouth ☎ 508/540–2552) of-
RIDING fers lessons and trail rides by reservation Monday–Saturday.

Shopping
Europa (⊠ 628 W. Falmouth Hwy. [Rte. 28A], West Falmouth ☎ 508/ 540–7814) is a small boutique in a charming old house with a great selection of jewelry, accessories, gift items, and fun clothing at fair prices. A second room is devoted to lamps and lamp repair.

Falmouth

❹ *2 mi south of West Falmouth; 15 mi south of Bourne Bridge; 4 mi north of Woods Hole.*

Falmouth, the Cape's second-largest town, was settled in 1660 by Congregationalists from Barnstable who had been ostracized by their church and deprived of voting privileges and other civil rights for sympathizing with the Quakers (then the victims of severe repression). The town was incorporated in 1686 and named for Falmouth, England. The Falmouth area, sprawling over 44 square mi, includes eight villages: Falmouth, North Falmouth, West Falmouth, Hatchville, Teaticket, East Falmouth, Waquoit, and Woods Hole.

Much of Falmouth today is suburban, with a mix of old and new developments and a large year-round population. Many residents commute to other towns on the Cape, to southeastern Massachusetts, and even to Boston. The town has a quaint village center, with a typically old New England village green and a shop-lined Main Street. South of town center, Falmouth faces Nantucket Sound and has several often-crowded beaches popular with families. To the east, the Falmouth Heights neighborhood mixes inns, B&Bs, and private homes, nestled close together on residential streets leading to the sea. Bustling Grand Avenue, the main drag in Falmouth Heights, hugs the shore and the beach. Parks and ponds dot the town; one of the nicest, Grews Pond in Goodwill Park, is north of the town center—it's a lovely site for a picnic on a summer afternoon.

Today attractive old homes, some built by sea captains, flank the **Village Green,** which is listed on the National Register of Historic Places.

It served as a militia training field in the 18th century and a grazing ground for horses in the early 19th. Also on the green is the 1856 **Congregational Church,** built on the timbers of its 1796 predecessor, with a bell made by Paul Revere. The bell's cheery inscription reads: THE LIVING TO THE CHURCH I CALL, AND TO THE GRAVE I SUMMON ALL.

The **Falmouth Historical Society** maintains two museums that represent life in colonial Cape Cod. The 1790 **Julia Wood House** retains wonderful architectural details—a widow's walk, wide-board floors, lead-glass windows, and a colonial kitchen with wide hearth. Antique embroideries, baby shoes and clothes, toys and dolls, portraits, furniture, and the trappings of an authentically equipped doctor's office, all from the house's onetime owner, fill the premises. Out back, a re-creation of the Hallett Barn displays antique farm implements, a 19th-century horse-drawn sleigh, and other interesting items. The smaller **Conant House** next door, a 1794 half-Cape (an asymmetrical 1½-story building), holds military memorabilia, whaling items, scrimshaw, sailors' valentines, and a genealogical and historical research library. One collection includes books, portraits, and other items relating to Katharine Lee Bates, the native daughter who wrote "America the Beautiful." The Falmouth Historical Society also owns the 1812 white Cape house at 16 Main Street where Bates was born. Located off-site a couple of blocks away, the house is no longer open to the public, but a plaque out front commemorates Bates's birth in 1859.

Guides give tours of the museums, and a pretty formal garden with a gazebo and flagstone paths is adjacent. You can take a break with "Tea in Julia's Garden," with tea sandwiches, scones, and other refreshments, on Thursday from 1 to 3 in July and August. Free walking tours of the town are available Tuesday at 4 in July and August, as are historical trolley tours; call for prices and times. ☒ *Village Green, off Palmer Ave., Falmouth Center* ☎ *508/548–4857* ⊕ *www.falmouthhistoricalsociety. org* ☒ *Museums $4; tea $10, including museum admission* ☉ *June–Sept., Tues.–Sat. 10–4; Oct., weekends 1–4.*

❺ The **Charles D. and Margaret K. Spohr Garden,** 3 planted acres on Oyster Pond, is a pretty, peaceful, privately owned place. The springtime explosion of more than 700,000 daffodils gives way in turn to the tulips, azaleas, magnolias, flowering crab apples, rhododendrons, lilies, and climbing hydrangeas that inspire garden goers in summer. A collection of old millstones, bronze church bells, and ships' anchors decorates the landscape. ☒ *Fells Rd. off Oyster Pond Rd.* ☒ *Free* ☉ *Daily sunrise–sunset.*

Ⓒ Video-game rooms and candlepin bowling make the **Leary Family Amusement Center** a good place for children on a rainy day. (☒ 23 Town Hall Sq., off Rte. 28, Falmouth Center ☎ 508/540–4877)

Where to Stay & Eat

★ $–$$$ ✕ **Roo Bar City Bistro.** Sibling to the Chatham and Hyannis restaurants of the same name, the Roo Bar brings a distinctly urban hipness to Falmouth that is rarely seen on Cape Cod. The bar is a popular watering hole, and the menu—from the black bean and avocado pizza to the gorgonzola crusted filet mignon—has a global feel. ⊠ *285 Main St. (Rte. 28), Falmouth Center* ☎ *508/548–8600* ⊕ *www.theroobar.com* ☰ *AE, MC, V* ⊙ *No lunch.*

$–$$$ **Firefly Woodfire Grill and Bar.** Both the menu and the interior change seasonally here, but you can watch your food being prepared in the open kitchen year-round. Much of the food is cooked in the wood stone oven or on the woodfire grill for which the restaurant is named; try one of the pizzas, or any grilled meat or seafood dish. There's also a full bar with an extensive wine list and beer selection, in addition to its specialty cocktails. ⊠ *271 Main St.* ☎ *508/548–7953* ⊕ *www.fireflywoodfiregrill. com* ☰ *AE, D, MC, V.*

$–$$ ✕ **Quarterdeck Restaurant.** Part bar, part restaurant—but all Cape Cod—this spot is across the street from Falmouth's town hall, so the lunch talk tends to focus on local politics. The stained glass is not authentic, but the huge whaling harpoons certainly are. Low ceilings and rough-hewn beams seem a good match for the menu, which includes hearty sandwiches such as Reubens and grilled chorizo at lunch and specials at night. The swordfish kebab, skewered with mushrooms, onion, and green pepper and served over jasmine rice, is especially good. ⊠ *164 Main St. (Rte. 28), Falmouth Center* ☎ *508/548–9900* ☰ *AE, D, DC, MC, V.*

$–$$ **La Cucina Sul Mare.** Northern Italian and Mediterranean cooking is the Fodor'sChoice specialty at this classy and popular place. The staff is friendly and the ★ setting is both intimate and festive, if a bit crowded. Calamari, bruschetta, rigatoni à la vodka, and a variety of specials—including plenty of local fresh fish—adorn the menu. The zuppa de pesce, a medley of seafood sautéed in olive oil and garlic and finished in a white wine herb-and-tomato broth, is a specialty of the house. Make sure to come hungry—the portions here are huge—and expect a long wait during prime hours in season. ⊠ *237 Main St.* ☎ *508/548–5600* ☰ *AE, D, MC, V.*

¢–$$ ✕ **Homeport Café.** Between its name and its unlikely location in a Falmouth office park, you might be surprised to discover that the Homeport Café is in fact an authentic Korean restaurant. The menu includes healthy vegetarian wraps as well as more traditional fare such as *bulkoki* (marinated meat served with vegetables and rice), *jabchaebob* (noodles), and *kimchi* (spicy cabbage). Although this is primarily a take-out place, there are a few tables available for dining in. ⊠ *316 Gifford St.* ☎ *508/ 540–0886* ☰ *AE, D, MC, V* ⊙ *Closed Sun.*

¢–$ ✕ **Betsy's Diner.** A classic American treasure, Betsy's is a shiny, happy, busy place with a reassuring pink neon sign urging you to EAT HEAVY. The generous dining room, gleaming counter, and stools and booths by the big windows are done in pretty pastel mauve-and-cream tones. Memorabilia and neon grace the walls. Pancakes, waffles, and omelets are served all day, and typical dinner options include meat loaf and mashed potatoes, knockwurst and sauerkraut, and charbroiled pork chops. ⊠ *457 Main St. (Rte. 28), Falmouth Center* ☎ *508/540–0060* ⌨ *Reservations not accepted* ☰ *AE, D, MC, V* ⊙ *No dinner Sun.*

¢–$ ✕ **The Clam Shack.** Fried clams top the menu at this basic seafood joint right on Falmouth Harbor. The clams are crisp and fresh tasting; the meaty lobster roll and the fish-and-chips platter are good choices, too. Place your order at the counter and then take your tray to the picnic tables on the roof deck for the best views. More tables are on the dock in back, or you can squeeze into the tiny dining room. Just don't plan on a late night here—the Shack closes most evenings around 8. ⊠ *227 Clinton Ave., Falmouth Harbor* ☎ *508/540–7758* ▭ *No credit cards* ⊗ *Closed early Sept.–late May.*

¢ ✕ **Maryellen's Portuguese Bakery.** It's easy to drive right past this no-frills spot hidden behind a Dairy Queen. Take a seat at the counter or at one of the few tables, and then order up breakfast with a Portuguese twist. Try the savory Portuguese omelet, filled with spicy *linguica* (sausage), parsley, onions, and cheese, or the French toast made with Portuguese bread. The lunch menu starts with BLTs and burgers but quickly moves on to kale soup and *cacoilha* (marinated pork). ⊠ *829 Main St., near Falmouth Heights Rd.* ☎ *508/540–9696* ▭ *No credit cards* ⊗ *No dinner.*

$$$–$$$$ ✕▦ **Coonamessett Inn.** At this delightful old-Cape-style inn-restaurant, five buildings of one- or two-bedroom suites ring a landscaped lawn that leads to a scenic wooded pond. Rooms are casually decorated, with bleached wood or pine paneling and New England antiques or reproductions. A large collection of Cape artist Ralph Cahoon's work appears throughout the inn. In the main dining room, a few contemporary flourishes enhance the traditional menu; you can still find rack of lamb and baked-stuffed lobster, but you might also see cumin-scented scallops with Israeli couscous. ⊠ *311 Gifford St., at Jones Rd., 02540* ☎ *508/548– 2300* 🖷 *508/540–9831* ⊕ *www.capecodrestaurants.org/coonamessett* ➥ *28 suites, 1 cottage* ⚅ *Restaurant, cable TV, bar; no smoking* ▭ *AE, D, MC, V* ᠐᠐᠐ *CP.*

$$$$ ▦ **Inn on the Sound.** At this stylish inn, perched on a bluff overlooking Vineyard Sound, the living room and nine of the guest rooms face the water. Guest rooms have queen-size beds and unfussy contemporary furnishings such as natural oak tables, unbleached cottons, and ceiling fans; four have private decks. Common areas include an art-laden living room with a boulder fireplace, oversize windows, and modern white couches; a bistrolike breakfast room; and a porch with even more stunning water views. ⊠ *313 Grand Ave., Falmouth Heights 02540* ☎ *508/ 457–9666 or 800/564–9668* 🖷 *508/457–9631* ⊕ *www.innonthesound. com* ➥ *10 rooms* ⚅ *Cable TV, beach; no a/c, no kids under 18, no smoking* ▭ *AE, D, MC, V* ᠐᠐᠐ *CP.*

★ $$$$ ▦ **La Maison Cappellari at Mostly Hall.** With its deep, landscaped yard and wrought-iron fence, this elegant inn with a wraparound porch resembles a private estate. (The house got its name when a young guest is said to have exclaimed, "Look! It's mostly hall!") The imposing 1849 Italianate house has an upscale European style with painted murals in several bedrooms; the Tuscan Room's walls suggest an intimate Tuscan garden. Three of the rooms are more traditionally decorated, with canopy beds and antiques. Breakfast is served in the formal parlor or outside on the veranda. Although the inn is steps from the town center, you can lounge in the gardens and feel a world away. ⊠ *27 Main St. (Rte. 28), 02540* ☎ *508/548–3786 or 800/682–0565* 🖷 *508/548–*

5778 ⊕ *www.mostlyhall.com* ⇆ *6 rooms* ⚲ *Bicycles, library; no in-room TV, no kids under 16, no smoking* ⊟ *AE, D, MC, V* ⊗ *Closed mid-Dec.–mid-Apr.* ⎮◎⎮ *BP.*

$$$$ ⊡ **Scallop Shell Inn.** At this swank inn one block from the sea, you can
Fodor'sChoice find all the comforts of home, and then some. Check in at your leisure,
★ help yourself to the top-shelf bar, choose from nearly 100 videos, and even toss in a load of laundry (detergent supplied). Breakfast is a four-course feast, and you can help yourself to popcorn, yogurt, or other snacks throughout the day. If you're headed for the beach, the inn supplies beach chairs, towels, and coolers. The contemporary-style rooms are not large, but they're well-designed, with bedside reading lamps and in-room VCRs; additional luxury comes from the featherbeds and hand-painted sinks. ⊠ *16 Massachusetts Ave., Falmouth Heights 02540* ☎ *508/ 495–4900 or 800/249–4587* 🖷 *508/495–4600* ⊕ *www.scallopshellinn. com* ⇆ *7 rooms* ⚲ *In-room safes, cable TV, billiards, recreation room, laundry facilities* ⊟ *AE, DC, MC, V* ⎮◎⎮ *BP.*

$$$–$$$$ ⊡ **Baileys by the Sea.** Spectacular ocean views are the lure at this 1874 Victorian house opposite Vineyard Sound, where you can settle into a rocker on the wraparound porch, with picture windows on three sides. Owners Liz and Jerry Bailey have decorated their home with a comfortable mix of Victorian pieces and Asian antiques that they acquired when they lived in Japan. The best rooms face the ocean; the spacious third-floor Tokyo room has a particularly stellar vista. Morning menus might include omelets or apple-pecan pancakes, and in the afternoon you can head back to the porch for fresh-baked sweets—and a glass of Bailey's. ⊠ *321 Grand Ave., Falmouth Heights 02540* ☎ *508/548–5748 or 866/548–5748* 🖷 *508/548–5748* ⊕ *www. baileysbythesea.com* ⇆ *6 rooms* ⚲ *Cable TV, some in-room VCRs; no kids under 10 (in season), no smoking* ⊟ *AE, MC, V* ⊗ *Closed Nov.–Apr.* ⎮◎⎮ *BP.*

$$$–$$$$ ⊡ **Holiday Inn.** This chain hotel is a dependable option for families. A tried-and-true comfort formula has been applied here: large rooms with contemporary furnishings, suites with king-size beds, and a large pool area surrounded by patio furniture and greenery. The Kansas City Steakhouse restaurant is open for breakfast and dinner year-round, and serves Cape Cod specialties as well as huge quantities of beef. The hotel is adjacent to a pond and is close to Falmouth Center. ⊠ *291 Jones Rd., 02540* ☎ *508/540–2000 or 800/465–4329* 🖷 *508/ 548–2712* ⊕ *www.holidayinn-falmouth.com* ⇆ *93 rooms, 5 suites* ⚲ *Restaurant, room service, cable TV, indoor pool, gym, no-smoking rooms* ⊟ *AE, D, DC, MC, V.*

$$$–$$$$ ⊡ **Palmer House Inn.** This turn-of-the-20th-century Queen Anne home stands on a tree-lined street, just a short stroll from Falmouth's village green. The Victorian interior is pretty if slightly overdone, with heavy period furniture, endless lace, and ornate stained-glass windows. One good bet is the third-floor Tower Room, which has a view across the treetops. The large rooms in the 1910 carriage house are also airier, with more tailored appointments, and four newer rooms, all with whirlpool baths, are less ornate. There's a two-bedroom suite in a separate cottage (where young children are permitted). A candlelight breakfast is served and afternoon refreshments are available. ⊠ *81 Palmer Ave., 02540* ☎ *508/548–1230 or 800/472–2632* 🖷 *508/540–1878* ⊕ *www. palmerhouseinn.com* ⌨ *16 rooms, 1 suite* ⚴ *Some in-room hot tubs, cable TV, bicycles; no kids under 10 (except in cottage), no smoking* ▭ *AE, D, DC, MC, V* ⦿| *BP.*

★ **$$$–$$$$** 🏠 **Wildflower Inn.** Innkeepers Phil and Donna Stone call their decorating style "old made new again": tables are constructed from early-1900s pedal-sewing-machine bases, and a sideboard was once a '20s Hotpoint electric stove. Each of the rooms—two with whirlpool tubs—is also innovatively decorated. The bed in the romantic Moonflower Room sits under the eaves and is draped in netting, while the cheerful Geranium Room has a white-iron bed topped with a geranium-print comforter. Donna cooks using edible wildflowers; one morning the five-course breakfast might include sunflower crepes; the next, calendula corn muffins. ⊠ *167 Palmer Ave., 02540* ☎☎ *508/548–9524 or 800/294–5459* ⊕ *www.wildflower-inn.com* ⌨ *5 rooms, 1 cottage* ⚴ *Some in-room hot tubs; no room phones, no TV in some rooms, no kids under 12, no smoking* ▭ *AE, MC, V* ⦿| *BP.*

$$$ 🏠 **Capt. Tom Lawrence House.** A lawn shaded by old maple trees surrounds this pretty white house, which is steps from downtown yet set back from the street enough to feel secluded. Built in 1861 for a whaling captain, the intimate B&B has romantic rooms with antique and painted furniture, Laura Ashley or Ralph Lauren linens, French country wallpaper, and thick carpeting. An efficiency apartment is bright, spacious, and suitable for families, with a fully equipped eat-in kitchen. Breakfast and afternoon snacks are served near the fireplace in the common room. ⊠ *75 Locust St., 02540* ☎ *508/548–9178* 🖷 *508/457–1790* ⊕ *www.captaintomlawrence.com* ⌨ *6 rooms, 1 efficiency* ⚴ *Kitchen, refrigerators, cable TV, bicycles; no a/c (except in efficiency), no room phones, no kids under 12 (except in efficiency), no smoking* ▭ *AE, MC, V* ⦿| *BP.*

$$–$$$ 🏠 **Admiralty Inn.** This large roadside motel outside Falmouth Center has several types of rooms and suites, and its child-friendly facilities make it a good bet for families. Standard rooms have two queen-size beds or one queen-size and one Murphy bed. King Jacuzzi rooms have king-size beds and whirlpool tubs in the bedroom. Town-house suites have cathedral ceilings with skylights, two baths (one with whirlpool), a loft with a king-size bed, a living room with a sofa bed, and a queen- or king-size bed. Children under 12 stay free. ⊠ *51 Teaticket Hwy. (Rte. 28), 02540* ☎ *508/548–4240 or 800/341–5700* 🖷 *508/457–0535* ⊕ *www. vacationinnproperties.com* ⌨ *70 rooms, 28 suites* ⚴ *Restaurant, some in-room hot tubs, refrigerators, cable TV, 2 pools, hot tub, bar, no-smoking rooms* ▭ *AE, D, DC, MC, V.*

Nightlife & the Arts

THE ARTS The **College Light Opera Company** (⊠ Highfield Theatre, off Depot Ave. ☎ 508/548–0668 ⊕ www.collegelightopera.com) presents nine musicals or operettas for one week each, the results of a summer program involving music and theater majors from colleges around the country. The company includes more than 30 singers and an 18-piece orchestra. Be forewarned: the quality can vary from show to show. The **Cape Cod**

Theatre Project (☎ 508/457–4242 ⊕ www.capecodtheatreproject.org) helps develop new American plays through a series of staged readings. Each summer the project presents three or four readings, which are followed by audience discussion with the playwright. Productions have included works by Gloucester Stage Company director Israel Horovitz and by Pulitzer Prize winners Lanford Wilson and Paula Vogel. Performances take place at **Falmouth Academy** (✉ 7 Highfield Dr., off Depot Ave., Falmouth). Falmouth's summer **town-band concerts** (✉ Scranton Ave. ☎ 508/548–8500 or 800/526–8532) are held in Marina Park on Thursday evening starting at 8.

NIGHTLIFE **Coonamessett Inn** (✉ 311 Gifford St. ☎ 508/548–2300) has dancing to soft piano, jazz trios, or other music in its lounge on weekends year-round.

Nimrod Inn (✉ 100 Dillingham Ave., Falmouth Center ☎ 508/540–4132) presents jazz and contemporary music at least six nights a week year-round.

Sports & the Outdoors

BASEBALL The **Falmouth Commodores** (✉ 790 E. Main St. [Rte. 28] ☎ 508/432–6909 ⊕ www.falcommodores.org) of the collegiate Cape Cod Baseball League play home games at Guv Fuller Field from mid-June to mid-August.

BEACHES Some Falmouth hotels and motels will sell daily resident parking permits to guests, so do ask if you plan to drive to the beach.

A bit removed from the hubbub of town, with swaying beach grass and a salt pond behind, the narrow **Falmouth Beach,** on Surf Drive, faces Nantucket Sound and Martha's Vineyard. Lifeguards watch the beach in season, and there are portable toilets. You need a resident parking sticker to park in the beach lot in season.

Falmouth Heights Beach on Grand Avenue is an often-crowded arc of sand on Nantucket Sound, backed by a row of inns and B&Bs. The beach has lifeguards (in summer) and portable toilets. There's a small strip of metered parking on Grand Avenue between Walden Avenue and Crescent Park Avenue.

Grews Pond in Goodwill Park, a pretty tree-lined freshwater pond with a sandy beach and lifeguarded swimming area, is popular with local families. You can find several sites for picnicking, along with rest rooms, and a volleyball net; there's also a playground nearby. You can enter the park from Route 28 just north of Jones Road or from Gifford Street opposite St. Joseph's Cemetery. Parking is free.

Surf Drive Beach, a family-friendly sandy cove on Surf Drive, faces Nantucket Sound with views out toward the Vineyard. The beach has restrooms and showers as well as lifeguards, and public parking is available; in summer the daily parking fee is $10.

BIKING The **Shining Sea Trail** is an easy 3½-mi route between Locust Street, Falmouth, and the Woods Hole ferry parking lot. It follows the coast, providing views of Vineyard Sound and dipping into oak and pine woods;

a detour onto Church Street takes you to Nobska Light. A brochure is available at the trailheads. If you're going to Martha's Vineyard with your bike, you can park your car in one of Falmouth's Steamship Authority lots and ride the Shining Sea Trail to the ferry. (The free shuttle buses between the Falmouth lots and the Woods Hole ferry docks also have bike carriers; ⇨ Boat and Ferry Travel *in* Smart Travel Tips A to Z).

Corner Cycle (⊠ 115 Palmer Ave., Falmouth ☎ 508/540–4195) rents bikes (including tandems and children's bikes) by the hour, day, or week. It also rents Burley trailers for carrying small children and does on-site repairs. The shop is two blocks from the Shining Sea Trail. **Holiday Cycles** (⊠ 465 Grand Ave., Falmouth Heights ☎ 508/540–3549) has surrey, tandem, and other unusual bikes.

FISHING Freshwater ponds are good for perch, pickerel, trout, and more; you can obtain the required license (along with rental gear) at tackle shops, such as **Eastman's Sport & Tackle** (⊠ 150 Main St. [Rte. 28], Falmouth ☎ 508/548–6900).

Patriot Party Boats (⊠ 227 Clinton Ave., Falmouth Harbor ☎ 508/548–2626, 800/734–0088 in Massachusetts ⊕ www.patriotpartyboats.com) has deep-sea fishing from party or charter boats. Advance bookings are recommended, particularly for weekend trips.

ICE-SKATING Fall through spring, skaters take to the ice at the **Falmouth Ice Arena** (⊠ 9 Skating La., off Palmer Ave. ☎ 508/548–7080, 508/548–6940 pro shop ⊕ www.falmouthicearena.com). You can rent skates from the pro shop.

RUNNING To run in the world-class **SBLI Falmouth Road Race** (✑ Box 732, Falmouth, 02541 ☎ 508/540–7000 ⊕ www.sblifalmouthroadrace.com) in mid-August, send a self-addressed, stamped envelope to request an entry form. The race typically closes to entrants in early spring.

TENNIS & The huge **Falmouth Sports Center** (⊠ 33 Highfield Dr. ☎ 508/548–7433)
RACQUETBALL has three outdoor and six indoor tennis courts and two racquetball-handball courts, as well as steam rooms and saunas, a full health club, and physical therapist services. Day and short-term rates are available.

Shopping

★ **Bean & Cod** (⊠ 140 Main St. [Rte. 28], Falmouth Center ☎ 508/548–8840 or 800/558–8840 ⊕ www.beanandcod.com), a specialty food shop, sells cheeses, breads, and picnic fixings, along with pastas, coffees and teas, and unusual condiments. The store also packs and ships gift baskets.

Eight Cousins Children's Books (⊠ 189 Main St. [Rte. 28], Falmouth Center ☎ 508/548–5548) is the place to find reading material for toddlers through young adults. In addition to nice sections on oceans and marine life, Native American peoples, and other Cape topics, the well-stocked shop also carries audiotapes and games.

Howlingbird (⊠ 91 Palmer Ave., Falmouth Center ☎ 508/540–3787) stocks detailed hand-silk-screened marine-theme T-shirts and sweatshirts, plus hand-painted cards and silk-screened hats and handbags.

Maxwell & Co. (✉ 200 Main St. [Rte. 28], Falmouth Center ☏ 508/540–8752) has traditional men's and women's clothing with flair from European and American designers, handmade French shoes and boots, and leather goods and accessories.

Rosie Cheeks (✉ 233 Main St. [Rte. 28], Falmouth Center ☏ 508/548–4572), whose name was inspired by the owner's daughter, specializes in creative women's clothing and jewelry, with a particularly nice selection of hand-knit sweaters.

Woods Hole

❻ *4 mi southwest of Falmouth, 19 mi south of the Bourne Bridge.*

The village of Woods Hole, which dangles at the Cape's southwestern tip, has a unique personality shaped by its substantial intellectual community. As a major departure point for ferries to Martha's Vineyard, it draws crowds of through traffic in season. Well known as a center for international marine research, Woods Hole is home to several major scientific institutions. The National Marine Fisheries Service was here first, established in 1871 to study fish management and conservation. In 1888 the Marine Biological Laboratory (MBL), a center for research and education in marine biology, moved in across the street. Then in 1930 the Woods Hole Oceanographic Institution (WHOI) arrived, and the U.S. Geological Survey's Branch of Marine Geology followed suit in the 1960s.

Most of the year Woods Hole is a peaceful community of intellectuals quietly going about their work. In summer, however, the basically one-street village overflows with the thousands of scientists and graduate students who come from around the globe either to participate in summer studies at MBL, WHOI, or the National Academy of Sciences conference center or to work on independent research projects. A handful of waterside cafés and shops along Water Street compete for the most bicycles stacked up at the door. Parking, limited to a relatively small number of metered spots on the street, can be nearly impossible. If you're coming from Falmouth to wander here, either ride your bicycle down the straight and flat Shining Sea Trail or take the Cape Cod Regional Transit Authority's WHOOSH trolley (⇨ Trolley Travel *in* The Upper Cape A to Z).

What accounts for this incredible concentration of scientific minds is, in part, the variety and abundance of marine life in Woods Hole's unpolluted waters, and the natural deepwater port. In addition, researchers have the opportunity for an easy interchange of ideas and information and the stimulation of daily lectures and discussions (many open to the public) by important scientists. The pooling of resources among the various institutions makes for economies of scale that benefit each while allowing all access to highly sophisticated equipment.

Scientific forces join together at the **Marine Biological Laboratory–Woods Hole Oceanographic Institution Library** (✉ 7 Marine Biological Laboratory St., off Water St. ⊕ www.mbl.edu), one of the best collections of biological, ecological, and oceanographic literature in the world. On top of its access to more than 200 computer databases, the library subscribes to more than 5,000 scientific journals in 40 languages, with complete collections of most. During World War II the librarian made arrangements with a German subscription agency to have German periodicals sent to neutral Switzerland to be stored until the end of the war. Thus the library's German collections are uninterrupted, where even those of many German institutions are incomplete. All journals are always accessible, as they cannot be checked out, and because the library is open 24 hours a day. The Rare Books Room contains photographs, monographs, and prints, as well as journal collections that date from 1665.

Unless you are a scientific researcher, the only way you can get to see the library is by taking the **Marine Biological Laboratory tour** (☎ 508/289–7623). The one-hour tours (mid-June–August, weekdays at 1, 2, and 3), led by retired scientists, include an introductory slide show as well as stops at the library, the Marine Resources Center (where living sea creatures collected each day are kept), and one of the many working research labs. Call for reservations and meeting instructions at least a week in advance if possible.

The **Woods Hole Oceanographic Institution** is the largest independent, private oceanographic laboratory in the world. Several buildings in the village of Woods Hole house its shore-based facilities; others are on a 200-acre campus nearby. During World War II its research focused on underwater explosives, submarine detection, and the development of antifouling paint. Today its $93 million annual budget helps to operate many laboratories with state-of-the-art equipment. A graduate program is offered jointly with MIT. WHOI's several research vessels roam the world's waters. Its staff led the successful U.S.–French search for the *Titanic* (found about 400 mi off Newfoundland) in 1985.

The Woods Hole Oceanographic Institution is open to the public only on guided tours, but you can learn about it at the small **WHOI Exhibit Center,** with videos and exhibits on the institution and its various projects, including research vessels. **One-hour walking tours** (☎ 508/289–2252) of the institution and its piers are offered in July and August, weekdays at 10:30 and 1:30; tours begin at the WHOI Information Office at 93 Water Street and are free, but reservations are required. ✉ *15 School St.* ☎ *508/289–2663* ⊕ *www.whoi.edu* ✎ *$2 suggested donation* ☉ *Late May–early Sept., Mon.–Sat. 10–4:30, Sun. noon–4:30; Apr., Nov., and Dec., Fri. and Sat. 10–4:30, Sun. noon–4:30; early May–late May and early Sept.–Oct., Tues.–Sat. 10–4:30, Sun. noon–4:30.*

☺ The **National Marine Fisheries Service Aquarium** displays 16 tanks of regional fish and shellfish. Magnifying glasses and a dissecting scope help you examine marine life, and several hands-on pools hold banded lobsters, crabs, snails, starfish, and other creatures. The top attraction is two harbor seals, on view in the outdoor pool near the entrance in sum-

Fodor'sChoice
★

A DAY ON MARTHA'S VINEYARD

THE DOUBLE LIFE OF THIS ISLAND reveals itself in two seasons: from late May through early September the quieter (some might say the real) Vineyard morphs into a vibrant, celebrity-studded place. Edgartown floods with people who come to wander narrow streets flanked with elegant boutiques, stately whaling captains' homes, and luxurious inns. The busy main port, Vineyard Haven, welcomes day-trippers fresh off ferries and private yachts to browse in its shops carrying everything from wampum and sea-glass jewelry to chic fashions. Oak Bluffs, where pizza and ice cream emporiums reign supreme, attracts diverse crowds with its boardwalk-town air and nightspots that cater to high-spirited, carefree youth. Around the island, pristine white-sand beaches beckon.

Most people know the Vineyard's summer persona, but in many ways its other self has even more appeal, as the island in the off season is a place of peace and simple beauty. Drivers traversing country lanes through the agricultural center of the island find time to linger over pastoral and ocean vistas without being pushed along by a throng of other cars, bicycles, and mopeds. In nature reserves, the voices of summer are gone, leaving only the sounds of birdsong and the crackle of leaves underfoot. Private beaches are open to the public, and the water sparkles under crisp, blue skies. Whichever season you want to experience, you can make the trip by ferry to this island south of the western end of Cape Cod in 35 minutes to 1¾ hours from Woods Hole, Falmouth, or Hyannis.

The Vineyard is roughly triangular, with maximum distances of about 20 mi east to west and 10 mi north to south. The western end of the Vineyard, known as "up-island"—from the nautical expression of going "up" in degrees of longitude as you sail west—is more rural and wild than the eastern down-island end, which includes Vineyard Haven, Oak Bluffs, and Edgartown. Conservation land claims almost a quarter of the island, with preservationist organizations constantly acquiring more. The Land Bank, funded by a tax on real-estate transactions, is a leading group, set up to preserve as much of the island in its natural state as is possible and practical.

The many ways to spend a day here may tempt you to stay longer. You might want to spend a short time in Vineyard Haven (Tisbury is its official name) before getting rural up-island or heading for a beach. Or you can go straight to tony Edgartown to stroll past the antique white houses, pop into some of the museums that make up the excellent Vineyard Museum and Oral History Center, and shop. If you just want to have fun, Oak Bluffs, with its harbor scene, colorful Carpenter Gothic Victorian cottages, and nearby beaches, will be the place to go. If you want to see a little bit of everything, an itinerary for a day on the Vineyard follows below. You can bring over a car (reservations are essential in summer) or rent one. To get around without your own wheels, use the convenient year-round shuttle buses or the seasonal minibuses that run between down-island towns and up-island villages such as Chilmark and Menemsha and sights such as the lighthouse and red cliffs at Aquinnah. Taxis are another option, or you can choose pedal power and explore miles of bike trails at your own pace.

When making your dining plans, keep in mind that Vineyard Haven, West Tisbury, Menemsha, and Aquinnah are all "dry" towns—it's strictly BYOB.

For visitor information, contact the **Martha's Vineyard Chamber of Commerce** (✉ Beach Rd. 🕭 Box 1698, Vineyard Haven 02568 ☎ 508/693–0085 ⊕ www.mvy.com), two blocks from the Vineyard Haven Ferry. For information on travel by ferry from Cape Cod, see Boat and Ferry Travel in Smart Travel Tips A to Z.

Vineyard Haven. After disembarking from the ferry, spend some time exploring the area around your port of arrival. "Vineyard Heaven," the local moniker for Vineyard Haven, is a cozy little town clustered around a picturesque harbor of tall ships and private yachts. Just a two-minute walk from the harbor, the **Black Dog Bakery** (⊠ 11 Water St., ☎ 508/693–4786) makes a great post-ferry stop for pastries, breads, and other treats. If you've admired the signature T-shirts sporting the image of a black lab that pop up on travelers around the world, now's your chance to buy one of your own at the **Black Dog General Store** (⊠ 3 Water St. ☎ 508/696–8182), next door to the bakery.

Stroll uphill to **Main Street**, which is lined from end-to-end with tempting shops, restaurants, lodgings, and historical sites. Unlike other parts of the island, this commercial center of the island hums year round. The center of Main Street, both geographically and ideologically, is the **Bunch of Grapes Bookstore** (⊠ 44 Main St. ☎ 508/693–2291), known for its outstanding selection of books, and for the book signings that headline notables like Hillary Clinton and Vineyard resident David McCullough.

After exploring the rest of the island, stop in at the famous **Black Dog Tavern** (⊠ 20 Beach St. Ext. ☎ 508/693–9223) for dinner before heading back to the Cape—conveniently, it's just steps from the ferry.

Oak Bluffs. From Vineyard Haven, head to nearby Oak Bluffs. A microcosm of the diversity that makes the island as a whole so appealing, O.B., as those who live here call it, offers visitors a mix of honky-

tonk, charm, and history. Young and old will want to take a spin on the **Flying Horses Carousel** (⊠ Oak Bluffs Ave., ☎ 508/693–9481), the oldest operating merry-go-round in the country, where grabbing for the brass ring turns into a friendly competition. The activity-charged **Circuit Avenue** neighborhood is peppered with funky shops and enticing eateries ranging from a trio of superb ice cream parlors to family-friendly restaurants and trendy bistros.

Nearby in distance but conjuring another era, some 400 colorfully painted "gingerbread cottages" built in the late 19th century make up **Wesleyan Grove**, originally a campground for Methodists who flocked here to listen to the preachings of John Wesley. More recently, Oak Bluffs has attracted talented artists and craftspeople.

Edgartown. A stroll through charming Edgartown will complete your exploration of the east side of the Vineyard. Even more so than the other down-island towns of Vineyard Haven and Oak Bluffs, this enclave of Greek Revival ship captains' houses is a walking town par excellence. Its appeal for architecture buffs is complemented by the eclectic boutiques and restaurants often housed within historical frameworks. A coterie of classy inns offers sumptuous accommodations.

For a walk on the "wild" side, you need only hop on the Chappy Ferry in Edgartown and disembark five minutes later on the island of Chappaquiddick. This haven for seekers of solitude and green space comprises the 500-acre **Cape Pogue Wildlife Refuge** and the adjoining 200-acre **Wasque Reservation** (enter at the east end of Wasque Rd.), and **Mytoi**, a 14-acre Japanese garden on Dike Rd.

Before leaving Edgartown, visit **South Beach**, also called Katama Beach, a

CloseUp

gorgeous 3-mi-long stretch of barrier beach on Katama Road.

West Tisbury. After lunch, head westward to the bucolic heart of the island, West Tisbury. Spread over its 34 square mi are a winery, a strawberry farm, a llama farm, and hundreds of cows, sheep, and onion patches. In summer, the Saturday farmers' market and the annual agricultural fair, held for four days in mid- to late August since 1859, are popular with residents and visitors.

Alley's General Store (⊠ State Rd. ☎ 508/693–0088), now owned by the native Wampanoag tribe, has been in continuous operation since 1858. This old-fashioned general store is the nerve center of the rural community, and has everything from groceries to sundries and more. *The Polly Hill Arboretum* (⊠ 809 State Rd. ☎ 508/693–9426) comprises 60 acres of some 2,000 species of native plants raised from seeds and lovingly tended by horticulturist Polly Hill, now in her 90s, and is a delightful place to wander, learn, and appreciate natural beauty.

Chilmark. Continuing into the up-island territory of Chilmark, the contrast is pleasantly jolting. Rolling green farmland bounded by the ocean, stunning old stonewalls, and rambling farmhouses set a tranquil tone that carries over into the charming fishing village of *Menemsha.* The pace is unhurried and the scenery absorbing. If it's summertime, be sure to join the queue for a snack at *The Bite* (⊠ Basin Rd. ☎ 508/645–9239) for arguably the best clam chowder and fried seafood around.

Aquinnah. Conclude the day with a visit to Aquinnah. Previously known as Gay Head, this westernmost town on the island is the only community in Massachusetts that continues to have a substantial Native American presence in the 20th century,

with descendents of the mainland Wampanoag tribe. The most outstanding natural feature is the magnificent clay cliffs formed by glaciers millions of years ago and now designated a national landmark. Most visitors admire the brilliantly colored cliffs from a distance, but if curiosity gets the best of you, follow the wooden boardwalk to the beach down below. Two caveats: it's forbidden to remove any of the clay, and this is unofficially a nude beach. From late June–mid-September, Friday–Sunday evenings, the 160-year-old *Aquinnah Lighthouse* (⊠ Lighthouse Rd. ☎ 508/645–2211) opens its doors for a few hours for sunset viewing.

— by James W. Rohlf

mer; you can watch their feedings daily at 11 and 4. ⊠ *Corner of Albatross and Water Sts.* ☎ *508/495–2267, 508/495–2001 recorded information* ⊕ *www.nefsc.nmfs.gov/nefsc/aquarium* 🎫 *Free; donations accepted* ⊙ *Call for hrs.*

need a break?

Pie in the Sky (⊠ 10 Water St. ☎ 508/540–5475), a small bakery with indoor and outdoor seating, sells cookies, pastries, and coffees, as well as sandwiches. The Oreo cookie bars are truly decadent.

The **Woods Hole Historical Museum** (formerly known as the Bradley House Museum) is a three-building complex that houses paintings, a restored Woods Hole Spritsail boat, boat models, and a model of the town as it looked in the 1890s. One room is filled with elegant ladies' clothing from the late 1800s. The archives hold old ships' logs, postcards, newspaper articles, maps, diaries, and photographs; more than 200 tapes of oral history provided by local residents; and a 100-volume library on maritime history. Free guided walking tours of the village take place Tuesday at 4 in July and August; tours depart from the museum, which is across from the Martha's Vineyard ferry parking lot. ⊠ *573 Woods Hole Rd.* ☎ *508/548–7270* ⊕ *www.woodsholemuseum.org* 🎫 *Donations accepted* ⊙ *Museum mid-June–mid-Oct., Tues.–Sat. 10–4; archives year-round, Tues. and Thurs. 10–2.*

The 1888 **Episcopal Church of the Messiah,** a stone church with a conical steeple and a small medicinal herb garden in the shape of a Celtic cross, is a good place for some quiet time. The garden, enclosed by a holly hedge, has a bench for meditation. Inscriptions on either side of the carved gate read ENTER IN HOPE and DEPART IN PEACE. ⊠ *22 Church St.* ☎ *508/548–2145* ⊕ *www.messiahweb.org* 🎫 *Free* ⊙ *Daily sunrise–sunset.*

Impressive **Nobska Light** (⊠ Church St.) has spectacular views from its base of the nearby Elizabeth Islands and of Martha's Vineyard, across Vineyard Sound. The 42-foot cast-iron tower, lined with brick, was built in 1876 with a stationary light. It shines red to indicate dangerous waters or white for safe passage. Since the light was automated in 1985, the adjacent keeper's quarters have been the headquarters of the Coast Guard group commander—a fitting passing of the torch from one safeguarder of ships to another. The lighthouse is not open to the public except during special tours.

Where to Stay & Eat

$$$ ✕ **Landfall.** Request a window table overlooking the water at this classic Cape seafood spot, where lobster pots, buoys, and other nautical paraphernalia hang from the ceilings. Lobster, fried clams, and baked scrod lead off the menu of traditional seafood fare. Though the kids will need their restaurant manners, it's still family friendly, and the children's allyou-can-eat specials are a great value. ⊠ *2 Luscombe Ave.* ☎ *508/548–1758* ⊕*www.woodshole.com/landfall* ▭*AE, MC, V* ⊙ *Closed Dec.–Mar. and Mon.–Wed. Apr.–late May and early Sept.–Nov.*

$$–$$$ **Captain Kidd Restaurant & Bar.** The stately bar, festive atmosphere, and a small number of cozy tables that cluster around a wood stove and overlook Eel Pond make this a year-round favorite for locals. Fish, chicken, steak and pasta are the staples, served in a publike atmosphere. Free Internet access is available. ⊠ *77 Water St.* ☎ *508/548–8563* ▤ *AE, MC, V.*

★ **$$–$$$** ✕ **Fishmonger's Café.** The seafood-centered menu at this top Woods Hole choice is ambitious, particularly the inventive daily specials. The hearty *bruschetta* (broiled bread slices) with ricotta, basil, and olives is a treat, and many grilled seafood dishes come with tropical fruit glazes, such as a mango and cilantro sauce over grilled salmon. Vegetarians have lots of options here, too. The main dining room overlooks the water, and there's a handsome wood bar. ⊠ *56 Water St.* ☎ *508/540–5376* ⌂ *Reservations not accepted* ▤ *AE, MC, V* ☉ *Closed mid-Dec.–mid-Feb. and Tues. early Sept.–Mar.*

$–$$ ✕ **Shuckers World Famous Raw Bar and Cafe.** Some of the harborside tables at this casual nautical-theme restaurant are so close to the dock that you almost feel as if you're sitting in the bobbing sailboats. The menu ranges from jerk chicken to pasta primavera to lobster ravioli, but it's best to stick with the grilled fish and other simple seafood dishes. The "world-famous" lobster boil—a boiled lobster, steamed clams and mussels, and an ear of corn—is justifiably popular. ⊠ *91A Water St.* ☎ *508/540–3850* ⊕ *www.woodshole.com/shuckers* ▤ *AE, D, MC, V* ☉ *Closed mid-Oct.–mid-May, and Mon.–Thurs. mid-May–late May and early Sept.–mid-Oct.*

$$–$$$ ⊡ **Capeside Cottage.** This classic Cape house, built in 1942, has country-style rooms with the same basic touches: double beds, lace curtains, and fluffy quilts. A tiny cottagelike room out back, next to the kidney-shape in-ground pool, has a double bed and a sleeper sofa but no kitchen. You can eat breakfast out by the pool or in the comfortable common room, which has a fireplace and lots of amenities, including a refrigerator and an assortment of teas, as well as a TV and VCR. ⊠ *320 Woods Hole Rd., 02543* ☎ *508/548–6218 or 800/320–2322* 🖶 *508/457–7519* ⊕ *www.capesidecottage.com* ↯ *6 rooms* ⌂ *Pool; no room phones, no room TVs, no smoking* ▤ *MC, V* ⧆ *BP.*

$$–$$$ ⊡ **Sands of Time Motor Inn and Harbor House.** Essentially two lodgings in one, this property on a hill above Woods Hole village houses both a motel and a Victorian-era inn. In the family-friendly motor inn, the furnishings are standard motel-style; the best views, looking out to the water, are from the second-floor rooms. The Harbor House is more eclectic—a canopy bed here, a claw-foot tub there; some rooms have fireplaces or private patios. ⊠ *549 Woods Hole Rd., 02543* ☎ *508/548–6300 or 800/841–0114* 🖶 *508/457–0160* ⊕ *www.sandsoftime.com* ↯ *35 rooms* ⌂ *Cable TV, pool; no smoking* ▤ *AE, D, DC, MC, V* ☉ *Closed mid-Nov.–Mar.* ⧆ *CP.*

$$–$$$ ⊡ **Woods Hole Passage.** A century-old carriage house and barn have been converted into a romantic showcase. The large rose-hue common room radiates comfort with its lace curtains and overstuffed furniture. One guest room (the smallest) is in the main house; the others are in the restored barn, where the upstairs rooms have soaring ceilings. Gregarious and helpful owner Deb Pruitt sells Martha's Vineyard ferry tickets at cost so you can avoid lines at the dock. You can have breakfast on the patio in the lovely yard, or early risers can request "breakfast-in-a-bag" to take on the road. Kids are accepted, by prior arrangement. ⊠ *186 Woods Hole Rd., 02540* ☎ *508/548–9575 or 800/790–8976* ⊟ *508/540–4771* ⊕ *www.woodsholepassage.com* ↪ *5 rooms* ⚲ *Bicycles, croquet, horseshoes; no room phones, no room TVs, no smoking* ⊟ *AE, D, DC, MC, V* ⦿ *BP.*

Nightlife & the Arts

The **Cape Cod Theatre Project** (☎ 508/457–4242 ⊕ www.tcctp.com) (⇨Falmouth) helps develop new American plays through a series of staged readings each summer. Performances are held in the **Woods Hole Community Hall** (⊠ Water St., Woods Hole) or at **Falmouth Academy** (⊠ 7 Highfield Dr., off Depot Ave., Falmouth). The **Woods Hole Folk Music Society** (⊠ Community Hall, Water St. ☎ 508/540–0320 ⊕ www.arts-cape.com/whfolkmusic) presents professional and local folk and blues in a smoke- and alcohol-free environment, with refreshments available during intermission. Concerts by nationally known performers take place the first and third Sunday of the month from October to April. **Woods Hole Theater Company** (⊠ Community Hall, Water St. ☎ 508/540–6525 ⊕ www.woodsholetheatercompany.org), the community's resident theater group since 1974, presents several productions each year, generally between late spring and early fall.

Shopping

Handworks (⊠ 68 Water St. ☎ 508/540–5291), tucked in the back of the Community Hall building next to the drawbridge, is a cooperative arts-and-crafts gallery showcasing the work of local artists.

East Falmouth & Waquoit

5 mi northeast of Woods Hole.

These bucolic villages (well, bucolic once you leave Route 28 and its strip malls) have much to offer nature lovers. East Falmouth and Waquoit sit on narrow fingers of land that poke out toward Nantucket Sound, so water is never far away here, and comes in the form of quiet inlets and marshy bays rather than the crashing surf of the open ocean. The residential neighborhoods here, with both seasonal and year-round homes, often end in dirt lanes that lead to the water. Menauhant Beach, the nicest beach in these towns, sits on a thin sliver of land with the sound on one side and a grass-lined cove on the other. Inland, the land is more rural, with a number of farms (and farm stands) still operating. Note that as you head east from Falmouth Center on Route 28, the street signs change names as you travel through different areas. The road is Main Street until you pass Falmouth Heights Road, when Route 28 becomes Davis Straits. Farther east it becomes Teaticket Highway, then East Falmouth Highway, and then Waquoit Highway.

❼ Overseen by the Massachusetts Audubon Society, **Ashumet Holly and Wildlife Sanctuary** is true to its name and its original plantsman, Wilfred Wheeler, with its 1,000-plus holly trees and shrubs composed of 65 American, Asian, and European varieties. Like Heritage Museums and Gardens in Sandwich, this 45-acre tract of woodland, shady groves, meadows, and hiking trails was purchased and donated by Josiah K. Lilly III to preserve local land. Grassy Pond is home to numerous turtles and frogs, and in summer 35 nesting pairs of barn swallows live in the open rafters of the barn. Maps for self-guided tours cost $1. Tours to nearby Cuttyhunk Island (on a 50-foot sailing vessel) leave Woods Hole every Sunday from mid-July to early October; trips run from 9 to 5 and cost $50. ⊠ *286 Ashumet Rd., East Falmouth* ☎ *508/362–1426* ⊕ *www.massaudubon.org* ✉ *$4* ☉ *Trails daily sunrise–sunset.*

☼ **Waquoit Bay National Estuarine Research Reserve** encompasses 2,500 acres of estuary and barrier beach around the bay, making it a good birding site. **South Cape Beach** is part of the reserve; you can lie out on the sand or join one of the interpretive walks. **Flat Pond Trail** runs through several different habitats, including fresh- and saltwater marshes. **Washburn Island** (☎ 877/422–6762 camping permit) is accessible by boat (your own) or by Saturday-morning tours (call to reserve); it offers 330 acres of pine barrens and trails, swimming, and 11 wilderness campsites (a permit is required). At the **reserve headquarters,** a 23-acre estate, an exhibit center includes displays about the bay's plants and animals, the Cape Cod watershed, and local Wampanoag culture. An interactive exhibit, outside on the lawn, allows you to trace the path of a raindrop; pick up a ball (the pseudo-raindrop) and follow its journey from cloud to land to river and on through the water cycle. In July and August the center has nature programs for children and families, as well as a Saturday-afternoon open house from 2 to 4 PM with family programs and a Tuesday-evening lecture-performance series (bring picnics). ⊠ *Rte. 28, 3 mi west of Mashpee rotary, Waquoit* ☎ *508/457–0495* ⊕ *www.waquoitbayreserve.org* ☉ *Exhibit center late June–early Sept., Mon.–Sat. 10–4; late May–late June, weekdays 10–4.*

Tony Andrews Farm and Produce Stand has pick-your-own strawberries (June), peas and beans (June and July), herbs (July and August), and tomatoes (August), as well as other produce on the stand. The farm schedules hayrides in fall, and a haunted house is set up in October. You can pick your own pumpkins in fall and choose your Christmas tree in December. ⊠ *394 Old Meeting House Rd., East Falmouth* ☎ *508/548–4717* ☉ *June–Oct.; call for hrs and for information about special events.*

Coonamessett Farm operates a farm store where you can assemble your own gift baskets or purchase produce and specialty foods, as well as a small café serving soups, salads, baked goods, and beverages. Members of the farm's Pick-Your-Own club ($15-per-year membership; non-Cape residents can buy a one-day membership for $5) can pick strawberries, lettuces, herbs, rhubarb, and other fruits and vegetables. Members can also tour the greenhouses and fields, learn about hydroponic growing systems, and visit the animals (call ahead to arrange tours). The farm also rents canoes for use on the adjacent Coonamessett Pond. ⊠ *277*

Hatchville Rd., East Falmouth ☎ *508/563–2560* ⊕ *www. coonamessettfarm.com* ⊙ *Call for seasonal hrs.*

Rows and rows of grapevines—8,000 in all—line the fields of Kristina and Antonio Lazzari's **Cape Cod Winery.** It now produces six wines; the Nobska red won a bronze medal at an International Eastern Wine Competition. ⊠ *681 Sandwich Rd., East Falmouth* ☎ *508/457–5592* ⊕ *www. capecodwinery.com* ⊙ *July and Aug., tastings Wed.–Sun. noon–4; late May, June, and Sept.–late Nov., tastings weekends noon–4.*

Where to Stay & Eat

¢–$ ╳ **McGann's of Falmouth Pub and Restaurant.** McGann's calls itself "a touch of Ireland on Cape Cod," and the McGann family should know—they also have a pub in the town of Doolin, County Galway, Ireland. The place does have the slightly frayed grit of an Irish country tavern, and the bar food comes with an Irish twist: Irish-style fish-and-chips, Gaelic chicken in an Irish whiskey and bacon sauce. Though Guinness reigns, the bar has 20 beers on draft. There's live music Friday, Saturday, and Sunday; Thursday is karaoke night. ⊠ *734 Teaticket Hwy. (Rte. 28), East Falmouth* ☎ *508/540–6656* ⌂ *Reservations not accepted* ▤ *AE, D, MC, V.*

¢ ╳ **Moonakis Café.** Breakfast gets high marks at this cheery café. You'll find all the standards and then some—eggs, pancakes, fruit salad—all nicely done. The chunky hash browns are fried with just the right amount of onions, and if the omelet with roasted tomatoes, olives, and goat cheese is on the menu, it's an excellent choice. Also recommended (if you're not on a diet) are the decadent Belgian waffles buried under strawberries, bananas, and whipped cream. Specials are always offered and change frequently. ⊠ *460 Waquoit Hwy. (Rte. 28), Waquoit* ☎ *508/ 457–9630* ▤ *No credit cards* ⊙ *No dinner.*

$$–$$$ ▦ **Green Harbor Waterfront Lodging.** Although the modest motel rooms here are clean and adequate, it's the friendly summer camplike feel that makes the Green Harbor great for families. There are old-fashioned lawn swings, a swimming pool, umbrella-topped picnic tables, barbecue grills, and the main attraction—the waterfront. It's not open ocean here but a peaceful tree-lined inlet, with rowboats and pedal boats for guests' use. Some of the no-frills rooms in the 1960s-vintage motel have microwaves and small refrigerators; others have kitchenettes. A spacious three-bedroom cottage has three full baths, an eat-in kitchen, and a living room with a fireplace and two sofa beds. ⊠ *134 Acapesket Rd., East Falmouth 02536* ☎ *508/548–4747 or 800/548–5556* ⊟ *508/540–1652* ⊕ *www.gogreenharbor.com* ↝ *34 rooms, 1 cottage* ⌂ *Picnic area, some kitchenettes, some microwaves, some refrigerators, cable TV, pool, wading pool, boating, volleyball, laundry facilities, some pets allowed (fee); no smoking* ▤ *AE, D, DC, MC, V* ⊙ *Closed Nov.–Apr.*

$$–$$$ ▦ **Cape Wind.** If you're traveling with children who need space to run, this gray-shingle motel is a good choice. The rooms face a broad green lawn that slopes down to the bay, where rowboats and pedal boats are available. The rooms are decidedly basic, with standard motel furnishings; some have been updated more recently than others—so ask before you reserve. All have refrigerators and coffeemakers, and some have microwaves while others have kitchenettes. The spacious one-bedroom apartment has a private terrace, but its half-basement location makes the interior rather dark. ⊠ *34 Maravista Ext., Teaticket, East Falmouth 02536* ☎ *508/548–3400 or 800/267–3401* 🖷 *508/495–0316* ⊕ *www.capewind. com* ⤳ *31 rooms, 1 apartment* ⚒ *Some kitchenettes, some microwaves, some refrigerators, pool, boating; no smoking* ▤ *D, MC, V* ⊗ *Closed Nov.–Mar.*

Sports & the Outdoors

BEACHES **Menauhant Beach,** on Menauhant Road in East Falmouth, is a long, narrow stretch of sand with a pond behind in a quiet residential neighborhood. Its slightly more secluded location means it can be a bit less crowded than the beaches near Falmouth Center. The beach has lifeguards, restrooms, outdoor showers, and a small snack bar. Public parking is available; in season the fee is $10.

Mashpee

❽ *7 mi east of East Falmouth, 10 mi south of Sandwich.*

Mashpee is one of two Massachusetts towns (the other is Aquinnah, formerly known as Gay Head, on Martha's Vineyard) with both municipally governed and Native American–governed areas. In 1660 the missionary Reverend Richard Bourne gave a 16-square-mi parcel of land to the Wampanoags (consider the irony—an outsider "giving" Native people their own land). Known as the Mashpee Plantation and governed by two local sachems, it was the first Native American reservation in the United States. In 1870 Mashpee was founded as a town. In 1974 the Mashpee Wampanoag Tribal Council was formed to continue its government with a chief, a supreme sachem, a medicine man, and clan mothers. More than 600 residents are descended from the original Wampanoags, and some continue to observe their ancient traditions. Today, several resort-residential communities have developed in the Mashpee area; the largest, New Seabury, is a full-fledged resort with apartment units available to vacationers and has one of the best golf courses on the Cape. Mashpee, with its villagelike Mashpee Commons mall, has also become a popular shopping destination. Yet away from the stores, the town retains a more rural character, with wooded roads, inland ponds, and reminders of the area's original settlers.

The **Old Indian Meeting House** was originally built on Santuit Pond in 1684 and was later moved to its present site on Route 28. The oldest standing church on Cape Cod, the meetinghouse is still used by the Mashpee tribe for worship and meetings. In summer, memorials and religious events are held, some incorporating traditional Wampanoag practices. ⊠ *Meeting House Rd. off Rte. 28* ☎ *508/477–0208* ⊗ *Hrs vary; call ahead.*

The **Old Indian Burial Ground,** near the meetinghouse on Meeting House Road, is an 18th-century cemetery with headstones typical of the period, intricately carved with scenes and symbols and inscribed with witty sayings.

In a cavernous former church building, the **Cape Cod Children's Museum** welcomes kids with interactive play, science exhibits, a 30-foot pirate play ship, a portable planetarium, and other playtime activities. The museum is best suited for preschoolers and children in the early elementary grades. ⊠ *577 Great Neck Rd. S* ☎ *508/539–8788* ⊕ *www. capecodchildrensmuseum.pair.com* 🎟 *$4* ⊙ *Mon.–Sat. 10–5, Sun. noon–5. Reduced hrs in winter; call before visiting.*

Perfect for bird-watching, fishing, or canoeing, the **Mashpee River Woodlands** occupy 391 acres along the Mashpee River. More than 8 mi of trails meander through the marshlands and pine forests. Park on Quinaquisset Avenue, River Road, or Mashpee Neck Road (where there's a public landing for canoe access). Trail maps are available at the Mashpee Chamber of Commerce (⇨ Visitor Information *in* The Upper Cape A to Z). The trails are open daily, dawn to dusk.

Where to Stay & Eat

$$–$$$
Fodor'sChoice
★

✕ **Bleu.** Chef Frederic Feufeu, a native of the Loire Valley, brings the flavors of France to Cape Cod. From bistro classics to haute cuisine and sophisticated lunch sandwiches to decadent desserts, the flavors are astounding. Seasonal specialties include planked salmon and a cassoulet of duck leg confit, navy pea beans, and garlic sausage. There's also a jazz brunch on Sunday. ⊠ *7 Market St., Mashpee Commons* ☎ *508/ 539–7907* ⊟ *AE, D, MC, V.*

$–$$
✕ **The Flume.** Under new ownership since January 2004, the Flume now has a brand-new look and menu. Chef–owner Ken McNulty fuses Southern Italian cuisine with traditional Cape Cod flavors and changes the menu frequently; specialties include roasted veal tenderloin and seafood *fra diavolo*. Dinners are complemented by an extensive wine list and light background music, and the desserts are all homemade. ⊠ *13 Lake Ave., off Rte. 130* ☎ *508/477–1456* ⊟ *MC, V* ⊙ *Closed late Nov.–late Apr. No lunch.*

$$
✕ **Popponesset Inn.** The surroundings, more so than the lobster rolls, grilled swordfish, steak, and other offerings, are exceptional here. The site is a gem, with old Cape Cod saltbox houses, lovely Nantucket Sound in the background, and perfect evening light. The restaurant has a lounge called Poppy's and comprises several small dining rooms, some with skylights and others looking over the water through glass walls. Sit outside, either under the tent or at one of the umbrella tables. You can dance to a band on some weekends. The Popponesset is in the New Seabury Resort. ⊠ *Shore Dr.* ☎ *508/477–1100* ⊕ *www.newseabury.com* ⊟ *AE, DC, MC, V* ⊙ *Closed mid-Oct.–late Apr. Closed Mon.–Thurs. Sept.and Oct. No lunch Sept. and Oct.*

¢–$$
✕ **Marketplace Raw Bar.** At this funky little seafood joint, you can pull up a bar stool and chow down on giant lobster rolls, littlenecks, cherrystones, oysters, steamers, and peel-your-own shrimp, all easily washed down with a local brew or a rum punch. Despite a few picnic tables out back, the scene here is more "bar" than "seafood shack." There's live music some nights, too. ⊠ *Popponesset Marketplace, New Seabury* ☎ *508/539–4858* ⊟ *AE, MC, V* ⊙ *Closed late Oct.–early Apr.*

★ **$$$–$$$$** ✕⊞ **New Seabury Resort and Conference Center.** On Nantucket Sound, this self-contained resort community rents apartments in some of its 13 "villages." Maushop Village, for example, is an oceanfront complex of buildings, with rugosa roses trailing over picket fences; the interiors attractively mix Cape-style and modern furnishings. Town-house units in Sea Quarters have solariums with whirlpool baths and gas-log fireplaces. All units have full kitchens and washer-dryers. Among the amenities (many of them seasonal) are fine oceanfront dining, a 3-mi private beach and an oceanfront pool, and the shops at Popponesset Marketplace. Golf and other packages are available. ⊠ *Off Great Neck Rd. S* ⬧ *Box 549, New Seabury 02649* ☏ *508/477–9400 or 800/999–9033* 🖷 *508/477–9790* ⊕ *www.newseabury.com* ➲ *140 1- or 2-bedroom units* ⬧ *2 restaurants, some in-room hot tubs, kitchens, 2 18-hole golf courses, 16 tennis courts, 2 pools, health club, beach, boating, bicycles, shop, laundry facilities* ☰ *AE, DC, MC, V.*

Nightlife & the Arts

Bobby Byrne's Pub (⊠ Mashpee Commons, Rtes. 28 and 151 ☏ 508/477–0600) is a comfortable pub with an outdoor café, a jukebox, and good light and full menus. The **Boch Center for the Performing Arts** (☏ 508/477–2580 ⊕ www.bochcenterarts.com) presents top-name performers year-round, as well as the Annual New England Jazz Festival in late August. Plans are under way to construct a complex of buildings, including an amphitheater to accommodate 2,000 people, on an idyllic 10-acre tract of countryside in Mashpee. Until the complex is completed in mid-2006, performances are held at Mashpee Commons, in the Mashpee High School auditorium, or at other local venues. The 90-member **Cape Symphony Orchestra** (☏ 508/362–1111 ⊕ www.capesymphony.org) comes to Mashpee in July for its annual Sounds of Summer Pops Concert (it also performs an August concert in Orleans). The performance takes place at the Mashpee Commons.

Sports & the Outdoors

BEACHES **Attaquin Park Beach** (⊠ End of Lake Ave. off Rte. 130, near Great Neck Rd. N) is a pretty, sandy place, with a spectacular view of the interconnecting Mashpee and Wakeby ponds, the Cape's largest freshwater expanses. It's popular for swimming, fishing, and boating, but resident parking stickers are required in season.

South Cape Beach is a 2½-mi-long state and town beach on warm Nantucket and Vineyard sounds, accessible via Great Neck Road south from the Mashpee rotary. You can walk to get a bit of privacy on this beach, which is wide, sandy, and pebbly in parts, with low dunes and marshland. The only services are portable toilets, although lifeguards are on duty in season. A hiking trail loops through marsh areas and ponds, linking it to the Waquoit Bay National Estuarine Research Reserve. A $7 parking fee is charged from late May through early September.

GOLF **New Seabury Country Club** (⊠ Shore Dr., New Seabury ☏ 508/477–9111) has a superior 18-hole, par-72 championship layout on the water as well as an 18-hole, par-70 course. Both are open to the public October–May, depending on availability; reservations two days in advance are recommended, and proper attire is required.

HIKING &
WALKING
The 4 mi of walking trails at **Lowell Holly Reservation** (⊠ S. Sandwich Rd. off Rte. 130 ☎ 781/821–2977 ⊕ www.thetrustees.org), administered by the Trustees of Reservations, wind through American beeches, hollies, white pines, and rhododendrons on a peninsula between Mashpee and Wakeby ponds. The reservation has picnic tables and a little swimming beach. A small free parking area is open year-round, and an additional parking lot opens from late May to early September ($6).

In summer, the **Mashpee Conservation Commission** (☎ 508/539–1400 Ext. 540 for schedules) has information about free naturalist-led guided walks of Mashpee's woods and conservation areas. Family nature walks, animal scavenger hunts, and "pond scoops" to explore aquatic life are a few of the activities offered for kids and their parents; sunrise walks on South Cape Beach and natural history tours of the Lowell Holly Reservation are also on the program.

Shopping

Mashpee Commons (⊠ Junction of Rtes. 28 and 151 ☎ 508/477–5400) has about 80 stores, including restaurants, art galleries, and a mix of local boutiques and national chains, in an attractive village square. There's also a multiscreen movie theater and free outdoor entertainment in summer. Some of the more unique shops include **M. Brann & Co.** (☎ 508/477–0299), a creative home-and-gift shop that carries everything from funky refrigerator magnets and unusual candlesticks to hand-crafted glassware, one-of-a-kind lamps, mirrors, and furniture, with many of the works by New England artists; **Signature Gallery** (☎ 508/539–0029), a high-end crafts gallery and store (with branches in Boston and in Westport, Connecticut) that stocks contemporary crafts, including textiles, ceramics, prints, and glass; and **Cape Cod Toys** (☎ 508/477–2221), crammed full of anything the children might possibly need, including beach toys, board games, and science projects.

Popponesset Marketplace (⊠ Off Great Neck Rd. S, New Seabury, 2½ mi south of Rte. 28 from Mashpee rotary ☎ 508/477–9111), open from late spring to early fall, has 20 shops (boutique clothing, antiques), eating places (a raw bar, pizza, ribs, Ben & Jerry's), miniature golf, and weekend entertainment (bands, fashion or puppet shows, sing-alongs).

THE UPPER CAPE A TO Z

To research prices, get advice from other travelers, and book travel arrangements, visit www.fodors.com.

AIRPORTS

Barnstable Municipal Airport is the main air gateway on the Cape.

🚺 Airport Information **Barnstable Municipal Airport** ⊠ 480 Barnstable Rd., north of the Rte. 28 rotary, Hyannis ☎ 508/775–2020.

BOAT & FERRY TRAVEL

Year-round ferries to Martha's Vineyard leave from Woods Hole. Seasonal Vineyard ferries leave from Falmouth. For details *see* Boat and Ferry Travel *in* Smart Travel Tips A to Z.

BUS TRAVEL

Peter Pan Bonanza offers direct bus service to Bourne, Falmouth, and the Woods Hole steamship terminal from Boston's Logan Airport, downtown Boston, Providence (Rhode Island), Fall River, and New Bedford, as well as connecting service from New York, Connecticut, and Providence's T. F. Green Airport. Some of the buses from Boston also make stops in Wareham. Bonanza runs a service between Bourne, Falmouth, and Woods Hole year-round. Plymouth & Brockton Street Railway provides bus service to Provincetown from downtown Boston and Logan Airport, with stops en route. The Logan Direct airport express service bypasses downtown Boston and stops in Plymouth, Sagamore, Barnstable, and Hyannis. For general information on Cape buses, *see* Bus Travel *in* Smart Travel Tips A to Z.

🚌 Bus Depots **Bonanza Bus Terminals** ✉ South Station Bus Terminal, 700 Atlantic Ave., Boston ☎ 617/720–4110 ✉ Depot Ave., Falmouth ☎ 508/548–7588 ✉ Steamship Authority Piers, Woods Hole ☎ 508/548–5011. **Hyannis Transportation Center** ✉ 215 Iyannough Rd., Hyannis ☎ 508/775–8504. **Plymouth & Brockton Street Railway Terminals** ✉ South Station Bus Terminal, 700 Atlantic Ave., Boston ☎ 508/746–0378.

🚌 Bus Lines **Bonanza Bus Lines** ☎ 508/548–7588 or 800/556–3815 ⊕ www.bonanzabus.com. **Plymouth & Brockton Street Railway** ☎ 508/746–0378 ⊕ www.p-b.com.

BUS TRAVEL WITHIN THE UPPER CAPE

The Cape Cod Regional Transit Authority's SeaLine, H2O Line, Barnstable Villager, and Hyannis Villager buses travel between the Upper and Lower Cape. Service is not frequent—buses depart once every hour or two, depending on the time of day—so check the schedule before you set out. To travel between Falmouth and Woods Hole, the WHOOSH trolley, also run by the Cape Cod Regional Transit Authority, is convenient. Their detailed Web site shows the real-time position of the buses.

FARES & SCHEDULES The SeaLine buses begin running around 6:30 AM and operate until about 8 PM; call or check the Web site for exact details. Fares vary by distance, between $1 and $3.50. The WHOOSH trolley departs every 20 minutes between 9:30 AM and 7:10 PM Monday through Friday (every 30 minutes on Saturday and Sunday); there's also hourly service on Friday and Saturday evenings between 7:30 and 10:30 PM. Regular adult fare is $1 per ride. You can buy a one-day unlimited ride pass for $3.

🚌 **Cape Cod Regional Transit Authority** ☎ 508/385–8326, 800/352–7155 in Massachusetts ⊕ www.capecodtransit.org.

CAR TRAVEL

If your destination is Sagamore, Sandwich, or points east along Cape Cod Bay, cross the Sagamore Bridge to reach U.S. 6 or Route 6A. If you're headed for Bourne, Falmouth, Woods Hole, or Mashpee, take the Bourne Bridge instead and pick up Route 28 south. To reach East Falmouth or Mashpee, get off Route 28 at either Route 151 or Brick Kiln Road to bypass Falmouth Center—both rejoin Route 28 east of Falmouth. If you're not in a hurry, get off the main highways and seek out the Upper Cape's more scenic byways. Route 6A heading east from Sandwich is a heavily traveled but still scenic route that parallels Cape Cod Bay all the way to Orleans. Watch for cars turning suddenly, though, as there are shops and side roads along many stretches of 6A. Heading from the Bourne Bridge toward Falmouth, County Road and Route 28A are prettier alternatives to Route 28, and Sippewisset Road meanders near Buzzards Bay between West Falmouth and Woods Hole. Just remember that some of these roads travel through residential areas, so keep your speed down.

PARKING In Sandwich, very limited free parking is available on Main Street; the town does not have a municipal parking lot. In downtown Falmouth, street parking is available along Main Street, and there's a large parking lot adjacent to the Falmouth Chamber of Commerce office; it's between Main Street and Katharine Lee Bates Road. Parking in Woods Hole is extremely limited in summer, so a good strategy is to park in Falmouth and take the WHOOSH trolley (⇨ Trolley Travel, *below*). It's also an easy bike ride from Falmouth to Woods Hole along the Shining Sea bike path. If you're planning to park in Woods Hole en route to Martha's Vineyard, note that the parking lots by the dock are frequently full. Signs along Route 28 will direct you to the nearest lot with space available; free shuttles take you from the parking lots to the ferry docks.

TRAFFIC Traffic can be heavy in the Falmouth area, particularly on Route 28—both north and east of the town center—during the morning and evening rush hours. Traffic is heaviest between 8 and 9 AM and between 4 and 5:30 PM, and throughout the day on summer Saturdays.

CHILDREN IN THE UPPER CAPE

SIGHTS & Libraries usually offer regular children's story hours or other programs;
ATTRACTIONS check them out on a rainy day. Hours are listed in the newspapers each week. The Army Corps of Engineers Junior Ranger Program for children ages 6–12 offers various summer activities that teach kids about the Cape Cod Canal and the area's natural history; kids must be accompanied by an adult. Also good for families are star watches, beach and dune walks, and other nature programs. The Cape Cod Baseball League has summer day camps and clinics, run by the individual teams, for children ages 5–13; most teams have six weeks of camp, typically weekday mornings. The Green Briar Nature Center runs one-day and multiday nature programs, with classes geared to ages four to five, six to eight, and nine and up. Sample programs include Nature Detectives, a Cape Cod Safari, and Canoe Adventures. At the Waquoit Bay National Estuarine Research Reserve, there are various summer programs for kids, including junior ranger activities that are generally one-hour programs at South Cape Beach for ages 6–12 (accompanied by an adult).

🗗 Local Information **Army Corps of Engineers Junior Ranger Program** ☎ 508/759-4431. **Cape Cod Baseball League** ☎ 508/432-6909 ⊕ www.capecodbaseball.org. **Green Briar Nature Center** ☎ 508/888-6870 ⊕ www.thorntonburgess.org. **Waquoit Bay National Estuarine Research Reserve** ☎ 508/457-0495.

EMERGENCIES

Falmouth Hospital has a 24-hour emergency room. For rescues at sea call the Coast Guard. Boaters should use Channel 16 on their radios. The CVS pharmacy in Falmouth closes at 10 PM Monday–Saturday and 9 PM Sunday.

🗗 Doctors & Dentists **Falmouth Walk-In Medical Center** ✉ 309 Teaticket Hwy. [Rte. 28], East Falmouth ☎ 508/540-6790. **Mashpee Family Medicine** ✉ 5 Industrial Dr., off Rte. 28, Mashpee ☎ 508/477-4282.

🗗 Emergency Services **Ambulance, fire, police** ☎ 911 or dial township station. **Coast Guard** ☎ 508/548-5151 in Woods Hole, 508/888-0335 in Sandwich and Cape Cod Canal.

🗗 Hospital **Falmouth Hospital** ✉ 100 Ter Heun Dr., Falmouth ☎ 508/548-5300.

🗗 Hotline **Massachusetts Poison Control Center** ☎ 800/682-9211.

🗗 Late-Night Pharmacy **CVS** ✉ 105 Davis Straits, Falmouth ☎ 508/540-4307 ⊕ www.cvs.com.

LODGING

APARTMENT & HOUSE RENTALS Donahue Real Estate lists both apartments and houses for summer rental in the Falmouth area. Real Estate Associates lists properties, some pricey, ranging from beach cottages to waterfront estates, with a focus on more expensive houses. It covers Falmouth, Bourne, and Mashpee, on the Upper Cape.

🗗 Local Agents **Donahue Real Estate** ✉ 850 Main St., Falmouth 02540 ☎ 508/548-5412 🖷 508/548-5418 ⊕ www.falmouthhomes.com. **Real Estate Associates** ✉ Rtes. 151 and 28A ⬭ Box 738, North Falmouth 02556 ☎ 508/563-7173 🖷 508/563-6943 ⊕ www.realestateassc.com.

TAXIS

🗗 Taxi Company **All Village Taxi** ✉ Falmouth ☎ 508/540-7200.

TOURS

Patriot Boats has two-hour day and sunset cruises from Falmouth Harbor on the 74-foot schooner *Liberté II*. Another sunset cruise, which operates on Friday and Saturday evenings, passes six lighthouses in the Falmouth area. Rates and schedules vary.

🗗 Fees & Schedules **Patriot Boats** ✉ 227 Clinton Ave., Falmouth ☎ 508/548-2626, 800/734-0088 in Massachusetts ⊕ www.patriotpartyboats.com.

TROLLEY TRAVEL

The Cape Cod Regional Transit Authority runs seasonal trolleys in Falmouth, Mashpee, Hyannis, Yarmouth, and Dennis. Fares and times vary; call for more information.

🗗 **Cape Cod Regional Transit Authority** ☎ 508/385-8326, 800/352-7155 in Massachusetts ⊕ www.capecodtransit.org.

VISITOR INFORMATION

The Cape Cod Chamber of Commerce is open year-round, Monday–Saturday 9–5 and Sunday 10–4. The year-round visitor information center on Route 25, in a rest area about 3 mi west of the Bourne Bridge, is open daily 9–5 (with extended hours 8 AM–10 PM from late May to mid-October). The Cape Cod Canal Region, which includes Sandwich, Bourne, and Wareham, has information centers at the Sagamore rotary, at a train depot in Buzzards Bay, and on Route 130 in Sandwich (near the intersection with U.S. 6).

🚹 Tourist Information : **Cape Cod Canal Region** ✉ 70 Main St., Buzzards Bay 02532 ☎ 508/759-6000 ⊕ www.capecodcanalchamber.org. **Cape Cod Chamber of Commerce** ✉ Junction of U.S. 6 and 132, Hyannis ☎ 508/362-3225, 888/332-2732, Rte. 25 visitor information center ⊕ www.capecodchamber.org. **Falmouth Chamber of Commerce** ✉ 20 Academy La. ⊕ Box 582, 02541 ☎ 508/548-8500 or 800/526-8532 ⊕ www.falmouthchamber.com. **Mashpee Chamber of Commerce** ✉ N. Market St., Mashpee Commons [Rte. 151], 02649 ☎ 508/477-0792, 800/423-6274 outside Massachusetts ⊕ www.mashpeechamber.com.

THE MID CAPE

3

CHOW DOWN ON FRESH FRIED SEAFOOD
at local favorite Cap'n Frosty's ⇨*p.87*

PAY HOMAGE TO JFK
in his summer hometown ⇨*pp. 96–97*

REVISIT THE "GOOD OLD DAYS"
at Hallet's country drugstore ⇨*p.81*

COMMUNE WITH NATURE
on the Cape Cod Rail Trail ⇨*p.90*

ROCK OUT AT A CONCERT
at the Cape Cod Melody Tent ⇨*p.105*

Revised by
Lori A. Nolin

MORE A COLLOQUIALISM than a proper name, the designation "Mid Cape" refers to central Cape Cod, the most heavily populated—and touristed—part of the peninsula. To the north lies tranquil Cape Cod Bay, laced with wide beaches, inlets, creeks and marshes. The tides on the bay are dramatic—at dead low some beaches double in size as the tidal flats stretch out for hundreds to thousands of feet. The calmer waters on the bay side make these beaches particularly suitable for kids, and when the tide is out, they can explore and play in the tidepools left behind.

The main thoroughfare through the north side of the Mid Cape is Route 6A, a scenic section that dates from 1684, making it one of the first major roads constructed on Cape Cod. Alternately called Old King's Highway, Main Street, and Hallet Street, the road winds through the villages of West Barnstable, Barnstable, Cummaquid, Yarmouth Port, and Dennis, with north-side harbors and beaches just a short drive from village centers. A mix of residential and commercial, Route 6A is lined with antique captains' mansions and farmhouses that are now private homes, bed-and-breakfasts, art galleries, restaurants, and antiques shops. Protected by a historical society, colors and architecture along the road are kept to the standards set by early settlers.

On the south side of the Mid Cape, sunbathers flock to the expansive beaches along Nantucket Sound. The main thoroughfare here is the busy and overdeveloped Route 28, which passes through Centerville, Osterville, Hyannis, West and South Yarmouth, and Dennisport. This stretch, particularly between West Yarmouth and Dennisport, is the original vacationland of Cape Cod, a tawdry mecca of strip motels, clam shacks, miniature golf courses, ice-cream parlors, and tacky T-shirt outlets. A draw for families in its 1960s heyday, the area hasn't seen much renovation since. However, stray from the congestion of Route 28, and the serenity of soft sand and quiet back roads await. It's hard to get too lost on the Cape—you can't go far off the main roads without hitting water—so poking around is worth the risk.

Between Routes 6A and 28 is the "mid" of the Mid Cape, a mostly residential area with some historic sections, a few quiet freshwater ponds, and the commercial sections of Hyannis. Nearby are tony Osterville and Hyannis Port, a well-groomed enclave and site of the Kennedy compound.

Exploring the Mid Cape

The Mid Cape includes the towns of Barnstable, Yarmouth, and Dennis, each divided into smaller townships and villages. The town of Barnstable, for example, consists of Barnstable Village, West Barnstable, Cotuit, Marstons Mills, Osterville, Centerville, and Hyannis, with the smaller quasi villages (distinguished by their separate postal codes), of Craigville, Cummaquid, Hyannis Port, West Hyannis Port, and Wianno. Yarmouth contains Yarmouth Port, along on the north shore, and the mid- and south villages of West Yarmouth and South Yarmouth. The town of Dennis's villages are easy to remember: Dennis, West Dennis, South Dennis, East Dennis, and Dennisport. Route 6A winds along the north shore through tree-shaded scenic towns and village centers, while Route 28 dips south through some of the more overdeveloped parts of the Cape. Generally speaking, if you want to avoid malls, heavy traffic, and cheesy motels, stay away from Route 28 from Falmouth to Chatham.

About the Restaurants

The Mid Cape is chock-full of eateries, ranging from sedate, high-end haute cuisine houses such as Hyannis's Paddock, the Regatta of Cotuit, and Dennis's Red Pheasant to family places such as Barbyann's in Hyannis and the Red Cottage in Dennis. Expect good fun and great eats at the area's dozens of clam shacks and other supercasual restaurants along Route 28 in Yarmouth and Dennis. If you simply want lots of choices, head to Barnstable and its villages, particularly Hyannis, where a stroll down Main Street will bring you to a dozen fine restaurants ranging from lunch joints to Thai, Italian, Cajun, and upscale American dining establishments.

About the Hotels

On the northern (bay) side, Route 6A from Barnstable to Dennis has dozens of B&Bs, many in the elegant former homes of sea captains. In contrast, Route 28 on the south side has row after row of lodgings, from tacky roadside motels to medium-range family hotels, with larger seaside resorts along the side roads on Nantucket Sound. Main Street, Hyannis, is lined with motels, while several inns and B&Bs perch on side streets leading to Hyannis Harbor and Lewis Bay.

WHAT IT COSTS					
	$$$$	$$$	$$	$	¢
RESTAURANTS	over $30	$20–$30	$15–$20	$10–$15	under $10
HOTELS	over $220	$140–$220	$100–$140	$80–$100	under $80

Restaurant prices are per person for a main course at dinner. Hotel prices are for a standard double room in high season, excluding 5.7% state tax and gratuities. Some inns add a 15% service charge.

Timing

In summer the Mid Cape bustles with tourists. But from Columbus Day weekend through April, the Mid Cape is a peaceful collection of towns and villages, with beaches (no fees) for strolling, trails for walking and biking, and a wealth of shopping and entertainment. While the year-round population has ballooned in the last decade, the off-season is still a laid-back and welcome time to catch the best of the Cape minus the crowds. Fall sees bursts of color in the easily accessed forests and marshes; winter brings a slower pace of life and a holiday spirit that locals love to celebrate with Christmas strolls featuring tours of shops, B&Bs, and old homes. Spring is also quiet, as the Mid Cape awakens to blooming trees, warmer days, reopened B&Bs, newly

Numbers in the text correspond to numbers in the margin and on the Mid Cape map.

The crowded belly of the Cape is a center of activity unlike any other here, except perhaps Provincetown at the height of its summer crush. **Hyannis** ⑪–⑭ is the hub of Cape Cod, with plenty to do and see. Take a cruise around the harbor or go on a deep-sea fishing trip. There are shops and restaurants along Main Street and plenty of amusements for the youngsters. Kennedy fans might want to spend time at the JFK Museum. End the day with a concert at the Cape Cod Melody Tent. **Barnstable** ①, the county seat, has plenty of its own history and the wonderful Sandy Neck Beach to keep you occupied. Scenic Route 6A passes through **Yarmouth Port** ② and **Dennis** ⑤. There are beaches and salt marshes, museums, walking trails, and old graveyards all along this route if you feel like stopping. Yarmouth Port's **Bass Hole Boardwalk** ④ makes for a particularly beautiful stroll. In Dennis there are historic houses to tour, the Cape Museum of Fine Arts will introduce you to the work of Cape-associated artists, and the Cape Cod Rail Trail provides a premier path for bicyclists. Toward the end of the day, head for Scargo Hill and climb 30-foot **Scargo Tower** ⑥ to watch the sun set. At night you could catch a film at the Cape Cinema, on the grounds of the **Cape Playhouse** ⑦. The south shore has plenty of activities for kids, from **Centerville** ⑩ to **Dennisport** ⑲.

3

landscaped golf courses, and flower festivals. Boats come out of hibernation—the Hyannis Whale Watcher Cruises, for instance, starts its program in May.

Barnstable

① *11 mi east of Sandwich; 4 mi north of Hyannis.*

With nearly 50,000 year-round residents, Barnstable is the largest town on the Cape. It's also the second oldest—it was founded in 1639, two years after Sandwich. You can get a feeling for its age in Barnstable Village, on and near Main Street (Route 6A), a lovely area of large old homes dominated by the Barnstable County Superior Courthouse. Behind the courthouse are the county lockup and a complex of government buildings, all best avoided. In the Village Hall is the Barnstable Comedy Club, one of the oldest community theater groups in the country. Just north of the village are the marshes and beaches of Cape Cod Bay, including beautiful Sandy Neck Beach, as well as busy Barnstable Harbor. The Cape Cod Conservatory of Music and Arts and Cape Cod Community College are also in the vicinity.

The **Olde Colonial Courthouse,** built in 1772 as the colony's second courthouse, is the home of the historical society **Tales of Cape Cod** (✉ 3018 Main St. [Rte. 6A] ☎ 508/362–8927). The society hosts a weekly slide-illustrated lecture on Tuesday in July and August, plus special events in the shoulder seasons: in May there's a lecture during Maritime Week, and in June there's one during Heritage week. In September, a "mystery" bus trip takes visitors to areas of historic interest. From the courthouse take a peek across the street at the old-fashioned English gardens at **St. Mary's Episcopal Church.**

The **Sturgis Library,** established in 1863, is in a 1644 building listed on the National Register of Historic Places. Its holdings date from the 17th century and include hundreds of maps and land charts, the definitive collection of Cape Cod genealogical material ($5 daily fee for nonresidents), and an extensive maritime history collection. ⊠ *3090 Main St. (Rte. 6A)* ☎ *508/362–6636* ⊕ *www.sturgislibrary.org* ☉ *Mon., Wed., Thurs., and Fri. 10–5, Tues. 1–8, Sat. 10–4.*

Barnstable's maritime past is on display at the **Trayser Museum Complex.** On the National Register of Historic Places, the complex's red-painted brick main building houses a small collection of maritime exhibits—telescopes, captains' shaving boxes, items brought back from voyages, ship models, and paintings—as well as ivory, Sandwich glass, and arrowheads. The downstairs is a re-creation of the building as it looked in 1856, when it served as a customs house; don't miss the ornate bronze Corinthian columns. A restored customs-keeper's office with an original safe and a view of the harbor are on the second floor. Also on the grounds are a jail, circa 1690, with two cells bearing former inmates' graffiti, and a carriage house with early tools, fishing implements, and a 19th-century horse-drawn hearse. ⊠ *3353 Main St. (Rte. 6A)* ☎ *508/362–2092* ⊕ *www.barnstablepatriot.com/ trayser* ⊠ *$2 suggested donation* ☉ *Mid-June–mid-Oct., Thurs.–Sun. 1:30–4:30.*

If you're interested in Cape history, the **Nickerson Memorial Room** at **Cape Cod Community College** has the largest collection of information on Cape Cod, including books, records, ships' logs, oral-history tapes, photographs, and films. It also has materials on the neighboring islands of Martha's Vineyard and Nantucket. ⊠ *2240 Iyanough Rd., off Rte. 132, West Barnstable* ☎ *508/362–2131 Ext. 4342* ⊕ *www.capecod.mass. edu* ☉ *Mon., Wed., and Fri. 8:30–4:30.*

Where to Stay & Eat

$$–$$$ ✕ **Dolphin Restaurant.** For the scoop on local politics, keep your ears attuned and eavesdrop at the Dolphin. A popular spot among local political figures, for decades this has been the place in town where opinions clash and deals are cut. The dark, inviting interior has a colonial feel. Lunch favorites include the shrimp and crab melt, rib-eye steak and fish and chips. The small but welcoming bar is a good spot to chow down if you're dining solo. ⊠ *3250 Main St. (Rte. 6A)* ☎ *508/362–6610* ⊕ *www.thedolphinrestaurant.com* ⊟ *AE, MC, V* ☉ *No lunch Sun.*

$–$$$ ✕ **Barnstable Tavern & Grille.** This handsome old building right in the village center, across from the courthouse, holds both a formal restaurant and a more relaxed tavern. Fresh seafood dishes and the Tavern Keeper's Special (a medley of seafood in a casserole) are local favorites. Lunch fare is lighter and includes burgers, salads, and sandwiches. Look for

Beaches

Beach lovers will find numerous Shangri-Las throughout the Mid Cape. Sandy Neck, a peninsular strip of land that stretches across the north side of Barnstable Harbor, is one of the Top 10 on Cape Cod, perfect for those who like gentle surf and long shoreline walks. Also on the north side of the Mid Cape, Dennis's Corporation Beach and Mayflower Beach are great places for kids, with wide tidal flats, snack huts, and restrooms. South-side beaches, on Nantucket Sound, include the busy Craigville Beach in Centerville, popular with college students on break, and Kalmus Park Beach in Hyannis, with a windy surf that attracts world-class windsurfers. Yarmouth's best beaches lie along its Nantucket Sound side and include Seagull Beach and Parker's River Beach.

3

In and among Mid Cape towns are a number of freshwater kettle ponds, created by receding glaciers eons ago. Pond beaches are usually not as crowded as ocean beaches and have plenty of appeal for those who like cooling off in gentle water without the salt and sand. In Yarmouth Port, Dennis Pond attracts families to its shallow swimming area. Dennis's Scargo Lake has two public beaches, and Hathaway's Pond in Barnstable has a nice beach and restrooms.

Biking

Bike enthusiasts are well served on the Mid Cape: the scenic 25-mi Cape Cod Rail Trail begins in South Dennis, following the paved right-of-way of the old Penn Central Railroad, and ends in South Wellfleet.

Nightlife & the Arts

Since you can pass an art gallery almost every minute on the drive along Route 6A between Barnstable and Dennis, you should stop in at some of these places, such as Cummaquid Fine Arts, which carries original contemporary art that's a decided improvement over the ubiquitous paintings of rowboats on beaches. Other gallery centers are on Main Street in both Hyannis and Osterville.

The Mid Cape is a hub for summertime entertainment. The Cape Cod Melody Tent, in Hyannis, has attracted such internationally well-known performers as comedians Bill Cosby and George Carlin and singers Jimmy Cliff and Lyle Lovett. The Melody Tent—which really is a tent, albeit a large and comfortable one with a revolving stage—also produces children's matinee theater, with regular summer shows such as *Sleeping Beauty* and *The Frog Prince.* Your theater needs can also be sated at the Cape Playhouse in Dennis, one of the country's oldest summer repertory theaters. Big stars who have come this way in the past include Henry Fonda, Gregory Peck, and Bette Davis. The Cape Playhouse also offers children's theater during the season. The Barnstable Comedy Club on Route 6A in Barnstable Village presents drama, sketches, and, yes, comedic works throughout the summer.

Nightlife is abundant in the Mid Cape, from bistros and bars that have regular entertainment—think Hyannis's Roadhouse Café for jazz—to hip dance clubs like the Blue Room in Hyannis and heart-and-soul blues beats at Harry's down the street. Special events such as the Boston Pops Esplanade Orchestra's Pops by the Sea concert, held on the Hyannis Village Green in August, are listed in local newspapers weekly. Check out listings in the *Register,* the *Barnstable Patriot,* and the Tuesday and Friday editions of the *Cape Codder,* as well as the pullout section "Cape Week" in the Friday edition of the *Cape Cod Times.* You can pick up any of these publications at local supermarkets and convenience stores.

Sports & the Outdoors

Numerous fishing and tour boats depart Hyannis Harbor, Barnstable Harbor, and Dennis's Sesuit Harbor for trips ranging from deep-sea fishing excursions to harbor fishing, a favorite with the kids. Barnstable Harbor is also the launch point for Hyannis Whale Watcher Cruises, which operates from spring through early fall. Canoeing and sea kayaking are excellent around the bay's marshy inlets, and windsurfing is popular at Hyannis's Kalmus Park Beach. Dennis's Swan River is great for kayaking and canoeing, and the Bass River, a border separating Yarmouth and Dennis, has river sightseeing excursions on a small boat, as well as fishing and, if you've got the permit, clamming.

Conservation-land walking trails are found in Yarmouth and Dennis, including a Dennis trail set up for hikers with vision impairments.

Shopping

Throughout the villages and towns of the Mid Cape, and—particularly along Route 6A and the main streets of Hyannis, Centerville, Osterville, and Dennisport—are numerous boutiques, crafts shops, bookstores, antiques centers, candy shops (saltwater taffy, yes, but also exquisite chocolates and homemade fudge), and galleries. In general, look to the smaller towns and villages for specialty crafts items such as Nantucket baskets, wicker furniture, and bird-watching esoterica. The huge Cape Cod Mall, between Routes 132 and 28 in Hyannis, has clothing boutiques such as Ann Taylor Loft, Gap, and Abercrombie & Fitch; jewelry stores; specialty shops; and the anchor stores Macy's, Filene's, and Sears Roebuck. Everyone is wild about Christmas Tree Shops, a local chain with stores in Yarmouth Port, West Yarmouth, West Dennis, and Hyannis that sells all sorts of amusing things at discount prices, including lava lamps, lanai furniture, candles, and cookies.

---

live music on the patio Friday night. ⊠ *3176 Main St. (Rte. 6A)* ☎ *508/362–2355* ▤ *AE, MC, V.*

$–$$ ✕ **Whistleberries.** Most people settle for takeout from this tiny sandwich shop, but the lucky few who manage to grab one of the three counter spots or two tables are in for a treat. Breakfast is fresh muffins; "scrambled" eggs (they're actually steamed by the cappuccino machine); bagels; or burrito sandwiches stuffed with cheese, bacon, veggies, rice, beans, and sour cream. For lunch, try a wrap—there are many tempting choices, from barbecued chicken, turkey, or roast beef to specialties such as the Mediterranean, with red pepper, hummus, tabbouleh, tomato, onion, and feta cheese folded up in a spinach tortilla. ⊠ *3261 Main St. (Rte. 6A)* ☎ *508/362–6717* ▤ *No credit cards* ⊘ *Closed Sun. No dinner.*

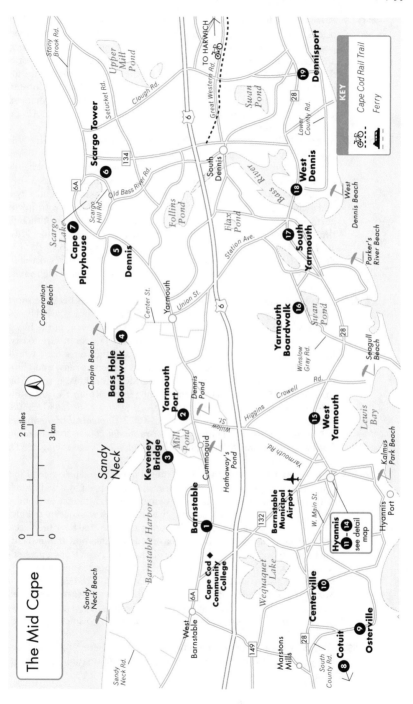

The Mid Cape

2 miles

3 km

KEY

🚲⋯ Cape Cod Rail Trail

🚢--- Ferry

Sandy Neck

Stony Brook Rd.

Upper Mill Pond

Setucket Rd.

Clough Rd.

TO HARWICH 🚲

Great Western Rd.

Swan Pond

19 Dennisport

6

28

Scargo Tower 6

134

Lower County Rd.

6A

Old Bass River Rd.

South Dennis

18 West Dennis

West Dennis Beach

Scargo Hill Rd.

Follins Pond

Bass River

Flax Pond

Cape 7 Playhouse

Scargo Lake

5 Dennis

Station Ave.

17 South Yarmouth

Parker's Beach

Center St.

Union St.

6

Corporation Beach

Chapin Beach

Bass Hole 4 Boardwalk

Yarmouth 2 Port

Dennis Pond

Yarmouth

Yarmouth Boardwalk 16

Swan Pond

28

Seagull Beach

Keveney Bridge 3

Mill Pond

Cummaquid

Hathaway's Pond

Willow St.

Higgins

Crowell Rd.

Winslow Gray Rd.

Yarmouth Rd.

West 15 Yarmouth

Lewis Bay

Barnstable Harbor

Barnstable 1

Cape Cod Community College ◆

Barnstable Municipal Airport

W. Main St.

Kalmus Park Beach

Hyannis Port

Sandy Neck Beach

Sandy Neck Rd.

West Barnstable

6A

132

Wequaquet Lake

Hyannis 11–14 see detail map

Centerville 10

149

28

Marstons Mills

South County Rd.

8 Cotuit

Osterville 9

★ ¢–$$ ✕ **Mill Way Fish and Lobster.** This combination seafood market and lunch place sits right on Barnstable Harbor, giving it access to the freshest seafood possible. It's tiny, with a fistful of outside picnic tables on a wooden deck and limited parking, but the fried clams and fish sandwiches are worth the inevitable wait. Arrive hungry and try the fat onion rings or the almost-too-big-for-lunch clambake, which comes with chowder, lobster, steamers, and an ear of corn. Mill Way is open until 7 for early dinners. ⊠ *275 Mill Way* ☎ *508/362–2760* ⊕ *www.millwayfish.com* ▭ *AE, D, MC, V* ⊙ *Closed Oct.–Mar.*

★ $$$ ▦ **Acworth Inn.** This historic 1860 house 1 mi east of Barnstable Village has four large rooms and a spacious two-room suite. The rooms are decorated with soft pastels, lacy designer linens, and tasteful hand-painted furniture. The suite, with modern furnishings, also has a fireplace, whirlpool tub, TV–VCR, and refrigerator. Breakfast is family-style and includes granola, fresh muffins or homemade coffee cake, fruit, yogurt, and an entrée that might use herbs from the inn's gardens. Although the inn is not designed for small kids, inquire about bringing older kids. ⊠ *4352 Main St. (Rte. 6A)* ⬨ *Box 256, Cummaquid 02637* ☎ *508/ 362–3330 or 800/362–6363* 🖷 *508/375–0304* ⊕ *www.acworthinn. com* ⇨ *4 rooms, 1 suite* ⊘ *No room phones, no TV in some rooms, no smoking* ▭ *AE, D, MC, V* ⦿ *BP.*

$$$ ▦ **Ashley Manor.** Set behind hedges and a wide lawn, this B&B is a short walk from the village. The inn has preserved its antique wide-board floors and has open-hearth fireplaces, one with a beehive oven, in the living room, the dining room, and the keeping room. The rooms are toasty, too—all but one have a working fireplace, and the suites have whirlpool tubs. Antique and country furnishings, Oriental rugs, and glimmers of brass and crystal create an elegant feel. Breakfast is served on the backyard terrace or in the formal dining room. Room TVs are available upon request. ⊠ *3660 Main St. (Rte. 6A)* ⬨ *Box 856, 02630* ☎ *508/ 362–8044 or 888/535–2246* 🖷 *508/362–9927* ⊕ *www.ashleymanor.net* ⇨ *2 rooms, 4 suites* ⊘ *Dining room, in-room data ports, some in-room hot tubs, tennis court, bicycles; no kids under 14, no smoking.* ▭ *D, MC, V* ⦿ *BP.*

★ $$$ ▦ **Beechwood Inn.** Debbie and Ken Traugot's yellow and pale green 1853 Queen Anne house has gingerbread trim and is wrapped by a wide porch with wicker furniture and a glider swing. Although the parlor is pure mahogany-and-red-velvet Victorian, guest rooms (all with queen- or king-size beds) have antiques in lighter Victorian styles; several have fireplaces, and one has a bay view. Bathrooms have pedestal sinks and antique lighting fixtures. Breakfast is served in the dining room, which has a pressed-tin ceiling, a fireplace, and lace-cover tables. Afternoon tea and homemade snacks are also available. ⊠ *2839 Main St. (Rte. 6A), 02630* ☎ *508/ 362–6618 or 800/609–6618* 🖷 *508/362–0298* ⊕ *www.beechwoodinn. com* ⇨ *6 rooms* ⊘ *Dining room, refrigerators, bicycles; no room phones, no TV in some rooms, no kids under 12, no smoking* ▭ *AE, D, MC, V* ⦿ *BP.*

$$$ ▦ **Cobb's Cove.** Henri-Jean Studley and Evelyn Chester's offbeat hideaway surrounded by lush, wild gardens is the destination for a quiet,

romantic hideaway. The interior has huge wood beams, rough burlap walls, and heavy wooden doors studded (just as they were in the olden days) with nail heads. Each of the large guest rooms has a dressing area and a private bath with whirlpool tub. From the two top-floor rooms, you can enjoy the spectacular view of Cape Cod Bay. A Count Rumford–designed fireplace dominates the rustic dining room, where breakfast is served. ⊠ *31 Powder Hill Rd.* ⚐ *Box 208, 02630* ☏ *877/378–5172* ⚏ *508/362–9356* ⊕ *www.cobbscove.com* ⚐ *6 rooms* ♨ *In-room hot tubs; no a/c, no room phones, no room TVs, no kids, no smoking* ⊟ *AE, D, MC, V* ⦿ *BP.*

★ **$$$** ⛪ **The Highpointe Inn.** Debbie and Rich Howard's intimate haven is nestled high on a hill, overlooking dunes, the Great Salt Marsh, and the Bay at Sandy Neck. Although just minutes from historic Route 6A, the inn transports you to a dreamlike getaway. The light and airy B&B offers casual luxury at its best. Each of the inn's three rooms inspire serenity with comforting colors, decor, and magical views. Breakfast includes Rich's famed french toast and Debbie's homemade goodies. ⊠ *70 High St.* ⚐ *Box 346, West Barnstable 02668* ☏ *508/362–4441 or 888/362–4441* ⚏ *508/362–4401* ⊕ *www.thehighpointeinn.com* ⚐ *3 rooms* ♨ *Refrigerators, exercise room, putting green; no room phones, no room TVs, no kids under 16, no smoking* ⊟ *AE, D, MC, V* ⊗ *Closed Nov.–Apr.* ⦿ *BP.*

$$$ ⛪ **Honeysuckle Hill.** Innkeepers Mary and Bill Kilburn ran an inn in Vermont before relocating to the Cape, and their experience and graciousness shine through in lots of little touches: a guest fridge stocked with sodas and water bottles, beach chairs with umbrellas (perfect for nearby Sandy Neck Beach), and an always-full cookie jar. The airy, country-style guest rooms in this 1810 Queen Anne–style cottage have lots of white wicker, featherbeds, checked curtains, and pastel-painted floors. The spacious second-floor Wisteria Room overlooking the lush yard is a particularly comfortable retreat, and the screened-in porch is a peaceful place for early-morning coffee. ⊠ *591 Rte. 6A, West Barnstable 02668* ☏ *508/362–8418 or 866/444–5522* ⚏ *508/362–8386* ⊕ *www.honeysucklehill.com* ⚐ *4 rooms, 1 suite* ♨ *No room phones, no kids under 12, no smoking, no TV in some rooms* ⊟ *AE, D, MC, V* ⦿ *BP.*

$$$ ⛪ **Lamb and Lion Inn.** Lamb and Lion occupies a 1740 farmhouse and barn, as well as several additions, with rooms and suites gathered around a courtyard and large swimming pool. Inside, some rooms are summery, with blue-and-white-stripe wallpaper and wicker chairs, while others are more staid, furnished with antiques and dark woods. The Innkeeper's Pride Suite has a fireplace and sunken tub that opens to a private deck; the rustic Barn-Stable, in the original barn, has three sleeping lofts that can accommodate six. Amenities include pickups and drop-offs from local ferries and the Barnstable Municipal Airport. ⊠ *2504 Main St. (Rte. 6A)* ⚐ *Box 511, Barnstable 02630* ☏ *508/362–6823 or 800/909–6923* ⚏ *508/362–0227* ⊕ *www.lambandlion.com* ⚐ *4 rooms, 6 suites* ♨ *Cable TV, pool, hot tub, shop, airport shuttle, some pets allowed (fee); no kids in season* ⊟ *MC, V* ⦿ *CP.*

Nightlife & the Arts

The **Barnstable Comedy Club** (✉ Village Hall, Rte. 6A ☎ 508/362–6333 ⊕ www.barnstablecomedyclub.com), the Cape's oldest amateur theater group (it was founded in the 1920s), gives much-praised musical and dramatic performances throughout the year. Some folks who appeared here before they made it big are Geena Davis, Frances McDormand, and Kurt Vonnegut, a past president of the BCC.

Sports & the Outdoors

BEACHES Hovering above Barnstable Harbor and the 4,000-acre **Great Salt Marsh, Sandy Neck Beach** stretches some 6 mi across a peninsula that ends at **Sandy Neck Light.** The beach is one of the Cape's most beautiful—dunes, sand, and sea spread endlessly east, west, and north. The marsh used to be harvested for salt hay; now it's a haven for birds, which are out and about in the greatest numbers in morning and evening, during low tide, and during spring and fall migration. The lighthouse, standing a few feet from eroding shoreline at the tip of the neck, has been out of commission since 1952. It was built in 1857 to replace an 1827 light, and it used to run on acetylene gas. It's now privately owned and no longer accessible from the beach. If you like to hike, ask at the ranger station for a trail brochure. The main beach at Sandy Neck has lifeguards, a snack bar, restrooms, and showers. As you travel east along Route 6A from Sandwich, Sandy Neck Road is just *before* the Barnstable line, although the beach itself is in West Barnstable. ✉ *Sandy Neck Rd., West Barnstable* ⊒ *Parking $10 late May–early Sept.* ☉ *Daily 8 AM–9 PM, but staffed only until 5 PM.*

Hathaway's Pond (✉ Off Phinney's La.) is a freshwater pond with a beach, restrooms, and a lifeguard (in season).

FISHING **Aquarius Charters Inc.** (✉ Barnstable Harbor ☎ 508/362–9617 ⊕ www.aquariussportfishing.com) supplies all gear on its 35-foot boat to catch bass, blues, tuna, and shark and offers four-, six-, and eight-hour trips for up to six people. Reservations are recommended.

WHALE- On **Hyannis Whale Watcher Cruises** out of Barnstable Harbor, a naturalist
WATCHING narrates and comments on whale sightings and the natural history of Cape Cod Bay. Trips last about four hours, there are concessions on board, and in July and August you can cruise at sunset, too. Reservations are recommended. ✉ *Millway Marina, off Phinney's La.* ☎ *508/362–6088 or 888/942–5392* ⊕ *www.whales.net* ⊒ *$26* ☉ *May–Oct.*

Shopping

Black's Handweaving Shop (✉ 597 Rte. 6A, near Rte. 149, West Barnstable ☎ 508/362–3955), in a barnlike shop with working looms, makes beautiful handwoven goods in traditional and jacquard weaves. If you don't see what you want on display, you can commission it.

Maps of Antiquity (✉ 1022 Rte. 6A, West Barnstable ☎ 508/362–7169) sells original and reproduction maps of Cape Cod, New England, and other parts of the world. Some date to the 1700s.

West Barnstable Tables (⌧ 2454 Meetinghouse Way [Rte. 149] West Barnstable ☎ 508/362–2676) has exquisite handcrafted tables, chairs, chests, and other furniture made from the finest woods.

The decor changes seasonally at **Whippletree** (⌧ 660 Rte. 6A, West Barnstable ☎ 508/362–3320 ⊕ www.thewhippletree.com), the 1779 barn where Christmas decorations and country gift items hang from the rafters year round. Goods include German nutcrackers, from Prussian soldiers to Casanovas.

Yarmouth Port

❷ *4 mi northeast of Hyannis; 21 mi east of the Sagamore Bridge; 4 mi east of Barnstable.*

Once known as Mattacheese, or "the planting lands," Yarmouth was settled in 1639 by farmers from the Plymouth Bay Colony. Yarmouth Port wasn't incorporated as a separate village until 1829. By then the Cape had begun a thriving maritime industry, and men turned to the sea to make their fortunes. Many impressive sea captains' houses—some now B&Bs and museums—still line the always-enchanting Route 6A, as well as side streets, and Yarmouth Port has some real old-time stores in town. A mile's drive north of Route 6A is the small but lovely Gray's Beach, where a boardwalk at the section called Bass Hole stretches hundreds of feet over the wide marsh and where the Callery-Darling conservation land trails loop through forest and marshland.

☼ Visit the **Edward Gorey House Museum** to explore the eccentric illustrations and offbeat humor of the late acclaimed artist in his home. The exhibitions, including displays of his drawings and rantings of oddball characters, reveal the mysterious psyche of the sometimes dark but always playful Gorey. The museum also promotes Gorey's lifelong dedication to animal welfare with interactive learning. ⌧ *8 Strawberry La.* ☎ *508/362–3909* ⊕ *www.edwardgoreyhouse.org* ☜ *$5* ⊙ *May–Sept., Wed.–Sat. 10–5, Sun. noon–5; Oct.–Apr., Thurs.–Sat. 11–4, Sun. noon–4.*

★ For a peek into the past, make a stop at **Hallet's,** a country drugstore preserved as it was in 1889, when it was opened by Thacher Hallet, the present owner's grandfather. Hallet served not only as druggist but also as postmaster and justice of the peace. At the all-marble soda fountain with swivel stools, you can order the secret-recipe ice cream soda and, in season, an inexpensive breakfast or lunch. Above Hallet's Store, the **Thacher Taylor Hallet Museum** displays photographs and memorabilia of Yarmouth Port and the Hallet family. ⌧ *139 Hallet St. (Rte. 6A)* ☎ *508/362–3362* ☜ *Donations accepted for museum* ⊙ *Apr.–mid-Nov.; call for hrs.*

The 1886 **Village Pump** (⌧ 220 Main St.), a black wrought-iron mechanism long used for drawing household water, is topped by a lantern and surrounded by ironwork with cutouts of birds and animals. In front is a stone trough that was used for watering horses. It's across from the Parnassus Book Service. The 1696 **Old Yarmouth Inn** (✉ 223 Main St. [Rte. 6A], near Summer St. ☎ 508/362–9962), near the village pump, is the Cape's oldest inn and a onetime stagecoach stop.

The **Botanical Trails of the Historical Society of Old Yarmouth,** behind the post office (✉ 231 Main St.), provides a good look at the area's flora in 50 acres of oak and pine woods and a pond, accented by blueberries, lady's slippers, Indian pipes, rhododendrons, and hollies. Stone markers and arrows point out the 2 mi of trails; you'll find trail maps in the gatehouse mailbox. Just beyond the historical society's trails, you can find **Kelley Chapel,** built in 1873 by a father for his daughter, who was grieving over the death of her child. An iron woodstove and a pump organ dominate the simple interior. ✉ *Off Main St. (Rte. 6A)* 🎟 *$1 suggested donation* ☉ *Gatehouse July–Aug., daily 1–4. Trails during daylight hrs year-round.*

The 1780 **Winslow Crocker House** is an elegantly symmetrical two-story Georgian with 12-over-12 small-pane windows and rich paneling in every room. Crocker was a well-to-do trader and land speculator; after his death, his two sons built a wall dividing the house in half. The house was moved here from West Barnstable in 1936 by Mary Thacher, who donated it—along with her collection of 17th- to 19th-century furniture, pewter, hooked rugs, and ceramics—to the Society for the Preservation of New England Antiquities, which operates it as a museum. ✉ *250 Main St. (Rte. 6A)* ☎ *508/362–3021* 🎟 *$5* ☉ *June–mid-Oct., weekends, tours at 11, 12, 1, 2 and 3.*

Built in 1840 onto an existing 1740 house for a sea captain in the China trade, then bought by another, who swapped it with a third captain, the **Captain Bangs Hallet House** is a white Greek Revival building with a hitching post out front and a weeping beech in back. The house and its contents typify a 19th-century sea captain's home, with pieces of pewter, china, nautical equipment, antique toys, and clothing on display. The kitchen has the original 1740 brick beehive oven and butter churns. ✉ *11 Strawberry La., off Rte. 6A* ☎ *508/362–3021* 🎟 *$3* ☉ *June–mid-Oct., Thurs.–Sun. 1–4, tours at 1, 2, and 3.*

Purchased in 1640 and established as a prosperous farm in the late 1700s, the **Taylor-Bray Farm** (✉ Bray Farm Rd. ☎ 508/385–6499 ⊕ www.taylorbrayfarm.org) is listed on the National Register of Historic Places. The farm is occasionally open to the public by appointment through the caretaker-tenants. Call for information. The farm has picnic tables, walking trails, and a great view of the tidal marsh.

For a scenic loop with little traffic, turn north off Route 6A in town onto Church Street or Thacher Street, then left onto Thacher Shore Road. In fall this route is especially beautiful, with its impressive stands of blazing-red burning bush. Wooded segments alternate with open views of marsh. Keep bearing right, and at the WATER STREET sign, the dirt road on the right will bring you to a wide-open view of marshland as it meets the bay. Don't drive in too far, or you may get stuck. As you come out, ❸ a right turn will take you to **Keveney Bridge,** a one-lane wooden bridge over marshy Mill Pond, and back to Route 6A.

One of Yarmouth Port's most beautiful areas is Bass Hole, which stretches from Homer's Dock Road to the salt marsh. **Bass Hole Boardwalk** (⊠ Trail entrance on Center St. near Gray's Beach parking lot) extends over a marshy creek; amid the salt marshes, vegetated wetlands, and upland woods meander the 2½-mi **Callery-Darling nature trails.** Gray's Beach is a little crescent of sand with still water good for kids—but don't go beyond the roped-in swimming area, the only section where the current isn't strong. At the end of the boardwalk, benches provide a place to relax and look out over abundant marsh life and, across the creek, the beautiful, sandy shores of Dennis's Chapin Beach. At low tide you can walk out on the flats for almost a mile. It's a far cry from the days when an 18th-century harbor here was the site of a schooner shipyard.

Where to Stay & Eat

$$–$$$$ ✕ **Abbicci.** Unassuming from the outside, Abbicci tells an entirely different story on the inside, with stunning explosions of color and a handsome black-slate bar. One of the first to bring northern Italian cooking to Cape Cod, chef-owner Marietta Hickey has remained true to the tradition and ahead of the crowd with heartier dishes in the winter months and fish and elegant pastas for summer. She prepares rich and full-tasting fare; one of the most pleasing is roast rack and grilled leg of lamb with a Cabernet mint demi-glace. ⊠ *43 Main St. (Rte. 6A)* ☎ *508/362–3501* ⊕ *www.abbiccirestaurant.com* ☐ *AE, D, DC, MC, V.*

$$–$$$ ✕ **Inaho.** Yuji Watanabe, the chef-owner of the Cape's best Japanese
Fodor'sChoice restaurant, makes early morning journeys to Boston's fish markets to
★ shop for the freshest local catch. His selection of sushi and sashimi is vast and artful, and vegetable and seafood tempura come out of the kitchen fluffy and light. If you're a teriyaki lover, you can't do any better than the chicken's beautiful blend of sweet and sour. One remarkable element of the restaurant is its artful lighting: small pinpoint lights on the food accentuate the presentation in a dramatic way. The serene and simple Japanese garden out back has a traditional koi pond. ⊠ *157 Main St. (Rte. 6A)* ☎ *508/362–5522* ☐ *MC, V* ☺ *Closed Mon. No lunch.*

$–$$$ ✕ **Old Yarmouth Inn Restaurant & Tavern.** Established in 1696, this inn—the oldest on Cape Cod—now primarily functions as a restaurant (rooms are available in season). The restaurant comprises a main dining room, which is bright and airy, and two smaller and more intimate ones, plus the wood-paneled Tavern, which has a full bar and serves more casual fare. Fresh ingredients are a priority, so the menu changes seasonally, but the wide range of meat, poultry, seafood, and pasta dishes infused with clever combinations of familiar flavors offers something for just about everyone. The Sunday brunch is popular. Reservations are recommended. ⊠ *223 Rte. 6A* ☎ *508/362–9962* ⊕ *www.oldyarmouthinn. com* ☐ *AE, D, MC, V* ☺ *Closed Mon., Jan.–May.*

$$–$$$ ▦ **Blueberry Manor.** The living room of this 19th-century Greek Revival pairs Victorian furnishings with modern amenities, including a TV–VCR, a stereo, and a stash of puzzles, games, and books. Guest-room furnishings are traditional, but there are no fussy lace treatments or curio shelves. The Lavender Room has a queen-size four-poster bed with a handmade quilt, an antique armoire, and a modern bath under the eaves. The Rose Room has an exquisitely painted queen-size bed and cheery pink walls. The Willow Garden Suite, with a loft and fireplace, accommodates up to four and is suitable for a family. The fruit from the blueberry bushes in the lush yard turns up in homemade coffee cakes and other baked goods. ⊠ *438 Main St. (Rte. 6A), 02675* ☎ *508/362–7620* 📠 *508/362–0053* ⊕ *www.blueberrymanor.com* 🛏 *3 rooms, 1 suite* ♨ *No smoking* 🖃 *AE, MC, V* ¹⊘¹ *BP.*

$$–$$$ 🏨 **Liberty Hill Inn.** Smartly but traditionally furnished common areas—including the high-ceiling parlor, the formal dining room, and the wraparound porch—are a major draw to this dignified 1825 Greek Revival house. Guest rooms in both the main building and the carriage house are filled with a mix of old-world romantic charm and modern amenities; each is uniquely decorated, and some have whirlpool tubs. Breakfast might include blueberry French toast or a frittata, and afternoon tea is also available. ⊠ *77 Main St. (Rte. 6A), 02675* ☎ *508/362–3976 or 800/821–3977* 📠 *508/362–6485* ⊕ *www.libertyhillinn.com* 🛏 *9 rooms* ♨ *Cable TV in some rooms; no kids in some rooms, no room phones, no smoking* 🖃 *AE, MC, V* ¹⊘¹ *BP.*

$$ 🏨 **Lane's End Cottage.** Owner-innkeeper Valerie Butler's house—with its English cottage garden and antiques-filled common room—indeed sits at the end of a dirt lane, moved here in 1860 by oxen to make room for the neighboring church. Each tasteful guest room has beds with firm mattresses, feather comforters, and white spreads. The first-floor Terrace Room has a fireplace and French doors that lead to a cobblestone patio. There's no air-conditioning, but the rooms have fans, and the cottage is shaded by trees. Dogs are welcome. ⊠ *268 Main St. (Rte. 6A), 02675* ☎ *508/362–5298* 🛏 *3 rooms* ♨ *Fans, library, some pets allowed; no a/c, no TV, no smoking* 🖃 *No credit cards* ¹⊘¹ *BP.*

$–$$ 🏨 **Village Inn.** Guest rooms, with wide pine floorboards, are snug in this old-fashioned 1795 sea captain's house. The Provincetown Room once served as the house's schoolroom; the original (but no longer used) light fixtures are still in place. The Wellfleet Room is tiny, but it's a great bargain for solo travelers. Families should note that the Brewster, Truro, and Hyannis rooms connect and that the first-floor Yarmouth Room is the most spacious, with its own library, bathroom with fireplace, and private entrance. The common rooms have as many books as some public libraries. Kids are welcome. ⊠ *92 Main St. (Rte. 6A)* 🖃 *Box 1, 02675* ☎ *508/362–3182* ⊕ *www.thevillageinncapecod.com* 🛏 *10 rooms, 8 with bath* ♨ *No a/c, no room phones, no TV in some rooms, no smoking* 🖃 *MC, V* ¹⊘¹ *BP.*

Nightlife & the Arts

Oliver's (⊠ 6 Bray Farm Rd., off Rte. 6A ☎ 508/362–6062) has live music in a variety of genres in its tavern on weekends year-round.

Sports & the Outdoors

BEACHES **Dennis Pond** (⊠ Off Summer St.) is a freshwater pond with a sandy beach, restrooms, and a seasonal snack bar. In season, a resident parking sticker is required.

Shopping

Cummaquid Fine Arts (✉ 4275 Rte. 6A, Cummaquid ☎ 508/362–2593) has works by contemporary resident Cape Cod artists, beautifully displayed in an old home.

Parnassus Book Service (✉ 220 Main St. [Rte. 6A] ☎ 508/362–6420), occupying a three-story 1840 former general store, has a huge selection of old and new books—Cape Cod, maritime, Americana, antiquarian, and others—and is a great place to browse. Its book stall, outside on the building's side, is open 24 hours a day and works on the honor system—tally up your purchases and leave the money in the mail slot. Parnassus also carries Robert Bateman's nature prints.

Peach Tree Designs (✉ 173 Main St. [Rte. 6A] ☎ 508/362–8317) carries home furnishings and decorative accessories, some from local craftspeople, all beautifully made.

Dennis

❺ *4½ mi north of South Yarmouth; 4 mi east of Yarmouth Port; 5 mi north of Dennisport.*

The backstreets of Dennis still retain the colonial charm of seafaring days. The town was named for the Reverend Josiah Dennis and incorporated in 1793. There were 379 sea captains living in Dennis when fishing, salt making, and shipbuilding were the main industries, and the elegant houses they constructed—now museums and B&Bs—still line the streets. In 1816 Dennis resident Henry Hall discovered that adding sand to his cranberry fields' soil improved the quality and quantity of the fruit. The following decades saw cranberry farming and tourism become the Cape's main commercial enterprises. Dennis has a number of conservation areas and nature trails and numerous freshwater ponds for swimming. The village center has antiques shops, general stores, a post office, and ice cream shops. There's also a village green with a bandstand, which hosts occasional summer concerts.

West Dennis and Dennisport, off Route 28 on the south shore of the Cape (the triceps, if you will), are covered separately below.

The **Josiah Dennis Manse,** a saltbox house with add-ons, was built in 1736 for the Reverend Josiah Dennis. Inside, the home reflects life in Reverend Dennis's day. A child's room includes antique furniture and toys, the keeping room has a fireplace and cooking utensils, and the attic exhibits spinning and weaving equipment. Throughout you'll see china, pewter, and portraits of sea captains. The Maritime Wing has ship models, paintings, and nautical artifacts. On the grounds is a 1770 one-room schoolhouse, furnished with wood-and-wrought-iron desks and chairs. ✉ *77 Nobscussett Rd., at Whig St.* ☎ *508/385–2232* ⌨ *Donations accepted* ☉ *Late June–Sept., Tues. 10–noon, Thurs. 2–4.*

❻ On a clear day, from the top of **Scargo Tower,** you'll have unbeatable views of Scargo Lake, the village's scattered houses below, Cape Cod Bay, and distant Provincetown. A wooden tower built on this site in 1874 was one of the Cape's first tourist attractions; visitors would pay 5¢ to climb to the top for the views. That tower burned down, and the present all-stone 30-foot tower was built in 1901 to replace it. Winding stairs bring you to the top; don't forget to read the unsightly, but amusing, graffiti on the way up. Expect crowds at sunrise and sunset. ⊠ *Scargo Hill Rd., off Rte. 6A or Old Bass River Rd.* ⚐ *Free* ☉ *Daily sunrise–sunset.*

need a break?

Dip into homemade ice cream and frozen yogurt at the **Ice Cream Smuggler** (⊠ 716 Main St. [Rte. 6A] ☎ 508/385–5307), across the street from the town green and cemetery.

For Broadway-style dramas, comedies, and musicals, as well as kids' plays, you can attend a production at the **Cape Playhouse,** the oldest professional summer theater in the country. In 1927 Raymond Moore, who had been working with a theatrical troupe in Provincetown, bought an 1838 former Unitarian Meeting House and converted it into a theater. The original pews still serve as seats. The opening performance was *The Guardsman,* starring Basil Rathbone; other stars who performed here in the early days, some in their professional stage debuts, include Bette Davis (who first worked here as an usher), Gregory Peck, Lana Turner, Ginger Rogers, Humphrey Bogart, Tallulah Bankhead, and Henry Fonda, who appeared with his then-unknown 20-year-old daughter, Jane. Cape resident Shirley Booth was such an admirer of the Playhouse that she donated her Oscar (for *Come Back Little Sheba*) and her Emmy (for *Hazel*) to the theater; both are on display in the lobby during the season. Behind-the-scene tours are also given in season; call for a schedule. The Playhouse offers children's theater on Friday morning during July and August. Also on the 26-acre property, now known as the Cape Playhouse Center for the Arts, are a restaurant, the **Cape Museum of Fine Arts,** and the **Cape Cinema,** whose exterior was designed in the style of the Congregational church in Centerville. Inside, a 6,400-square-foot mural of heavenly skies—designed by Massachusetts artist Rockwell Kent, who also designed the gold-sunburst curtain—covers the ceiling. ⊠ *820 Main St. (Rte. 6A)* ☎ *508/385–3911 or 877/385–3911* ⊕ *www.capeplayhouse.com* ☉ *Call for tour schedule.*

need a break?

Indulge in sumptuous baked goods at **Buckie's Biscotti** (⊠ 780 Main St. [Rte. 6A] ☎ 508/385–4700 ⊕ www.buckiesbiscotti.com), just behind the Dennis Post Office near the **Cape Playhouse.** Have a slice of pie—try the Italian homestyle ricotta or the key lime, arguably the Cape's best—or another tasty treat, then wash it all down with a cappuccino or latté.

The **Cape Museum of Fine Arts** has a permanent collection of more than 850 works by Cape-associated artists. Important pieces include a portrait of a fisherman's wife by Charles Hawthorne, the father of the Provincetown art colony; a 1924 portrait of a Portuguese fisherman's daughter by William Paxton, one of the first artists to summer in Provincetown; a collection of wood-block prints by Varujan Boghosian, a member of Provincetown's Long Point Gallery cooperative; an oil sketch by Karl Knaths, who painted in Provincetown from 1919 until his death in 1971; and works by abstract expressionist Hans Hoffman and many of his students. The museum also hosts film festivals, lectures, art classes, and trips. On Wednesday from 10 AM to 1 PM, admission is free (but donations are accepted). ☒ *60 Hope La., on grounds of Cape Playhouse, off Rte. 6A* ☎ *508/385–4477* ⊕ *www.cmfa.org* ☜ *$7* ☉ *Late May–mid-Oct., Mon.–Sat. 10–5, Sun. noon–5; mid-Oct.–Jan. and early Apr. to late May, Tues.–Sat. 11–5, Sun. noon–5, Jan. to early Apr., Mon.–Sat. 10–4, Sun. noon–4.*

Where to Stay & Eat

$$–$$$$ ✕ **Red Pheasant.** This is one of the Cape's best cozy country inns, with
Fodor'sChoice a consistently good kitchen, where hearty American food is prepared
★ with elaborate sauces and herb combinations. For instance, rack of lamb is served with an intense port-and-rosemary reduction, and exquisitely grilled veal chops come with a dense red wine and portobello mushroom sauce. In fall look for the specialty game dishes, including venison and quail. Try to reserve a table in the more intimate Garden Room. The expansive wine list is excellent. Men may want to wear a jacket. ☒ *905 Main St. (Rte. 6A)* ☎ *508/385–2133 or 800/480–2133* ⊕ *www.redpheasantinn.com* ☜ *Reservations essential* ▤ *D, MC, V* ☉ *No lunch.*

$$–$$$ ✕ **Gina's by the Sea.** Some places are less than the sum of their parts; Gina's is more. The funky old building is tucked into a sand dune, so that the aroma of fine northern Italian cooking blends with a fresh breeze off the bay. The dining room is tasteful, cozy, and especially wonderful in fall when the fireplace is blazing. Blackboard specials could include angel-hair pasta or linguine with clams. If you don't want a long wait, come early or late. An enthusiastic staff rounds out the experience. ☒ *134 Taunton Ave.* ☎ *508/385–3213* ☜ *Reservations not accepted* ▤ *AE, MC, V* ☉ *Closed Dec.–Mar. and Mon.–Wed. Oct.–Nov.*

★ **$$–$$$** ✕ **Scargo Café.** With the Cape Playhouse right across the street, this café is a favorite before- and after-show haunt. There's plenty of seafood on the menu, like the "seafood romance" with clams, scallops, and shrimp, but carnivores can also take delight, with such dishes as ginger duckling, rack of lamb, and twin filet mignons. Lighter meals include scallops harpooned on a skewer and tucked in bacon and an Asian-style fish sandwich served with seaweed salad. An added plus: the kitchen stays open until 11 PM in summer. ☒ *799 Main St. (Rte. 6A)* ☎ *508/385–8200* ⊕ *www.scargocafe.com* ▤ *AE, D, MC, V.*

$–$$ ✕ **Cap'n Frosty's.** A great stop after the beach, this is where locals go to
Fodor'sChoice get their fried seafood. The modest joint has a regular menu that includes
★ ice cream, a small specials board, and a counter where you order and take a number written on a french fries box. The staff is young and hard working, pumping out fresh fried clams and fish-and-chips on paper plates. All frying is done in 100% canola oil, and rice pilaf is offered as a substitute for fries. There's seating inside as well as outside on a shady brick patio. ☒ *219 Main St. (Rte. 6A)* ☎ *508/385–8548* ☜ *Reservations not accepted* ▤ *No credit cards* ☉ *Closed early Sept.–Mar.*

¢ ✕ **Red Cottage Restaurant.** Up Old Bass River Road just ½-mi north of
Fodor'sChoice the town hall, the Red Cottage is indeed a red cottage and serves break-
★ fast and lunch year-round. Locals pack this place even in the off-sea-

son and you can expect a wait in the summer. The cottage is a no-frills, friendly place with food that runs the gamut from decadent stuffed french toast specials to a list of health-conscious offerings with egg whites, "lite" cheese and turkey bacon. The grill is in plain view; if you want to watch your meal being cooked, the swivel stools at the counter have the best angle. Bottomless cups of coffee are served in an interesting collection of mismatched mugs. The breakfasts are better than the lunches, but both are no-nonsense and just plain reliably good. ⊠ *36 Old Bass River Rd.* ☎ *508/394–2923* ♠ *Reservations not accepted* ⊟ *No credit cards* ◌ *No dinner.*

¢ ✕ **Grumpy's Restaurant.** In 2004 Grumpy's expanded its restaurant to pack in more tables and counter space to meet year-round demand. From baked goods to waffles and eggs done any way you like them, Grumpy's jump-starts your day with generous portions for breakfast and lunch. Get there early to avoid a line that often curls out the door. ⊠ *1408 Rte. 6A* ☎ *508/385–2911* ♠ *Reservations not accepted* ⊟ *No credit cards* ◌ *No dinner.*

$$–$$$$ ▥ **Scargo Manor.** This 1895 sea captain's home has a prime location on Scargo Lake, with a private beach and dock. Inside, innkeepers Larry and Debbie Bain display a collection of art and antiques amidst the Victorian furnishings. There's plenty of room to spread out on the big screened porch, in the sitting room or more formal living room, or in the cozy third-floor reading room. If you want a lake view, choose the cozy all-blue Hydrangea Room, with a pineapple-top four-poster bed and a skylight overhead. For more space, the Captain Howe's Suite has a king-size canopy bed, plus a separate sitting room with a working fireplace that's bigger than the guest rooms at many other B&Bs. Kids are welcome. ⊠ *909 Main St. (Rte. 6A), 02638* ☎ *508/385–5534 or 800/ 595–0034* ⊟ *508/385–9791* ⊕ *www.scargomanor.com* ⇆ *4 rooms, 2 suites* ♿ *Cable TV, beach, boating, bicycles; no room phones, no smoking, no pets* ⊟ *AE, D, DC, MC, V* ⫶⊙⫶ *BP.*

$$–$$$ ▥ **Isaiah Hall B&B Inn.** Lilacs and pink roses trail along the white picket fence outside this historic 1857 Greek Revival farmhouse on a quiet residential road near the bay. Innkeepers Jerry and Judy Neal set the scene for a romantic getaway with guest rooms that have country antiques, floral-print wallpapers, and such homey touches as quilts and Priscilla curtains. In the attached carriage house, rooms have three walls stenciled white and one knotty pine, and some have small balconies overlooking a wooded lawn with gardens, grape arbors, and berry bushes. The carriage-house suite has a king-size bed, a separate sitting area with a pullout couch, and a refrigerator. Common areas such as the dining room are elegant. Make-it-yourself popcorn, tea, coffee, and soft drinks are always available. ⊠ *152 Whig St.* ⊡ *Box 1007, 02638* ☎ *508/ 385–9928 or 800/736–0160* ⊟ *508/385–5879* ⊕ *www.isaiahhallinn. com* ⇆ *9 rooms, 1 suite* ♿ *Picnic area, in-room data ports, in-room VCRs, badminton, croquet; no kids under 7, no smoking, no pets* ⊟ *AE, D, MC, V* ⫶⊙⫶ *CP.*

FodorŝChoice
★

Nightlife & the Arts

The oldest professional summer theater in the country is the **Cape Playhouse** (⊠ 820 Main St. [Rte. 6A] ☎ 508/385–3911 or 877/385–3911

⊕ www.capeplayhouse.com), an 1838 former Unitarian Meeting House, where top stars appear each summer. The playhouse also mounts kid's shows on Friday morning in July and August. On the grounds of the Cape Playhouse is the artsy **Cape Cinema** (☎ 508/385–2503 ⊕ www. capecinema.com), which shows foreign and first-run films throughout the summer.

Lost Dog Pub (⊠ 1374 Rte. 134 ☎ 508/385–6177) offers basic pub eats and a relaxed social atmosphere, and is a popular place for locals and visitors to grab a beer after a long day.

The **Nau-Sets** (⊠ Dennis Senior Center, Rte. 134 ☎ 508/255–9327 or 508/430–9929 ✍ 6$) holds weekly square dances on Tuesday.

Reel Art (⊠ 60 Hope La. ☎ 508/385–4477) at the Cape Museum of Fine Arts shows avant-garde, classic, art, and independent films on weekends September through April. Call for a schedule.

Sports & the Outdoors

BEACHES Parking at all Dennis beaches is $10 a day in season for nonresidents.

Chapin Beach (⊠ Chapin Beach Rd.) is a lovely dune-backed bay beach with long tidal flats so you can walk far out at low tide. It has no lifeguards or services.

Corporation Beach (⊠ Corporation Rd.) has lifeguards, showers, restrooms, and a food stand. At one time a packet landing owned by a corporation of the townsfolk, the beautiful crescent of white sand backed by low dunes now serves a decidedly noncorporate use as a public beach.

Mayflower Beach (⊠ Dunes Rd. off Bayview Rd.) at low tide reveals hundreds of feet of tidal flats. The beach has restrooms, showers, lifeguards, and a food stand.

For freshwater swimming, **Scargo Lake** (⊠ Access off Rte. 6A or Scargo Hill Rd.) has two beaches with restrooms, playgrounds, and a picnic area. The sandy-bottom lake is shallow along the shore, which is good for kids. It's surrounded by woods and is stocked for fishing.

BIKING A guidebook published by the Dennis Chamber of Commerce includes bike tours and maps. You can rent bikes from a number of places along the 25-mi Cape Cod Rail Trail. **Barbara's Bike Shop** (⊠ 430 Rte. 134 ☎ 508/760–4723) is at the Rail Trail entrance.

You can pick up the Cape Cod Rail Trail at several points along its path. In fact, riding the entire trail in one day doesn't do justice to its sights and side trips (though it certainly can be done). Many bicyclists, especially those with small kids, prefer the piecemeal method since they can relax and enjoy the sights—and not turn their legs into jelly.

The ride in Dennis starts as a flat, straight spin through a small pine forest, a good warming-up exercise. Your first road crossing is at busy Great Western Road, one of the town's major thoroughfares, after which you'll pass Sand Pond and Flax Pond in Harwich. The Dennis part of the trail is short, but it's worth starting here for the ample parking at

CloseUp

RIDING THE RAIL TRAIL

N THE LATE 1800S visitors to Cape Cod could take the train from Boston all the way to Provincetown. But with the construction of the Sagamore and Bourne bridges in the mid-1930s, the age of the automobile truly arrived on the Cape. Today, although passenger trains no longer serve Cape Cod, the former train paths provide another, more leisurely way to explore the Cape—by bicycle. For many people, riding the trail through the fragrant woods is as quintessential a Cape experience as leaping into the cold Atlantic on a dune-backed beach.

The Cape's premier bike path, the Cape Cod Rail Trail, was constructed in 1978 and extended in the mid-1990s and now offers a scenic ride from South Dennis to South Wellfleet. Following the paved right-of-way of the old Penn Central Railroad, it's 25 mi long, passing salt marshes, cranberry bogs, ponds, and Nickerson State Park, which has its own path.

Some serious bikers whiz along at top speed, but that's not the only way to travel. Along the way there are plenty of tempting places to veer off to spend an hour or two on the beach, to stop for lunch or ice cream, or just to smell the pine trees and imagine what the Cape looked like years ago. The terrain is easy to moderate in difficulty and is generally quite flat, making it great for youngsters.

The trail starts at the parking lot off busy Route 134 south of U.S. 6, near Theophilus Smith Road in South Dennis, a far-from-scenic place that will make you appreciate the trail even more. It ends at the post office in South Wellfleet. The Dennis Chamber of Commerce will give you a free rail trail map with distance markings to various points along the trail. It also notes the location of parking lots en route if you want to cover only a segment: in Harwich (across from Pleasant Lake Store on

Pleasant Lake Avenue), in Brewster (at Nickerson State Park), and in Eastham (at the Salt Pond Visitor Center). Several bike shops near the trail in Dennis, Brewster, and Eastham can also provide information as well as convenient rentals.

If you want to ride the entire length and back in one day, you're in for a long ride. Experienced rail-trailers suggest doing the trail in segments, perhaps starting in the middle near Nickerson State Park and looping to one end and back. If you want to return to your starting point by public transportation, the easiest way is to start in Dennis, ride to Orleans, and catch the bike-rack-equipped H2O Line bus back to Dennis; contact the Cape Cod Regional Transit Authority for a schedule and route information.

The Cape Cod Rail Trail is popular with in-line skaters and pedestrians as well as bicyclists. Remember that wheels yield to heels, so cyclists should give walkers the right of way. Pass slower traffic on the left, and call out a warning before you pass. Kids under 13 must wear helmets. The trail can get crowded at times, especially in summer; if you prefer solitude (or cooler temperatures), set out earlier in the morning or later in the afternoon.

Busy bike trails share the same fate as roads: maintenance projects and expansion. A 3-mi spur leads from the rail trail through Harwich to the Chatham line; eventually this spur will go into Chatham center. Also in the works are plans to extend the trail westward into Yarmouth. **Nickerson State Park** (☎ 508/896–3491 ⊕ www.state.ma.us/mhd/paths/webrt. htm) maintains the rail trail; to view a map of the route before you leave home, go to their Web site.

— By Carolyn Heller

the trail's entrance and for the several bike-rental places that set up shop on Route 134.

FISHING Sesuit Harbor, on the bay side of Dennis off Route 6A, is busy with fishing and pleasure boats. Several are available for fishing charters. The **Bluefish** (⊠ Sesuit Harbor ☐ Box 113, Dennis 02638 ☎ 508/385–7265 ⊕ www.sunsol.com/bluefish) makes four-, six-, and eight-hour trips. The **LAD-NAV** (⊠ Sesuit Harbor ☐ Box 2002, East Dennis 02641 ☎ 508/385–8150 ⊕ www.lad-nav.com) takes as many as six anglers per trip on a 36-foot fishing vessel.

Shopping

Antiques Center of Cape Cod (⊠ 243 Rte. 6A ☎ 508/385–6400) is a large and busy market populated by more than 160 dealers offering furniture, artwork, jewelry, china, clocks, books, antique dolls, and other collectibles.

Armchair Bookstore (⊠ 619 Main St. [Rte. 6A] ☎ 508/385–0900) carries a large selection of new releases, plus numerous books about Cape lore, history, and sights. Also on hand are cards and knickknacks and a kid's section with books, games, and toys.

Emily's Beach Barn (⊠ 708 Main St. [Rte. 6A] ☎ 508/385–8328) has fashionable women's beachwear, from bathing suits and wraps to sun hats and summer dresses and tops.

★ **Robert C. Eldred Co.** (⊠ 1483 Main St. [Rte. 6A] East Dennis ☎ 508/385–3116 ⊕ www.eldreds.com) holds more than two dozen auctions per year, dealing in Americana; estate jewelry; top-quality antiques; marine, Asian, American, and European art; tools; and dolls. Its "general antiques and accessories" auctions put less-expensive wares on the block.

Ross Coppelman, Goldsmith. (⊠ 1439 Rte. 6A, East Dennis ☎ 508/385–7900 ⊕ www.rosscoppelman.com). Peek into the tiny workshop as you enter this showroom and you can get a sense of how handcrafted Ross Coppelman's designs truly are. For more than 30 years, the self-taught goldsmith has been designing rings, necklaces, and other original jewelry out of high-karat gold, semiprecious gemstones, and other materials. Customized wedding bands are a popular specialty.

Fodor'sChoice **Scargo Pottery** (⊠ 30 Dr. Lord's Rd. S, off Rte. 6A ☎ 508/385–3894
★ ⊕ www.scargopottery.com) is in a pine forest, where potter Harry Holl's unusual wares—such as his signature castle birdhouses—sit on tree stumps and hang from branches. Inside are the workshop and kiln, plus work by Holl's four daughters. With luck you can catch a potter at the wheel; viewing is, in fact, encouraged.

Cotuit

❽ *9 mi southwest of Barnstable; 2½ mi southeast of Mashpee.*

Once called Cotuit Port, this charming little town was formed around seven homesteads belonging to the family of 18th-century trader Winslow Crocker. Much of the town lies along and just south of Route 28, west of Osterville and east of Mashpee, and its center is not much more than a crossroads with a post office, old-time coffee shop, local pizza parlor, and general store, which all seem unchanged since the 1940s. Large waterfront estates line sections of Main Street and Ocean View Drive, where small coves hide the uncrowded Loop Beach and Ropes Beach. It's best to get to the beaches by bike, since traffic is light and beach parking is for residents only.

The **Cahoon Museum of American Art** is in one of the old Crocker family buildings, a 1775 Georgian colonial farmhouse that was once a tavern and an overnight way station for travelers on the Hyannis–Sandwich stagecoach line. Displays include selections from the permanent collection of American primitive paintings by Ralph and Martha Cahoon along with other 19th- and early 20th-century artists. Special exhibitions, classes, talks, and demonstrations are held throughout the summer. ⊠ *4676 Falmouth Rd. (Rte. 28)* ☎ *508/428–7581* ⊕ *www. cahoonmuseum.org* ⊡ *$3* ☉ *Feb.–Dec., Tues.–Sat. 10–4.*

The first motor-driven fire-fighting apparatus on Cape Cod, a 1916 Model T chemical fire engine, is in the **Santuit-Cotuit Historical Society Museum,** behind the **Samuel Dottridge Homestead,** which itself dates from the early 1800s. ⊠ *1148 Main St.* ☎ *508/428–0461* ⊡ *Free* ☉ *Mid-June–mid-Oct., Thurs.–Sun. 2:30–5.*

Cotuit Library (⊠ 871 Main St. ☎ 508/428–8141 ⊕ www.library.cotuit. ma.us) has a noncirculating set of luxurious leather-bound classics.

Where to Stay & Eat

$$$–$$$$ ✕ **Regatta of Cotuit.** This restaurant is in a restored colonial stagecoach inn filled with wood, brass, and Oriental carpets. The classic yet original fare includes pâtés of rabbit, veal, and venison and a signature seared loin of lamb with cabernet sauce, surrounded by chèvre, spinach, and pine nuts. Chef Heather Allen's signature premium fillet of buffalo tenderloin is prepared differently each night, with seasonal starches and vegetables. The cozy taproom has its own bar menu. ⊠ *4631 Falmouth Rd. (Rte. 28)* ☎ *508/428–5715* ⊕ *www.regattaofcotuit.com* ⌔ *Reservations essential* ⊟ *AE, MC, V.*

¢ ✕ **The Mills.** With just 20 tables and a six-seat lunch counter, this busy breakfast and lunch spot has local and imported fans lining up to sample *linguica* (sausage) and cheese omelets, blueberry or cranberry pancakes, and thick-cut (and intriguingly named) Texas French toast. The Mills also serves up fresh baked muffins, scones, and breads. Lunch is homemade soups and sandwiches, including burgers and veggie burgers. ⊠ *Rte. 149, just north of Cotuit, Marstons Mills* ☎ *508/428–9814* ⊕ *www.millsrestaurant.com* ⊟ *No credit cards* ☉ *No dinner Sat.–Thurs.*

$$$ ⌂ **Josiah Sampson House.** Guest rooms in this 1793 Federal-style home have canopy beds, needlepoint rugs, antiques, and air-conditioning. Hannah's Room, the most spacious, has a queen-size four-poster bed, built-in window seats, and a massive working fireplace. Upstairs, the Sampson Room has an extra-large bathroom and a view of the backyard. Tennis privileges ($10 for 1½ hours) are available at the Kings Grant

Racquet Club next door. ⊠ *40 Old Kings Rd., off Main St.* ⅅ *Box 226, 02635* ☎ *508/428–8383 or 877/574–6873* 🖷 *508/428–0116* ⊕ *www. josiahsampson.com* ⇨ *6 rooms, 1 suite* ⚭ *Outdoor hot tub, bicycles; no room phones, no room TVs, no kids under 10, no smoking* ⊟ *AE, MC, V* ⏁◎ *BP.*

Sports & the Outdoors
The **Cotuit Kettleers** of the collegiate Cape Cod Baseball League play home games at **Lowell Park** (⊠ Lowell St., 2 mi south of Rte. 28 ☎ 508/428–3358 ⊕ www.kettleers.org) from mid-June to mid-August.

Shopping
The **Sow's Ear Antique Company** (⊠ 4698 Rte. 28 ☎ 508/428–4931), in a house that dates from the late 1600s next to the Cahoon Museum, specializes in folk art—dolls, ship's models, wood carvings, antique quilts, and paintings.

Osterville

❾ *3 mi east of Cotuit; 7 mi southwest of Barnstable.*

A wealthy Barnstable enclave southwest of the town center, Osterville is lined with elegant waterfront houses, some of which are large "cottages" built in the 19th century, when the area became popular with a monied set. You'll find that most beaches in the village, including the impressive **Dowses Beach,** are restricted to residents-only parking. Despite its haute homes, the village of Osterville retains the small-town charm that permeates the Cape; its Main Street and Wianno Avenue area houses a collection of trendy boutiques and jewelry shops mixed with a library, a post office, and country stores. The village's festivals of Daff O'ville Day (late April) and Christmas Stroll (mid-December) are heavily attended.

The **Osterville Historical Society Museum,** in an 1824 sea captain's house, has antiques, dolls, and exhibits on Osterville's history. Two wooden-boat museums, each showcasing various sailing vessels, as well as the Cammett House (dating from the late 18th century) are also on the property. ⊠ *155 W. Bay Rd.* ☎ *508/428–5861* ⊠ *$2* ◷ *Late June–Oct., Thurs.–Sun. 1:30–4:30.*

> **need a break?**
>
> **Gone Chocolate** (⊠ 858 Main St. ☎ 508/420–0202) will tempt you with old-fashioned chocolate-pecan turtles, saltwater taffy, ice cream, and other confections.

Where to Eat
$$–$$$$ ✕ **Five Bays Bistro.** With its stylish feel and creative menu, this contemporary bistro wouldn't be out of place in Boston or Manhattan. Dishes such as Asian spring rolls or tuna with wasabi sauce draw inspiration from the East, while others—perhaps a linguine, duck, and artichoke appetizer or an entrée of seared halibut with shallot risotto—have more of a Mediterranean flavor. If you wear black, you won't clash with the eclectic artwork on the bright yellow walls. ⊠ *825 Main St.* ☎ *508/ 420–5559* ⊟ *AE, D, MC, V* ◷ *No lunch.*

$$–$$$ ✕ **Wimpy's.** No, this is not a fast-food hamburger joint but a Cape standby with an extensive menu that favors Italian food and fried fish, from chicken piccata to a seafood platter. Wimpy's numerous and loyal clientele fills a big family dining room, a sunny atrium, and a dark traditional tavern that has cozy booths and a fine old bar. Opt for the more inventive specials such as tortilla-crusted salmon topped in a caper sauce or a simple prime rib (when available). You can get takeout here, too. ⊠ *752 Main St.* ☎ *508/428–6300, 508/428–3474 takeout* ▭ *AE, DC, MC, V.*

Sports & the Outdoors

Holly Hill Farm (⊠ 240 Flint St., Marstons Mills ☎ 508/428–2621 ⊕ www.hollyhillstable.com) offers horseback-riding instruction and day camp but no trail rides.

Shopping

★ **Oak & Ivory** (⊠ 1112 Main St. ☎ 508/428–9425 ⊕ www.oakandivory. com) specializes in Nantucket lightship baskets made on the premises, as well as gold miniature baskets and scrimshaw. China, gold jewelry, and other gifts round out the selection.

Centerville

🔟 *2½ mi northeast of Osterville; 4 mi southwest of Barnstable.*

Centerville was once a busy seafaring town, a history evident in the 50 or so shipbuilders' and sea captains' houses along its quiet, tree-shaded streets. Offering the pleasures of sheltered ocean beaches on Nantucket Sound, such as **Craigville Beach,** and of freshwater swimming in Lake Wequaquet, it has been a popular vacation area since the mid-19th century. Shoot Flying Hill Road, named by Native Americans, is the highest point of land on the Cape, with panoramic views of Plymouth and Provincetown to the north and of Falmouth and Hyannis to the south.

In a 19th-century house, the **Centerville Historical Society Museum** has furnished period rooms, Sandwich glass, miniature carvings of birds by Anthony Elmer Crowell, models of ships, marine artifacts, military uniforms and artifacts, antique tools, perfume bottles (dating from 1760 to 1920), historic costumes and quilts, and a research library. Each summer there are special costume exhibits or other shows. ⊠ *513 Main St.* ☎ *508/ 775–0331* ▣ *$4* ⊙ *June–Oct., Mon.–Sat. noon–5.*

The **1856 Country Store** (⊠ 555 Main St. ☎ 508/775–1856 or 888/750–1856 ⊕ www.1856countrystore.com) still sells penny candy, except that these days each candy costs at least 25 pennies. The store also carries newspapers, coffee, crafts, jams, and all kinds of gadgets and toys. You can sip your coffee—and take a political stance—by choosing a wooden bench out front, one marked DEMOCRAT and the other REPUBLICAN.

need a break? Sample a variety of creamy homemade flavors at **Four Seas Ice Cream** (⊠ 360 S. Main St. ☎ 508/775–1394 ⊕ www. fourseasicecream.com), a tradition for generations of summer visitors. It's open from late May to mid-September until 10:30 PM.

The **Centerville Library** (✉ 585 Main St. ☎ 508/790–6220 ⊕ www.centervillelibrary.org) has a 42-volume noncirculating set of transcripts of the Nuremberg Trials.

Where to Stay

$$–$$$ ▦ **Tradewinds Inn.** This 6-acre property, overlooking the Atlantic Ocean and Lake Elizabeth, has large, family-friendly ocean-view rooms. There are also three efficiencies with fully equipped kitchenettes (refrigerator, stove, microwave, and cooking utensils), but skip the less attractive non-water-view rooms in the detached buildings. The furnishings are simple but appealing, including whitewashed furniture and floral quilts. A small, sandy beach is down the path from the main lodge. The wicker-festooned, knotty-pine-paneled lobby has a fireplace and a cocktail bar. ✉ 780 Craigville Beach Rd. ⌖ Box 477, 02632 ☎ 508/775–0365 or 877/444–7966 🖷 508/790–1404 ⊕ www.twicapecod.com ⤳ 28 rooms, 4 suites, 3 efficiencies ⌂ Some kitchenettes, cable TV, putting green, beach, lobby lounge; no smoking ▭ AE, MC, V ⊗ Closed Nov.–Apr. ⦿⦿ CP.

Sports & the Outdoors

Craigville Beach, on Craigville Beach Road, is a long, wide strand that is extremely popular with the collegiate crowd. The beach has lifeguards, showers, restrooms, and there's food nearby. A $10 parking fee is charged in summer.

Many road races are held in season, and the **Hyannis Sprint I Triathlon** (☎ 508/477–6311) takes place at Craigville Beach in early summer.

Hyannis

❶–❶ *3½ mi east of Centerville; 23 mi east of the Bourne Bridge.*

Hyannis was named for the Native American Sachem Iyanno, who sold the area for £20 and two pairs of pants. Perhaps he would have sold it for far more had there been any indication that Hyannis would become known as the "home port of Cape Cod" or that the Kennedys would have pitched so many tents here. Hyannis is effectively the transportation center of the Cape; it's near the airport, and ferries depart here for Nantucket and (in season) Martha's Vineyard. The busy roads feeding into the town are lined with big-box stores you'll find anywhere.

A bustling year-round hub of activity, Hyannis has the Cape's largest concentration of businesses, shops, malls, hotels and motels, restaurants, and entertainment venues. Main Street is lined with used-book and gift shops, jewelers, clothing stores, summer-wear and T-shirt shops, and ice-cream and candy stores, but the street can have a somewhat forlorn, down-at-the-heels feeling, as the malls outside downtown have taken their toll on business. There are, however, plenty of good eateries, both fun and fancy.

Perhaps best known for its association with the Kennedy clan, the Hyannis area was also a vacation site for President Ulysses S. Grant in 1874 and later for President Grover Cleveland. Hyannis is making an effort to preserve its historical connection with the sea. By 1840 more than 200 shipmasters had established homes in the Hyannis–Hyannis

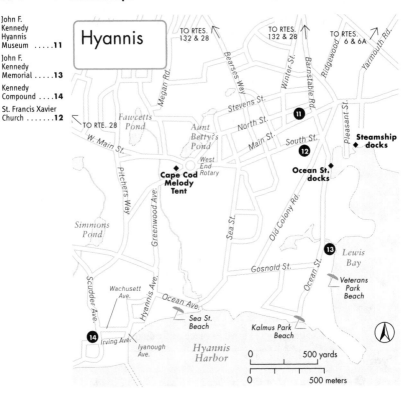

Port area. Aselton Park (at the intersection of South and Ocean streets) and the Village Green on Main Street are the sites of events celebrating this history, and Aselton Park marks the starting point of the scenic Walkway to the Sea, which extends to the dock area.

Three parallel streets run through the heart of town. Busy, shop-filled Main Street runs one-way from east to west; South Street runs from west to east; and North Street is open to two-way traffic. The airport rotary connects with heavily trafficked Routes 132 and 28 and with U.S. 6. Off Ocean Street and Sea Street lie several excellent beaches, including Kalmus Park Beach, renowned for its stiff winds and hordes of windsurfers, and the smaller Veterans Park Beach, next to the Kennedy Memorial.

⓫ In Main Street's Old Town Hall, the **John F. Kennedy Hyannis Museum** explores JFK's Cape years (1934–63) through enlarged and annotated photographs culled from the archives of the JFK Library near Boston, as well as a seven-minute video narrated by Walter Cronkite. The gift shop sells mugs, T-shirts, and presidential memorabilia. ⊠ *397 Main St., Downtown Hyannis* ☎ *508/790–3077* ☜ *$5* ☉ *Mid-Apr.–Oct., Mon.–Sat. 9–5, Sun. and holidays noon–5; Nov.- early Dec., mid-Feb.–mid-Apr., Thurs.–Sat. 10–4, Sun. and holidays noon–4.*

⑫ The **St. Francis Xavier Church** (✉ 347 South St., Downtown Hyannis ☎ 508/771–7200 ⊕ www.sfxp.org) is where Rose Kennedy and her family worshiped during their summers on the Cape; the pew that John F. Kennedy used regularly is marked by a plaque.

Beyond the bustling docks where waterfront restaurants draw crowds and where ferries, harbor tour boats, and deep-sea fishing vessels come **⑬** and go, the quiet esplanade by the **John F. Kennedy Memorial** (✉ Off Ocean St. south of Channel Point, Hyannis Harbor) overlooks boat-filled Lewis Bay. JFK loved to sail these waters, and in 1966 the people of Barnstable erected a plaque and fountain pool here in his memory. Adjacent to the memorial is **Veterans Park,** with a beach, a tree-shaded picnic and barbecue area, and a playground.

Hyannis Port became a hot spot for Americans during the Kennedy pres-**⑭** idency, when the **Kennedy Compound** became the summer White House. The days of hordes of Secret Service men and swarms of tourists trampling down the bushes are gone, and the area is once again a community of quietly posh estates, though the Kennedy mystique is such that tourists still seek it out. The best way to get a glimpse of the compound is from the water on one of the many harbor tours or cruises.

Joseph P. and Rose Kennedy bought their house here—the largest one, closest to the water—in 1929 as a healthful place to summer with their soon-to-be-nine kids. (Son Ted bought the house before his mother's death in 1995.) Sons Jack and Bobby bought neighboring houses in the 1950s. Jack's is the one at the corner of Scudder and Irving, with the 6-foot-high stockade fence on two sides. Bobby's is next to it, with the white fieldstone chimney. Ted bought a home on Squaw Island, a private island connected to the area by a causeway at the end of Scudder Avenue. It now belongs to his ex-wife, Joan. Eunice (Kennedy) and Sargent Shriver have a house near Squaw Island, on Atlantic Avenue.

The compound is relatively self-sufficient in terms of entertainment: Rose Kennedy's former abode (with 14 rooms and nine baths) has a movie theater, a private beach, a boat dock, a swimming pool, a tennis court, and a sports field that was the scene of the famous Kennedy touch-football matches. Maria Shriver, Caroline Kennedy Schlossberg, and other family members have had their wedding receptions here. In the summer of 1999 family members waited here, with local and international media lining the streets, for confirmation of John F. Kennedy Jr.'s death in a plane crash off Martha's Vineyard. He and his wife, Carolyn Bessette Kennedy, were flying her sister, Lauren Bessette, to the Vineyard before continuing on to a cousin's wedding in Hyannis; all three were killed.

Hyannis Public Library (✉ 401 Main St., Downtown Hyannis ☎ 508/775–2280) has a case full of books on JFK.

☙ Perfect for a rainy day, **Smith Family Amusement** is replete with bowling lanes, video-game rooms, and that old seaside favorite, Skee-ball. ✉ *441 Main St., Downtown Hyannis* ☎ *508/775–3411* ☉ *Daily; hrs vary.*

A VISIT TO THE GRAY LADY

NANTUCKET HOLDS THE DISTINCTION of being the only place in the United States where an island, town, and county have the same name. The island of Nantucket is a one- to two-hour trip south of Hyannis or Harwich Port by ferry, and its historic homes, stunning beaches, and rolling moors that make it an aesthetic world unto itself. In summer, the 3- by 14-mi island brims with activity as people descend to explore the well-preserved streets of Nantucket Town. Greek Revival houses and museums such as the Whaling Museum carry echoes of the mid-19th century, when this was the world's foremost whaling port. Nantucket was a busy place, dubbed the Gray Lady of the Sea by sailors because of fogs that swept in quickly. Today Nantucket's increasing chicness is balanced by a dedication to preserving the island's natural beauty—no billboards or neon here—as well as all manner of sophisticated pleasures: superlative restaurants, sumptuous B&Bs, and fine boutiques and antiques shops.

More than a few people find themselves mildly disoriented upon arrival as they disembark from the ferries—while the journey from the Cape is pretty much southward, by the time the boat rounds Brant Point to enter the harbor, it's facing due west. Once you reach Nantucket's dreamy shores, the island's inviting villages await. Summertime always brings with it a flood of visitors and bustle, but this is the place for true nature enthusiasts any time of year: 50% of the island is conservation lands. These areas are the residents' pride, chock-full of flora, fauna, and delicious scents from berries and flowering plants. Preserving the pristine nature of the island is always top priority.

Although Nantucket is, for the most part, a pleasantly sleepy place, you can find some action in Nantucket Town, the heart of the island. For a bird's eye panorama of the island, climb the First Congregational Church Tower. From there you can see Muskeget and Tuckernuck islands. In Nantucket Town you can learn about the island's history, including its flora and fauna. Meander the cobblestone streets of town center and see the homes of sea captains, built in the heyday of whaling. Main Street of Nantucket Town, at the core of the historic district, has an east–west orientation, stemming from Straight Wharf out to Madaket Road, which proceeds 6 mi west to Madaket Beach. Milestone Road, accessed from a rotary at the end of Orange Street off Main Street, is a straight, 8-mi shot to Siasconset, known more commonly as Sconset.

If you want to spend time shopping on the island, most stores and galleries are in Nantucket's commercial district along Main, Broad, Center, and South Beach streets. You are more likely to find high-quality locally crafted handmade goods here than the tacky tourist shops that dot much of the mainland. One local treasure is the Nantucket Lightship Basket, hand-woven skillfully and topped with ornamentation sketched into scrimshaw or rosewood. Nantucket sailors invented the baskets in the early 1800s to give as gifts to their families on the island. A new one will cost hundreds of dollars; a vintage one woven on the lightships will sell for thousands.

Outside of town center, the island's lush natural habitat and scenic villages are beautiful, tranquil places to explore. You'll want to use a map if you plan on straying from the main roads, however; many of the smaller roads through conservation areas and villages are unpaved, and some are unmarked as well. A useful assortment of maps are available for free at the Nantucket Visitor Services and Information Bureau in the center of town; the bike shops along the Nantucket Town piers have them as well. Bicycle, moped, or your own feet are the preferred modes of transportation here. Not only is this the easiest (and sometimes the only) way to get to some of the beaches and conservation areas, but the residents will appreciate it as well—many of them choose to get around the island this way themselves.

Sconset, the easternmost part of the island, is a tranquil village where driveways of crushed white shells lead to tiny rose-covered cottages. Stroll through the village's small unpaved streets and continue on to nearby beaches, bogs, and conservation areas. Milestone Bog comprises more than 200 acres of working cranberry bogs; it's a spectacular sight, especially during the harvest in early autumn. The conservation land surrounding the bogs are also home to Altar Rock. Nestled among the hillocks of Polpis, Altar Rock is the island's highest point, at a mere 100 feet. Views are incredible just about everywhere in Nantucket, but they are especially impressive here. Madaket is in the opposite direction of Sconset heading out of town, near the western tip of the island. This fishing village is speckled with creeks, ponds, and marshes. You can bike here from Nantucket town via the 5½-mi Madaket Bike Path, which extends all the way to Madaket Beach, known for its beautiful sunsets. The town's other beach, Eel Point, is part of a conservation area of the same name and is accessible only by foot. Eel Point is better for wading and bird-watching rather than actual swimming—the 100-yard-long sandbar attracts a variety of nesting birds and keeps the beach's waters shallow and calm.

All Nantucket beaches (the island has more than 100 mi of sandy shoreline) are open to the public, a point of local pride. A half dozen or so town-supervised beaches have amenities such as snack bars and lifeguard stations; the rest are the purview of solitary strollers. The northerly, Nantucket Sound–side beaches are nearly always placid, while the ocean-side beaches are known for big round waves that will lift you off your feet. Outer beaches, such as Madaket and Sconset, present further challenges with strong sidelong currents. But even if you don't swim, you can still savor walking along the beach.

Like the original settlers and the early tourists, most people who visit Nantucket today come to escape—from cities, from stress. Nantucket has a bit of nightlife, including two raucous year-round dance clubs, but that's not what the island is about. It's about gray-shingle cottages, covered with pink roses in summer, about daffodil-lined roads in spring. It's about moors swept with salt breezes and scented with bayberry. Perhaps most of all, it's about rediscovering a quiet place within yourself and within the world, getting back in touch with the elemental and taking it home with you when you go.

For visitor information, contact the **Nantucket Chamber of Commerce** (✉ 48 Main St., 02554 ☎ 508/228–1700 ⊕ www.nantucketchamber.org). The **Nantucket Visitor Services and Information Bureau** (✉ 25 Federal St., 02554 ☎ 508/228–0925) provides information on activities, museums, restaurants, and accommodations. For information on travel by ferry from Cape Cod, see Boat & Ferry Travel in Smart Travel Tips A to Z.

— by James W. Rohlf

off the beaten path

CAPE COD POTATO CHIPS FACTORY – There's a standing invitation on the back of the bag: come for a free factory tour and get free samples of the crunchy all-natural chips hand-cooked in kettles in small batches. ⊠ *Independence Dr. to Breeds Hill Rd., off Rte. 132* ☎ *508/775–3358* ⊕ *www.capecodchips.com* ⊗ *Weekdays 9–5; call for off-season hrs.*

Where to Stay & Eat

$$–$$$$
Fodor'sChoice
★

✕ **The Paddock.** The Paddock is synonymous with excellent formal dining on the Cape. Its authentic Victorian style includes sumptuous upholstery in the main dining room and old-style wicker on the breezy summer porch. The menu is traditional yet deceptively innovative, combining fresh ingredients in novel ways. Pistachio encrusted halibut with citrus beurre blanc is but one example. The steak au poivre, with several varieties of crushed peppercorns, is masterful; the fire-roasted salmon comes with black bean chili and mango salsa. ⊠ *W. Main St. rotary, next to Melody Tent, West End* ☎ *508/775–7677* ⊕ *www. paddockcapecod.com* ▤ *AE, DC, MC, V* ⊗ *Closed mid-Nov.–Mar.*

$$–$$$
✕ **Penguins Seagrill.** Owner-chef Bobby Gold experiments carefully and never loses sight of the fresh grilled seafood he prepares so well. Baked stuffed lobster (from 1 to 3 pounds) is outstanding, served with crabmeat stuffing topped with fresh sea scallops. There are a number of excellent pasta dishes, again with seafood, such as pasta Fiore (shrimp, scallops, and lobster with mushrooms, scallions, sherry, and cream sauce on angel-hair pasta). All the breads and desserts are homemade. The bi-level dining room has wood and brick and carvings of sea life galore. ⊠ *331 Main St., Downtown Hyannis* ☎ *508/775–2023* ▤ *AE, D, DC, MC, V* ⊗ *Closed Mon. No lunch.*

$$–$$$
Fodor'sChoice
★

✕ **Roadhouse Café.** Candlelight flickers off the white-linen tablecloths and dark-wood wainscoting at this smart choice for a night out. Popular dishes include the pepper-and-goat-cheese appetizer and shrimp and basil pesto over linguine. In the more casual bistro and the mahogany bar, you can order from a separate menu, which includes thin-crust pizza as well as burgers and lighter fare. On Monday night year-round in the bistro is excellent straight-ahead jazz, with such regulars as pianist Dave McKenna and Lou Colombo (the trumpet-playing father of owner Dave). There's a piano bar the rest of the week from early July to early September; it continues on Friday and Saturday in the off-season. ⊠ *488 South St., Downtown Hyannis* ☎ *508/775–2386* ⊕ *www.roadhousecafe. com* ⟡ *Reservations essential* ▤ *AE, D, MC, V* ⊗ *No lunch.*

$$–$$$
✕ **RooBar.** A bit of Manhattan on Main Street, RooBar has a dark, sophisticated feel, with good music, low light, and a hip bar scene. A wood-fired oven produces "hand-spun to order" pizzas such as scallop and prosciutto with asparagus. Other world-beat choices include littlenecks in a tomato-caper-wine broth and grilled filet mignon served with potato leek tart, walnut gorgonzola crust and port wine demi-glace. The owner is a member of actor Christopher Reeve's family, and a portion of all profits goes to the Christopher Reeve Foundation for Spinal Cord Research. ⊠ *586 Main St., Downtown Hyannis* ☎ *508/778–6515* ⊕ *www. theroobar.com* ▤ *AE, MC, V* ⊗ *Closed Mon. in off-season. No lunch.*

★ **$–$$$** ✕ **Alberto's Ristorante.** End a day of sightseeing at this relaxing and intimate dinner spot, which serves tender veal, lamb, chicken, aged sirloin, and succulent seafood in romantic dining rooms warmed by fireplaces. There's live entertainment a few nights a week, including jazz piano Friday and Saturday. Summertime means sunset dinners at candlelit tables along Main Street. ✉ *360 Main St.* ☎ *508/778–1770* ⊕ *www.albertos.net* ☐ *AE, MC, V.*

$–$$$ ✕ **Baxter's Fish N' Chips.** Since fried seafood is a Cape staple, you may want to pay homage to one of the best Fry-o-lators around. Right on Hyannis Harbor, it's been a favorite of boaters and bathers alike since 1955. Generous portions of fried clams are delicious and cooked hot to order. The picnic tables outside, some set up on an old floating ferry, allow you to lose no time in the sun while eating lobster, fish-and-chips, or something from the raw bar. If the weather's not on your side, there's indoor seating overlooking the harbor. A passageway off the dining room leads to Baxter's Boat House Club, slightly more upscale and with the same menu, though no one under 21 is permitted there. ✉ *Pleasant St., Hyannis Harbor* ☎ *508/775–4490* ⊕ *www.baxtersboathouse.com* ⌛ *Reservations not accepted* ☐ *AE, DC, MC, V* ☺ *Closed mid-Oct.–Apr. and weekdays early Sept.–mid-Oct.*

$–$$$ ✕ **Harry's.** This place serves up sizable portions of Cajun and creole dishes with great spices. The menu includes a number of meal-size sandwiches and blackened local fish that's done to perfection, with a jambalaya that makes you wonder if there isn't a bayou nearby. It's also a prime location for music: you can hear blues, zydeco, and folk music nightly year-round. ✉ *700 Main St., West End* ☎ *508/778–4188* ⊕ *www. harrysbluesbar.com* ⌛ *Reservations not accepted* ☐ *AE, DC, MC, V.*

$$ ✕ **Misaki.** Tucked away on quieter West Main Street, Misaki serves authentic Japanese food in an intimate setting. The menu has a diverse array of traditional Japanese dishes, such as vegetable tempura, yaki soba, and chicken or beef teriyaki, but the sushi and sashimi—made from the freshest raw fish and prepared by an experienced master sushi chef—are the real stars here. Try the tuna rolls, which are delectably soft and silky. Two traditional Japanese "sitting booths" are available; call ahead to reserve one for an even more authentic dining experience (shoes must be removed). For meals on the go, there's also a take-out menu—the lunch specials are a great deal. Reservations are recommended on weekends. ✉ *379 W. Main St.* ☎ *508/771–3771* ⊕ *www.misakisushi.com* ☐ *AE, MC, V.*

$–$$ ✕ **Barbyann's.** For a reasonably priced family meal, try the steak, seafood, pizza, burgers, or one of the child-pleasing (if hardly authentic) Mexican dishes here. Best of all are the Buffalo chicken wings, hot and spicy and filling. There's an outdoor patio with umbrella tables, and early-bird specials are offered Monday–Thursday. ✉ *120 Airport Rd.* ☎ *508/ 775–9795* ⌛ *Reservations not accepted* ☐ *AE, D, DC, MC, V.*

$–$$ ✕ **Brazilian Grill.** The Cape has a strong Brazilian population, and you
Fodor'sChoice can find many of these residents, plus plenty of satisfied visitors, at this
★ all-you-can-eat *churrascaria*, a Brazilian barbecue. Waiters circulate through the dining room offering more than a dozen grilled meats—beef, pork, chicken, sausage, even quail—on long swordlike skewers. You can

help yourself to a buffet of salads and side dishes, including *farofa* (a couscous-like dish made of manioc), plantains, rice, and beans. The atmosphere is often loud and jovial. For dessert, the homemade flan is the best anywhere. Reservations are recommended on weekends. ⊠ *680 Main St., West End* ☎ *508/771–0109* ⊟ *AE, D, DC, MC, V.*

★ **$–$$** ✕ **Fazio's Trattoria.** Set in an old Italian bakery building, Fazio's looks like the trattoria it is, with wood floors, high ceilings, and a deli case full of fresh pasta, breads, and cheeses (not for sale). There's also an espresso and cappuccino bar. Chef Tom Fazio's menu leans on fresh ingredients and herbed pastas, such as thick, rough-cut black pepper tagliatelle with sausage and eggplant chunks in a garlicky tomato sauce. All ravioli, pastas, and breads are homemade. Gourmet pizzas also available. Take home some fresh cannoli for dessert. ⊠ *294 Main St., Downtown Hyannis* ☎ *508/775–9400* ⊕ *www.fazio.net* ⊟ *AE, MC, V* ⊗ *No lunch.*

$–$$ ✕ **Sam Diego's.** The bar has a busy social scene, and the menu has satisfying Tex-Mex burritos, enchiladas, and fajitas. Crispy deep-fried ice cream served in a giant goblet is a house favorite along with any flavor margarita. The prop-shop furnishings may be a little cheesy—sombreros, Aztec birds, and the like—but the place is fun, friendly, and popular with families. Weekday lunches, there's an all-you-can-eat chili and taco bar, and dinner is served nightly until midnight. ⊠ *950 Iyanough Rd. (Rte. 132)* ☎ *508/771–8816* ⊕ *www.samdiegos.com* ⊟ *AE, D, MC, V.*

$–$$ ✕ **Star City Grill.** Formerly known as Starbucks (not the ubiquitous coffee chain), this restaurant has been completely revamped by its owners and now has a swanky new look to go with its new name. Now with two bars, the house special drinks and martinis are better than ever. So is the food, which includes all the basic American nuts and bolts like burgers and sandwiches to heartier entrees. As dinner winds down, live entertainment and a solid bar scene take over. ⊠ *624 Iyanough Rd. (Rte. 132)* ☎ *508/778–6767* ⚬ *Reservations essential on weekends* ⊟ *AE, D, DC, MC, V.*

$–$$ ✕ **Ying's.** The huge menu at this little pan-Asian place combines Thai, Korean, and Japanese cuisines. Ying's sushi and sashimi combos are artful, and its wealth of curried Thai seafood, noodles, and fried rice dishes ranges from spicy to, well, really spicy. For something different, try the Korean *bibimbap* (vegetables, beef, and egg on rice with hot sauce). Tables are set up by the windows, and there's a sushi bar as well as a small lounge area with a selection of Asian beers. Try the sweet and thick Thai iced tea—you won't need dessert. But if you do, the fried ice cream is a treat. For similar food with nightlife, check out Ying's other restaurant, **The Blue Anchor Cafe,** on Main Street. ⊠ *59 Center St., East End* ☎ *508/790–2432* ⊟ *AE, MC, V* ⊗ *No lunch weekends.*

$$$–$$$$ ▦ **Breakwaters.** If these weathered-gray-shingle cottages were any closer to Nantucket Sound, they'd be in it. These privately owned condos rent by the week (or day if vacancies occur); divided into one-, two-, and three-bedroom units, the cottages offer all the comforts of home. Each unit has one or two full baths; kitchens with microwave, coffeemaker, refrigerator, toaster, and stove; TV and phone (local calls are free); and a deck or patio with grill and picnic table. Most have water views. An in-ground heated pool is less than 200 feet from the lifeguarded town beach. Excluding Sunday, there is daily maid service. ⊠ *432 Sea St.* ⬧ *Box 118, 02601* ☎☎ *508/775–6831* ⊕ *www.capecod.com/breakwaters* ⬧ *19 cottages* ⬧ *Kitchens, microwaves, refrigerators, cable TV, pool, beach, babysitting; no smoking, no a/c, no pets* ▭ *No credit cards* ⊘ *Closed mid-Oct.–Apr.*

$$$–$$$$ ▦ **Cape Codder Resort.** Don't let the kids spy the indoor wave pool here— a fantasy of waves, waterfalls, and water slides—or you'll never get out to see anything else on the Cape. Although it's set on a rather unattrac- tive stretch of Route 132, this sprawling, family-friendly motel-style com- plex has quite a few amenities. The rooms range from basic to more elaborate; the Cape Codder rooms are more upscale than the standard "deluxe" ones. The best rooms face the inner courtyard, overlooking the lawn or the "beach" (a stretch of sand that's used for seasonal clam bakes). The suites are huge, including several with spiral staircases lead- ing up to a sleeping loft. ⊠ *1225 Iyanough Rd., 02601* ☎ *508/771– 3000 or 888/297–2200* ⊟ *508/771–6564* ⊕ *www.capecodderresort.com* ⬧ *252 rooms, 8 suites* ⬧ *2 restaurants, room service, in-room data ports, room TVs with movies and video games, tennis court, pool, exercise equip- ment, spa, volleyball, wine bar, playground, meeting rooms* ▭ *AE, D, DC, MC, V.*

$$$–$$$$ ▦ **Four Points by Sheraton Hyannis Resort.** It's hard to beat the Shera- ton, with its beautifully landscaped grounds, extensive services and pampering, and superior resort facilities, including a popular golf course open to the public and a recently added spa. The lobby area is elegant; the rooms, if unremarkable in decor, feature private balconies or patios and particularly comfortable mattresses. ⊠ *Scudder La., West End rotary, 02601* ☎ *508/775–7775, 800/325–3535 reservations* ⊟ *508/778–6039* ⊕ *www.sheraton.com* ⬧ *224 rooms* ⬧ *Restau- rant, room service, in-room data ports, in-room VCRs, 18-hole golf course, putting green, 2 tennis courts, 2 pools (1 indoor), health club, spa, pub, business services, meeting rooms, no-smoking rooms* ▭ *AE, D, DC, MC, V.*

$$$–$$$$ ▦ **Simmons Homestead Inn.** At this 1820 former sea captain's estate, each room in the main house or the detached barn is named for an animal. They have antique, wicker, or canopied four-poster beds topped with brightly colored quilts; some have fireplaces, and some, like the large, cheery Bird Room, have private decks. You can borrow the 10-speed mountain bikes, and Simmons Pond is a short jaunt on the property's trail. Gregarious innkeeper Bill Putman encourages you to return each evening for a wine-and-socializing hour. He'll also be happy to show you his collection of antique cars or his 384 types of single malt scotch whiskeys. Note that Putman—a smoker himself— allows smoking in some public spaces. Kids are welcome. ⊠ *288 Scudder Ave.* ⬧ *Box 578, Hyannis Port 02647* ☎ *508/778–4999 or 800/637–1649* ⊟ *508/790–1342* ⊕ *www.simmonshomesteadinn.com* ⬧ *12 rooms, 2 suites* ⬧ *Hot tub, bicycles, billiards, some pets allowed (fee), no-smoking rooms; no a/c, no room phones, no room TVs* ▭ *AE, D, MC, V* ⧎ *BP.*

$$–$$$$ ▨ **Anchor-In.** Most rooms have harbor views and small balconies overlooking the water at this inviting motel on the north end of Hyannis Harbor. Its simple street-side appearance belies its spacious accommodations and extensive grounds. Some rooms have refrigerators, while the larger deluxe and executive rooms have wraparound porches. Lisa and Skip Simpson deliver the warm, personal service of a small B&B. Ferries for Nantucket and Martha's Vineyard are just around the corner. ⊠ *1 South St., 02601* ☎ *508/775–0357* 🖷 *508/775–1313* ⊕ *www. anchorin.com* ⇥ *43 rooms* ⚸ *In-room data ports, some refrigerators, cable TV, pool* ▤ *AE, D, MC, V.*

$–$$$$ ▨ **Capt. Gosnold Village.** An easy walk from the beach and town, this colony of motel rooms and pink-shutter cottages is ideal for families. Kids can ride their bikes around the quiet street, and the pool is fenced in and watched by a lifeguard. In some rooms walls are attractively paneled with painted pine; floors are carpeted, and simple furnishings are colonial or modern. All cottages have decks and gas grills and receive maid service daily (except Sunday). Choose from efficiency units or one-to three-bedroom cottages. Cottages aren't air-conditioned, although you can rent an a/c unit if you need it. ⊠ *230 Gosnold St., 02601* ☎ *508/ 775–9111* ⊕ *www.captaingosnold.com* ⇥ *18 cottages* ⚸ *Picnic area, cable TV, pool, basketball; no a/c, no pets.* ▤ *MC, V* ⊙ *Closed Nov.–mid-Apr.*

$$$ ▨ **Comfort Inn Cape Cod.** All the rooms at this cinder-block motel just off the highway have white-oak-veneer furnishings and include one king-size or two double beds, a table and chairs or a desk and chair, and a wardrobe. Some king rooms have sofa beds. The quietest rooms are those on the top floor that face the pond and woods; all have free HBO and Nintendo, and pets are allowed. Kids under 18 stay free. Although the location is convenient to the highway, keep in mind that Route 132 is extremely busy during the summer months. ⊠ *1470 Iyanough Rd. (Rte. 132), 02601* ☎ *508/771–4804, 800/228–5150 reservations* 🖷 *508/790–2336* ⊕ *www.comfortinn-hyannis.com* ⇥ *103 rooms, 1 suite* ⚸ *Cable TV with movies and video games, indoor pool, gym, hot tub, sauna, meeting room, some pets allowed, no-smoking rooms* ▤ *AE, D, DC, MC, V* ۞ *CP.*

$–$$$ ▨ **Hyannis Inn Motel.** The second-oldest motel in Hyannis, the main building of this modest two-story spot served as press headquarters during JFK's presidential campaign. The main building's immaculate rooms have double, queen-size, or king-size beds; some have whirlpool tubs. The newer deluxe rooms—built in 1981 in a separate wing out back—are larger, sunnier, and quieter (they don't face Main Street) and have queen-or king-size beds, sleeper sofas, walk-in closets, and refrigerators. The restaurant serves breakfast only. Kids under 12 stay free. ⊠ *473 Main St., 02601* ☎ *508/775–0255 or 800/922–8993* 🖷 *508/771–0456* ⊕ *www.hyannisinn.com* ⇥ *77 rooms* ⚸ *Restaurant, in-room data ports, some in-room hot tubs, some refrigerators, cable TV, indoor pool, sauna, pub, no-smoking rooms* ▤ *AE, D, MC, V* ⊙ *Closed early Nov.–Feb.*

¢–$$$ ▨ **Cape Cod Inn.** This centrally located inn on downtown Main Street is squarely placed within walking distance of all of Hyannis's major sights. The no-frills rooms have large double beds; most, unfortunately, have views of the drab parking lot. The inn is attached to the Duck Inn Pub, a popular local hangout, where breakfast is served. ✉ *447 Main St., 02601* ☎ *508/775–3000* 🖷 *508/771–1457* ➥ *37 rooms, 1 suite* ♨ *Restaurant, cable TV, indoor pool, bar* 🚭 *AE, D, MC, V* ⭐ *CP.*

★ **$–$$** 🏨 **Sea Breeze Inn.** Each room in this comfortable cedar-shingle B&B two blocks from the beach has antique or canopied beds and is simply decorated with quilts or floral comforters and well-chosen antiques. There's also an efficiency unit with a stove and refrigerator. Breakfast is served in the dining room or in the outdoor gazebo, surrounded by winsome gardens. ✉ *270 Ocean Ave., at Sea St., 02601* ☎ *508/771–7213* 🖷 *508/862–0663* ⊕ *www.seabreezeinn.com* ➥ *13 rooms, 1 efficiency* ♨ *Kitchenette, refrigerator; no a/c (except in efficiency), no room TVs, no smoking, no pets* 🚭 *AE, D, MC, V* ⭐ *CP.*

Nightlife & the Arts

THE ARTS   The **Boston Pops Esplanade Orchestra** (☎ 508/362–0066 ⊕ www.artsfoundationcapecod.org/Fleet.html) wows a crowd with its annual Pops by the Sea concert, held in August at the Hyannis Village Green. Each year a celebrity guest conductor strikes up the band for a few selected numbers; past baton bouncers have included Olympia Dukakis, Joan Kennedy, Mike Wallace, Art Buchwald, Maya Angelou, and Sebastian Junger.

In 1950 the actress Gertrude Lawrence and her husband, producer-manager Richard Aldrich, opened the **Cape Cod Melody Tent** (✉ 21 W. Main St., at West End rotary, West End ☎ 508/775–5630, 800/347–0808 for tickets ⊕ www.melodytent.com) to showcase Broadway musicals and concerts. Today it's the Cape's top venue for pop concerts and comedy shows; performers who have played here, in the round, include Aretha Franklin, the Doobie Brothers, Tom Jones, Ziggy Marley, Ani DiFranco, Anne Murray, Kenny Rogers, and Crosby, Stills & Nash. The Tent also hosts a Wednesday-morning children's theater series in July and August.

The 90-member **Cape Symphony Orchestra,** under former D'Oyly Carte Opera conductor Royston Nash, gives regular classical and children's concerts with guest artists September through May. Performances are held at the Barnstable Performing Arts Center at **Barnstable High School** (✉ 744 W. Main St. ☎ 508/362–1111 ⊕ www.capesymphony.org).

Opera New England of Cape Cod (☎ 508/771–3600 schedules, locations, and reservations) has two or three performances a year, in spring and fall, by the National Lyric Opera Company.

In July and August **town-band concerts** (☎ 508/362–5230 or 877/492–6647) are held on Wednesday evening starting at 7:30 on the Town Green on Main Street.

NIGHTLIFE   **The Beechtree Bar** (✉ 599 Main St. ☎ 508/771–3272) is part of Bubba's BBQ&Clam Shack, tucked just behind the restaurant off Main Street. The centerpiece (and namesake) of this outdoor bar is an enormous beech tree. This hotspot attracts a younger crowd in summer.

The Blue Room (✉ 415 Main St. ☎ 508/778–7200) features DJs spinning the latest hits and techno mixes. There's a big dance floor, lots of space to mingle, several bars and an outdoor deck.

The British Beer Company (✉ 412 Main St. ☎ 508/771–1776 ⊕ www.britishbeer.com) has a hearty selection of beers from stouts to pilsners and has live entertainment—usually local rock bands—most nights. The BBC also has other branches on the Cape in Sandwich and Falmouth.

Bud's Country Lounge (✉ 3 Bearses Way, at Rte. 132 ☎ 508/771–2505) has pool tables and provides live country music, dancing, and line-dancing lessons year-round.

Club 477 (✉ 477 Yarmouth Rd., East End ☎ 508/771–7511), in the old Hyannis train station, is the Upper and Mid Cape's only gay club. There's a piano bar on the lower level and a dance bar on the upper floor with music almost as hot as the crowd.

★ **Harry's Blues Bar** (✉ 700 Main St., ☎ 508/778–4188 ⊕ www.harrysbluesbar.com) is hopping every night all year-round, drawing blues lovers of all ages. Expect to see 21-year-olds and 70-year-olds dancing up a sweat side by side. Owner Laddie Durham fills the creole joint with the crowd-pleasing bands and her top-notch hospitality. In summer, crowds spill over from inside onto the two decks.

The Hyport Brewing Company (✉ 720 Main St. ☎ 508/775–8289 ⊕ www.hyportbrew.com) offers a variety of brews made on-site and nighttime entertainment through the summer (call for schedule). Try the "Flounder," a six-brew sampler.

The **Prodigal Son** (✉ 10 Ocean St., Downtown Hyannis ☎ 508/771–1337) showcases some of the best up-and-coming bands and musicians in New England. The lineup includes acoustic, blues, jazz, and rock, and even spoken-word performers. The high-octane java keeps the joint jumpin'. Call for a schedule.

Pufferbellies (✉ 183 Iyanough Rd. [Rte. 28] ☎ 508/790–4300 or 800/233–4301), in an old railroad roundhouse by the Hyannis tracks, is the Mid Cape's largest dance club, with several dance floors of swing, country line dancing, and DJ tunes, as well as eats, Internet terminals, and even volleyball courts.

The **Roadhouse Café** (✉ 488 South St., Downtown Hyannis ☎ 508/775–2386) has great jazz year-round.

★ After dinner, **The Roo Bar** (✉ 586 Main St. ☎ 508/778–6515 ⊕ www.theroobar.com) turns up the music and morphs into the place to see and be seen on Cape Cod. The Manhattan-esque haunt draws large crowds of attractive twenty- and thirtysomethings; expect to see lines of people out the door in summer. Personable bartenders and staff boost the already lively atmosphere.

The **Star City Grill** (✉ 645 Iyanough Rd. ☎ 508/778–6767) presents live acoustic entertainment in its bar many nights year-round.

Sports & the Outdoors

BASEBALL The **Hyannis Mets** (☎ 508/420–0962 ⊕ www.hyannismets.org) of the collegiate Cape Cod Baseball League play home games at **McKeon Field** (⊠ High School Rd., Downtown Hyannis) from mid-June to mid-August.

BEACHES **Kalmus Park Beach,** at the south end of Ocean Street, is a fine, wide sandy beach with an area set aside for windsurfers and a sheltered area that's good for kids. It has a snack bar, restrooms, showers, and lifeguards. The parking fee is $10 in season.

Veterans Park, next to the John F. Kennedy Memorial on Ocean Street, has a small beach that's especially good for kids; it's sheltered from waves and fairly shallow. There are picnic tables, barbecue facilities, showers, and restrooms. The parking fee is $10 in season.

BIKING **Cascade Motor Lodge** (⊠ 201 Main St., Downtown Hyannis ☎ 508/775–9717), near the bus and train station, rents three-speed and mountain bikes by the half day, full day, and week.

BOATING **Eastern Mountain Sports** (⊠ 1513 Iyanough Rd. [Rte. 132] ☎ 508/362–8690) rents kayaks and camping gear.

Sailing tours aboard the catboat *Eventide* (⊠ Ocean St. Dock, Hyannis Harbor ☎ 508/775–0222) include several one- and two-hour cruises through Hyannis Harbor and out into Nantucket Sound, such as a nature tour and a sunset cruise.

Hy-Line (⊠ Ocean St. Dock, Hyannis Harbor ☎ 508/778–2600 ⊕ www.hy-linecruises.com) offers cruises on replicas of old-time Maine coastal steamers. The one-hour tours of Hyannis Harbor and Lewis Bay include a view of the Kennedy compound and other points of interest.

FISHING **Hy-Line** (⊠ Ocean St. Dock, Hyannis Harbor ☎ 508/790–0696 ⊕ www.hy-linecruises.com) leads fishing trips on a walk-on basis in spring and fall, but reservations are mandatory in summer.

GOLF **Four Points by Sheraton Hyannis Resort** (⊠ Scudder La., West End rotary, West End ☎ 508/775–7775) has a beautifully landscaped, challenging 18-hole par-3 course called Twin Brooks open to nonguests. You may bump into some famous faces; many performers from the Cape Cod Melody Tent tee off here while in town.

HEALTH & **Barnstable Athletic Club** (⊠ 55 Attucks La., Independence Park, off Rte. FITNESS CLUBS 132 ☎ 508/771–7734) has four racquetball-wallyball courts (wallyball is volleyball played on a racquetball court), a squash court, basketball, an aerobics room, whirlpools, sauna and steam rooms, and cardiovascular and free-weight equipment. Day care, and day and short-term memberships are available.

Hyannis Athletic Club (⊠ Sheraton Hyannis Hotel, Scudder La., West End rotary, West End ☎ 508/862–2535) has two outdoor tennis courts, a fitness club, and indoor and outdoor pools. Day and short-term memberships are available.

ICE-SKATING   The **Joseph P. Kennedy Jr. Memorial Skating Rink** (✉ 141 Bassett La., Downtown Hyannis ☎ 508/790–6345), named for the late Kennedy scion and war hero, offers skating October through March, with special times reserved for teenagers, youngsters, and families; skate rentals are available.

MINIATURE GOLF   **Cape Cod Storyland Golf** is a 2-acre miniature golf course set up as a mini–Cape Cod, with each of the 18 holes modeled after different Cape towns. The course winds around small ponds and waterfalls, a full-size working gristmill, and reproductions of historic Cape buildings. There's an additional charge of $5 for the bumper boats. ✉ *70 Center St., by railroad depot, East End* ☎ *508/778–4339* ✎ *$7* ☉ *Apr.–Oct., daily 9 AM–midnight.*

Shopping

Cape Cod Mall (✉ Between Rtes. 132 and 28 ☎ 508/771–0200 ⊕ www.capecodmall.com), the Cape's largest, has 120 shops, including department stores like Macy's and Marshall's, and a 12-screen movie complex.

Christmas Tree Shops (✉ 655 Iyanough Rd. [Rte. 132] ☎ 508/778–5521 ⊕ www.christmastreeshops.com), a Cape mainstay, are a bargain shoppers' haven. Take home Cape souvenirs at a great discount and just about anything you might need—or not need—to decorate your home. The Hyannis store is the largest on the Cape.

Colonial Candle of Cape Cod (✉ 388 Main St., Downtown Hyannis ☎ 508/771–2790 or 508/771–3916) is wall-to-wall top-notch Cape-made candles in dozens of scents, including those specific to Cape Cod, like cranberry and bayberry.

Nantucket Trading Company (✉ 354 Main St., Downtown Hyannis ☎ 508/790–3933), sort of a local version of Pier 1, sells neat necessities for your home, including edibles, table linens, cooking gadgets, and kitchen accessories.

The handsome flagship **Puritan of Cape Cod** (✉ 408 Main St., Downtown Hyannis ☎ 508/775–2400) store carries upscale clothing brands from North Face to Eileen Fisher and Ralph Lauren and also sells outdoor gear. Service is great here; there are also five other stores around the Cape.

West Yarmouth

⑮ *4 mi south of Yarmouth Port; 3 mi east of Hyannis.*

The commercial hub of West Yarmouth (and the major road through the town) is, for better or worse, Route 28—the part of the Cape people love to hate. As you pass through the area—likely very slowly in summer traffic—it's one motel, strip mall, nightclub, and miniature golf course after another. In 1989, as *Cape Cod Life* magazine put it, "the town [began] to plant 350 trees in hopes that eventually the trees' leaves, like the fig leaf of Biblical lore, [would] cover the shame of unkempt overdevelopment." Regardless of the glut of tacky tourist traps, there are some interesting sights in the little villages along the way. So take Route 28 if you want to intersperse amusements with your sightseeing, because you really can amuse yourself to no end here. A sensible option if you want to avoid this road entirely: take speedy U.S. 6 to the exit nearest what you want to visit and then cut south across the interior. If you must travel the Route 28 area, take Buck Island Road, which runs north of and parallel to much of the busy route in West and South Yarmouth.

Yelverton Crowe settled the village of West Yarmouth in 1643, after acquiring the land from a Native American sachem. The deal they struck was that Crowe could have as much land as he could traverse in an hour in exchange for an "ox-chain, a copper kettle . . . and a few trinkets." The first settlers were farmers; when Central Wharf near Mill Creek was built in the 1830s, the town turned to more commercial ventures as it became headquarters for the growing packet service that ferried passengers from the Cape to Boston.

Listed on the National Register of Historic Places, the 1710 **Baxter Grist Mill,** by the shore of Mill Pond, is the only mill on Cape Cod powered by an inside water turbine; the others use either wind or paddle wheels. The mill was converted to the indoor metal turbine in 1860 because of the pond's low water level and the damage done to the wooden paddle wheel by winter freezes. The original metal turbine is displayed on the grounds, and a replica powers the restored mill. A videotape tells the mill's history. ⊠ *Rte. 28, across from Baxter Ave.* ☎ *508/362–3021* ⊕ *www.hsoy.org/historic/baxtermill.htm* ⊡ *Free* ☉ *Early June–early Sept., call for schedule.*

16 A unique and lovely walking trail, the **Yarmouth Boardwalk** (⊠ Off Meadowbrook La.) stretches through swamp and marsh and leads to the edge of Swan Pond, a pretty pond ringed with woods. To get here, take Winslow Gray Road northeast from Route 28, turn right on Meadowbrook Lane, and take it to the end.

An entertaining, educational, and occasionally hokey stop for kids, **ZooQuarium** has sea-lion shows, a petting zoo with native wildlife, wandering peacocks, aquariums, and educational programs, plus pony rides in summer. The Children's Discovery Center presents changing exhibits such as *Bone Up on Bones* (all about skeletons), *Zoo Nutrition* (in which kids prepare meals), and the self-explanatory *Scoop on Poop.* ⊠ *674 Main St. (Rte. 28)* ☎ *508/775–8883* ⊕ *www.zooquariumcapecod.net* ⊡ *$9* ☉ *Mid-Feb.–June and Sept.–late Nov., daily 9:30–5; July and Aug., daily 9:30–6.*

need a break? **Jerry's Seafood and Dairy Freeze** (⊠ 654 Main St. [Rte. 28] ☎ 508/775–9752), open year-round, serves fried clams and onion rings, along with thick frappes (milk shakes), frozen yogurt, and soft ice cream at good prices.

Where to Stay & Eat

$$–$$$ ✕ **The Yarmouth House Restaurant.** This festive family-owned restaurant has built a strong local following over the years. The menu has classic

Italian dishes like chicken Parmesan and veal marsala, as well as traditional grilled steaks and plenty of fresh seafood dishes. Try filet mignon à la neptune (topped with lobster meat and hollandaise sauce). Accompany your meal with a selection from their long list of beers, wines, and specialty cocktails. Early-bird specials, Sunday specials, and a kids' menu are available. ☒ *335 Rte. 28* ☎ *508/771–5454* ⊕ *www. yarmouthhouse.com* ☐ *AE, D, MC, V.*

★ ¢ ✕ **Keltic Kitchen.** If you like to start your day with a substantial meal, stop into this friendly café for a traditional Irish breakfast—eggs, sausage, rashers (bacon), black and white pudding, home fries or beans, tomato, and brown bread or scones. The potato pancakes with sour cream and scallions are tasty, too, as are the more "American" options, including French toast and omelets. At midday, you can still get breakfast, or choose from an assortment of sandwiches that might include corned beef or burgers. Just don't come by too late; the kitchen closes around 2 PM. ☒ *415 Rte. 28* ☎ *508/771–4835* ☐ *No credit cards* ☉ *No dinner.*

★ $–$$ ⊡ **Inn at Lewis Bay.** Affordable and beautiful, this 1920s Dutch Colonial overlooks Lewis Bay, a short walk from the beach. Janet Vaughn, who owns the inn with her husband, David, is an avid quilter; her work tops the antique or canopy beds and adorns the walls in the country-style rooms. Each room has a name and a theme; Whale Watch, with its distinctive navys and maroons, is one of two rooms with water views. Bountiful breakfasts are served in the dining room or on the spacious front porch, which is also a pleasant place for afternoon tea and home-baked cookies. The Whale Watch and Sea Grass rooms are air-conditioned. ☒ *57 Maine Ave., 02673* ☎ *508/771–3433 or 800/962–6679* 🖷 *508/790–1186* ⊕ *www.innatlewisbay.com* ➷ *6 rooms* ☖ *Dining room; no a/c in some rooms, no room phones, no room TVs, no kids under 12, no smoking* ☐ *AE, MC, V* ⦿| *BP.*

$–$$ ⊡ **Mariner Motor Lodge.** Although Route 28 is crowded and more commercial than serene, it's also home to several value-packed hotels. The Mariner, near the Hyannis–West Yarmouth line, is a good family lodging and a bargain. Although the rooms are standard-issue motel—think basic furnishings like floral bedcovers and carpets that can take a direct hit from a spilled soft drink—the outdoor pool is heated and large, and a heated indoor pool, with an oversize whirlpool hot tub, is great for rainy days. Also on-site are a miniature golf course and vending machines for snacks. Kids stay free, and weekday rates are reduced. ☒ *573 Rte. 28, 02673* ☎ *508/771–7887 or 800/445–4050* 🖷 *508/771–2811* ⊕ *www.mariner-capecod.com* ➷ *100 rooms* ☖ *Coffee shop, in-room safes, refrigerators, cable TV, miniature golf, 2 pools (1 indoor), hot tub, no-smoking rooms* ☐ *AE, D, MC, V.*

$ ⊡ **Americana Holiday Motel.** If you want the convenience of staying on Route 28, this family-owned and -operated strip motel is a good choice. All rooms have cable TV and a phone; those in the rear Pine Grove section overlook serene sea pines and one of the motel's three pools rather than traffic snarls. The two-room suites have a bedroom plus a separate living room with a sleeper sofa and VCR. In the off-season the rates simply can't be beat. Price includes Continental breakfast. ☒ *99 Main St. (Rte. 28), 02673* ☎ *508/775–5511 or 800/445–4497* 🖷 *508/790–*

0597 ⊕ *www.americanaholiday.com* ↝ *117 rooms, 19 suites* ♻ *Coffee shop, refrigerators, cable TV, some in-room VCRs, putting green, 3 pools (1 indoor), hot tub, sauna, shuffleboard, playground* ⊟ *AE, D, DC, MC, V* ⭑◉⭑ *BP.*

Nightlife & the Arts

Cape Cod Irish Village (✉ 512 Main St. [Rte. 28] ☎ 508/771–0100) has dancing to two- or three-piece bands performing traditional and popular Irish music year-round. The crowd is mostly couples and people over 35.

Mill Hill Club (✉ 164 Rte. 28 ☎ 508/775–2580) has more than 20 TVs, live music, hypnotist acts, the occasional men's and women's bikini contests, and Brazilian nights. The crowd is young—and loud.

West Yarmouth's summertime **town-band concerts** are held on Monday in July and August at 7 PM at **Mattacheese Middle School** (✉ Off Higgins Crowell Rd. ☎ 508/778–1008).

Sports & the Outdoors

BEACHES **Seagull Beach** (✉ Seagull Rd., off South Sea Ave.), a long, wide beach along Nantucket Sound, has restrooms and a seasonal concession stand. There's a $10 parking fee in season.

FISHING **Truman's** (✉ 608 Main St. [Rte. 28] ☎ 508/771–3470) can supply you with a required freshwater license and rental gear.

Shopping

The **Cranberry Bog Outlet Stores** (✉ Rte. 28 ☎ No phone) are on the edge of a working cranberry bog. Bass, Van Heusen, and Izod are a few of the shops here.

South Yarmouth

⓱ *3 mi east of West Yarmouth; 6 mi east of Hyannis.*

The Bass River divides the southern portions of the towns of Yarmouth and Dennis. People also generally refer to the area of South Yarmouth as Bass River. Here you can find charter boats, boat and kayak rentals, as well as a river cruise, plus seafood restaurants and markets. Like West Yarmouth, the town has its stretch of blight and overdevelopment on Route 28, but it also has some nice beaches that are good for families. For a good indication of what the town looked like in the late 19th century, take a drive down Pleasant Street and the Main Street section south of Route 28 to view old homes in the Federal and Greek Revival styles. This section along Bass River was home to the elite businessmen, bankers, and sea merchants.

South Yarmouth was once known as Quaker Village for the large numbers of Quakers who settled the area in the 1770s after a smallpox epidemic wiped out the local Native American population. The 1809 **Quaker Meeting House** is still open for meetings. Two separate entrance doors and the partition down the center were meant to divide the sexes. The adjacent cemetery has simple markers with no epitaphs, an expression of the Friends' belief that all are equal in God's eyes. Behind the cemetery is a circa-1830 one-room Quaker schoolhouse. ⊠ *58 N. Main St.* ☎ *508/398–3773* ⊘ *Services Sun. at 10.*

★ ☾ **Pirate's Cove** is the most elaborate of the Cape's many miniature golf setups, with a hill, a waterfall, a stream, and the 18-hole Blackbeard's Challenge course. ⊠ *728 Main St. (Rte. 28)* ☎ *508/394–6200* 🗒 *$7* ⊘ *July and Aug., daily 9 AM–11 PM; late Apr.–June, Sept. and Oct., most days 10–8, but call.*

☾ For rainy-day fun, the **Ryan Family Amusement Center** offers video-game rooms, Skee-Ball, and bowling. There's a snack bar that serves pizza, sandwiches, and beer and wine. ⊠ *1067 Main St. (Rte. 28)* ☎ *508/394–5644* ⊘ *Daily; hrs vary.*

Where to Stay & Eat

$$–$$$ ✕ **The Skipper.** This classic Cape restaurant has been getting better and better since its inception in 1936. Sit downstairs in the nautical-theme main room or upstairs on the outside deck with terrific views of Nantucket Sound. The menu is an odd but compelling mix of classic New England seafood, Italian favorites, and international dishes, from Thai pasta to Jamaican jerk chicken. The Skipper is open in season for breakfast, lunch, and dinner. ⊠ *152 South Shore Dr.* ☎ *508/394–7406* ⚄ *Reservations not accepted* ⊟ *AE, D, MC, V* ⊘ *Closed Nov.–Mar.*

¢–$$ ✕ **Ardeo.** Despite its unpromising location in a shopping plaza, this smart-casual Mediterranean bistro has built a local following for its pizzas, pastas, salads, panini, and Middle Eastern fare. Some may find the food more Americanized than authentic, but it's tasty nonetheless. There's something for everyone here—you could bring the kids, or your grandparents, or a group of pals, and it's a good choice for vegetarians, too. ⊠ *23V Whites Path, Union Station Plaza* ☎ *508/760–1500* ⊕ *www.ardeocapecod.com* ⊟ *AE, D, MC, V.*

$$$–$$$$ ▦ **Capt. Farris House.** Steps from the Bass River Bridge dividing South
Fodor$Choice Yarmouth and West Dennis and a short spin away from congested
★ Route 28 sits this imposing 1845 Greek Revival home. Owners Steve and Patty Bronstein carefully tune in to the needs of their guests while maintaining a casual, our-house-is-your-house attitude. The large rooms and suites have either antique or canopied beds, plush comforters, fancy drapes, and deep tile baths (all but one with a whirlpool tub). Some have fireplaces and sundecks. Breakfast is served in the formal dining room or in the greenhouse-style interior courtyard and might include quiche with pumpkin-pecan scones or thick French toast. Baked goods and coffee are available after hours. There's also a well-rounded videotape library stocked with recent releases. ⊠ *308 Old Main St., 02664* ☎ *508/760–2818 or 800/350–9477* ᵬ *508/398–1262* ⊕ *www.captainfarris.com* ⇨ *5 rooms, 4 suites* ⚄ *Dining room, some in-room hot tubs, cable TV, in-room VCRs, Internet; no kids under 12, no smoking* ⊟ *AE, D, MC, V* ⦿❙ *BP.*

$$$–$$$$ ▦ **Ocean Mist.** This three-story, upscale motel-style resort sits on its own private (if tiny) beach on Nantucket Sound. The rooms have modern furnishings, cable TV, and either wet bars (with sink and refrigerator) or fully stocked kitchenettes. The duplex loft suites are a step above,

with cathedral ceilings, a sitting area with pullout sofa, skylights, and one or two private balconies. ✉ *97 South Shore Dr., 02664* ☎ *508/398–2633 or 800/248–6478* 🖷 *508/760–3151* ⊕ *www.capecodtravel.com/oceanmist* ⇥ *32 rooms, 31 suites* ⟶ *Coffee shop, some kitchenettes, some minibars, some refrigerators, cable TV, indoor pool, hot tub, beach, laundry facilities, no-smoking rooms* ▤ *AE, D, MC, V* ⊙ *Closed Dec.–mid-Feb.* ⦿ *CP (in season).*

$$–$$$$ ▦ **Seaside.** Right on a Nantucket Sound beach, this 5-acre village of Cape-style cottages (studios and one- or two-bedroom units) has a view of scalloped beaches in both directions. Seaside was built in the 1940s, and the furnishings vary from cottage to cottage, as each is individually owned. All have kitchens or kitchenettes, and many have wood-burning fireplaces. The oceanfront cottages, right off a strip of grass set with lounge and Adirondack chairs, have the best view. Cottages in the adjacent pine grove are generally very pleasant, too. Rentals are by the week in summer. ✉ *135 South Shore Dr., 02664* ☎ *508/398–2533* 🖷 *508/398–2523* ⇥ *43 cottages* ⟶ *Picnic area, some kitchens, some kitchenettes, cable TV, beach; no a/c, no room phones* ▤ *D, MC, V* ⊙ *Closed mid-Oct.–Apr.*

$$–$$$ ▦ **Belvedere B&B.** Elisha Baker, a local sea captain, built this quaint Federal home around 1820. The Hamilton Room is the most spacious, with some frilly touches: lace curtains, a lacy bedspread, and old pink-velvet chairs. Romantics may prefer the Boston Room, with green wicker chairs, a two-person whirlpool tub, and a queen-size bed topped with a rose quilt. The Virginia Anthony Room (with pink-and-white quilts on the twin four-posters) and the Florilla Room (with a queen-size bed and white wicker furnishings) are small but sunny; they share a bath. For privacy, consider the Coach House, an efficiency unit behind the main house. Breakfast is served in the formal dining room or on the screened-in porch. ✉ *167 Old Main St., 02664* ☎ *508/398–6674 or 800/288–4080* 🖷 *508/398–6674* ⊕ *www.belvederebb.com* ⇥ *4 rooms, 2 with bath, 1 efficiency* ⟶ *Dining room, cable TV in some rooms; no room phones, Internet; no smoking* ▤ *AE, D, MC, V* ⦿ *BP.*

Nightlife & the Arts

Feel as if it's been too long since you last fox-trotted? **Betsy's Ballroom** (✉ 528 Forest Rd. ☎ 508/362–9538) has Saturday-night ballroom dancing year-round to live bands on the Cape's largest dance floor. The bands deliver swing, waltzes, and fox-trot 8 PM–11 PM. It's BYO for drinks and snacks; Betsy will provide the ice and cups. Admission is $8.50.

Sports & the Outdoors

BASEBALL The **Yarmouth-Dennis Red Sox** of the collegiate Cape Cod Baseball League play home games at **Red Wilson Field** (✉ Station Ave. ☎ 508/394–9387 ⊕ www.ydredsox.org) from mid-June to mid-August.

BEACHES The **Flax Pond** (✉ N. Main St. between High Bank and Great Western Rds.) recreation area has freshwater swimming, a lifeguard, and ducks, but no sand beach, just pine needle–covered ground. There's a pine-shaded picnic area with grills, as well as tennis and basketball courts and plenty of parking.

Parker's River Beach (⊠ South Shore Dr.), a flat stretch of sand on warm Nantucket Sound, is perfect for families. It has a lifeguard, a concession stand, a gazebo and picnic area, a playground, outdoor showers, and restrooms. There's a $10 parking fee in season.

BIKE RENTAL **Outdoor Shop** (⊠ 50 Long Pond Dr. ☎ 508/394–3819) rents bikes and mopeds and does repairs.

GOLF **Blue Rock Golf Course** (⊠ Off Great Western Rd. ☎ 508/398–9295) is a highly regarded, easy-to-walk 18-hole, par-3, 3,000-yard public course crossed by a pond. The pro shop rents clubs; reservations are mandatory in season.

HEALTH & **Mid Cape Racquet Club** (⊠ 193 White's Path ☎ 508/394–3511 ⊕ www.
FITNESS CLUBS midcaperacquet.com) has one racquetball, one squash, and nine indoor tennis courts; indoor basketball; a sauna, steam room, and whirlpools; massage services; and a free-weight and cardiovascular room—plus day care. It also offers spinning, kickboxing, and body pump classes. Daily rates are available.

SOCCER The **Cape Cod Crusaders,** of the D-3 League, play action-packed home matches at the Alan Carlsen Field at **Dennis-Yarmouth Regional High School** (⊠ Station Ave. ☎ 508/394–1171 ⊕ www.capecodcrusaders.com) from May to mid-August.

West Dennis

❶❽ *6 mi south of Dennis; 1 mi east of South Yarmouth.*

In another one of those tricks of Cape geography, the village of West Dennis is actually south of South Dennis, on the east side of the Bass River. Dennisport is farther east, near the Harwich town line. If you're driving between West Dennis and Harwich, Lower County Road, with occasional glimpses of the sea between the cottages and beachfront hotels, is a more scenic alternative to overdeveloped Route 28.

Where to Stay & Eat

$–$$$ ✕ **Christine's.** This family-run restaurant is sprawling, spacious, and a little generic—the type that attracts bus tours—with a big bar in its own room, a private function room, and a separate entertainment lounge with a glittering stage featuring cabaret acts, comedians, impersonators, and bands. The menu is mostly typical American fare, with basic Italian dishes and some seafood and steak. Lebanese specials include a pine-nut and almond-crusted haddock with tahini, and grilled *kafta* (ground lamb and beef with Lebanese spices) served with almond rice and hummus. To help work off dinner, there's dancing year-round. ⊠ *581 Main St. (Rte. 28)* ☎ *508/394–7333* ▭ *AE, D, MC, V.*

★ $–$$$ ✕ **Ocean House.** Overlooking Nantucket Sound, this restaurant has spectacular views to match the food and service. Sunday brunches (reservations strongly recommended) are decadent, with various carving stations, omelets, pancakes, and waffles made to order, and oysters and shrimp on ice, to name just a few of the selections. For dinner, try apple mustard-glaze Atlantic salmon with potato gnocchi, followed by caramelized sugar-encrusted vanilla bean crème brûlée for dessert. Chef

Tim Miller changes the menu seasonally. ⊠ *Depot St.* ☎ *508/394–0700* ▤ *AE, D, MC, V.*

¢–$$ ✕ **Kream 'N Kone.** After a fire and a dispute between the proprietors, this summer favorite has a new location, but the food remains as good as ever. This is how it's been since 1953: order up some fried clams and a shake or a soda, get a number, wait five minutes, and sit down to some of the best fast-food anywhere. The fried food will overflow your paper plate onto a plastic tray, but it's so good that what you thought you'd never be able to finish somehow vanishes. The onion rings in particular are a knockout. At times the prices seem surprisingly high, but the quality and quantity of what you get are well worth the splurge. ⊠ *Corner of Rtes. 134 and 28* ☎ *508/394–0808* ▤ *MC, V* ⊙ *Closed Nov.–Jan.*

$$$$ ▦ **Lighthouse Inn.** On a small private beach adjacent to West Dennis Beach, this traditional Cape resort has been in family hands since 1938. The main inn was built around a still-operational 1855 lighthouse. Along a landscaped lawn are 23 individual one- to three-bedroom cottages made entirely of shingles and five larger buildings with multiple guest rooms. Cottages have decks, fireplaces, two double (or one double and one king-size) beds, and sitting areas (but no kitchens). In the main inn are five guest rooms, a living room, a library, and a waterfront restaurant serving New England fare. In summer, supervised kids' activities give parents some private time. ⊠ *1 Lighthouse Rd.* ⊡ *Box 128, 02670* ☎ *508/398–2244* 🖷 *508/398–5658* ⊕ *www.lighthouseinn.com* ➫ *40 rooms, 23 cottages* ⌂ *Restaurant, room service, in-room data ports, refrigerators cable TV, miniature golf, tennis court, pool, beach, fishing, billiards, shuffleboard, bar, library, nightclub, recreation room, kid's programs (ages 3–12), playground* ▤ *MC, V* ⊙ *Closed mid-Oct.–mid-May* ⍟⏀ *BP.*

$$–$$$ ▦ **Shady Hollow Inn.** Dedicated vegetarians, owners Ann Hart and David Dennis found B&B travel a challenge, so they opened their own veggie-friendly inn. Their breakfasts, which might include omelets, dairy-free baked goods, or a tofu quiche, are designed to appeal to anyone, from foodies to strict vegans. By prior arrangement, they can also prepare vegetarian dinners. Furnishings in their comfortable home are Mission-style; the guest rooms have quilt-topped beds, and the largest—the airy first-floor Westwind—has a striking painted mantle. ⊠ *370 Main St., South Dennis 02660* ☎ *508/394–7474* ⊕ *www. shadyhollowinn.com* ➫ *4 rooms, 2 with bath* ⌂ *In-room VCRs, bicycles; no a/c in some rooms, no room phones, no kids under 10, no smoking* ▤ *MC, V* ⍟⏀ *BP.*

★ $–$$ ▦ **Beach House Inn.** This is the kind of house you'd expect when Nantucket Sound is your backyard: shingles weathered gray from the salt air, white wicker and natural oak furniture that's practical yet comfortable, and walls of glass that frame the beauty—and sometimes ferocity—of Mother Nature. Some rooms have brass or four-poster beds, and all have ceiling fans and decks. The best room is Room 2, with its waterfront deck and a private staircase leading to the inn's beach. The common room has a TV and a wide assortment of hit movies on video. You can cook meals on the barbecue grills or in the fully equipped kitchen. From mid-June though Labor Day, rooms must be rented by the week. A continental breakfast is provided from May through mid-October. ⊠ *61 Uncle Stephen's Rd., Box 494, 02670* ☎ *508/398–4575, 617/489–4144 Columbus Day–Memorial Day* ↬ *7 rooms* ⟨ *Cable TV, beach, playground; no smoking* ⊟ *No credit cards.*

Nightlife & the Arts

Christine's (⊠ 581 Main St. [Rte. 28] ☎ 508/394–7333) stages nightly entertainment in season in its 300-seat showroom. Concerts, sometimes with dancing, include name bands from the 1950s to 1970s, Top 40 bands, or jazz. There are also stand-up comedy nights. Off-season the schedule includes live entertainment and dancing to a DJ on weekends, as well as special events.

The **Sand Bar** (⊠ Lighthouse Rd. ☎ 508/398–7586) presents the boogie-woogie piano playing of local legend Rock King, who's been tickling the ivories—and people's funny bones—since the 1960s. The club is closed from mid-October to mid-May.

In season, you can dance to a DJ and live bands at **Sundancer's** (⊠ 116 Main St. [Rte. 28] ☎ 508/394–1600). It's closed December and January.

Sports & the Outdoors

BEACHES The **West Dennis Beach** (⊠ Lighthouse Rd. off Lower County Rd.) is one of the best on the south shore. A breakwater was started here in 1837 in an effort to protect the mouth of Bass River, but was abandoned when a sandbar formed on the shore side. It's a long, wide, and popular sandy beach, stretching for 1½ mi, with marshland and the Bass River across from it. Popular with windsurfers, the beach also has bathhouses, lifeguards, a playground, concessions, and parking for 1,000 cars. Nonresidents pay a $10 parking fee per day in season.

ICE-SKATING You can ice-skate at the **Tony Kent Arena** (⊠ 8 Gages Way, South Dennis ☎ 508/760–2400) fall though spring and on Saturday in summer. Keep your eyes peeled: this is where Nancy Kerrigan and Paul Wylie train. Rental skates are available.

JOGGING **Lifecourse** (⊠ Bob Crowell Rd. and Old Bass River Rd., South Dennis) is a 1½-mi jogging trail through woods, with 20 exercise stations along the way. It's part of a recreation area that includes basketball and handball courts, ball fields, a playground, and a picnic area.

Dennisport

🔟 *1 mi east of West Dennis; 10 mi west of Chatham.*

The Mid Cape's last southern village is Dennisport, a prime summer-resort area, with gray-shingle cottages, summer houses and condominiums, and lots of white picket fences covered with rambling roses. The Union Wharf Packing Company operated here in the 1850s, and sail makers and ship chandlers lined the shore. Sunbathers now pack the sands where sea clams once laid primary claim.

need a break? Set in a rustic mid-19th-century barn decorated with a working nickelodeon, the **Sundae School Ice Cream Parlor** (⊠ 387 Lower County Rd. ☎ 508/394–9122), open mid-April–mid-October, serves great homemade ice cream, frozen yogurt, real whipped cream, and old-fashioned sarsaparilla and cream soda from an antique marble soda fountain.

Where to Stay & Eat

$–$$$ ╳**Clancy's.** A local landmark on the bucolic Swan River, Clancy's is popular, with a parking lot that's often jammed by 5 PM, so expect a substantial wait during peak hours in season. This is an enormous operation, with long family tables, round tables, booths, a deck overlooking the river, and two bars. On the seemingly endless menu are several variations of nachos, salads, and chili. Clancy's likes to be creative with the names of its dishes, so you can find items such as steak Lucifer (sirloin topped with lobster, asparagus, and béarnaise sauce) and a Sunday-brunch menu with the likes of crab, steak, or eggs Benny. ⊠ *8 Upper County Rd.* ☎ *508/394–6661* ⊕ *www.clancysrestaurant.com* ⚌ *Reservations not accepted* ⊟ *AE, DC, MC, V.*

$–$$$ ╳**Swan River Seafood Restaurant.** From the right table you can have a beautiful view of the Swan River marsh and Nantucket Sound beyond at this informal little eatery, which turns out great fresh fish in both traditional and creative preparations. Besides the usual fried and broiled choices, try mako shark au poivre or scrod San Sebastian, simmered in garlic broth with littleneck clams. ⊠ *5 Lower County Rd.* ☎ *508/394–4466* ⊟ *AE, MC, V* ⊘ *Closed mid-Sept.–late May. No lunch weekdays late May–mid-June.*

$–$$$$ ▥ **The Corsair and Cross Rip.** These motels, built side by side, offer clean and crisp rooms, many with captivating beach views. Rooms in the main motel buildings range from smaller "value" units with one queen bed to pricier deluxe accommodations with kitchenettes and sitting areas, plus a few spacious condo-style suites. Three large three- and four-bedroom vacation houses are also available for rent; they can sleep up to 12 and are fully equipped with luxurious amenities. Decor in the motel buildings is more basic, but between the oceanfront location (there are three private beaches) and the extensive facilities, you can spend little time in your room. There are also laundry facilities on-site. Suites and houses require a one-week minimum stay in season. ⊠ *33 and 41 Chase Ave.* ☎ *508/398–2279 or 800/889–8037* ⊕ *www.corsaircrossrip.com* ⤹ *37 rooms, 2 suites* ⚘ *Picnic area, some kitchens, some kitchenettes, refrigerators, cable TV, 2 pools (1 indoor), hot tub, video game room, laundry facilities; no smoking* ⊟*AE, D, MC, V* ⊘ *Closed late Oct.–Mar.*

$$$–$$$$ ▥ **Pelham House.** The ocean-side Pelham House, south of Route 28,
Fodor'sChoice is a modern (if not particularly exciting) collection of spacious rooms
★ strategically angled to maximize ocean views. Atop the property's ocean-facing section are several "penthouse" rooms with sitting areas,

excellent views of Nantucket Sound, and more upscale furniture. But the location is what really generates a buzz—with about 400 feet of private beachfront, it's a great place to spend all day in the sun and sand. A complimentary full breakfast is served in season, a continental breakfast in the cooler months. ⊠ *14 Sea St.* ⊕ *Box 38, 02639* ☎ *508/398–6076 or 800/497–3542* 🖷 *508/760–3999* ⊕ *www.pelhamhouseresort.com* ⤳ *37 rooms, 2 suites* ⚭ *Refrigerators, cable TV, tennis court, pool, beach; no a/c in some rooms* ▤ *AE, D, MC, V* ⊗ *Closed Nov.–Mar.* ⍑⊖⍳ *BP.*

$$–$$$ ⊡ **English Garden Bed & Breakfast.** Anita and Joe Sangiolo—she's a former actress and he's a retired engineer—have turned their comfortable 1922 home into an equally comfortable B&B. The eight rooms are done in a cheerful country style, with quilts, four-poster or iron beds, and pine armoires; four rooms have ocean views. The adjacent carriage house has two modern suites, each with a bedroom, separate living area with a gas fireplace, and kitchenette. Beach chairs and towels are provided (the house is just a block from the sand), and Joe has put together a meticulously detailed notebook of things-to-do ideas. Film buffs take note: one of the two guest parlors has a TV–VCR and a collection of classic movies. ⊠ *32 Inman Rd., 02639* ☎ *508/398–2915 or 888/788–1908* 🖷 *508/398–2852* ⊕ *www.theenglishgardenbandb.com* ⤳ *8 rooms, 2 suites* ⚭ *In-room data ports, kitchenette, cable TV; no kids under 10 (except in suites), no smoking* ▤ *AE, D, MC, V* ⊗ *Closed Nov.–mid-Apr.* ⍑⊖⍳ *BP.*

$$–$$$ ⊡ **The Garlands.** There are innumerable strip motels and cottage colonies lining Old Wharf Road in Dennisport, but few places provide comfort and views to match this bi-level motel-style complex. There are 20 units in all; 18 are two-bedroom suites. Each unit has a fully equipped kitchen, private sundeck or patio, and daily maid service. The oceanfront VIP suites, simply named A and B (two bedrooms) and C and D (one bedroom), are the best picks here—the nearly floor-to-ceiling windows offer unobstructed water views; at high tide you're almost in the surf. ⊠ *117 Old Wharf Rd.* ⊕ *Box 506, 02639* ☎ *508/398–6987* ⤳ *20 suites* ⚭ *Kitchen, cable TV, beach; no a/c, some ceiling fans* ▤ *No credit cards* ⊗ *Closed mid-Oct.–mid-Apr.*

Nightlife & the Arts

Improper Bostonian (⊠ Rte. 28 ☎ 508/394–7416), open only in summer, has a mix of live music and DJ-spun dance tunes several nights a week and attracts a young crowd.

Karl's Landmark Cafe (⊠ 645 Main St. ☎ 508/398–5551), open only in summer, shares patrons with **Improper Bostonian** across the street. Live music and DJs entertain to a dancing crowd.

Sports & the Outdoors

Cape Cod Waterways (⊠ 16 Main St. [Rte. 28] ☎ 508/398–0080) rents canoes, kayaks, and electric paddleboats for leisurely travel on the Swan River.

Shopping

Cape Cod Shoe Mart (⊠ 271 Main St. [Rte. 28] ☎ 508/398–6000) has such brand names as Capezio, Dexter, Clark, Esprit, Nike, Reebok, L. A. Gear, and Rockport.

THE MID CAPE A TO Z

To research prices, get advice from other travelers, and book travel arrangements, visit www.fodors.com.

AIR TRAVEL

Airline service is extremely unpredictable because of the seasonal nature of Cape travel—carriers come and go, while others juggle their routes.

CARRIERS Cape Air/Nantucket Airlines flies direct from Boston to Hyannis and Provincetown year-round and from New Bedford to Martha's Vineyard and Nantucket. Cape Air has joint fares with Continental, Delta, Midwest Express, and US Airways and ticketing and baggage agreements with eight major U.S. airlines and with KLM. For charters, contact Cape Air.

US Airways Express flies nonstop from Boston and New York to Hyannis year-round. Connect in Boston with the airline's other routes. Westchester Air offers charter service from White Plains, New York, to and from Hyannis, Martha's Vineyard, and Nantucket.

🛫 Airlines & Contacts **Cape Air/Nantucket Airlines** ☎ 508/771-6944 or 800/352-0714 ⊕ www.flycapeair.com. **US Airways Express** ☎ 800/428-4322.

AIRPORTS

Barnstable Municipal Airport is in Hyannis, minutes from Barnstable village.

🛫 Airport Information **Barnstable Municipal Airport** ⊠ 480 Barnstable Rd., Rte. 28 rotary ☎ 508/775-2020.

BOAT & FERRY TRAVEL

Year-round ferries to Nantucket leave from Hyannis. Seasonal ferries to Martha's Vineyard also depart from Hyannis. For details *see* Boat & Ferry Travel *in* Smart Travel Tips A to Z.

BUS TRAVEL

Plymouth & Brockton Street Railway provides bus service to Provincetown from downtown Boston and Logan Airport, with stops in Barnstable, Hyannis, and other towns en route. The Logan Direct airport express service bypasses downtown Boston and stops in Plymouth, Sagamore, Barnstable, and Hyannis.

🚌 Bus Depots **Hyannis Transportation Center** ⊠ 215 Iyanough Rd., Hyannis ☎ 508/775-8504 ⊕ www.capecodtransit.org. **Plymouth & Brockton Street Railway Terminals** ⊠ South Station Bus Terminal, 700 Atlantic Ave., Boston ☎ 508/746-0378.

🚌 Bus Line **Plymouth & Brockton Street Railway** ☎ 508/746-0378 ⊕ www.p-b.com.

BUS TRAVEL WITHIN THE MID CAPE

The Cape Cod Regional Transit Authority operates several bus services that link Cape towns. All buses are wheelchair-accessible and equipped with bike racks. The SeaLine operates along Route 28 Monday–Saturday between Hyannis and Woods Hole (average fare is $3.50 one-way from Hyannis to Woods Hole). Its many stops include Mashpee Commons, Falmouth, and the Woods Hole Steamship Authority docks. The SeaLine connects in Hyannis with the Plymouth & Brockton line, as well as the Villager, another bus line that runs along Route 132 between Hyannis and Barnstable Harbor. The driver will stop when signaled along the route.

The b-bus service is a fleet of minivans that will transport passengers door to door between any towns on the Cape. You must register in advance to use the b-bus; phone the Cape Cod Regional Transit Authority between 1 and 4 PM on weekdays to sign up. After you are enrolled, call for reservations between 8 AM and 4 PM on weekdays; reservations may be made up to a week in advance. Service runs seven days a week, year-round. The cost is $2 per ride, plus 10¢ per mile, half that for senior citizens.

The H20 Line offers daily regularly scheduled service year-round between Hyannis and Orleans along Route 28. The Hyannis–Orleans fare is $3.50; shorter trips cost less. Buses connect in Hyannis with the SeaLine, Villager, and Plymouth & Brockton lines.

🚍 **Cape Cod Regional Transit Authority** ☎ 508/385-8326, 800/352-7155 in Massachusetts ⊕ www.capecodtransit.org.

CAR RENTALS

You can rent wheels at Barnstable Municipal Airport (⇨ Airports, *above*).

🚗 Major Agencies **Avis** ☎ 508/775-2888 or 800/831-2847 ⊕ www.avis.com. **Budget** ☎ 508/790-8050 or 800/527-0700 ⊕ www.budgetrentacar.com. **Hertz** ☎ 508/775-5825 or 800/654-3131 ⊕ www.hertz.com. **National** ☎ 508/771-4353 or 800/227-7368 ⊕ www.nationalcar.com.

🚗 Local Agency **Rent-A-Wreck of Hyannis** ☎ 508/771-9667 or 888/486-1470 ⊕ www.rentawreck.com.

CAR TRAVEL

U.S. 6 and Routes 6A and 28 are heavily congested eastbound Friday evening, westbound Sunday afternoon, and in both directions on Saturday in summer.

PARKING Throughout the Mid Cape, most museum and other attractions have at least small parking lots. In Hyannis, there's street parking along both sides of Main Street.

TRAFFIC Route 28, along the Cape's southern edge, can get very congested during the morning and evening rush hours, particularly in and around Hyannis. On rainy summer days, the shopping areas, both along Route 28 and on Route 132 near the Cape Cod Mall, get especially clogged.

DISABILITIES & ACCESSIBILITY

The Cape Cod Disability Access Directory, available from the Cape Cod Chamber of Commerce or online (⊕ www.capecoddisability.org), has detailed information about accessibility Cape-wide. For more information on this and other resources, *see* Disabilities & Accessibility *in* Smart Travel Tips A to Z.

EMERGENCIES

Cape Cod Hospital has a 24-hour emergency room. Mid Cape Medical Center is open weekdays 8–5, Saturday 8–3, and Sunday 8–1. Dental Associates of Cape Cod accepts emergency walk-ins. For rescues at sea, call the Coast Guard. Boaters should use Channel 16 on their radios.

🚩 Doctors & Dentists **Dental Associates of Cape Cod** ⊠ 262 Barnstable Rd., Hyannis ☎ 508/778-1200. **Mid Cape Medical Center** ⊠ 489 Bearses Way, at Rte. 28, Unit A-4, Hyannis ☎ 508/771-4092.

🚩 Emergency Services **Ambulance, fire, police** ☎ 911 or dial township station. **Coast Guard** ☎ 508/888-0335 in Sandwich and Cape Cod Canal, 508/945-0164 in Chatham ⊕ www.uscg.mil.

🚩 Hospital **Cape Cod Hospital** ⊠ 27 Park St., Hyannis ☎ 508/771-1800 ⊕ www.capecodhealth.org.

🚩 Hotline **Massachusetts Poison Control Center** ☎ 800/682-9211.

🚩 24-Hour Pharmacy **CVS** ⊠ 176 North St., Hyannis ☎ 508/775-8346 ⊕ www.cvs.com.

KIDS IN THE MID CAPE

SIGHTS & ATTRACTIONS Libraries usually offer regular kids story hours or other programs; check them out on a rainy day. Hours are listed in the newspapers each week. The Cape Cod Baseball League has summer day camps and clinics, run by the individual teams, for kids ages 5–13; most teams have six weeks of camp, typically weekday mornings. In Hyannis, the Cape Cod Melody Tent has a kids theater series on Wednesday mornings in July and August. The Cape Playhouse in Dennis also offers children's theater on Friday morning in July and August. The Cape Cod Museum of Fine Arts has summer workshops for kids, as well as kids' classes year-round; call for program details.

🚩 Local Information **Cape Cod Baseball League** ☎ 508/432-6909 ⊕ www.capecodbaseball.org. **Cape Cod Melody Tent** ☎ 508/775-9100. **Cape Cod Museum of Fine Arts** ☎ 508/385-4477. **Cape Playhouse** ☎ 508/385-3911 or 877/385-3911.

LODGING

APARTMENT & HOUSE RENTALS Rentals throughout the Mid Cape are handled by Century 21, Sam Ingram Real Estate. Great Vacations Inc. specializes in locating vacation rentals in Brewster, Dennis, and Orleans. Peter McDowell Associates offers a wide selection of properties for rent by the week, month, or season; the company also rents larger homes for family reunions and other gatherings. Most places are in Dennis. Waterfront Rentals covers Bourne to Truro, listing everything from condos to estates.

🚩 Local Agents **Century 21, Sam Ingram Real Estate** ⊠ 938 Rte. 6A, Yarmouth Port 02675 ☎ 508/362-1191 or 800/676-3340 📠 508/362-7889 ⊕ www.century21samingram.com. **Great Vacations Inc.** ⊠ 2660 Rte. 6A, Brewster 02631 ☎ 508/896-2090. **Peter McDowell Associates** ⊠ 585 Main St. [Rte. 6A], Dennis 02638 ☎ 508/385-9114 or 888/

385-9114 ✉ 11 Main St. [Rte. 28], Dennisport 02639 ☎ 508/394-5400 or 800/870-5401 ⊕ www.capecodproperties.com. **Waterfront Rentals** ✉ 20 Pilgrim Rd., West Yarmouth 02673 ☎ 508/778-1818 ⛶ 508/771-3563 ⊕ www.waterfrontrentalsinc.com.

CAMPING   Eastern Mountain Sports rents tents and sleeping bags. Sandy Terraces is a seasonal family nudist campground.

🔳 **Eastern Mountain Sports** ✉ 1513 Rte. 132, Hyannis ☎ 508/362-8690 ⊕ www. emsonline.com. **Sandy Terraces** ⛺ Box 98, Marstons Mills 02648 ☎ 508/428-9209.

MEDIA

The *Cape Cod Times* is the region's main local daily newspaper. The *Barnstable Patriot* focuses on the Mid Cape; it's a weekly newspaper.

TAXIS

There are taxi stands at the Hyannis airport, the Hyannis bus station, and the Capetown Mall, across the street from the Cape Cod Mall. In Hyannis call Checker Taxi for pickups. Dick's Taxi will pick you up and has a stand at the airport. John's Taxi & Limousine picks up in Dennis and Harwich only but will take passengers all over the Cape. Town Taxi is found at several locations around Hyannis, including Capetown Mall, the bus station, and on W. Main Street.

🔳 Taxi Companies **Checker Taxi** ☎ 508/771-8294. **Dick's Taxi** ☎ 508/428-4918. **John's Taxi & Limousine** ☎ 508/394-3209. **Town Taxi** ☎ 508/771-5555 or 888/771-8696.

TOURS

Cape Cod Duck Mobile takes you on a land-and-sea tour of downtown Hyannis and the harbor in a restored U.S. military amphibious vehicle. These 45-minute narrated tours depart on the hour, roll through downtown, then splash into Lewis Bay to cruise past the Kennedy compound and other sights. Tickets go on sale daily at 9 and in summer often sell out quickly. Tours run frequently between 10 and 5 June through Labor Day; call for details about where to purchase tickets and for spring and fall schedules. Admission for the tour is $14.

Hy-Line runs one-hour narrated boat tours of Hyannis Harbor, including a view of the Kennedy compound. Sunset and evening cocktail cruises are also available; ticket prices for all tours range between $12 and $15. Bass River Cruises offers 1½-hour narrated tours of the Bass River, past windmills, marshlands, and old captains' houses, all seen from a 49-passenger aluminum boat with an awning. Trips cost $12.50 and run Memorial Day to Columbus Day at 11, 1, 4, and 6, and there's a snack bar on board.

Cape Cod Soaring Adventures offers glider flights and lessons out of Marstons Mills.

The Cape Cod Central Railroad offers two-hour, 42-mi narrated rail tours from Hyannis to the Cape Cod Canal (admission $15) late May through October; trains generally run Tuesday to Sunday, but call for a schedule. You can have your fill of cranberry bogs, marshes, and woodlands, as well as such unusual sights as the Barnstable House of Corrections, where you'll spot inmates farming in the fields. From Hyannis, sit on the right side of the train for the best views. The second hour and its narration are a bit subdued, as you're traveling back the way you came, but the scenery and loud whistle blasts ought to keep you alert and engaged. There's also a three-hour, adults-only dinner train where you can settle back and watch the scenery as you nosh. The summer dinner train runs Wednesday through Sunday, and the cost is $56.95 per person. Another dinner train, created for families, with a kids' menu and activities, runs on Tuesday evening, $34.95 per person, $24.95 for kids under 12. A lunch train operates on Tuesday and Wednesday in June, July, and August for $34.95 per person.

🖪 Fees & Schedules **Bass River Cruises** ✉ Rte. 28, West Dennis, just east of Bass River Bridge ☎ 508/362-5555. **Cape Cod Central Railroad** ✉ Hyannis Train Depot, 252 Main St., Hyannis ☎ 508/771-3800 or 888/797-7245 ⊕ www.capetrain.com. **Cape Cod Duck Mobile** ✉ 447 Main St., Hyannis ☎ 508/790-2111 or 888/225-3825. **Cape Cod Soaring Adventures** ☎ 508/420-4201. **Hy-Line** ✉ Ocean St. dock, Pier 1 ☎ 508/778-2600 or 800/492-8082 ⊕ www.hy-linecruises.com.

TROLLEY TRAVEL

The Cape Cod Regional Transit Authority runs seasonal trolleys in Falmouth, Mashpee, Hyannis, Yarmouth, and Dennis. Fares and times vary; call for more information.

🖪 **Cape Cod Regional Transit Authority** ☎ 508/385-8326, 800/352-7155 in Massachusetts ⊕ www.capecodtransit.org.

VISITOR INFORMATION

The Cape Cod Chamber of Commerce is open year-round, Monday–Saturday 9–5 and Sunday 10–4.

🖪 Tourist Information **Cape Cod Chamber of Commerce** ✉ Junction of U.S. 6 and 132 ⌖ Box 790, Hyannis 02601 ☎ 508/862-0700 or 888/332-2732 ⊕ www.capecodchamber.org. **Dennis** ✉ Junction of Rtes. 28 and 134, West Dennis ⌖ Box 275, South Dennis 02660 ☎ 508/398-3568 or 800/243-9920 ⊕ www.dennischamber.com. **Hyannis** ✉ 1481 Rte. 132, 02601 ☎ 508/362-5230 or 877/492-6647 ⊕ www.hyannis.com. **Yarmouth** ✉ 657 Rte. 28, West Yarmouth 02673 ✉ Box 479, South Yarmouth 02664 ☎ 508/778-1008 or 800/732-1008 ⊕ www.yarmouthcapecod.com ✉ Information center ✉ U.S. 6 heading east between exits 6 and 7 ☎ 508/362-9796.

THE LOWER CAPE

4

VIEW A SPECTACULAR SUNSET
at First Encounter Beach ⇨*p.167*

WATCH BASEBALL'S FUTURE ALL-STARS
at a Cape League game ⇨*p.155*

INDULGE IN A SEVEN-COURSE MEAL
at the esteemed Chillingsworth ⇨*p.134*

HAVE A COLORFUL STAY
at Kadee's Gray Elephant ⇨*p.161*

SOAK UP THE DRAMATIC VIEW
from Chatham Light on a foggy day ⇨*p.148*

Revised by
Lori A. Nolin

SPECKLED WITH STILL-ACTIVE CRANBERRY BOGS, sturdy trees, and pasture, the Lower Cape exudes a peaceful residential aura. You won't find roadways cluttered with minigolf complexes, trampolines, or bumper boats here. While an influx of year-round residents has transformed much of the Upper Cape into a commuter's haven, the Lower Cape still has a quiet sense of history and simple purpose.

Rich in history and Cape flavor, Brewster and Harwich stand opposite one another in the area just shy of the elbow. Harwich, inland, has antique homes, rambling old burial grounds, and a modest town center with shops, restaurants, museums, churches, and public parks. Brewster is similarly historic; examples of Victorian, Greek Revival, and colonial architecture abound, most of it meticulously preserved. Many homes have been converted to welcoming guesthouses and bed-and-breakfasts, while others are privately owned.

The traditional, elegant town of Chatham perches dramatically at the end of the peninsular elbow. It's here the Atlantic begins to wet the shores of the Cape, sometimes with frightening strength. Chatham has shown vulnerability to the forces of nature over the years, as little by little its shores have succumbed to the insatiable sea.

North of Chatham is Orleans, supply center of the Lower and Outer Capes, replete with large grocery chains and shopping plazas. The famed Nauset Beach is here, its dune-backed shores crammed with sun-seeking revelers in summer. Orleans does have a rich history; you just have to leave the maze of industry to find it. Continuing north, you can reach Eastham, a town often overlooked because of its position on busy U.S. 6, but perfectly charming if you know where to look.

The Lower Cape is blessed with large tracts of open space, set aside for conservation. South of Chatham, the Monomoy National Wildlife Refuge is a twin-island bird sanctuary. Here dozens of species of birds are free to feed, nest, and expand their numbers without human meddling. Recreation seekers should head straight to Nickerson State Park in Brewster to frolic in freshwater ponds or enjoy a serene bike ride under the shade of trees. In Eastham, where the Cape Cod National Seashore officially begins, the Salt Pond Visitor Center has a wealth of area information, educational programs, and guided tours.

Exploring the Lower Cape

The towns of Harwich, Chatham, Brewster, Orleans, and Eastham comprise the Lower Cape. Of these, only Brewster and Orleans touch Route 6A. Harwich, Chatham and Orleans span Route 28, but don't fear. Although known for traffic, Route 28's congestion eases as the road winds toward the Lower Cape. Eastham sits along Route 6. While Route 6 is the fastest way to get to all the towns, it's a worthwhile drive to amble along Routes 28 or 6A. On the way, picturesque harbors, scenic side roads, the towns' Main Streets, antique stores, romantic inns, and colonial homes dot the landscape. Follow 28 into Chatham and make your way to the Chatham Lighthouse for breathtaking views of Nantucket Sound.

About the Restaurants

In what began as a highly controversial policy change, most Cape towns—including Chatham, Orleans, Eastham, Brewster, and Harwich—banished smoking from restaurants and bars. Now that some time has passed, everyone has adjusted. Smokers retreat for a break outdoors and businesses are back to booming despite the policy.

Each town has its own batch of treasured and traditional restaurants, and all will be crowded in summer. A significant number of restaurants close their doors once the crowds thin in October—including the beloved fried-seafood shacks—but plenty remain open throughout the year. Fresh seafood is a major staple.

If you are celebrating a milestone or hoping to delight someone special, Brewster's Chillingsworth impresses with French-country elegance. The Chatham Bars Inn romances an era of gentle tranquillity. If you're undecided, a stroll down Chatham's Main Street will tempt your palate. The restaurants in Orleans, Brewster, Harwich, and Eastham are spread out through the towns, but top restaurants like the Brewster Fish House are worth finding.

About the Hotels

Money made in early maritime fortunes helped build exquisite historic homes, many of which are now unique and lovely inns. Chatham is blessed with dozens of these aged beauties, most with all the modern conveniences. B&Bs and intimate guesthouses are the primary lodging choices, but even larger hotels such as Chatham Bars Inn and the Chatham Wayside Inn capture the charm of Old Cape Cod. Expect fewer hotel and motel options on this part of the Cape. However, outside town centers are a few roadside or waterfront hotel complexes, usually a bit softer on the budget and welcoming to families with small children.

Brewster is essentially a B&B kind of town, offering lodging in former sea captains' homes. Harwich and Orleans have a mixture of both family-friendly hotel complexes and lovingly restored inns. Eastham has quite a few large-scale hotels along U.S. 6, including the Sheraton. Don't expect to find bargains here during the high season.

Other options include camping or weekly cottage rentals; all towns have the Cape's trademark cottage colonies. Note that in summer these must be secured well in advance, usually through a local real estate agent.

	WHAT IT COSTS				
	$$$$	$$$	$$	$	¢
RESTAURANTS	over $30	$20–$30	$15–$20	$10–15	under $10
HOTELS	over $220	$140–$220	$100–$140	$80–$100	under $80

Restaurant prices are per person for a main course at dinner. Hotel prices are for a standard double room in high season, excluding 5.7% state tax and gratuities. Some inns add a 15% service charge.

Numbers in the text correspond to numbers in the margin and on the Lower Cape and Chatham maps.

Brewster ❶ is an eclectic mix of antiques shops, museums, an old gristmill open to the public, freshwater ponds for swimming or fishing, the beach and tidal flats to explore when the water is low, and miles of biking and hiking trails through **Nickerson State Park ❹**. Don't miss the **Cape Cod Museum of Natural History ❸**, which will take a couple of hours to explore. Main Street in the handsome town of **Chatham ❻–⓫** is perfect for strolling, shopping, and dining. A trip to the Monomoy Islands is a must for bird-watchers. Back in town, you can watch glassblowing in process at the Chatham Glass Company, visit the Old Atwood House and Railroad Museums, and drive over to take in the view from Chatham Light.

On the way north from Chatham, take the less commercial end of Route 28 to **Orleans ⓬**, driving alongside sailboat-speckled views of Pleasant Bay. Try to allow time for a good long bike ride on the Cape Cod Rail Trail or for an afternoon relaxing at Nauset Beach. **Eastham ⓭** is the next stop on the way up the arm, where the **Fort Hill Area ⓮** has the historic Penniman House Museum and some wonderful walks along the adjacent trails. Stop at the National Seashore's **Salt Pond Visitor Center ⓯** for some interesting information about the area, then take the bike trails to Coast Guard Beach and Nauset Light, with a view of the Three Sisters Lighthouses, now settled in a small park area.

4

Timing

Although the crowds of summer are testament to the appeal of the Lower Cape and its spectacular beaches, outdoor pursuits, crafts and art shows, concerts, and special events, the region is becoming a popular year-round destination. Because of the ocean-side climate, spring and fall are simply lesser shades of full-blown summer. In late May and early June businesses closed in the winter months open their doors, lodging rates are lower, and the agonies of summertime traffic, long waits at restaurants, and parking restrictions at area beaches can all be avoided. September, October, and even November are the same. The waters usually remain warm enough to swim well into October, and seasonal businesses do their best to rid their stocks of merchandise by having generous sales.

You won't get the expected splendors of New England foliage on the Lower Cape, because the landscape changes are subtle. Swaying salt-marsh grasses turn golden, cranberry bogs explode in a vividness of ruby harvest, and the ocean relaxes into a deep, deep blue. The light becomes softer and its patterns more dramatic on both land and sea. In the towns of Harwich, Brewster, and Orleans, where the soil is substantial enough to support mighty oaks and maples, the colors of autumn do peer through. A drive along Route 6A under the canopy of changing leaves is just as breathtaking as a summer jaunt past blooming gardens.

Brewster

❶ *6 mi north of Chatham; 5 mi west of Orleans; 20 mi east of Sandwich.*

Celebrating its history as a seafaring community, Brewster honors its heritage by calling itself the Sea Captains' Town. Historic Route 6A, the Old King's Highway, winds through the center of town. This road, the old stagecoach route, was once nearly the only one at this end of the Cape, and both residents and legislators are determined to keep it well-preserved. Homes and businesses must adhere to historic detail—there are no neon signs, no strip malls—only the gentle facades of a graceful era.

Named for Plymouth leader William Brewster, the area was settled in 1659 but was not incorporated as a separate town until 1803. In the early 1800s, Brewster was the terminus of a packet cargo service from Boston. In 1849 Thoreau wrote that "this town has more mates and masters of vessels than any other town in the country." Many mansions built for sea captains remain, and quite a few have been turned into handsome B&Bs. In the 18th and 19th centuries, the bay side of Brewster was the site of a major salt-making industry. Of the 450 saltworks operating on the Cape in the 1830s, more than 60 were here.

Brewster's location on Cape Cod Bay makes it a perfect place to learn about the natural history of the Cape. The Cape Cod Museum of Natural History is here, and the area is rich in conservation lands, state parks, forests, freshwater ponds, and brackish marshes. When the tide is low in Cape Cod Bay, you can stroll the beaches and explore tide pools up to 2 mi from the shore on the Brewster flats. When it's high tide, the water is relatively warm and very calm for swimming. Both Nickerson State Park and the Punkhorn Parklands offer up thousands of acres through which to wander.

Windmills used to be prominent in Cape Cod towns; the Brewster area once had four. The 1795 **Higgins Farm Windmill** (⊠ Off Rte. 6A, just west of the Cape Cod Museum of Natural History, West Brewster)—an octagonal-type mill shingled in weathered pine with a roof like an upturned boat—was moved here in 1974 and has been restored. The millstones are original. At night the mill is often spotlighted and makes quite a sight.

On the grounds of the Higgins Farm Windmill, the one-room **Harris-Black House** dates to 1795. The restored building is today partially furnished, and is dominated by a brick hearth and original woodwork. ⊠ *Off Rte. 6A, just west of Cape Cod Museum of Natural History, West Brewster* ☎ *508/896–9521* ☞ *Free* ⊙ *Mid-June to mid-Oct., Thurs.-Sat. 1–4.*

❷ A short drive from Route 6A is the **Stony Brook Grist Mill,** a restored, operating 19th-century fulling mill (a mill that shrinks and thickens cloth), now also a museum. The old mill's waterwheel slowly turns in a small, tree-lined brook. Inside, exhibits include old mill equipment and looms;

4

Beaches

The Lower Cape is straddled by four major bodies of water: the bracing and grand Atlantic Ocean, and three more mild-mannered bays—Nantucket Sound, Pleasant Bay, and Cape Cod Bay. If you prefer freshwater swimming you can try the many ponds—some left over from the ancient glacial carving of the peninsula—sprinkled throughout the entire area.

On the south side, Harwich Port, Harwich, and Chatham dip into the shallower and warmer Nantucket Sound. The beaches here, which tend to be divided into smallish partitions designated according to public or private ownership, are popular with families, ice-cream trucks, jet skiers, and windsurfers. Harwich and Chatham swimmers can also find a spot along Pleasant Bay. The waters here are very shallow, which makes it ideal for kayaks, canoes, and swimmers.

Brewster's glory is Cape Cod Bay, and dozens of beaches (public and private) extend for acres at low tide. Although swimmers won't have much luck at this time, treasure hunters can stroll the sands, keeping an eye out for shells and creatures left behind by the retreating waters. There's plenty of room to wander on the bay side, and you won't find a better spot to catch the nightly sunset.

The Lower Cape's ocean beaches are unbroken by dictates of ownership or man-made barriers from Chatham onward, so you're free to roam. Note that Chatham's ocean beaches are easily accessible by bike or foot, but there's no parking for cars. Orleans has Nauset Beach, a Cape favorite. In Eastham the National Seashore and the town maintain several beaches with exhilarating ocean swimming.

Biking

The Cape's top bike route, the 25-mi Cape Cod Rail Trail, follows the paved right-of-way of the old Penn Central Railroad, from South Dennis to South Wellfleet. You can pick up the trail in Harwich, Brewster, Orleans, or Eastham. Nickerson State Park, in Brewster, has 8 mi of its own forested trails, some with access to the rail trail. From the Salt Pond Visitor Center in Eastham, take a jaunt off the rail trail for meandering paths leading to Nauset Beach, Coast Guard Beach, and beautiful Nauset Marsh. Cyclists in Chatham can follow the little green signs that denote the Chatham Bike Route—but use caution, as the roadway is shared with folks in cars who are taking in the view just as eagerly as you are. The trail runs beside the ocean and all the stunningly majestic homes that dominate the waterfront.

Nightlife & the Arts

Chatham's Main Street is lined with galleries and studios showcasing local and national artists. In Orleans weekly outdoor art shows sell the works of local painters and craftspeople and have free demonstrations. Eastham and Harwich also host outdoor arts-and-crafts forays. Harwich's biggie is the Professional Arts and Crafts Festival, held in July and August.

The theater tradition remains strong throughout the Lower Cape. In Harwich, the Harwich Junior Theatre stages performances year-round and offers children's classes in the summer. Community theater dominates the scene in Orleans and Chatham. Off-season, Eastham shines with the First Encounter Coffee House, a teetotaler's haven for local music and poetry readings. In Brewster, the professional Cape Cod Repertory Theatre stages productions both indoors and out under the stars. Popular and free town-band concerts are held all over the Cape, and other concerts are presented by various church groups and community organizations. There's a continuous, lively schedule of events throughout the summer in each town; pick up a free guide at information centers and stores.

Nightlife on the Lower Cape is never wild, but it's certainly not dull. Local bands liven things up at favored watering holes in Orleans, Chatham, and Harwich including the Chatham Squire, Land Ho! in Orleans, Brewster's rustic Woodshed, and the spirited Irish Pub in West Harwich. More peaceful nighttime diversions include solitary beach walking by moonlight, and stargazing (watch for the extraordinary Perseid meteor shower display in August). The National Seashore schedules storytelling nights around a beach bonfire.

Sports & the Outdoors

Cape Cod, especially the Lower and Outer regions, is an outdoor playground. From Eastham to Provincetown, the Cape Cod National Seashore offers miles of hiking and biking trails, several historic sites, and many beautiful, natural places to explore. The Cape's rivers, ponds, inlets, and harbors are great for canoeing or kayaking. Whether on your own or as part of a guided tour (the Cape Cod Museum of Natural History, in Brewster, has a full schedule of such trips), these peaceful ventures provide a break from the crowds and an up-close look at the local flora and fauna. Several rental shops offer equipment and instruction in Eastham, Orleans, and elsewhere. Ambitious anglers in search of striped bass, bluefish, flounder, or cod will find plenty of charter boats for hire. In general, fishing is a tremendous industry on Cape Cod, both commercial and recreational.

In Eastham, the National Seashore's Salt Pond Visitor Center maintains walking and biking trails in the woods and around Nauset Marsh. In Brewster, the Punkhorn Parklands include nearly 2,000 acres open to walkers, horseback riders, and mountain bikers. From Chatham, you can hike over to Morris Island (mindful of the tides), which affords spectacular views of the ocean and the dunes.

Shopping

In Cape Cod, you can buy everything from a sweatshirt to a handcrafted reproduction of an early-American brass lantern. Absent on the Lower Cape are the national chain stores so popular on the mainland and on the Upper Cape. Out in these parts, stores are individually owned and carry a selection of unique merchandise. The area, however, does have its fill of kitsch-laden gift shops, selling all manner of magnets, T-shirts, mugs, and beach towels— all emblazoned with local themes such as lobsters and lighthouses. Cape Cod has long been a center for artists and craftspeople, who have been inspired by the natural environment. The tourist trade helps sustain them, as most artisans spend the winter creating and replacing stock of ceramics, jewelry, works in fabric, sculpture, paintings, photography, or glass wiped out with visitors' dollars the season before.

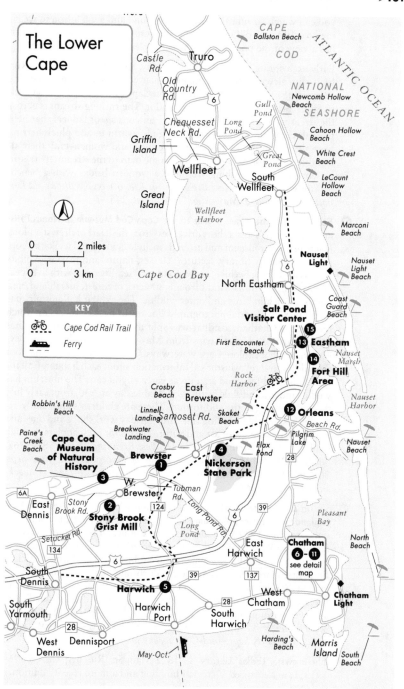

The Lower Cape

CAPE
Ballston Beach
COD
Castle Rd.
Truro
Old Country Rd.
NATIONAL
Newcomb Hollow Beach
SEASHORE
Gull Pond
Chequesset Neck Rd.
Long Pond
Cahoon Hollow Beach
Griffin Island
White Crest Beach
Wellfleet
Great Pond
LeCount Hollow Beach
South Wellfleet
Great Island
Wellfleet Harbor
Marconi Beach
Nauset Light
Nauset Light Beach
Cape Cod Bay
North Eastham
Coast Guard Beach
Salt Pond Visitor Center
First Encounter Beach
15
13 Eastham
Nauset Marsh
14
Fort Hill Area
Nauset Harbor
Rock Harbor
12 Orleans
Crosby Beach
East Brewster
Beach Rd.
Robbin's Hill Beach
Linnell Landing
Samoset Rd.
Skaket Beach
Pilgrim Lake
Nauset Beach
Paine's Creek Beach
Breakwater Landing
28
Cape Cod Museum of Natural History
Brewster
1
Flax Pond
3
4
Nickerson State Park
W. Brewster
Tubman Rd.
East Dennis
Stony Brook Rd.
2
124
Long Pond Rd.
39
Pleasant Bay
North Beach
Setucket Rd.
Stony Brook Grist Mill
134
Long Pond
East Harwich
Chatham 6-11 see detail map
South Dennis
39
137
Chatham Light
South Yarmouth
Harwich 5
West Chatham
Harwich Port
South Harwich
28
West Dennis
Dennisport
May-Oct.
Harding's Beach
Morris Island
South Beach

KEY
🚲 Cape Cod Rail Trail
⛴ Ferry

0 — 2 miles
0 — 3 km

you can watch cornmeal being stone-ground and get a lesson in weaving on a 100-year-old loom. Out back, across wooden bridges, a bench has a view of the pond and of the sluices leading into the mill area.

Early each spring, in April and early May, Stony Brook's **Herring Run** boils with alewives (herring) making their way to spawning waters; it's an amazing sight. The fish swim in from Cape Cod Bay up Paine's Creek to Stony Brook and the ponds beyond it. The rushing stream is across the street from the mill. The herring run consists of ladders that help the fish climb the rocky waters. Seagulls swarm in and pluck herring from the run into mid-air, while fishermen–and women–grab their allowable quota for bait. Farther down the path to the stream, there's an ivy-covered stone wishing well and a wooden bridge with a bench. ⌧ *Stony Brook Rd., West Brewster, off Rte. 6A* ☎ *No phone* ✆ *Donations accepted* ☼ *May–Aug., Thurs.–Sat. 2–5.*

☾ ❸ For nature enthusiasts, a visit to the **Cape Cod Museum of Natural History** is a must; it's just a short drive west from the heart of Brewster along Route 6A. The museum and grounds include guided field walks, a shop, a natural-history library, lectures, classes, nature and marine exhibits such as a working beehive, and a pond- and sea-life room with live specimens. Walking trails wind through 80 acres of forest, marshland, and ponds, all rich in birds and other wildlife. The exhibit hall upstairs has a wall display of aerial photographs documenting the process by which the famous Chatham sandbar was split in two. The museum also has guided canoe and kayak trips from May through September and several cruises that explore Cape waterways. Onboard naturalists point out the wildlife and relay historical information about each habitat. Call for tour times and fees, and sign up as early as you can. The museum has wildlife movies and slide lectures on Wednesday at 7:30, from early July through August, in the auditorium. There are children's and family activities in summer, including full- and half-day workshops and one- and two-week day camps of art and nature classes for preschoolers through grade 9. ⌧ *869 Main St. (Rte. 6A), West Brewster* ☎ *508/896–3867, 800/479–3867 in Massachusetts* ⊕ *www.ccmnh.org* ✆ *$5* ☼ *June–Sept. 30, daily 10–4; Apr.–May 30, Wed.–Sun. 10–4; Oct. 1–Dec. 31, weekends 10–4, except Christmas.*

☾ Set on a re-created 19th-century common with a picnic area, the **New England Fire & History Museum** exhibits 35 antique vehicles, including the only surviving 1929 Mercedes-Benz fire engine. Other highlights are the late Boston Pops conductor Arthur Fiedler's private collection of firefighting memorabilia, 14 mannequins in historical uniforms depicting firefighters through the centuries, a Victorian apothecary shop, an animated diorama of the Chicago Fire of 1871 complete with smoke and fire, a historic working forge, and medicinal herb gardens. Guided tours are given. Group tours are by appointment. ⌧ *1439 Main St. (Rte. 6A), West Brewster* ☎ *508/896–5711* ✆ *$6* ☼ *Mid-May–early Sept., weekdays 10–4; early Sept.–mid-Oct., weekends noon–4.*

The **Brewster Ladies' Library** (⌧ 1822 Main St. [Rte. 6A] ☎ 508/896–3913) is in a restored Victorian building and a more recent addition.

Fodor'sChoice
★

At the junction of Route 124, the **Brewster Store** (✉ 1935 Main St. [Rte. 6A] ☎ 508/896–3744 ⊕ www.brewsterstore.com) is a local landmark. Built in 1852 as a church, it's a typical New England general store with such essentials as the daily papers, penny candy, and benches out front for conversation. The Brewster Scoop out back serves ice cream mid-June through early September. Upstairs, the old front of the store has been re-created, and memorabilia from antique toys to World War II bond posters are displayed. Downstairs there's a working antique nickelodeon.

need a break?

If you need a quick break, **Hopkins House Gift and Bakery** (✉ 2727 Main St., East Brewster ☎ 508/896–9337) is the perfect pit stop. Wash down a chewy hermit cookie, baked with molasses and raisins, with some strong, hot coffee. Have an assortment of cookies, muffins, and snack bars boxed up for the road. A home-furnishings shop attached to the bakery might tempt you to stretch your legs a while longer.

Known as the Church of the Sea Captains, the handsome **First Parish Church** (✉ 1969 Main St. [Rte. 6A] ☎ 508/896–5577), with Gothic windows and a capped bell tower, is full of pews marked with the names of famous Brewster seamen. Out back is an old graveyard where militiamen, clergy, farmers, and sea captains rest side by side. The church hosts a summer musical program, including the ever-popular Tanglewood marionette show, Tuesday–Thursday mornings at 9:30.

The **Brewster Historical Society Museum,** in an 1830s house, has a sea captain's room with paintings and artifacts, an 1890 barbershop, a child's room with antique toys and clothing, a room of women's period gowns and accessories, and other exhibits on local history and architecture. Out back, a ¼-mi nature trail over dunes leads to the bay. ✉ *3371 Main St. [Rte. 6A], East Brewster* ☎ *508/896–9521* ⊠ *Free* ⊙ *June and Sept., weekends 1–4; July and Aug., Tues.–Fri. 1–4.*

For a lovely hike or run through the local wilds, try the **Punkhorn Parklands,** with freshwater kettle-hole ponds and 45 mi of scenic trails meandering through 800 acres of meadows, marshes, and pine forests. ✉ *End of Run Hill Rd., off Stony Brook Rd., West Brewster.*

☚ ❹ **Nickerson State Park**'s 1,961 acres were once part of a vast estate belonging to Roland C. Nickerson, son of Samuel Nickerson, a Chatham native who became a multimillionaire and founder of the First National Bank of Chicago. Today the land is open to the public for recreation. Roland and his wife, Addie, lavishly entertained such visitors as President Grover Cleveland at their private beach and hunting lodge in English country-house style, with coachmen dressed in tails and top hats and a bugler announcing carriages entering the front gates.

Like a village unto itself, the estate gardens provided much of the household's food, supplemented by game from its woods and fish from its ponds. It also had its own electric plant and a 9-hole golf course by the water. The enormous mansion Samuel built for his son in 1886 burned to the ground 20 years later, and Roland died two weeks after the event. The even grander stone mansion built to replace it in 1908 is now part of the Ocean Edge resort. In 1934 Addie donated the land for the state park in memory of Roland and their son, who died during the 1918 flu epidemic.

The park consists of acres of oak, pitch pine, hemlock, and spruce forest dotted with seven freshwater kettle ponds formed by glacial action. Some ponds are stocked with trout for fishing. You can swim in the ponds, canoe, sail, motorboat, bike along 8 mi of paved trails that have access to the Cape Cod Rail Trail, picnic, and cross-country ski in winter. Bird-watchers seek out the thrushes, wrens, warblers, woodpeckers, finches, larks, Canada geese, cormorants, great blue herons, hawks, owls, ospreys, and other species that frequent the park. Occasionally, red foxes and white-tailed deer are spotted in the woods. Both tent and RV camping are extremely popular here, and nature programs are offered in season. A map of the park is available on-site. ⊠ *3488 Rte. 6A, East Brewster* ☎ *508/896–3491* ⊕ *www.state.ma.us/dem/parks/nick.htm* ▣ *Free* ☉ *Daily dawn–dusk.*

need a break? **Box Lunch** (⊠ 302 Underpass Rd. near Cape Cod Rail Trail crossing, Brewster, South Brewster ☎ 508/896–1234), famous for its unique "rollwiches," is quickly spreading around the Cape. This location has the same tasty selection of breakfast and lunch roll-ups, perfect for a break and a bite while on the Cape Cod Rail Trail or just touring around. In summer the Box Lunch stays open until 9 PM; it closes at 4 PM when the weather turns cooler.

Where to Stay & Eat

$$$$ ✕ **Chillingsworth.** Generally regarded as the crown jewel of Cape restau-
Fodor's Choice rants, Chillingsworth combines formal presentation with an excellent
★ French menu and a diverse wine cellar to create a memorable dining experience. Super-rich risotto, roast lobster, and grilled venison are favorites. Dinner in the main dining rooms is prix fixe only and though it may seem pricey at first glance, it includes seven courses—appetizer, soup, salad, sorbet, entrée, "amusements," and dessert, plus coffee or tea. À la carte options for lunch, dinner, and Sunday brunch are served in the more casual, patio-style Garden Room. Inquire about on-site guest rooms if you decide to extend your stay. ⊠ *2449 Main St. (Rte. 6A), East Brewster* ☎ *508/896–3640* ⊕ *www.chillingsworth.com* ▤ *AE, DC, MC, V* ☉ *Closed late Nov.–late May; Mon. mid-June–late Nov.; and some weekdays late May–mid-June and mid-Oct.–late Nov.*

$$–$$$ ✕ **Spark Fish.** "Spark" refers to a wood-fire grill, which the kitchen uses often. Owner Steven Parrott's menu emphasizes simple ingredients—fresh herbs, garlic, and fruit salsas—and lets the flavors of local seafood, quality meats, and good vegetables shine through without complicated sauces. The inside is as unfussy as the menu and, like the food, is more about elegant understatement than elaborate decoration. A full wine list is available. The canopy-covered outdoor deck is the place to be in warm weather. In the off-season, there's comfortable fireside dining. ⊠ *2671 Rte. 6A, East Brewster* ☎ *508/896–1067* ▤ *MC, V.*

$–$$$ ⊞ **Brewster Fish House.** Long overshadowed by its pricier neighbors, the
Fodor'sChoice   Fish House finally has carved a niche for itself: Cape Cod standards like
★   classic scrod and New England boiled dinner share billing with tradi-
tional preparations of duck, rack of lamb, Cornish hen, and tenderloin
of beef. Locals are known to drive from all points of the Cape, as far
as Falmouth, for what is considered the freshest fish. The wine list in-
cludes a flavorful selection of by-the-glass offerings. ⊠ *2208 Rte. 6A,
South Brewster* ☎ *508/896–7867* ⌖ *Reservations not accepted* ▤ *MC,
V* ☺ *Call for information about off-season closings.*

¢–$$$ ✕ **JT's Seafood.** Fresh and ample portions of fried seafood take center
stage at this casual joint, which is very popular with families. Pick from
several seafood platters, or gnaw on baby back ribs or burgers if you
need a break from the fruits of the sea. Several items, including corn
dogs, grilled cheese (lunch only), and peanut butter and jelly, are good
kid-friendly choices. Place your order at the counter and sit inside or
out. Leave your mark by sticking a pin in your town's name on the big
map by the order counter. Takeout is also available. ⊠ *2689 Main St.
(Rte. 6A)* ☎ *508/896–3355* ⌖ *Reservations not accepted* ▤ *MC, V.*

$$ ✕ **Brewster Inn and Chowder House.** The consistently excellent food at
this long-standing Cape institution continues to live up to its great rep-
utation among locals after all this time. Home cooking in the traditional
New England style is the rule; you'll find no fancy or fussy fusion
recipes here—just comfort food. Look for simple but tasty meat and
seafood standards, and don't miss the rich and full-bodied New England
clam chowder. The service is friendly, the prices are kind, and you won't
leave hungry. The restaurant serves lunch and dinner daily year-round.
⊠ *1993 Rte. 6A* ☎ *508/896–7771* ▤ *MC, V.*

$–$$ ✕ **Laurino's Cape Cod Tavern.** There's something timeless about this
eatery with warm wood paneling, generous booth-style seating, and red-
and-white-checkered tablecloths. Oven grinders, burgers, and specialty
pizzas that come in two sizes are mainstays. Try a Buffalo Chicken Pizza
or the Kitchen Sink, which, as you might expect, has plenty of toppings.
Lasagna, shrimp scampi, and mussels marinara are popular choices.
Nightly specials always include two baked fish selections. At the long,
friendly bar you can sit with a buddy over a beer and a big plate of Macho
Nachos. In summer live music serenades the late-night crowd. ⊠ *3668
Main St. (Rte. 6A), East Brewster* ☎ *508/896–6135* ⌖ *Reservations
not accepted* ▤ *AE, MC, V.*

$$$–$$$$ ⊞ **Brewster By The Sea.** Weather permitting, breakfast is served on the
patio overlooking a swimming pool and 2 acres of landscaped gardens
at this restored 1846 farmhouse on historic Route 6A. A fireplace is the
focal point in one guest room while another has a king-size canopy bed
and sliders that open to a private deck. Three more guest rooms, fur-
nished with authentic and reproduction antiques, fireplaces, and hot tubs,
are in an adjacent carriage house. ⊠ *716 Main St. (Rte. 6A), 02631*
☎ *508/896–3910 or 800/892–3910* 🖷 *508/896–4232* ⊕ *www.
brewsterbythesea.com* ⇥ *7 rooms, 2 suites* ⌂ *Some in-room hot tubs,
cable TV, pool, bicycles, Internet; no kids under 16, no smoking* ▤ *AE,
D, DC, MC, V* ⦿⧧ *BP.*

$$–$$$$ 🏨 **Captain Freeman Inn.** Architectural highlights of this 1866 Victorian
Fodor'sChoice built for a packet-schooner-fleet owner include a marble fireplace, her-
★ ringbone-inlay flooring, ornate Italian plaster ceiling medallions, and
12-foot ceilings. Guest rooms have hardwood floors, antiques and Vic-
torian reproductions, and beds with eyelet spreads and fishnet or lace
canopies. Eight rooms have queen-size canopy beds, sofas, fireplaces,
TVs with VCRs, and mini-refrigerators. French doors lead to small en-
closed porches with private hot tubs. Winter weekend cooking classes
are an off-season diversion. ⊠ *15 Breakwater Rd., 02631* ☎ *508/896–
7481 or 800/843–4664* 🖷 *508/896–5618* ⊕ *www.captainfreemaninn.
com* ⇌ *14 rooms* ⚲ *Some in-room hot tubs, cable TV, in-room VCRs,
pool, bicycles, badminton, croquet, Internet; no phones in some rooms,
no kids under 10, no smoking* ⊟ *AE, MC, V* ⦿| *BP.*

★ **$$–$$$$** 🏨 **Ocean Edge.** One of the Cape's only self-contained resorts, Ocean Edge
is a beachfront community where accommodations range from hotel
rooms in the conference center to one- to three-bedroom condominiums in the woods and two- to three-bedroom beachfront villas. Condominiums have full kitchens and washer-dryers; some units have
fireplaces, and many have ocean views. All rooms and condos have balconies or patios. There are a championship 18-hole golf course and tennis courts. Clambakes, concerts, and tournaments take place throughout
the summer. MAP plans are subject to availability. ⊠ *2907 Main St. (Rte.
6A), 02631* ☎ *508/896–9000 or 800/343–6074* 🖷 *508/896–9123*
⊕ *www.oceanedge.com* ⇌ *292 condominium units, 90 rooms* ⚲ *3
restaurants, room service, driving range, golf privileges, putting greens,
11 tennis courts, 6 pools (2 indoor), ponds, gym, saunas, beach, bicycles, basketball, pub, kids programs (ages 4–17), laundry facilities, concierge* ⊟ *AE, D, DC, MC, V.*

★ **$$–$$$** 🏨 **The Ruddy Turnstone.** Built in the early 1800s, this beautifully preserved
Cape homestead is on 3 gently rolling acres adjacent to a marsh. An-
tiques, quilts, pine-board floors covered with braided rugs (in the main
house), and original barn-board walls (in the Carriage House) take you
back in time. Rooms have queen-size beds and large baths, most with
shower-tub combos and fresh flowers. An upstairs common room offers an incredible vista of the marsh and bay beyond; another has a fireplace and small library. Country breakfast is served on the porch or in
the dining room. ⊠ *463 Main St. (Rte. 6A), 02631* ☎ *508/385–9871
or 800/654–1995* 🖷 *508/385–5696* ⊕ *www.theruddyturnstone.com*
⇌ *5 rooms* ⚲ *Dining room, cable TV; no room phones, no children
under 10, no smoking* ⊟ *MC, V* ⊘ *Closed Nov.–Apr.* ⦿| *BP.*

$$–$$$ 🏨 **Poore House Inn.** Indeed, this five-room 1837 home was once the town's
actual poor house, a shelter for widows and orphans. Today, you can
dwell alongside painted antiques and sleep beneath floral quilts and 19th-
century coverlets. The rooms are on the small side, but their prettiness
and lack of clutter make them comfortable. Each has a private bath,
though the one for room 3 is a quick scamper across the hall. A single
room has a twin bed for solo travelers or an extra body (the inn is not
suitable for those under eight) and there's even a larger, pet-friendly room.
Outside a beautiful yard and brick patio overlook the gardens and
greenhouse. ⊠ *2511 Main St. (Rte. 6A), 02631* ☎ *508/896–0004 or*

800/233–6662 ⊕ *www.capecodtravel.com/poore* 🏖 *5 rooms* ♿ *Meeting rooms, some pets allowed (fee); no room TVs, no kids under 8, no smoking* ▤ *AE, D, DC, MC, V* ☉ *Closed Nov.–mid-Apr.* 🍴 *CP.*

¢–$$$ 🏨 **Old Sea Pines Inn.** With its white-column portico and wraparound ve-
Fodor'sChoice randa overlooking a broad lawn, Old Sea Pines resembles a vintage sum-
★ mer estate. Climb the sweeping staircase to guest rooms decorated with
reproduction wallpaper, antiques, and framed old photographs. Some
are quite large; others have fireplaces. One of the more popular rooms
has a sitting area in an enclosed sunporch. Rooms in a newer building
are simple with bright white modern baths and cast-iron queen-size beds.
Some rooms have shared bathrooms. ✉ *2553 Main St. (Rte. 6A)* 📪 *Box
1070, 02631* ☎ *508/896–6114* 🖷 *508/896–7387* ⊕ *www.oldseapinesinn.
com* 🏖 *24 rooms, 19 with bath, 3 suites, 2 family-size rooms* ♿ *Restaurant, cable TV, Internet, meeting rooms; no a/c, no room phones, no
TV in some rooms, no kids under 8, no smoking* ▤ *AE, D, DC, MC,
V* ☉ *Closed Jan.–Mar.* 🍴 *BP.*

$$ 🏨 **Isaiah Clark House.** This former 18th-century sea captain's residence,
just west of the town proper, retains its wide-plank flooring and low,
sloping ceilings and has a varied selection of antiques. The original inhabitants are not forgotten here, from the scrawled signature of 13-year-
old son Jeremiah in a closet and framed historic documents and
photographs to the namesake of each of the rooms (all Clark family
women). Most rooms have queen-size four-poster or canopy beds,
braided rugs, and fireplaces. The extensive gardens yield some of the
fruit used in the homemade pies, muffins, and breads. ✉ *1187 Main
St. (Rte. 6A), 02631* ☎ *508/896–2223 or 800/822–4001* ⊕ *www.
isaiahclark.com* 🏖 *7 rooms* ♿ *Cable TV, Internet; no room phones, no
kids under 10, no smoking* ▤ *D, MC, V* 🍴 *BP.*

¢ ⚠ **Nickerson State Park.** Close to 2,000 acres of wooded landscape teem-
ing with wildlife, Nickerson State Park is the Cape's largest and most
popular camping site. Shaded by a canopy of white pine, hemlock and
spruce, the park is a nature-lover's haven. Wile away a summer afternoon trout fishing, walking, biking on 8 mi of paved trails, canoeing,
sailing, motorboating, or bird-watching; there are four ponds for
swimming, plus ocean beaches nearby. RVs must be self-contained. Maps
and schedules of park programs are available at the park entrance.
The park accepts campground reservations six months in advance, mid-
April through mid-October, and takes walk-ins only the rest of the
year. Reservation fees range from $12 to $50 and are slightly cheaper
for Massachusetts residents. ♿ *Grills, 4 ponds, playground, flush
toilets, dump station, drinking water, showers, fire grates, picnic tables, public telephone, general store, ranger station* 🏖 *420 sites,
some yurts* ✉ *3488 Main St. (Rte. 6A), 02631* ☎ *508/896–3491, 877/
422–6762 reservations* 🖷 *508/896–3103* ⊕ *www.state.ma.us/dem/
parks/nick.htm* 🏷 *Large yurt $30, small yurt $25, tent sites $12*
▤ *No credit cards.*

Nightlife & the Arts

The **Cape Cod Repertory Theatre Co.** (✉ 3379 Main St. [Rte. 6A], West
Brewster ☎ 508/896–1888) performs several impressive productions,
from original works to classics, in its indoor Arts and Crafts–style the-

ater way back in the woods. The season runs from May to November. Mesmerizing entertainment for children, in the form of lively outdoor (and often interactive) theater, is provided here, too. Performances of fairy tales, music, and folk tales are given on Tuesday and Friday mornings at 10 in June, July, and August. The theater is just west of Nickerson State Park.

Sunday evenings by the bay are filled with the sounds of the **town-band concerts,** held in the gazebo on the grounds of Drummer Boy Park (⊠ Rte. 6A, West Brewster). The park is about ½-mi west of the Cape Cod Museum of Natural History, on the western side of Brewster. Families with little ones will delight in the park's playground with its ornate wood facilities.

The **Woodshed** (⊠ 1993 Main St. [Rte. 6A] ☎ 508/896–7771), the rustic bar at the Brewster Inn, is a good place to soak up local color and listen to pop duos or bands that perform nightly. It's open from May through October.

Sports & the Outdoors

BASEBALL The **Brewster Whitecaps** (☎ 508/896–9284 in summer, 781/784–7409 in winter ⊕ www.brewsterwhitecaps.com) of the collegiate Cape Cod Baseball League play home games at Cape Cod Regional Tech High School (⊠ Rte. 124, Harwich) from mid-June to mid-August.

BEACHES **Flax Pond** in Nickerson State Park (⊠ 3488 Main St. [Rte. 6A], East Brewster ☎ 508/896–3491), surrounded by pines, has picnic areas, a bathhouse, and water-sports rentals.

Brewster's bay beaches all have access to the flats that at low tide make for very interesting tide-pool exploration. Eponymous roads to each beach branch off Route 6A; there's limited parking. All of the bay beaches require a daily, weekly, or seasonal parking pass, which can be purchased at the town hall (☎ 508/896–4511). **Breakwater Landing** is one of the most popular beaches in town and has an ample parking area. **Linnell Landing** has a smaller lot and tends to fill up quickly. A favorite among the toddler crowd and the sunset seekers, **Paine's Creek** also lacks a large lot, but if you get there early enough, you can find a spot. Harder to find down a dead-end street but worth it, **Robbin's Hill** is known for its intriguing tide pools. Farther east off Route 6A is **Crosby Beach,** ideal for beach walkers who can trek straightway to Orleans if they so desire.

BIKING The **Cape Cod Rail Trail** has many access points in Brewster, among them Long Pond Road, Underpass Road, and Nickerson State Park.

Brewster Bike (⊠ 442 Underpass Rd. ☎ 508/896–8149) carries a large selection of bikes.

Open in summer only but right alongside the Cape Cod Rail Trail is the tiny **Idle Times Bike Shop** (⊠ Rte. 6A, just west of Nickerson State Park, East Brewster ☎ 508/896–9242), with bikes both big and small for rent. You can't beat the proximity to the trail and the easy parking.

The **Rail Trail Bike Shop** (✉ 302 Underpass Rd. ☎ 508/896–8200) rents bikes, including children's bikes, and in-line skates. Parking is free, and there's a picnic area with easy access to the Rail Trail.

FISHING Many of Brewster's freshwater ponds are good for catching perch, pickerel, and other fish; five ponds are well stocked with trout. Especially good for fishing is Cliff Pond in Nickerson State Park. You'll need a **fishing license,** available from the town hall (✉ 2198 Main St. [Rte. 6A], East Brewster ☎ 508/896–4506).

GOLF The par-72, 18-hole **Captain's Golf Course** (✉ 1000 Freeman's Way, east of Rte. 6 ☎ 508/896–5100 or 877/843–9081) is an excellent public course.

Ocean Edge Golf Course (✉ Villages Dr., off Rte. 6A, East Brewster ☎ 508/896–5911), an 18-hole, par-72 course winding around five ponds, has Scottish-style pot bunkers and challenging terrain. Three-day residential and commuter golf schools are offered in spring and early summer.

HORSEBACK Instruction and trail rides to riders of all levels are available at **Moby**
RIDING **Dick Farm** (✉ 179 Great Fields Rd., West Brewster ☎ 508/896–3544).

Woodsong Farm (✉ 121 Lund Farm Way, South Brewster ☎ 508/896–5800) has instruction and day programs but no rentals or trail rides; it also has a horsemanship program for kids 5–18.

TENNIS The **Ocean Edge** resort (✉ 2907 Main St. [Rte. 6A], East Brewster ☎ 508/896–9000) has five clay and six Plexipave courts. It offers lessons and round-robins and hosts a tennis school, with weekend packages and video analysis.

Run by the town and open to the public at no charge are four **public tennis courts,** all just behind the fire and police stations on Route 6A. Two basketball courts are also for public use.

WATER SPORTS **Cape Cod Sea Camps** (✉ Box 1880, Brewster 02631 ☎ 508/896–3451) teaches team sports, archery, art, drama, sailing, and water sports to kids ages 7–17.

Jack's Boat Rentals (✉ Flax Pond, Nickerson State Park, Rte. 6A, East Brewster ☎ 508/896–8556) rents canoes, kayaks, Seacycles, Sunfish, pedal boats, and sailboards; guide-led kayak tours are also offered.

Shopping
B. D. Hutchinson (✉ 1274 Long Pond Rd., South Brewster ☎ 508/896–6395), a watch and clock maker, sells antique and collectible watches, clocks, and music boxes.

★ **Brewster Book Store** (✉ 2648 Main St. [Rte. 6A], East Brewster ☎ 508/896–6543 or 800/823–6543) prides itself on being a special Cape bookstore. It's filled to the rafters with all manner of books by local and international authors and has an extensive fiction selection and kids section. A full schedule of author signings and children's story times continues year-round.

HandCraft House (✉ 3996 Main St. [Rte. 6A], East Brewster ☎ 508/240–1412 or 888/826–4393) has "handmade in the USA" art for the home and garden, wood sculptures, handblown glass, stoneware, watercolors, and jewelry.

Kemp Pottery (✉ 258 Main St. [Rte. 6A], West Brewster ☎ 508/385–5782) has functional and decorative stoneware and porcelain, fountains, garden sculpture, pottery sinks, and stained glass.

Ivy covers the facade of **Kingsland Manor** (✉ 440 Main St. [Rte. 6A], West Brewster ☎ 508/385–9741), which has fountains in the courtyard, and everything "from tin to Tiffany"—including English hunting horns, full-size antique street lamps, garden and house furniture, weather vanes, jewelry, and chandeliers.

Kings Way Books and Antiques (✉ 774 Main St. [Rte. 6A], West Brewster ☎ 508/896–3639) sells out-of-print and rare books, including a large medieval section, plus small antiques, china, glass, silver, coins, and linens.

Lemon Tree Village (✉ Main St. [Rte. 6A, about 1 mi west of town center]) is a cheery shopping complex filled with many unusual stores. You can find garden statuary, top-of-the-line cooking implements, locally made arts and crafts, pottery, birding supplies, clothing, gifts, jewelry, and toys. There's even a café next door if all that shopping makes you hungry.

Open from April through October, the **Satucket Farm Stand** (✉ 76 Harwich Rd. [Rte. 124], just off Rte. 6A ☎ 508/896–5540) is a real old-fashioned farm stand. Most produce is grown on the premises, and you can fill your basket with the finest of the harvest, from home-baked scones and breads to fruit pies, produce, herbs, and flowers.

The **Spectrum** (✉ 369 Main St. [Rte. 6A], West Brewster ☎ 508/385–3322) carries a great selection of imaginative American arts and crafts, including pottery, stained glass, and art glass.

★ **Sydenstricker Galleries** (✉ 490 Main St. [Rte. 6A], West Brewster ☎ 508/385–3272) stocks glassware handcrafted by a unique process, which you can watch in-progress.

Harwich

❺ *3 mi east of Dennisport; 6 mi south of Brewster.*

Originally known as Setucket, Harwich separated from Brewster in 1694 and was renamed for the famous seaport in England. Like other townships on the Cape, Harwich is actually a cluster of seven small villages, including Harwich Port. Historically, the villages of Harwich were marked by their generous number of churches and the styles of worship they practiced—small villages often sprang up around these centers of faith.

Harwich and Harwich Port are the commercial centers, and although the two have very different natures, both have graceful old architecture and a rich history. Harwich Port is the more bustling of the two: brimming with shops, calm-water beaches, restaurants, and hotel complexes, it packs all manner of entertainment and frivolity along its roadways. Harwich is more relaxed, its commerce more centered, and its outlying areas graced with greenery, large shade trees, and historic homesteads. The Harwich Historical Society has a strong presence here, maintaining exhibits and artifacts significant to the town's past.

The Cape's famous cranberry industry took off in Harwich in 1844, and Alvin Cahoon was its principal grower at the time. Each September Harwich holds a **Cranberry Festival** to celebrate the importance of this indigenous berry; the festival is usually scheduled during the week after Labor Day. There are cranberry bogs throughout Harwich.

Three naturally sheltered harbors on Nantucket Sound make the town, like its English namesake, popular with boaters. You'll find dozens of elegant sailboats and elaborate yachts in Harwich's harbors, plus plenty of charter-fishing boats. Each year in August the town pays celebratory homage to its large boating population with a grand regatta, Sails Around the Cape.

Beaches are plentiful in Harwich, and nearly all rest on the warm and mild waters of Nantucket Sound. Freshwater ponds also speckle the area, ideal for swimming as well as small-scale canoeing and kayaking. Several conservation areas have miles of secluded walking trails, many alongside vivid cranberry bogs.

Once the home of a private school offering the first courses in navigation, the pillared 1844 Greek Revival building of the **Brooks Academy Museum** now houses the museum of the **Harwich Historical Society.** In addition to a large photo-history collection and exhibits on artist Charles Cahoon (grandson of cranberry grower Alvin), the sociotechnological history of cranberry culture, and shoe making, the museum has antique clothing and textiles, china and glass, fans, and toys. There's also an extensive genealogical collection for researchers. On the grounds is a powder house used to store gunpowder during the Revolutionary War, as well as a restored 1872 outhouse that could spur your appreciation for indoor plumbing. ⊠ *80 Parallel St.* ☎ *508/432–8089* ▣ *Donations accepted* ☉ *June–mid-Oct., Wed.–Sat. 1–4.*

☾ **Brooks Park** on Main Street (Route 28) is a good place to stretch your legs, with a playground, picnic tables, a ball field, tennis courts, and a bandstand where summer concerts are held.

☾ **Grand Slam Entertainment** has softball and baseball batting cages and pitching machines, including one with fastballs up to 80 mph and a Wiffleball machine for younger kids, plus a bumper-boat pool and a video-arcade room. ⊠ *322 Main St. (Rte. 28), Harwich Port* ☎ *508/430–1155* ▣ *10 pitches $1.50, 40 pitches $5, 100 pitches $10; bumper-boat pool ride $5* ☉ *Apr.–May and Sept.–mid-Oct., Mon.–Sat. 11–7, Sun. 11–9; June–Aug., daily 9 AM–10 PM.*

For children who have spent too much time in the car watching you drive,
☾ a spin behind the wheel of one of 20 top-of-the-line go-carts at **Bud's Go-Karts** may be just the thing. ⊠ *9 Sisson Rd., off Rte. 28, Harwich*

Port ☎ *508/432–4964* ✉ *$5 for 5 min* ☉ *June–early Sept., Mon.–Sat. 9 AM–11 PM, Sun. 10–11.*

☺ The **Trampoline Center** has 12 trampolines set up at ground level over pits for safety. ✉ *296 Main St. (Rte. 28), West Harwich* ☎ *508/432–8717* ✉ *$4 for 10 min* ☉ *Apr.–mid-June, weekends, hrs vary widely, call ahead; mid-June–early Sept., daily 9 AM–11 PM.*

Where to Stay & Eat

$$–$$$ ✕ **Cape Sea Grille.** Sitting primly on a side street off hectic Route 28, this gem stays free of crowds. Fresh flowers, white linens, and vibrant wall murals delight the eye while dinner teases the palate; specialties include local fish in savory marinades like roasted Calvados saffron reduction or orange-honey butter sauce. Chef-owner Douglas Ramler (formerly of Boston's noted Hamersley's Bistro) relies on the freshest ingredients to create an ever-changing menu. His wife, Jennifer, oversees the dining room. Dinner is served nightly from 5 in the summer; call for hours in the slower season. ✉ *31 Sea St., Harwich Port* ☎ *508/432–4745* ▭ *AE, D, MC, V* ☉ *Closed Nov.–early Apr.*

$$–$$$ ✕ **L'alouette.** Owners Danielle and Jean-Louis Bastres of France serve authentic French food in their casual restaurant. Look for traditional and rich selections such as duckling, rack of lamb, veal chops with portobello mushrooms, and chateaubriand, (a favorite). ✉ *787 Rte. 28, Harwich Port* ☎ *508/430–0405* ▭ *AE, DC, MC, V* ☉ *Closed late Feb.–mid-Mar.*

★ $$–$$$ ✕ **Country Inn Restaurant and Tavern.** Fresh flowers and candlelight grace the tables in the dining room while the tavern is cozy and dark. Off-season, a roaring fire enhances romance. The popular Country Inn Platter for Two is piled high with filet mignon, lobster, scallops, and shrimp scampi. Lazy-Man's Lobster is a local favorite; the kitchen staff does all the messy work, leaving you with nothing to do but enjoy the succulent feast. Live piano music cranks it up a notch on weekend nights. Saturday tends to be more lively, with lots of folks getting up to strut their stuff on the dance floor. ✉ *86 Sisson Ave. (Rte. 39), Harwich Port* ☎ *508/432–2769* ▭ *AE, MC, V.*

$$–$$$ ✕ **Buca's Tuscan Roadhouse.** This romantic roadhouse with crisp red-and-white-checkered tablecloth might transport you to Italy—and if it doesn't, the food will bring you that much closer. From *zuppe* to aged pecorino, gorgonzola, and ricotta salad with figs to veal scallopine with white wine, this is Italian fare taken far beyond traditional home-cooking and dressed with mouth-watering flavor. ✉ *4 Depot Rd., Harwich* ☎ *508/432–6900* ⊕ *www.bucasroadhouse.com* ▭ *MC, V.*

$–$$$ ✕ **400 East.** This big, dark restaurant buzzing with conversation is in a nondescript shopping plaza. The menu includes teriyaki chicken, prime rib, lobster ravioli, and baked scrod, but also has excellent pizza, with toppings such as wild mushrooms, blue cheese, or chicken sausage. Eating at the busy, U-shape bar is a good alternative to waiting for a table. The 400 has a cousin restaurant (also called the 400) on Main Street that is not as much fun. ✉ *1421 Rte. 39* ☎ *508/432–1800* ▭ *AE, D, MC, V.*

$–$$ ✕ **Brax Landing.** In this local stalwart perched alongside busy Saquatucket Harbor, you can get a menu tip-off as you pass by tanks full of steamers and lobsters in the corridor leading to the dining room. The restaurant sprawls around a big bar that serves specialty drinks like the Banzai (frozen piña colada with a float of dark rum). The swordfish and the Chatham scrod are favorites, both served simply and well. And if you've been after the ultimate lobster roll—and never thought you could get full on one—sample this one, bursting with the meat of a 1¼-pound lobster. There's a notable children's menu, and Sunday brunch, served from 10 to 2, is an institution. Even on chilly evenings, try to dine on the outdoor deck as the sun sets to truly experience the Cape's serenity. ⊠ *Rte. 28 at Saquatucket Harbor, Harwich Port* ☎ *508/432–5515* ⚇ *Reservations not accepted* ▤ *AE, DC, MC, V.*

¢ **Ay! Caramba Cafe.** There are no frills here, and there's lots of noise— the drinking crowd is young and very rowdy—but Ay! Caramba is great for filling up on authentic Mexican fare without cleaning out your wallet. Choose from tasty quesadillas, burritos, tostadas, and tacos, or go for one of the large combination plates, complete with rice and either refried beans or vegetables. The fish tacos and seafood quesadillas are especially good. Once you have your food, sidle up to the salsa bar, where three varieties are made throughout the day—but be sure to have your water handy for the hottest stuff. In warm weather, grab a seat on the outdoor patio. ⊠ *703 Main St., Harwich* ☎ *508/432–9800* ⊕ *www.aycarambacafe.com* ▤ *MC, V* ⊙ *Closed Sun. Sept.–Mar.*

$$$$ ▦ **Winstead Inn and Beach Resort.** Comprised of two distinct properties, the Winstead Inn and Beach Resort offer a two-for-one Cape Cod experience. Harking back to an earlier era, the Beach Resort sits on a private beach overlooking Nantucket Sound. From umbrella tables on the deck you can gaze at the sweep of coast and surrounding grasslands while enjoying a generous Continental breakfast (served poolside in warmer months). At the other end of the spectrum, the Winstead Inn is an in-town inn. Greenery surrounds the Gothic Victorian home, and many of the rooms have a view of the outdoor pool. Guests at either property share amenities and facilities at both locations. ⊠ *114 Parallel St., 02645* ⊠ *4 Braddock La., Harwich Port 02646* ☎ *508/432–4444 or 800/870–4405* ⊕ *www.winsteadinn.com* ⇆ *31 rooms* ⚇ *Some in-room hot tubs, some microwaves, cable TV, pool, Internet, meeting rooms; no a/c, no kids under 12, no smoking* ▤ *AE, MC, V* ⦿⦿ *CP.*

$$$–$$$$ ▦ **Augustus Snow House.** This grand old Victorian is the epitome of elegance. Common areas include the oak-panel front room, with tall windows and a fireplace, and a wicker-filled screened porch. A three-course breakfast is served in the stately dining room. Guest rooms have Victorian-print wallpapers, luxurious carpets, and antique and reproduction furnishings. All have quilts, TVs, and fireplaces; three rooms have hot tubs. The Carriage House Suite has a fireplace, dining area, kitchenette, and living room. Afternoon tea is served Thursday, Friday, and Saturday. ⊠ *528 Main St. (Rte. 28), Harwich Port 02646* ☎ *508/430–0528 or 800/320–0528* ⎙ *508/432–6638 Ext. 15* ⊕ *www.augustussnow.com* ⇆ *6 rooms; 1 suite* ⚇ *Some in-room hot tubs, kitchenette, ceiling fans, fireplaces, TVs; no a/c* ▤ *AE, D, MC, V* ⦿⦿ *BP.*

FodorśChoice
★

$$$–$$$$ 🖼 **Dunscroft by the Sea.** Romantic amenities include king- and queen-size lace-canopy and four-poster beds, two-person hot tubs, cotton robes, and some working fireplaces. A private beach overlooking the calming waters of Nantucket Sound is just a few paces away. There's also a honeymoon cottage suite. ⊠ *24 Pilgrim Rd., Harwich Port 02646* ☎ *508/432–0810 or 800/432–4345* ⊕ *www.dunscroftbythesea.com* ⇘ *8 rooms, 1 cottage* ⬩ *In-room hot tubs, beach* ⊟ *AE, MC, V* ⦿ *BP.*

$$–$$$ 🖼 **Seadar Inn.** More simple than elegant, the friendly Seadar Inn is just
Fodor'sChoice a stone's throw from Nantucket Sound. The only thing standing between
★ you and the beach is the small parking lot. Time it right and you can cross paths with the ice-cream truck on your way to fun in the sun. The homey, motel-style rooms are simple and practical in a colonial style, with knotty-pine walls and frilly curtains; some have water views. Suites are available for larger groups. There are outdoor grills for alfresco cooking. ⊠ *Braddock La. at Bank St. Beach, Harwich Port 02646* ☎ *508/432–0264 or 800/888–5250* ⊕ *www.seadarinn.com* ⇘ *23 rooms* ⊟ *AE, D, MC, V* ⊗ *Closed mid-Oct.–May* ⦿ *CP.*

Nightlife & the Arts

THE ARTS The **First Congregational Church** (⊠ Main St. at corner of Rtes. 39 and 124, Harwich ☎ 508/432–1053) closes its day of worship with Sunday-evening Candlelight Concerts at 7:30 from July through September.

Harwich Junior Theatre (⊠ 105 Division St., West Harwich ☎ 508/432–2002) gives theater classes for kids year-round and presents four family-oriented summer productions.

Town-band concerts in Harwich take place in summer on Tuesday at 7:30 in Brooks Park (☎ 508/432–1600).

NIGHTLIFE **Country Inn** (⊠ 86 Sisson Rd. [Rte. 39], West Harwich Port ☎ 508/432–2769) complements its dinner menu with dancing every Friday and Saturday evening. You can dance between courses to music of the 1940s with a piano player on Friday night and a pianist and bass player on Saturday evening after 7.

Irish Pub (⊠ 126 Main St. [Rte. 28], West Harwich ☎ 508/432–8808) has dancing to bands—playing Irish, American, and dance music—as well as sing-alongs, pool, darts, sports TV, and pub food in the bar.

Jake Rooney's Pub (⊠ 119 Brooks Rd., off Rte. 28, Harwich Port ☎ 508/430–1100) is a comfortable watering hole. Keno and live entertainment five nights a week make it a fun place to hang out with friends.

Sports & the Outdoors

BASEBALL The **Harwich Mariners** (⊠ Harwich High School, Oak St. ☎ 508/432–2000 ⊕ www.harwichmariners.org), of the collegiate Cape Cod Baseball League, play home games at Whitehouse Field from mid-June through mid-August.

BEACHES Harwich has 22 beaches, more than any other Cape town. Most of the ocean beaches are on Nantucket Sound, where the water is a bit calmer and warmer. Freshwater pond beaches are also abundant.

BOATING Whether you're in the mood to sail under the moonlight, hire a private charter, or learn to navigate yourself, **Cape Sail** (✉ 337 Saquatucket Harbor, off Rte. 28, Harwich Port ☎ 508/896–2730) can accommodate any whim.

Cape Water Sports (✉ 337 Main St. [Rte. 28], Harwich Port ☎ 508/432–5996) rents Sunfish, Hobie Cats, Lasers, powerboats, surf bikes, day sailers, and canoes and gives instruction.

In late August, the **Sails Around Cape Cod** regatta (☎ 508/430–1165) circumnavigates the Cape, a distance of 140 nautical mi, beginning at the east end of the Cape Cod Canal and ending at the west end.

FISHING Fishing trips are operated on a walk-on basis from spring through fall on the **Golden Eagle** (✉ Wychmere Harbor, Harwich Port ☎ 508/432–5611).

The **Yankee** (✉ Saquatucket Harbor, Harwich Port ☎ 508/432–2520) invites passengers in search of fluke, scup, sea bass, and tautog aboard its 65-foot party boat. Two trips depart daily Monday through Saturday; there's also one on Sunday. Reservations are recommended.

GOLF **Cranberry Valley Golf Course** (✉ 183 Oak St. ☎ 508/430–7560) has a championship layout of 18 well-groomed holes surrounded by cranberry bogs.

Harwich Port Golf Club (✉ South and Forest Sts., Harwich Port ☎ 508/432–0250) has a 9-hole course that's great for beginners.

Shopping

Cape Cod Braided Rug Co. (✉ 537 Main St. [Rte. 28], Harwich Port ☎ 508/432–3133) specializes in making braided rugs in all colors, styles, and sizes.

Carriage Barn Antiques (✉ 27 Rte. 28, West Harwich ☎ 508/430–4114) has dried and silk flower arrangements, folk art, and antiques.

820 Main Gallery (✉ 820 Main St. [Rte. 28], Harwich Port ☎ 508/430–7622) sells original works in oil, acrylics, watercolors and photography, as well as limited-edition prints by established local artists. The gallery specializes in regional land- and seascapes.

The **Potted Geranium** (✉ 188 Main St. [Rte. 28], West Harwich ☎ 508/432–1114) stocks country-inspired gifts and home-related items, including colorful wind flags, handcrafted items, and wind chimes.

Pottery Plus (✉ 551 Main St. [Rte. 28], Harwich Port ☎ 508/430–5240) sells the pottery of artist Scott Sullivan, as well as other works by local artists.

Wychmere Book & Coffee (✉ 587 Main St. [Rte. 28], Harwich Port ☎ 508/432–7868) is a place to savor the comforts of browsing, reading, and sipping good coffee. Special events with authors and a children's summer reading hour further enhance the scene.

Chatham

6–**11** *5 mi east of Harwich; 8 mi south of Orleans.*

Originally populated by Native Americans, Chatham came into the hands of white settlers from Plymouth in 1656, when William Nickerson traded a boat for the 17 square mi of land that make up the town. In 1712 the area separated from Eastham and was incorporated as a town; the surnames of the Pilgrims who first settled here still dominate the census list. Although Chatham was originally a farming community, the sea finally lured townspeople to turn to fishing for their livelihood, an industry that has held strong to this day.

At the bent elbow of the Cape, with water nearly surrounding it, Chatham has all the charm of a quietly posh seaside resort, with relatively little commercialism. And it's charming: gray-shingle houses with tidy awnings and cheerful flower gardens, an attractive Main Street with crafts and antiques stores alongside homey coffee shops, and a five-and-dime. It's a traditional town, where elegant summer cottages share the view with stately homes rich in Yankee architectural detail. In fact, this tiny town by the sea is where you'll find some of the finest examples of bow-roof houses in the country. Chatham's nowhere near as kitschy as Provincetown, but it's not overly quaint, either—it's casual and fun in a refined New England way.

Because of its location at the elbow, Chatham is not a town you just pass through—it's a destination in itself. Although it can get crowded in summer—and even on weekends during shoulder seasons—Chatham remains a true New England village. During summer months, the town bursts into bloom as hydrangeas blossom in shades of cobalt blue, indigo, and deep violet.

Its position on the confluence of Nantucket Sound and the Atlantic Ocean makes Chatham especially vulnerable to the destructive wrath of stormy seas. Many a home and beachfront have been lost to the tumultuous waters. But like any stalwart New England character, Chatham will continue to hold on to its fortunes, its past, and its future.

6 Authentic all the way, the **Railroad Museum** is in a restored 1887 depot. Exhibits include a walk-through 1910 New York Central caboose, old photographs, equipment, thousands of train models, and a diorama of the 1915 Chatham rail yards. ⊠ *153 Depot Rd., West Chatham* ☎ *No phone* 🖾 *Donations accepted* ☉ *Mid-June–mid-Sept., Tues.–Sat. 10–4.*

The **Play-a-round,** a multilevel wooden playground of turrets, twisting tubular slides, and jungle gyms, was designed with the input of local children and built by volunteers. There's a section for people with disabilities and a fenced-in area for small children. ⊠ *Depot Rd., across from Railroad Museum, West Chatham.*

On **Queen Anne Road** around Oyster Pond, half-Cape houses, open fields, and rolling pastures reveal the area's colonial and agricultural history.

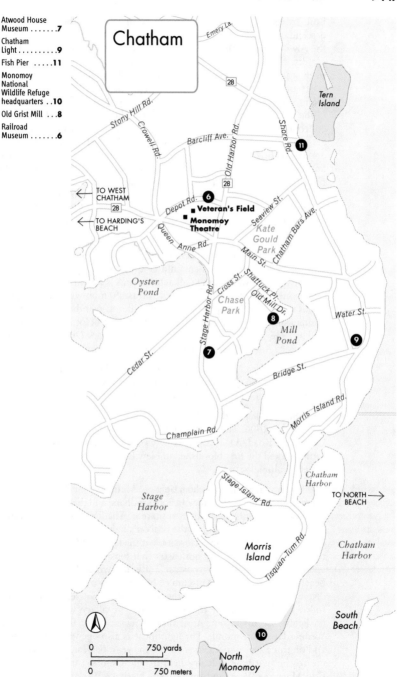

Chatham

Built by sea captain Joseph C. Atwood in 1752 and occupied by his descendants until it was sold to the Chatham Historical Society in 1926, the **Atwood House Museum** has a gambrel roof, variable-width floor planks, fireplaces, an old kitchen with a wide hearth and a beehive oven, and some antique dolls and toys. The New Gallery displays portraits of local sea captains. The Joseph C. Lincoln Room has the manuscripts, first editions, and mementos of the Chatham writer, and in the basement is an antique tool room. The 1974 Durand Wing has collections of seashells from around the world and threaded Sandwich glass, as well as Parian-ware figures, unglazed porcelain vases, figurines, and busts. In a remodeled freight shed are murals (1932–45) by Alice Stallknecht Wight portraying religious scenes in Chatham settings. On the grounds are an herb garden, the old turret and lens from the Chatham Light, and a simple camp house rescued from eroding North Beach. ⊠ *347 Stage Harbor Rd., West Chatham* ☎ *508/945–2493* ⊕ *www.chathamhistoricalsociety.org* ▱ *$3* ⊙ *Mid-June–Sept., Tues.–Fri. 1–4.*

The **Old Grist Mill,** one of a number of windmills still on the Cape, was built in 1797 by Colonel Benjamin Godfrey for the purpose of grinding corn. How practical the mill actually was is a matter of debate: for it to work properly, a wind speed of at least 20 mph was necessary, but winds more than 25 mph required the miller to reef the sails or to quit grinding altogether. The mill was moved to its present location from Miller Hill in 1956 and extensively renovated. ⊠ *Old Mill Dr. near Mill Pond* ▱ *Free* ⊙ *July and Aug., weekdays 10–3.*

Mill Pond is a lovely place to stop for a picnic. There's fishing from the bridge, and often the bullrakers can be seen at work, plying the pond's muddy bottom with 20-foot rakes in search of shellfish.

Stage Harbor, sheltered by Morris Island, is where Samuel de Champlain anchored in 1606. The street on its north side is, not surprisingly, called Champlain Road. A skirmish here between Europeans and Native Americans marked the first bloodshed in New England between Native people and colonial settlers.

★ ❾ The famous view from **Chatham Light** (⊠ Main St. near Bridge St., West Chatham)—of the harbor, the offshore sandbars, and the ocean beyond—justifies the crowds that gather to share it. The lighthouse is especially dramatic on a foggy night, as the beacon's light pierces the mist. Coin-operated telescopes allow a close look at the famous "Chatham Break," the result of a fierce 1987 nor'easter that blasted a channel through a barrier beach just off the coast; it's now known as North and South beaches. The Cape Cod Museum of Natural History in Brewster has a display of photos documenting the process of erosion leading up to and following the break. The U.S. Coast Guard auxiliary, which supervises the lighthouse, offers tours April through September on the first and third Wednesday of the month. The lighthouse is also open by appointment and on three special occasions during the year: Seafest, an annual tribute to the maritime industry held in mid-October; mid-May's Cape Cod Maritime Week; and June's Cape Heritage Week.

★ **Monomoy National Wildlife Refuge** is a 2,500-acre preserve including the Monomoy Islands, a fragile 9-mi-long barrier-beach area south of Chatham. Monomoy's North and South islands were created when a storm divided the former Monomoy Island in 1978. Monomoy was itself separated from the mainland in a 1958 storm. A haven for bird-watchers, the island is an important stop along the North Atlantic Flyway for migratory waterfowl and shore birds—peak migration times are May and late July. It also provides nesting and resting grounds for 285 species, including gulls—great black-backed, herring, and laughing—and several tern species. White-tail deer also live on the islands, and harbor and gray seals frequent the shores in winter. The only structure on the islands is the **South Monomoy Lighthouse**, built in 1849. If you want to spend a night in the house and on the island, contact Brewster's Cape Cod Museum of Natural History (☎ 508/896–3867 ⊕ www.ccmnh.org), which organizes such trips.

Monomoy is a quiet, peaceful place of sand and beach grass, of tidal flats, dunes, marshes, freshwater ponds, thickets of bayberry and beach plum, and a few pines. Because the refuge harbors several endangered species, activities are limited. Certain areas are fenced off to protect nesting areas of terns and the threatened piping plover. Several groups conduct tours of the islands, including the Massachusetts Audubon Society in South Wellfleet and the Cape Cod Museum of Natural History in Brewster, many with a focus on bird-watching. In season, the *Rip Ryder* (☎ 508/945–5450 ⊕ www.monomoyislandferry.com) will take you over from Chatham for some lone bird-watching. Rates vary greatly: if you catch a ride out with the seal-watching cruise, it's $14 per person; if you charter a private ride, rates are $45 per person round-trip or $10 per person for three or more passengers round-trip. Reservations are recommended.

❿ The **Monomoy National Wildlife Refuge headquarters,** on the misleadingly named Morris Island (it's connected to the mainland), has a visitor center and bookstore (⊠ Off Morris Island Rd., Morris Island ☎ 508/945–0594), open daily 8–4, where you can pick up pamphlets on Monomoy and the birds, wildlife, and flora and fauna found there. A ¾-mi interpretive walking trail around Morris Island, closed at high tide, gives a good view of the refuge and the surrounding waters. The area itself is open daily for exploring from dawn to dusk.

⓫ The **Fish Pier** (⊠ Shore Rd. and Barcliff Ave., North Chatham) bustles with activity when Chatham's fishing fleet returns, sometime between noon and 2 PM daily, depending on the tide. The unloading of the boats is a big local event, drawing crowds who watch it all from an observation deck. From their fishing grounds 3–100 mi offshore, fishermen bring in haddock, cod, flounder, lobster, halibut, and pollack, which are packed in ice and shipped to New York and Boston or sold at the fish market here. You might also see sand sharks being unloaded. Typically they are sent, either fresh or frozen, to French and German markets. Also here is *The Provider,* a monument to the town's fishing industry, showing a hand pulling a fish-filled net from the sea.

The **Eldredge Public Library** (⊠ 564 Main St. ☎ 508/945–5170) has a special genealogy department.

Known for their artful contemporary treatment of blown glass, Jim Holmes and Deborah Doane of the **Chatham Glass Company** create everything from candleholders to unique vases in a vast spectrum of colors. You can watch the fascinating process of glassblowing here. ⊠ *758 Main St.* ☎ *508/945–5547* ⊕ *www.chathamglass.com* ☉ *Late May–early Sept., Mon.–Sat. 10–5; early Sept.–late May, daily 10–5.*

need a break?

If you're looking for a fat and fancy sandwich, a morning bagel, or an afternoon cappuccino pick-me-up, stop in at the **Chatham Village Café** (⊠ 400 Main St. ☎ 508/945–2525) and choose from an impressive selection of food. Eat inside at one of the few tables for some good street-side people-watching, or head over to the Village Green for an impromptu picnic.

Where to Stay & Eat

★ **$$–$$$** ✕ **Chatham Squire.** If you order anything local here, you can't go wrong. The fish is as fresh and good as you get on Cape Cod, and the kitchen continues to innovate while still remaining true to its Cape roots. The calamari is always tender, the oysters a lovely mouthful. Expect a long wait in season, in which case you can visit the bar and pick up on local gossip. ⊠ *487 Main St.* ☎ *508/945–0945* ⊕ *www.thesquire.com* ≙ *Reservations not accepted* ☰ *AE, D, MC, V.*

$$–$$$ ✕ **Pate's.** This popular spot has been grilling up meats and local seafood since 1957. Succulent lamb chops, filet mignon, sirloin, and swordfish arrive at your table bearing the telltale stripes of the open flame. Seafood is a serious matter here. Take note: that baked lobster on your plate likely weighs in at more than 2 pounds. ⊠ *1260 Main St., West Chatham* ☎ *508/945–9777* ☰ *AE, MC, V* ☉ *Closed mid-Jan.–Apr.*

$$–$$$ ✕ **Pisces.** An intimate setting housed inside a colorful building, Pisces, as its name suggests, serves up coastal cooking—if it swims in local waters, they have it fresh. Fisherman's stew, crabmeat ravioli, and seared spice-rubbed tuna are among the tasty selections offered; complement your dinner with a selection from the extensive wine list. Reservations recommended. ⊠ *2653 Main St., West Chatham* ☎ *508/432–4600* ☰ *AE, MC, V.*

$$–$$$
Fodor'sChoice
★
✕ **Vining's Bistro.** An exceptionally inventive menu and a determination not to rest on its laurels make this restaurant a standout. The wood grill infuses many dishes with a distinctive flavor heightened further by the chef's use of zesty rubs and spices from all over the globe. The "Golden Triangle" curry mixes shrimp and chicken simmered in Madras and Indonesian curry. Spit-roasted Jamaican chicken competes with a portobello mushroom sandwich as the restaurant's signature dish. The restaurant is upstairs at the Gallery Building, and many windows look out on the art below. ⊠ *595 Main St.* ☎ *508/945–5033* ⊕ *www. viningsbistro.com* ≙ *Reservations not accepted* ☰ *AE, D, MC, V* ☉ *Closed mid-Jan.–Apr.*

$–$$$ ✕ **Christian's.** French and New England influences are found at this landmark town restaurant. The menu includes grilled prime meats and fresh Cape Cod seafood. The mahogany-panel bar and upstairs sunroom serve a lighter menu that remains strong on seafood but adds some Mexican influences, such as tacos and quesadillas, that are well suited to the summer. As attractive as the formal downstairs may be, the upstairs is more of a happening scene. ⊠ *443 Main St.* ☎ *508/945–3362* ⊕ *www. christiansrestaurant.com* 🖷 *508/945–8049* ▭ *DC, MC, V* ◑ *Closed weekdays Jan.–Mar.*

$–$$$ ✕ **Marley's.** Traditional New England fare often served with a decidedly international flair is what you'll find at Marley's. Scallops prepared with pineapple, rum, and brown sugar and topped with a coconut-macaroon crust are a favorite. Crab cakes and Cajun blackened salmon served with poached shrimp and crabmeat are house specialties. Steak, chicken pot-pie, lobster, and steamers round out the menu, which also includes several vegetarian dishes. Dinner is served April through November, lunch and dinner late May through mid-October. ⊠ *1077 Main St., West Chatham* ☎ *508/945–1700* ▭ *AE, MC, V.*

$$$$ ✕🖼 **Wequassett Inn Resort & Golf Club.** Twenty Cape-style cottages
Fodor'sChoice and an attractive hotel make up this traditionally elegant resort by the
★ sea. Set on 22 acres of shaded landscape partially surrounded by Pleasant Bay, the Wequassett is an informally upscale resort. An attentive staff, evening entertainment, fun in the sun, and golf at the exclusive Cape Cod National Golf Club are just a few of the benefits you can count on at Wequassett. Chef Bill Brodsky's creative globally inspired cuisine graces the menus of the three restaurants (the sophisticated Atlantic 28, elegant lounge-like Thoreau's, and the open-air Outer Bar & Grill), as well as at the Pool Bar & Grill, which serves cocktails, beverages, snacks, and light lunch fare poolside. After a day at the beach or on the links, retire to your spacious room and relax amid fresh pine furniture, floral bedcovers or handmade quilts, and overflowing window boxes. Or, sip a cocktail on the lawn outside your private cottage-style suite (no cooking facilities) overlooking Pleasant Bay. ⊠ *173 Orleans Rd. (Rte. 28), Pleasant Bay 02633* ☎ *508/432– 5400 or 800/225–7125* 🖷 *508/432–5032* ⊕ *www.wequassett.com* ⇨ *102 rooms, 2 suites* ♧ *3 restaurants, snack bar, room service, 4 tennis courts, pool, gym, windsurfing, boating, piano bar* ▭ *AE, D, DC, MC, V* ◑ *Closed Nov.–Mar.* ✴◫ *FAP.*

$$$–$$$$ ✕🖼 **Chatham Bars Inn.** Overlooking Pleasant Bay from atop a windswept bluff, Chatham Bars Inn is a grande dame hotel in the truest sense of the term. The ground-floor lobby gives way to the formal restaurant on one side and a porch-fronted lounge on the other. There are elegant guest rooms in the resort's main inn, and an additional 29 1- to 12-bedroom cottage-style suites (sans kitchens) dot 25 landscaped acres overlooking the ocean. Rooms and cottages are filled with hand-painted furnishings by local artists and colorful fabrics depicting sunny seaside scenes. It's on the pricey side, but if your wallet will allow, you'll feel coddled and catered to in this classic New England inn. ⊠ *Shore Rd., 02633* ☎ *508/ 945–0096 or 800/527–4884* 🖷 *508/945–5491* ⊕ *www.chathambarsinn. com* ⇨ *205 rooms* ♧ *3 restaurants, putting green, 3 tennis courts, pool, gym, beach, volleyball, bar, lobby lounge, babysitting, kids' programs (ages 4–teen)* ▭ *AE, DC, MC, V.*

$$$–$$$$
Fodor'sChoice
★ Captain's House Inn. A Victorian tile ceiling, wide-board floors, and elaborate moldings and wainscoting are just part of what makes Jan and Dave McMaster's inn one of the Cape's finest. Each room has its own personality. Some are quite large, and most have fireplaces. The Hiram Harding Room, in the bow-roof Captain's Cottage, has 200-year-old hand-hewn ceiling beams, a wall of raised walnut paneling, and a large, central working fireplace. Suites in the former stables are spacious and have hot tubs, fireplaces, TV–VCR, mini-refrigerators, and private patios or balconies. ⊠ *371 Old Harbor Rd., 02633* ☎ *508/945–0127 or 800/315–0728* 🖷 *508/945–0866* ⊕ *www.captainshouseinn.com* 🛏 *12 rooms, 4 suites* ♻ *Some in-room hot tubs, cable TV, in-room VCRs, bicycles, croquet, Internet; no kids under 12, no smoking* 🞉 *AE, D, MC, V* ⫟⦶ *BP.*

★ **$$$–$$$$** Chatham Wayside Inn. Once a stop on a turn-of-the-20th-century stagecoach route, the inn is still an oasis for weary travelers. Everything is crisp and colorful here, from the floral comforters and wallpapers to freshly painted walls and bright wall-to-wall carpeting. Some rooms have balconies, fireplaces, and hot tubs. The great location is smack in the center of town: you may not have to leave your room to hear the sounds of the weekly town-band concerts. ⊠ *512 Main St., 02633* ☎ *508/945–5550 or 800/391–5734* 🖷 *508/945–3407* ⊕ *www.waysideinn.com* 🛏 *56 rooms* ♻ *Restaurant, pool* 🞉 *AE, D, MC, V.*

$$$–$$$$ Cranberry Inn. Although close to the heart of town, the inn has a protected marsh area in its backyard—a fine spot from which to spy great blue herons and the occasional deer or fox. Billed as the oldest continuously operating lodging establishment in Chatham, the inn is filled with antique and reproduction furniture. Handmade quilts complete the picture. Rooms have telephones and televisions; some have fireplaces or balconies. ⊠ *359 Main St., 02633* ☎ *508/945–9232 or 800/332–4667* 🖷 *508/945–3769* ⊕ *www.cranberryinn.com* 🛏 *18 rooms* ♻ *Restaurant, cable TV; no kids under 12, no smoking* 🞉 *AE, D, MC, V* ⫟⦶ *BP.*

$$$–$$$$ Hawthorne Motel. This popular motel with a private beach overlooks Pleasant Bay, the Atlantic, and Chatham Harbor. Nearly all the rooms have stunning water views. Choose from spotless no-nonsense, simply decorated motel rooms or kitchenette efficiency units with small refrigerators, two heating plates, and a countertop sink work area; there's also a two-bedroom cottage (rented by the week in season) with full kitchen and a separate living–dining room, plus amenities like a VCR and an outdoor grill. The center of town is just a short walk away. ⊠ *196 Shore Rd., 02633* ☎ *508/945–0372* ⊕ *www.thehawthorne.com* 🛏 *16 rooms, 10 efficiencies, 1 cottage* ♻ *Some kitchenettes, refrigerators, cable TV; no smoking* 🞉 *AE, D, MC, V* ☼ *Closed mid-Oct.–mid-May.*

★ **$$$–$$$$** Queen Anne Inn. Built in 1840 as a wedding present for the daughter of a famous clipper-ship captain, the building first opened as an inn in 1874. Some of the large guest rooms have working fireplaces, balconies, and hot tubs. Lingering and lounging are encouraged—around the large heated outdoor pool, at the tables on the veranda, in front of the fireplace in the cozy sitting room, or in the plush parlor. The restaurant, which serves a delicious breakfast, is open to the public for dinner. ⊠ *70 Queen Anne Rd., 02633* ☎ *508/945–0394 or 800/545–4667*

🖷 *508/945–4884* 🌐 *www.queenanneinn.com* *31 rooms* *Restaurant, some in-room hot tubs, cable TV, 3 tennis courts, pool, bar, Internet, meeting rooms; no smoking* *AE, D, MC, V.*

$$$ Fodor'sChoice ★ **Moses Nickerson House.** Each room in this 1839 house has an individual look: one with dark woods, leathers, and English hunting antiques; another with a high canopy bed and a hand-hooked rug. Others have handmade quilts, floral wall coverings, and canopy or four-poster beds. Some rooms have gas-log fireplaces. The constants are the queen-size beds, TVs, phones, and computer hookups. Breakfast is served in a pretty glassed-in sunroom with views of the garden and fishpond. Innkeepers George and Linda Watts are especially hospitable, and their cheerful attitudes are infectious. ✉ *364 Old Harbor Rd., 02633* ☎ *508/945–5859 or 800/628–6972* 🖷 *508/945–7087* 🌐 *www.mosesnickersonhouse.com* *7 rooms* *Internet; no smoking* *AE, D, MC, V* *BP.*

$$–$$$ **Chatham Highlander.** A great bargain considering its location near the center of Chatham, this motel offers generously sized rooms on attractive grounds. Most rooms have double beds, though one has a king-size bed, and there are two efficiencies and a suite for larger families. ✉ *946 Main St., 02633* ☎ *508/945–9038* 🌐 *capecodtravel.com/highlander* *25 rooms, 2 efficiencies, 1 suite* *Some microwaves, some refrigerators, cable TV, 2 pools, Internet; no smoking* *AE, D, MC, V* *Closed late Nov.–Apr.*

Nightlife & the Arts

THE ARTS **Chatham Drama Guild** (✉ 134 Crowell Rd. ☎ 508/945–0510) stages productions year-round, including musicals, comedies, and dramas.

The **Creative Arts Center** (✉ 154 Crowell Rd. ☎ 508/945–3583) thrives year-round with classes, changing gallery exhibitions, demonstrations, lectures, and other activities.

In July and August the **Guild of Chatham Painters** presents an outdoor art gallery on Thursday and Friday from 9:30 to 5 on the lawn of the Main Street School (✉ Main St.).

The **Monomoy Theatre** (✉ 776 Main St. ☎ 508/945–1589) stages summer productions—thrillers, musicals, classics, modern drama—by the Ohio University Players.

Chatham's summer **town-band concerts** (✉ Kate Gould Park, Main St. ☎ 508/945–5199) begin at 8 on Friday and draw up to 6,000 people. As many as 500 fox-trot on the roped-off dance floor, and there are special dances for children and sing-alongs for all.

NIGHTLIFE **Chatham Squire** (✉ 487 Main St. ☎ 508/945–0945), with four bars including a raw bar, is a rollicking year-round local hangout, drawing a young crowd to the bar side and a mixed crowd of locals to the restaurant.

After great success in Hyannis and Falmouth, owners of **The Roo Bar** (✉ 907 Main St. ☎ 508/945–9988 🌐 www.theroobar.com) opened a third location in Chatham, transforming what was once a Friendly's into another elegant bar. Patrons enjoy an extensive wine list, great mixed drinks and varied entertainment, usually rock music, on the weekends.

Wequassett Inn Resort & Golf Club (✉ 173 Orleans Rd. [Rte. 28], Pleasant Bay ☎ 508/432–5400) has a jazz duo or piano music nightly in its lounge in July and August (jacket requested).

Sports & the Outdoors

BASEBALL The **Cape Cod Baseball League,** begun in 1885, is an invitational league of college players that counts Carlton Fisk, Ron Darling, and the late Thurman Munson as alumni. Considered the country's best summer league, it's scouted by all the major-league teams. Players have included Mo Vaughn and Nomar Garciaparra. Ten teams play a 44-game season from mid-June to mid-August; games held at all 10 fields are free. The **Chatham A's** games (✉ Veterans' Field, Main and Depot Sts. by rotary ☎ 508/996–5004 for schedule) are great entertainment.

Baseball clinics (✉ Veterans' Field, Main and Depot Sts. by rotary ☎ 508/432–6909), for kids 6 through 8, 9 through 12, and 13 through 17, are offered in one-week sessions by the Chatham A's in summer. The other nine town teams in the Cape league also conduct clinics (☎ 508/996–5004 information).

BEACHES If you're looking for a crowd-free sandy beach, boats at Chatham Harbor—such as the ***Rip Ryder*** (☎ 508/945–5450)—will ferry you across to North Beach ($10–$12 per person), which is a sand spit adjoining Orleans's Nauset Beach, to South Beach ($10), or to Monomoy ($45, or $10 per person for three or more passengers).

Outermost Harbor Marine (✉ Morris Island Rd., Morris Island ☎ 508/945–2030) runs shuttles to South Beach; rides cost $10 round-trip for adults. The cost includes parking.

Harding's Beach (✉ Harding's Beach Rd., off Barn Hill Rd., West Chatham), west of Chatham center, is open to the public and charges daily parking fees to nonresidents in season. Lifeguards are stationed in summer. This beach can get crowded, so plan to arrive early or late.

BIKING **Bert & Carol's Lawnmower & Bicycle Shop** (✉ 347 Orleans Rd. [Rte. 28], North Chatham ☎ 508/945–0137) rents bikes for all ages, shapes, and abilities.

Bikes & Blades (✉ 195 Crowell Rd. ☎ 508/945–7600) rents all manner of bikes as well as in-line skates.

BOATING **Monomoy Sail & Cycle** (✉ 275 Orleans Rd., North Chatham ☎ 508/945–0811) rents sailboards and Sunfish.

GOLF **Chatham Seaside Links** (✉ Seaview St., West Chatham ☎ 508/945–4774), a 9-hole course, is good for beginners.

SURFING The Lower and Outer Cape beaches, including North Beach in Chatham, are the best on the peninsula for surfing, which is tops when there's a storm offshore. Chatham does not have any surf shops, but you'll find them in nearby Orleans.

TENNIS **Chatham Bars Inn** (✉ Shore Rd. ☎ 508/945–0096 Ext. 1155) offers three waterfront all-weather tennis courts, open to the public by reservation for $30 an hour. You can also take lessons and visit the pro shop.

THE CAPE COD BASEBALL LEAGUE

A T THE BASEBALL HALL OF FAME in Cooperstown, New York, you can find a poster announcing a showdown between arch rivals Sandwich and Barnstable. The date? July 4, 1885. In the 100-plus years since that day, the Cape's ball-playing tradition has continued unabated, and if you're a sports fan, a visit to a Cape Cod Baseball League summer game is a must. To see a game on the Cape is to come into contact with baseball's roots. You'll remember why you love the sport, and you'll have a newfound sense of why it became the national pastime.

As they have since the 1950s, top-ranked college baseball players from around the country descend on the Cape when school lets out, in time to begin the season in mid-June. This is no sandlot, catch-as-catch-can scene. Each player joins one of the league's 10 teams, each based in a different town: the Bourne Braves, Wareham Gatemen, Falmouth Commodores, Cotuit Kettleers, Hyannis Mets, Dennis-Yarmouth Red Sox, Harwich Mariners, Brewster Whitecaps, Chatham Athletics (A's), and the Orleans Cardinals.

Players lodge with local families and work day jobs cutting lawns, painting houses, or giving baseball clinics in town parks. In the evening, though, their lives are given over to baseball as they don uniforms and head for the field.

The Cape League's motto is "Where the Stars of Tomorrow Shine Tonight." By latest count, one of every eight active major-league ballplayers spent a summer in the Cape League on the way up. You could build an all-star roster with names such as Nomar Garciaparra, Frank Thomas, Jeff Bagwell, Todd Helton, and Barry Zito.

To enshrine these heroes past, the Cape League inducted its first members into its Hall of Fame at the Heritage Museums & Gardens in Sandwich in January 2001. Among the 12 players honored were Thurman Munson, Mike Flanagan, Jeff Reardon, Mo Vaughn, and Frank Thomas.

Yet as good as the baseball is—you'll often see bunches of major-league scouts at a game—another great reason to come out to the ballpark is . . . the ballpark. Chatham's Veterans Field is the Cape's 3Com Park at Candlestick Point:, much like the San Francisco park, fog tends to engulf the games here. Orleans's Eldredge Park is a local favorite—immaculate, cozy, and comfortable. Some parks have bleachers, while in others it's up to you to bring your own chair or blanket and stretch out behind a dugout or baseline. Children are free to roam and can even try for foul balls—which they are, however, asked to return because, after all, balls don't grow on trees. When hunger hits, the ice-cream truck and hot-dog stand are never far away.

Games start at either 5 or 7, depending on whether the field has lights; there are occasionally afternoon games. Each team plays 44 games in a season, so finding one is rarely a problem (🌐 www. capecodbaseball.org. has information). And, best of all, they're always free. The Cape's baseball scene is so American, the ambience so relaxed and refreshing, it's tempting to invoke the old Field of Dreams analogy. But the league needs no Hollywood comparison. This is the real thing. It was built a long time ago, and they are still coming.

— Seth Rolbein

The town maintains two public tennis parks, one on Depot Road next to the Railroad Museum at No. 153 and the other at the middle school on Crowell Road.

Shopping

Main Street is a busy shopping area with a diverse range of merchandise, from the pocketbook-friendly to the pricier and more upscale. Here you'll find galleries, crafts, clothing stores, bookstores, and a few good antiques shops.

Cabbages and Kings Bookstore (⊠ 595 Main St. ☎ 508/945–1603) is a good independent bookstore. In addition to a full stock of literary and regional books, look for a host of unusual games, cards, and toys and a regular schedule of author appearances.

Cape Cod Cooperage (⊠ 1150 Queen Anne Rd., at Rte. 137, West Chatham ☎ 508/432–0788), in an old barn, sells woodenware made in a (more than) century-old tradition by an on-site cooper (barrel maker), as well as hand-decorated furniture and crafts supplies. Daily classes are available in everything from stenciling to basket making, from decorative painting to birdhouse building. Another location in Chatham (on Route 28) sells antiques and finely crafted Shaker furniture.

Chatham Glass Company (⊠ 758 Main St. ☎ 508/945–5547) is a glassworks where you can watch glass being blown, and buy it, too. Objects include marbles, Christmas ornaments, jewelry, and art glass.

Chatham Jam and Jelly Shop (⊠ 10 Vineyard Ave., at Rte. 28, West Chatham ☎ 508/945–3052) sells preserves such as cranberry with strawberries and Maine wild blueberry, nutty conserves, and ice cream toppings, all made on-site in small batches.

Clambake Celebrations (⊠ 1223C Main St. ☎ 508/945–7771 or 877/792–7771) prepares full clambakes, including lobsters, clams, mussels, corn, potatoes, onions, and sausage, for you to take out; it'll even loan a charcoal grill. The company also delivers via air year-round if necessary. The food is layered in seaweed in a pot and ready to steam.

The **East Wind Silver Co.** (⊠ 878 Main St. ☎ 508/945–8935) specializes in artful silver jewelry but also sells watercolor paintings, pottery, fountains, and Tiffany-style lighting.

Marion's Pie Shop (⊠ 2022 Main St. [Rte. 28], West Chatham ☎ 508/432–9439) sells homemade and home-style fruit breads, pastries, prepared foods such as lasagna, Boston baked beans, chowder base, and, of course, pies, both savory and sweet.

S. Wilder & Co. (⊠ 304 Rte. 28, North Chatham ☎ 877/794–5337) displays old-style colonial crafts. Handcrafted brass and copper lanterns are made here.

The **Spyglass** (⊠ 618 Main St. ☎ 508/945–9686) carries telescopes, barometers, writing boxes, maps, and other nautical antiques.

Yankee Ingenuity (⊠ 525 Main St. ☎ 508/945–1288) stocks a varied selection of unique jewelry and lamps and a wide assortment of unusual, beautiful trinkets at reasonable (especially for Chatham) prices.

Yellow Umbrella Books (⊠ 501 Main St. ☎ 508/945–0144) has an excellent selection of new books, many about Cape Cod, as well as used books.

en route   North of Chatham, Route 28 winds through wooded upland toward **Pleasant Bay,** from which a number of country roads will take you to a nice view of Nauset spit and the islands in the bay.

Orleans

⑫ *8 mi north of Chatham; 4 mi southwest of Eastham; 35 mi east of Sagamore Bridge.*

Named for Louis-Philippe de Bourbon, *duc d'Orléans* (duke of Orléans), who reputedly visited the area during his exile from France in the 1790s, Orleans was incorporated as a town in 1797. Historically, it has the distinction of being the only place in the continental United States to have received enemy fire during either world war. In July 1918 a German submarine fired on commercial barges off the coast. Four were sunk, and one shell is reported to have fallen on American soil.

Today Orleans is part quiet seaside village and part bustling center with strip malls. The commercial hub of the Lower Cape, Orleans is one of the more steadily populated areas, year-round, of the Lower Cape. Yet the town retains a fervent commitment to preserving its past, and residents, in support of local mom-and-pop shops, maintain an active refusal policy of many big-time corporations.

Orleans has a long heritage in fishing and seafaring, and many beautifully preserved homes remain from the colonial era. Much of this beauty is found in the small village of East Orleans, home of the town's Historical Society and Museum. In other areas of town, such as down by Rock Harbor, more modestly grand homes stand near the water's edge.

As you head north, this is the first Cape town to touch both Cape Cod Bay and the Atlantic Ocean. Nauset Beach, on the Atlantic, is enormously popular. Backed by towering dunes dotted with sea grass and colorful *rosa Rugosa,* this beach begins what could be a long but beautiful trek clear to the very tip of the Cape. Skaket Beach, just south of Rock Harbor, is the main bay-side beach and affords both scenic views and calm, warm waters for swimming.

A walk along Rock Harbor Road, a winding street lined with gray-shingle Cape houses, white picket fences, and neat gardens, leads to the bayside **Rock Harbor,** a former packet landing and site of a War of 1812 skirmish in which the Orleans militia kept a British warship from docking. In the 19th century Orleans had an active saltworks, and a flourishing packet service between Rock Harbor and Boston developed.

Today the former packet landing is the base of charter-fishing and party boats in season, as well as of a small commercial fishing fleet whose catch hits the counters at the fish market and small restaurant here. Sunsets over the harbor are spectacular.

The Community of Jesus, a religious community whose members come from a variety of Christian traditions, owns a large portion of the prime real estate in the Rock Harbor area. Their dramatic cathedral, the **Church of the Transfiguration,** showcases the work of local and international artisans, and reflects the community's dedication to the arts. Inside there's an organ with thousands of pipes (the largest is 37.5 feet long), authentic frescoes depicting Biblical scenes, colorful stained glass windows, and intricate mosaic work mixing religious themes with images of local flora and fauna. Guided tours of the church are at 3 PM Tuesday, Friday, and Saturday or by appointment; services are held several times a day and are open to the public. You are also free to explore the church and grounds on your own, but note that the community is closed to the public Wednesday and holidays. ⊠ *Rock Harbor Rd. across from Rock Harbor* ☎ *508/255–1054 or 508/255–6204 (tours)* ⊕ *www.communityofjesus.org* ⊠ *Free, donations accepted.*

need a break?	**Orleans Villa Pizza** (⊠ Rte. 6A ☎ 508/255–5111) is an unassuming year-round joint with the best pizza by the slice in town.

The 1890 **French Cable Station Museum** was the stateside landing point for the 3,000-mi-long transatlantic cable that originated in Brittany. Another cable laid between Orleans and New York City completed the France–New York link, and many important messages were communicated through the station. In World War I it was an essential connection between army headquarters in Washington and the American Expeditionary Force in France, and the station was under guard by the marines. By 1959 telephone service had rendered the station obsolete, and it closed. The equipment is still in place. ⊠ *41 S. Orleans Rd., East Orleans* ☎ *508/240–1735* ⊠ *Donations accepted* ☉ *June, Fri.–Sun. 1–4; July–early Sept., Mon.–Sat. 1–4.*

The **Jonathan Young Windmill,** a pretty if somewhat incongruous sight on the busy highway, is a landmark from the days of salt making in Orleans, when it would pump saltwater into shallow vaults for evaporation. A program explaining the history and operation of the mill demonstrates the old millstone and grinding process. ⊠ *Rte. 6A and Town Cove, East Orleans* ☉ *July and Aug., daily 11–4; June and Sept., weekends 11–4.*

need a break?	Grab a baked treat, chocolates of all varieties and any number of coffee concoctions at **The Chocolate Sparrow** (⊠ 5 Old Colony Way ☎ 508/240–2230)

☧ The **Academy of Performing Arts** (⊠ 5 Giddiah Hill Rd. ☎ 508/255–5510 ⊕ www.apa1.org) offers two-week sessions of theater, music, and dance classes to kids ages 8–12, with a show at the end of each session. It also schedules year-round classes for ages four to adult in dance, music, and drama. The academy's theater is at 120 Main Street.

Snow Library (⊠ Main St. and Rte. 28 ☎ 508/240–3760) has been in operation since around 1876; today there are kid's story hours and numerous lecture programs.

Where to Stay & Eat

$$–$$$$
Fodor'sChoice
★
✕ **Abba.** Bringing a much-needed dash of flavor to Orleans, Abba serves inspired pan-Mediterranean cuisine in an elegant and intimate setting. Chef and co-owner Erez Pinhas skillfully combines Middle Eastern, Asian, and Southern European flavors in such dishes as scallops with fettuccine and asparagus in a curry cream sauce or herb-crusted rack of lamb with gnocchi, green peas, Swiss chard, and olive sauce. Cushy pillows on the banquettes and soft candlelight flickering from Moroccan glass votives add a touch of opulence. Abba only serves dinner (reservations are recommended), but its adjacent café, **Abba to Go,** packages the same creative blend of flavors into a lighter, more casual, and less expensive menu. Choose from traditional tabbouleh, baba ghanouj, or falafel; specialty pizzas and sandwiches; or something from the extensive bakery selection. ⊠ *Old Colony Way and West Rd.* ☎ *508/255–8144* ⊕ *www.abbarestaurant.com* 🖃 *No credit cards* ⊙ *Closed Mon. No lunch.*

★ **$$–$$$$**
✕ **Nauset Beach Club.** Locals stand by this long-established eatery. The kitchen produces seasonally inspired regional Italian food with an emphasis on locally harvested seafood and produce. Choose from a fixed-price option (offered daily at two early seatings) or the regular menu for such favorites as pistachio-crusted roast rack of lamb or tagliatelle with lobster. The off-season warms up with wood oven–fired dishes; in fall and winter, truffles appear artfully in various presentations. Pastas and desserts are all homemade. The large Italian and American wine selection is excellent. ⊠ *222 Main St., East Orleans* ☎ *508/255–8547* ⊛ *Reservations essential* 🖃 *AE, D, DC, MC, V* ⊙ *No lunch.*

$$–$$$
✕ **Mahoney's Atlantic Bar and Grill.** The chef, a Mahoney who cooked for years at one of Provincetown's busiest restaurants, really knows his stuff. The lunch- and dinner-menu appetizers emphasize grilled vegetables and polenta, drunken shellfish steamed in ale, and tuna sashimi, a New Orleans classic. The bar is long and comfortable, and you can sip your California wine to live music Thursday and Saturday. ⊠ *28 Main St.* ☎ *508/255–5505* 🖃 *AE, MC, V.*

★ **$$–$$$**
✕ **The Old Jailhouse Tavern.** A big set of golden jailer's keys hangs at the entrance of this rambling restaurant, part of which was once an old stone lockup. The theme prevails throughout: the menu carries headings such as "A Light Sentence" for salads and appetizers and "The Lineup" for the sandwich list. Foods for sharing include a whole wheel of baked Brie with Boursin cheese, crackers, and fruit; and deep-fried fresh vegetables with ranch dip. Entrées tend toward basic seafood, steak, veal, and chicken dishes. The tavern has a long oak bar and bountiful flowers hanging from the atrium, plus an adjacent Courthouse room for group events. ⊠ *28 West Rd.* ☎ *508/255–5245* ⊛ *Reservations not accepted* 🖃 *D, MC, V.*

$–$$$ ✕ **The Beacon Room.** Adorned with crisp linens, frilly curtains, and wood furnishings, this bistro serves a nice mix of seafood and meats enhanced with sophisticated and inventive flavors. Start with the Gorgonzola, sun-dried cranberry, and walnut salad, and then move on to such delights as salmon and pasta sauté or the house favorite, chicken saltimbocca. There's a bit of everything here, from quesadillas to calamari. Each dish is treated with the same care and attention to quality. In warmer months, dinner on the garden patio is particularly gracious. An ambitious wine list complements the fine selection. ⊠ *23 West Rd.* ☎ *508/255–2211* ⌦ *Reservations not accepted* ⊟ *D, MC, V.*

$–$$$ ✕ **Kadee's Lobster & Clam Bar.** Kadee's serves good clams and fish-and-chips that you can grab on the way to the beach from the take-out window. Or sit down in the dining room for steamers and mussels, pasta and seafood stews, or the famous Portuguese kale soup. There's also a gift shop as well as a miniature golf course out back. Prices are the only serious drawback here. ⊠ *212 Main St.* ☎ *508/255–6184* ⌦ *Reservations not accepted* ⊟ *MC, V* ☉ *Closed early Sept.–late May and weekdays in early June.*

$–$$$ ✕ **Rosina's Cafe.** Originally a classic mom-and-pop Italian restaurant off Main Street, Rosina's has expanded into a full-blown full-service place. The pasta primavera makes the grade, as does Angela's stuffed halibut (often on special), a good chunk of fish stuffed with scallops, cheeses, pine nuts, bread crumbs, and garlic. The spaghetti puttanesca remains a rewarding signature dish. The wine list veers toward the conventional. ⊠ *15 Cove Rd.* ☎ *508/240–5513* ⊟ *AE, D, MC, V.*

$–$$ ✕ **Lobster Claw.** If you're over 6 feet tall, keep an eye out for the fishnets hanging from the ceiling in this goofy little seafood spot. Tables are lacquered turquoise, portions are huge, and the lobster roll is one of the best around. You can get all the Cape basics here: fish and seafood poached, broiled, baked, or fried, along with an assortment of steaks. The children's menu includes seafood and chicken tenders. The place gets packed to the gills, especially during its popular early-bird dining hours. ⊠ *Rte. 6A* ☎ *508/255–1800* ⌦ *Reservations not accepted* ⊟ *AE, D, DC, MC, V.*

$–$$ ✕ **The Yardarm.** Orleans's version of a roadhouse, the Yardarm feels smoky even though smoking is not allowed anymore. The TV over the bar is likely to be tuned to a sports game, and the only pool table in town is always busy (though it's not in use while dinner is being served). The hearty, well-cooked food is a great value, especially the baked sole, barbecued ribs or chicken, and the pot roast; thanks to the big portions, you can expect to take some of your dinner home. It's also a great place to stop in for a burger-and-beer lunch. ⊠ *48 Rte. 28* ☎ *508/255–4840* ⌦ *Reservations not accepted* ⊟ *AE, DC, MC, V.*

★ **¢–$$** ✕ **Land Ho!** Tried-and-true tavern fare is the rule at Orleans's flagship local restaurant. The scene is usually fun and boisterous. Dozens of homemade wooden signs hang from the rafters. The burgers and the sea-clam pie are both excellent—much better than the fish-and-chips. Blackboard specials change daily. This is a good place for a rainy-day lunch. On weekend nights, it livens up even more with the music of local bands. ⊠ *Rte. 6A and Cove Rd.* ☎ *508/255–5165* ⌦ *Reservations not accepted* ⊟ *AE, MC, V.*

¢–$$ ✕ **Sir Cricket's Fish and Chips.** For a beautifully turned-out fish sandwich, pull off the highway into this tiny local favorite, a hole-in-the-wall attached to the Nauset Lobster Pool. Built mainly for takeout, this no-frills fried-food joint does have three or four tiny tables and a soda machine. Try the fresh oyster roll or go for a full fisherman's platter. As you eat, check out the chair seats—each is an exquisitely rendered mini-mural of Orleans history or a personality painted by legendary local artist Dan Joy. ⊠ *Rte. 6A, near Stop & Shop* ☎ *508/255–4453* ⌂ *Reservations not accepted* ▭ *No credit cards.*

$$$–$$$$ ✕▦ **Orleans Inn.** Conveniently located just off Route 6A, this waterfront inn and restaurant housed in an 1875 sea captain's mansion has a cozy, down-to-earth feel. Rooms are charmingly appointed with classic wood furniture and floral quilts on the beds; the larger Waterfront suites have sitting areas and great views of the ocean. Local and long-distance phone calls are included in room rates. Common areas include a kitchenette with a microwave and toaster oven and a sitting room in the basement with a large TV and videos. The restaurant serves traditional standbys such as lobster, fish and chips, grilled sirloin, pasta dishes, and chicken Parmesan for lunch and dinner, plus daily specials that make creative use of familiar flavors. ⊠ *3 Old County Rd., off Route 6A, 02653* ☎ *508/255–2222* 🖷 *508/255–6722* ⊕ *www.orleansinn. com* ➥ *11 rooms* ⌂ *Restaurant, in-room data ports, refrigerators, cable TV, pub; no smoking* ▭ *AE, MC, V.*

$$–$$$ ✕▦ **Barley Neck Inn.** Spacious rooms are available in the hotel-like lodge, adjacent to the restaurant building. Televisions and small refrigerators are standard. The inn's restaurant, in a restored 1850s sea captain's house, is a popular destination. There's a semiformal dining room and a relaxed bar (the bar menu is cheaper). The chef prepares classic Cape fish dishes with a French influence; the innovative kitchen is known for its salsas and sauces. Off-season, relax fireside with Sunday afternoon live jazz. ⊠ *5 Beach Rd., East Orleans 02643* ☎ *508/255–8484, 508/255–0212 restaurant* 🖷 *508/255–3626* ⊕ *www.barleyneck.com* ➥ *18 rooms* ⌂ *2 restaurants, refrigerators, pool* ▭ *AE, MC, V* ⏐◎⏐ *CP.*

★ ¢–$$$ ▦ **Nauset House Inn.** You could easily spend a day trying out all the places to relax here. There's a parlor with comfortable chairs and a large fireplace, an orchard set with picnic tables, and a lush conservatory with a weeping cherry tree in its center. Rooms in both the main building and the adjacent Carriage House have stenciled walls, quilts, and unusual antique pieces, as well as hand-painted furniture, stained glass, and prints done by one of the owners. The beach is only ½-mi distant (they'll set you up with beach chairs and towels), and the attractions of town are close but not too close. ⊠ *143 Beach Rd.* ⏇ *Box 774, East Orleans 02643* ☎ *508/255–2195* ⊕ *www.nausethouseinn.com* ➥ *14 rooms* ▭ *D, MC, V* ⊗ *Closed Nov.–Mar.* ⏐◎⏐ *BP.*

★ $$ ▦ **Kadee's Gray Elephant.** A mile from Nauset Beach, next to shops, a grocery store, a farm stand, a post office, and Kadee's Lobster & Clam Bar, this centuries-old house has small vacation studio and one-bedroom apartments. With quilts and comforters in a mix of plaid and floral patterns layered on the beds, wicker painted lavender or green, and bright pink bows and flowers painted on furniture, they're a cheerful riot of color. Kitchens are fully equipped with microwaves, attractive glassware, irons and boards—even lobster crackers. ⊠ *216 Main St.* ⌖ *Box 86, East Orleans 02643* ☎ *508/255–7608* 🖶 *508/240–2976* ➲ *6–8 apartments* ♿ *Restaurant, microwaves, cable TV, miniature golf, shop; no smoking* ▤ *MC, V.*

$$ 🏨 **Orleans Holiday Motel.** Smack in the middle of a commercial area, this complex is not a totally peaceful place, but its position does put you in the midst of restaurants and other services; it's also an easy walk from the center of town. Motel rooms are set around the giant outdoor pool and have either two double, one queen-size, or two queen-size beds. There's a complimentary boat shuttle to Nauset Beach. ⊠ *Rtes. 6A and 28, 02643* ☎ *508/255–1514 or 800/451–1833* 🖶 *508/255–7284* ⊕ *www.orleansholiday.com* ➲ *45 rooms* ♿ *Picnic area, refrigerators, pool* ▤ *AE, MC, V* ⦿ *CP.*

★ **$–$$** 🏨 **Skaket Beach Motel.** Rooms in this convenient-to-everything motel on a busy roadside are well-sized; choose from standard, deluxe, or poolside. Outdoor facilities include horseshoes, a heated pool, and grills. ⊠ *203 Rte. 6A, 02643* ☎ *508/255–1020 or 800/835–0298* 🖶 *508/255–6487* ⊕ *www.skaketbeachmotel.com* ➲ *46 rooms* ♿ *Pool, croquet, horseshoes* ▤ *MC, V* ⊗ *Closed late Nov.–Mar.* ⦿ *CP.*

Nightlife & the Arts

The **Academy Playhouse** (⊠ 120 Main St. ☎ 508/255–1963), one of the oldest community theaters on the Cape, stages 12 or 13 productions year-round, including original works.

The **Cape & Islands Chamber Music Festival** (⌖ Box 2721, 02653 ☎ 508/945–8060) presents three weeks of top-caliber performances, including a jazz night, at various locations in August.

The 90-member **Cape Symphony Orchestra** (☎ 508/362–1111) sails into Orleans in late August for one of two Sounds of Summer Pops concerts (the other is in Mashpee in July). The performance takes place at the Eldredge Park, adjacent to the Nauset Middle School (⊠ Rte. 28 and Eldredge Pkwy.). Call for a year-round schedule of events.

The **Gloria Dei Artes Foundation** (☎ 508/255–3999 ⊕ www.gdaf.org) stages music and theatre events several times a year. The group is affiliated with the Community of Jesus; performances are held on the Community's grounds at Rock Harbor.

Joe's Beach Road Bar & Grille (⊠ Main St. at Beach Rd., East Orleans ☎ 508/255–0212) has live piano from Thursday through Sunday nights in summer; check for off-season entertainment schedules.

Land Ho! (⊠ Rte. 6A and Cove Rd. ☎ 508/255–5165) has live local bands frequently and throughout the year.

Mahoney's Atlantic Bar and Grill (⊠ 28 Main St. ☎ 508/255–5505) regularly has live jazz and blues in the bar area; call for times.

Free ocean-side concerts are held in the gazebo at **Nauset Beach** each Monday evening from 7 to 9 in July and August. The resident fried-clam shack stays open until 10.

Sports & the Outdoors

BASEBALL The **Orleans Cardinals** (☎ 508/255–0793) of the collegiate Cape Cod Baseball League play home games at Eldredge Park (⊠ Rte. 28) from mid-June to mid-August.

BEACHES The town-managed **Nauset Beach** (⊠ Beach Rd., Nauset Heights ☎ 508/240–3775)—not to be confused with Nauset Light Beach, up a ways at the National Seashore—is a wide 10-mi-long sweep of sandy ocean beach with low dunes and large waves good for bodysurfing or board surfing. The beach has lifeguards, restrooms, showers, and a food concession (something the National Seashore beaches lack). Despite its size, the massive parking lot often fills up when the sun is strong; it's best to arrive quite early or in the late afternoon if you want to claim a spot. The beach is open to off-road vehicles with a special permit. Daily parking fees of $10 are charged, or you can buy a one-week pass for $25, a two-week pass for $45, or a season pass for $65. Entrance is free with a resident sticker. For more information call the parks department.

Freshwater seekers can access **Pilgrim Lake** (⊠ Pilgrim Lake Rd. off Monument Rd. and Rte. 28, South Orleans) with the same parking and sticker fees as Nauset Beach.

Skaket Beach (⊠ Skaket Beach Rd., Namskaket ☎ 508/240–3775) on Cape Cod Bay is a sandy stretch with calm warm water good for children. It's a good place to watch motorboats, fishing charters, and sailboats as they leave the channel at Rock Harbor, not to mention the spectacular evening sunsets. There are restrooms, lifeguards, and a snack bar. Daily parking fees are the same as at Nauset Beach. For more information call the parks department.

BOATING **Arey's Pond Boat Yard** (⊠ 43 Arey's La., off Rte. 28, South Orleans ☎ 508/255–0994) has a sailing school with individual and group lessons.

FISHING Many of Orleans's freshwater ponds offer good fishing for perch, pickerel, trout, and more. The required fishing license, along with rental gear, is available at the **Goose Hummock Shop** (⊠ 15 Rte. 6A ☎ 508/255–0455).

The *Osprey* (☎ 508/255–4212) leaves Rock Harbor for both half- and full-day sportfishing trips. All tackle, bait, and cleaning services are provided.

Rock Harbor Charter Boat Fleet (⊠ Rock Harbor, Rock Harbor ☎ 508/255–9757, 800/287–1771 in Massachusetts) goes for bass and blues in the bay from spring through fall. Walk-ons and charters are both available.

ICE-SKATING Ice-skating, lessons, hockey, clinics, and camps are available at the **Charles Moore Arena** (⊠ O'Connor Way, east of Rte. 6 ☎ 508/255–5902 or 508/255–2971). Kids ages 9 through 14 ice-skate to DJ-spun rock and flashing lights at Rock Night, which takes place Friday from 8 to 10.

SPORTING GOODS—RENTALS **Nauset Sports** (⊠ Jeremiah Sq., Rte. 6A at rotary ☎ 508/255–4742) rents surf, body, skim, and wake boards; kayaks; wet suits; in-line skates; and tennis rackets.

For bike rentals just across the way from the Cape Cod Rail Trail, head to **Orleans Cycle** (✉ 26 Main St. ☎ 508/255–9115).

The Lower and Outer Cape beaches, including Nauset Beach in Orleans, are the best spots for surfing, especially when there's a storm offshore. For a surf report—water temperature, weather, surf, tanning factor—call ☎ 508/240–2229.

Pump House Surf Co. (✉ 9 Rte. 6A ☎ 508/240–2226) rents wet suits and surfboards, and sells boards and gear.

Shopping

Baseball Shop (✉ 26 Main St. ☎ 508/240–1063) sells licensed products relating to baseball and other sports—new and collectible cards (and nonsports cards) as well as hats, clothing, and videos.

Bird Watcher's General Store (✉ 36 Rte. 6A ☎ 508/255–6974 or 800/562–1512) stocks nearly everything avian but the birds themselves: feeders, paintings, houses, books, binoculars, calls, bird-theme apparel, and more.

Countryside Antiques (✉ 6 Lewis Rd., East Orleans ☎ 508/240–0525) specializes in European and Asian antique furniture, home-accent pieces, china, and silver.

Fancy's Farm Stand (✉ 199 Main St., East Orleans ☎ 508/255–1949) sells local produce, fresh sandwiches and roll-ups, salads (salad bar or prepared varieties), homemade soup, ice cream, fresh-baked breads, and other supplies for a great picnic. A wide assortment of flowers, both dried and fresh, are sold, adding great color to the beautiful, beamed old-style barn.

Heaven Scent You (✉ 13 Cove Rd. ☎ 508/240–2508) offers massage, spa services, and beauty treatments—everything you need for some relaxation and rejuvenation.

Karol Richardson (✉ 47 Main St. ☎ 508/255–3944) sells fine contemporary clothing, plus silk wraps and scarves, hats, shoes, handbags, and handcrafted jewelry. You'll pay well for the quality, but if you're fortunate enough to be around for one of the off-season warehouse sales, you'll hit the jackpot.

Kemp Pottery (✉ 9 Rte. 6A ☎ 508/255–5853) displays functional and decorative stoneware and porcelain, fountains, garden sculpture, sinks, and stained glass.

Oceana (✉ 1 Main St. Sq. ☎ 508/240–1414) has a beautiful selection of nautical-theme home accents, gifts, and jewelry, as well as colorful hooked rugs made by Cape artist Claire Murray.

The **Orleans Farmers' Market** (✉ Old Colony Way across from Capt'n Elmers ☎ 508/255–0951) is where to go for local delicacies such as fresh shellfish, produce, flowers, and homemade goodies. It opens at 8 on Saturday mornings throughout the summer. Be forewarned—early birds get the best selection, as things tend to disappear quickly.

SE. Mery Bookseller (✉ 43 Main St. ☎ 508/255–1545) is an independent bookstore with works by local authors and those who write on topics of regional interest. You'll also find an extensive collection of unique greeting cards and specialty items. Internet access is available on a sign-up fee basis.

XO Clothing (✉ 50 Main St. ☎ 508/255–4407) carries a full stock of designer warehouse excess at unbeatable prices. The inventory changes frequently, but expect scores of casual linen dresses, pants sets, shirts, and colorful cotton pieces.

ART & CRAFTS GALLERIES

The **Addison Art Gallery** (✉ 43 Rte. 28, ☎ 508/255–6200), in four rooms of a brick-red Cape house, represents more than two dozen regional artists. Peruse the collection of contemporary works, many of which are inspired by life on Cape Cod. The sculpture garden in the side yard is a perfect complement to the tasteful gallery. Receptions, where you can often meet the week's featured artist, are held from 5 to 7, Saturday nights, year-round.

The **Hogan Art Gallery** (✉ 39 Main St. ☎ 508/240–3655) showcases the colorful white-line woodblocks, paintings, and pastels by artist Ruth Hogan, as well as 20th-century American regional paintings by her husband, Frank. There's also a nice selection of painted furniture.

Left Bank Gallery (✉ 8 Cove Rd. ☎ 508/247–9172) carries an eclectic mix of handcrafted jewelry, fine art by both local and national artists, hand-painted furniture, pottery, and handmade clothing.

On Tuesday and Sunday in July and August, **Nauset Painters** (Tuesday ✉ Depot Sq. at Old Colony Way ✉ Sunday ✉ Sandwich Cooperative Bank, 51 Main St.) presents outdoor juried art shows.

The **Orleans Art Association** holds outdoor art shows from 10 to 5 each Thursday and Friday in July and August on the grounds of the American Legion Hall (✉ 137 Main St.).

At various times in June, July, and August, the **Orleans Professional Arts and Crafts Association** sponsors a giant outdoor show featuring the works of more than 100 artists and craftspeople on the grounds of the Nauset Middle School (✉ Rte. 28). For specific dates and times check the free town guide published by the Chamber of Commerce.

The **Star Gallery** (✉ 76 Rte. 6A ☎ 508/240–7827) specializes in contemporary and less traditional art by artists both local and beyond; watch for Saturday-evening artist receptions in July and August.

Tree's Place (✉ Rte. 6A at Rte. 28 ☎ 508/255–1330 or 888/255–1330), one of the Cape's best and most original shops, has a collection of handcrafted kaleidoscopes, as well as art glass, hand-painted porcelain and pottery, handblown stemware, jewelry, imported ceramic tiles, and fine art. Tree's displays the work of New England artists including Robert Vickery, Don Stone, and Elizabeth Mumford (whose popular folk art is bordered in mottoes and poetic phrases). Champagne openings are held on Saturday night in summer.

Eastham

⑬ *3 mi north of Orleans; 6 mi south of Wellfleet.*

Often overlooked on the speedy drive up toward Provincetown on U.S. 6, Eastham is a town full of hidden treasures. Unlike other towns on the Cape, it has no official town center or Main Street; the highway bisects Eastham, and the town is spread out on both Cape Cod Bay and the Atlantic. Amid the gas stations, convenience stores, restaurants, and large motel complexes, Eastham's wealth of natural beauty takes a little exploring to find.

One such gem is the National Seashore, which officially begins here. Beyond the commercial buildup lie thousands of acres of wooded areas, salt marshes and wild, open ocean beaches. The Salt Pond Visitor Center rests just off U.S. 6 and is one of Cape Cod National Seashore's main centers. This is a fine place to stop for information on the area; the center also hosts numerous nature and history programs and lectures and maintains a paved bike path. Nearby is the much-beloved Nauset Light, the red-and-white-stripe lighthouse saved from imminent destruction when it was moved from its perilous perch atop eroding cliffs. The Fort Hill area is another pretty spot, with lots of walking trails and a stately old mansion called the Penniman House.

It was here in 1620 that an exploring band of *Mayflower* passengers met the Nauset tribe on a bay-side beach, which they then named First Encounter Beach. The meeting was peaceful, but the Pilgrims moved on to Plymouth anyway. Nearly a quarter century later, they returned to settle the area, which they originally called by its Native American name, Nawsett. Eastham was incorporated as a town on June 7, 1651.

Like many other Cape towns, Eastham started as a farming community and later turned to the sea and to salt making for its livelihood; at one time there were more than 50 saltworks in town. A less typical industry that once flourished here was asparagus growing; from the late 1800s through the 1920s, Eastham was known as the asparagus capital of the United States. The runner-up crop, Eastham turnips, are still the pride of many a harvest table.

⑭ The road to the Cape Cod National Seashore's **Fort Hill Area** (✉ Fort Hill Rd., off U.S. 6) winds past the **Captain Edward Penniman House**, ending at a parking area with a lovely view of old farmland traced with stone fences that rolls gently down to **Nauset Marsh** and a red-maple swamp. Appreciated by bird-watchers and nature photographers, the 1-mi **Red Maple Swamp Trail** begins outside the Penniman House and winds through the area, branching into two separate paths, one of which eventually turns into a boardwalk that meanders through wetlands. The other path leads directly to Skiff Hill, an overlook with benches and informative plaques that quote Samuel de Champlain's account of the area from when he moored off Nauset Marsh in 1605. Also on Skiff Hill is Indian Rock, a large boulder moved to the hill from the marsh below. Once used by the local Nauset tribe as a sharpening stone, the rock is cut with deep grooves and smoothed in circles where ax heads were whetted.

The French Second Empire–style **Captain Edward Penniman House** was built in 1868 for a whaling captain. The impressive exterior is notable for its mansard roof; its cupola, which once commanded a dramatic view of bay and sea; and the whale-jawbone entrance gate. Though still in the process of renovation, the interior is open for guided tours or for browsing through changing exhibits. Call ahead to find out when tours are available. ⊠ *Fort Hill Rd., Fort Hill Area* ☎ *508/255–3421* 🏷 *Free* ☉ *Weekdays 1–4.*

The park at Samoset Road has as its centerpiece the **Eastham Windmill,** the oldest windmill on Cape Cod. A smock mill built in Plymouth in the early 1680s, it was moved to this site in 1793 and is the only Cape windmill still on the site where it was used commercially. The mill was restored by local shipwreck historian William Quinn and friends. The park often comes alive with town festivals and concerts, and occasionally demonstrations are given on the inner workings of the mill. Each September, just after Labor Day, Eastham celebrates its history and the change of the season with the annual Windmill Weekend, an event with a full roster of activities for all ages. ⊠ *U.S. 6 at Samoset Rd.* 🏷 *Free* ☉ *Late June–early Sept., Mon.–Sat. 10–5, Sun. 1–5.*

Frozen in time, the 1741 **Swift-Daley House** was once the home of Gustavus Swift, founder of the Swift meatpacking company. Inside the full Cape with bow roof you can find beautiful pumpkin-pine woodwork and wide-board floors, a ship's-cabin staircase that, like the bow roof, was built by ships' carpenters, and fireplaces in every downstairs room. The colonial-era furnishings include an old cannonball rope bed, tools, a melodeon, and a ceremonial quilt decorated with beads and coins. Among the antique clothing is a stunning 1850 wedding dress. Out back is a tool museum. ⊠ *U.S. 6, next to Eastham post office* ☎ *No phone* 🏷 *Free* ☉ *July and Aug., weekdays 1–4; Sept., Sat. 1–4.*

A great spot for watching sunsets over the bay, **First Encounter Beach** (⊠ End of Samoset Rd. off U.S. 6) is rich in history. Near the parking lot, a bronze marker commemorates the first encounter between local Native Americans and passengers from the *Mayflower,* led by Captain Myles Standish, who explored the entire area for five weeks in November and December 1620 before moving on to Plymouth. The remains of a navy target ship retired after 25 years of battering now rest on a sandbar about 1 mi out.

★ ☾ The Cape's most expansive national treasure, the **Cape Cod National Seashore,** was established in 1961 under the administration of President John F. Kennedy, for whom Cape Cod was home and haven. The 27,000-acre seashore, extending from Chatham to Provincetown, encompasses and protects 30 mi of superb ocean beaches; great rolling dunes; swamps, marshes, and wetlands; pitch pine and scrub oak forest; all kinds of wildlife; and a number of historic structures. Self-guided nature trails, as well as biking and horse trails, lace through these landscapes. Hiking trails lead to a red-maple swamp, **Nauset Marsh,** and to **Salt Pond,** in which breeding shellfish are suspended from floating "nurseries"; their offspring will later be used to seed the flats. Also in the seashore is the Buttonbush Trail, a nature path for people with vision impairments. A hike or bike ride to Coast Guard Beach leads to a turnout looking out over marsh and sea. A section of the cliff here was washed away in 1990, revealing remains of a prehistoric dwelling.

⑮ Salt Pond Visitor Center is the first visitor center of the Cape Cod National Seashore that you encounter as you travel down-Cape toward the tip (the other, the **Province Lands Visitor Center,** is in Provincetown). The Salt Pond Visitor Center is undergoing renovations; while it's closed, there will be a staffed temporary visitor station, but services will be limited. When it's fully operational, the Salt Pond center offers guided walks, tours, boat trips, demonstrations, and lectures from mid-April through Thanksgiving, as well as evening beach walks, campfire talks, and other programs in summer. The center includes a museum with displays on whaling and the old saltworks, as well as early Cape Cod artifacts including scrimshaw, the journal that Mrs. Penniman kept while on a whaling voyage with her husband, and some of the Pennimans' possessions, such as their tea service and the captain's top hat. A good bookstore and an air-conditioned auditorium showing films on geology, sea rescues, whaling, Henry David Thoreau, and Marconi are also here. Something's going on most summer evenings at the outdoor amphitheater, from slide-show talks to military-band concerts. ⊠ *Doane Rd. off U.S. 6* ☎ *508/255–3421* ⊕ *www.nps.gov/caco/places/saltpondvc.html* ⊠ *Free* ☉ *Mar.–June and Sept.–Dec., daily 9–4:30; July and Aug., daily 9–5; Jan. and Feb., weekends 9–4:30.*

Roads and bicycle trails lead to **Coast Guard and Nauset Light beaches** (⊠ Off Ocean View Dr.), which begin an unbroken 30-mi stretch of barrier beach extending to Provincetown—the "Cape Cod Beach" of Thoreau's 1865 classic, *Cape Cod.* You can still walk its length, as Thoreau did, though the Atlantic continues to claim more of the Cape's eastern shore every year. The site of the famous beach cottage of Henry Beston's 1928 book, *The Outermost House,* is to the south, near the end of Nauset spit. Designated as a literary landmark in 1964, the cottage was, alas, destroyed in the Great Blizzard of February 1978.

Moved 350 feet back from its perch at cliff's edge in 1996, the much-photographed red-and-white **Nauset Light** (⊠ Ocean View Dr. and Cable Rd. ⊕ www.nausetlight.org) still tops the bluff where the Three Sisters Lighthouses once stood; the Sisters themselves can be seen in a little land-locked park surrounded by trees, reached by paved walkways off Nauset Light Beach's parking lot. How the lighthouses got there is a long story. In 1838 three brick lighthouses were built 150 feet apart on the bluffs in Eastham overlooking a particularly dangerous area of shoals (shifting underwater sandbars). In 1892, after the eroding cliff dropped the towers into the ocean, they were replaced with three wooden towers. In 1918 two were moved away, as was the third in 1923. Eventually the National Park Service acquired the Three Sisters and brought them together here, where they would be safe, rather than returning them to the eroding coast. The Fresnel lens from the last working lighthouse is on display at the **Salt Pond Visitor Center.** Lectures on and guided walks to the lighthouses are conducted throughout the season. Call ☎ 508/240–2612 for schedules.

Where to Stay & Eat

¢–$$ ✕ **Fairway Restaurant and Pizzeria.** The friendly family-run Fairway specializes in Italian comfort food. Attached to the Hole in One Donut Shop (very popular among locals), the Fairway puts a jar of crayons on every paper-covered table and sells its own brand of root beer. Entrées come with salad and homemade rolls. Try the eggplant Parmesan or a well-stuffed calzone. You can order from the extensive breakfast menu from 6:30 to 11:30. ✉ *4295 U.S. 6* ☎ *508/255–3893* ♺ *Reservations not accepted* ▤ *AE, D, DC, MC, V.*

¢–$$ ✕ **The Friendly Fisherman.** Not just another roadside lobster shack with buoys and nets for decoration, this place is serious about its fresh seafood. It's both a great place to pick up ingredients to cook at home—there's a fish and produce market on-site—and a good bet for dining out on such favorites as fish-and-chips, fried scallops, and lobster. The market also sells homemade pies, breads, soups, stews, and pasta. ✉ *Rte. 6, North Eastham* ☎ *508/255–6770 or 508/255–3009* ▤ *AE, MC, V.*

$ ✕ **Beach Break Grill and Lounge.** All in all, this is an affordable and fun place to eat. It's a kitschy Hawaiian surfer-theme place, complete with old photos, long boards on the ceiling, and grassy adornments on the bar. The menu is basic and varied, with seafood, lots of burgers, fajitas, pasta, and steak. Pub food and late-night bites can be had in the lively bar, which also has a pool table. You might even find live entertainment rocking the joint on summer evenings. In fair weather, the outdoor deck is open for dining. ✉ *Main St. Mercantile off Rte. 6* ☎ *508/240–3100* ▤ *DC, MC, V.*

$$$–$$$$ 🏨 **Four Points Sheraton.** This hotel is at the entrance to the National Seashore. Rooms have views of the tropical indoor pool (with lush plants, pirate-theme bar, and resident live parrot), the parking lot, or the woods. Outside rooms are a little bigger and brighter and have mini-refrigerators. ✉ *3800 U.S. 6, 02642* ☎ *508/255–5000 or 800/533–3986* 🖷 *508/240–1870* ⊕ *www.fourpoints.com/eastham* ➴ *107 rooms, 2 suites* ♨ *Restaurant, room service, 2 tennis courts, 2 pools, gym, saunas, lobby lounge, no-smoking rooms* ▤ *AE, D, DC, MC, V* ⦿ *BP.*

$$$–$$$$ 🏨 **Penny House Inn.** Tucked behind a wave of privet hedge, this rambling gray-shingle inn's spacious rooms are furnished with antiques, collectibles, and wicker. The luxurious accomodations are cozy rather than stuffy; many are romantic, with whirlpool tubs, fireplaces, or both. Some rooms are larger, with sitting areas; suites have separate bedrooms and sitting rooms and can sleep up to 5. Take a dip in the saltwater pool, or indulge in a massage, facial, or mud wrap in the on-site spa room. Common areas include a Great Room with lots of windows and a selection of videos, a combination sunroom-library, and a garden patio with umbrella tables. A full homemade breakfast starts the day, and af-

ternoon tea is available. For a fee, you can arrange for a pass to use the facilities at Willy's Gym, just down the road. ⊠ *4885 County Rd. (U.S. 6), 02642* ☎ *508/255–6632 or 800/554–1751* 🖷 *508/255–4893* ⊕ *www. pennyhouseinn.com* ⇨ *9 rooms, 4 suites* ♢ *In-room data ports, some in-room hot tubs, some refrigerators, cable TV, in-room VCRs, saltwater pool, spa, library; no smoking* ⊟ *AE, D, MC, V* �"○" *BP.*

★ **$$$-$$$$** ⊞ **Whalewalk Inn.** This 1830 whaling master's home is on 3 landscaped acres. Wide-board pine floors, fireplaces, and 19th-century country antiques provide historical appeal. Rooms in the main inn have four-poster twin, double, or queen-size beds; floral fabrics; and antique or reproduction furniture. Suites with fully equipped kitchens are in the converted barn and guest house. A secluded saltbox cottage has a fireplace, kitchen, and private patio. Deluxe rooms in the carriage house have fireplaces, hot tubs, and air-conditioning. Breakfast is served in the cheerful sunroom or on the garden patio. ⊠ *220 Bridge Rd., 02642* ☎ *508/255–0617 or 800/440–1281* ⊕ *www.whalewalkinn.com* ⇨ *11 rooms, 5 suites* ♢ *Kitchens, some in-room hot tubs, bicycles; no smoking* ⊟ *MC, V* �"○" *BP.*

$$-$$$$ ⊞ **Over Look Inn.** If it weren't for the vivid-yellow paint job on this three-story inn, it would be lost among the trees, even though it's right along U.S. 6. Both the Cape Cod Rail Trail and the Salt Pond Visitor Center are just across the road from this 19th-century refuge. Victorian touches include graceful high ceilings and intricate interior wood molding. Each room has antiques, brass beds, and soft down comforters, plus a few modern amenities such as DVD players; some have genuine claw-foot tubs, which are great to slide into after a day at the beach. ⊠ *3085 U.S. 6, 02642* ☎ *508/255–1886* 🖷 *508/240–0345* ⊕ *www.overlookinn. com* ⇨ *14 rooms* ♢ *Cable TV, hot tub, massage, spa, recreation room* ⊟ *AE, D, MC, V* �"○" *BP.*

$$ ⊞ **Ocean Park Inn.** Rooms here are clean, simple, and straightforward. There are larger family units available—one with a fireplace—but most rooms are for double occupancy, with full- or queen-size beds. Take advantage of the adjacent Sheraton's indoor pool and tennis courts. ⊠ *Next to Four Points Sheraton, U.S. 6, 02642* ☎ *508/255–1132 or 800/862–5550* 🖷 *508/255–5250* ⇨ *55 rooms* ♢ *Picnic area, 2 tennis courts, 2 pools, gym, sauna, laundry facilities, no-smoking rooms* ⊟ *AE, D, DC, MC, V* ⊙ *Closed Nov.–Mar.*

¢-$$ ⊞ **Cove Bluffs Motel.** Nestled among the trees and within walking distance of Town Cove and several nature trails is this old-fashioned haven for nature-lovers and families. Settle into a standard motel room or choose a more self-sufficient getaway in studio or two-bedroom housekeeping units with stoves, refrigerators, and microwaves. Grounds include basketball courts, shuffleboard, swing sets, a playhouse, a sandbox, grills, and swinging hammocks in the shade. ⊠ *U.S. 6 and Shore Rd., 02642* ☎ *508/240–1616* ⊕ *www.capecod-orleans.com/covebluffs* ⇨ *5 rooms, 8 housekeeping units* ♢ *Pool, basketball, shuffleboard, laundry facilities, no-smoking rooms; no a/c* ⊟ *MC, V* ⊙ *Closed Nov.–Mar.*

¢ ⊞ **Hostelling International–Mid Cape.** On 3 wooded acres near the Cape Cod Rail Trail and a 15-minute walk from the bay, this hostel has cabins that sleep six to eight each; two can be used as family cabins. It has a common area and a kitchen, and there are a number of guest programs. ✉ *75 Goody Hallet Dr., 02642* ☎ *508/255–2785* ⊕ *www.usahostels. org* ⇆ *8 cabins* ♦ *Kitchen, Ping-Pong, volleyball; no a/c, no in-room TVs* ⊟ *MC, V* ⊙ *Closed mid-Sept.–mid-May.*

$ ◭ **Atlantic Oaks Campground.** This campground in a pine and oak forest is less than a mile north of the Salt Pond Visitor Center and minutes from Cape Cod National Seashore. Primarily an RV camp, it offers limited tenting as well. There are bikes for rent and direct access to the Cape Cod Rail Trail. Reservations are essential during the peak season. ♦ *Grills, playground, laundry facilities, flush toilets, full hookups, drinking water, showers, fire grates, picnic tables, electricity, public telephone, general store, swimming (pond and ocean)* ⇆ *99 RV sites, 30 tent sites* ✉ *3700 U.S. 6, 02642* ☎ *508/255–1437 or 800/332–2267* 🖶 *508/247–8216* ⊕ *www.atlanticoaks.com* 🏷 *Full hook-ups $49, partial hookups $35* ⊟ *D, MC, V* ⊙ *Open by prior appointment only Nov.–Apr.*

Nightlife & the Arts

The **Cape Cod National Seashore** (☎ 508/255–3421 information) sponsors summer-evening programs, such as slide shows, sunset beach walks, concerts by local groups or military bands, and campfire sing-alongs.

The **Eastham Painters Guild** holds outdoor art shows every Thursday, Friday, and holiday weekend from 9 to 5, July through October, at the Schoolhouse Museum (✉ Next to Salt Pond Visitor Center, off U.S. 6).

First Encounter Coffee House (✉ Chapel in the Pines, Samoset Rd. ☎ 508/255–5438) presents a mixture of professional and local folk and blues in a smoke-and-alcohol-free environment, with refreshments available during intermission. National acts are booked for the second and fourth Saturday. It's closed May and December.

Sea Dog Restaurant & Saloon (✉ 4100 Rte. 6 ☎ 508/255–2650 ⊕ www. seadogsaloon.com) serves pub food and drinks in a lively atmosphere. Live acoustic music is played year-round on varying nights; call for a schedule. Closed Tuesday.

Sports & the Outdoors

BEACHES On the bay side of the Outer Cape, **First Encounter Beach** (✉End of Samoset Rd. off U.S. 6) is open to the public and charges daily parking fees of $5 (Weekly and season passes are also available; call the town hall at ☎ 508/240–5972) to nonresidents in season. Parking fees or passes also apply to several other bay beaches and ponds, both saltwater and freshwater.

★ **Coast Guard Beach** (✉ Off Ocean View Dr.), part of the National Seashore, is a long beach backed by low grass and heathland. A handsome former Coast Guard station is also here, though it's not open to the public. The beach has no parking lot of its own, so park at the Salt Pond Visitor Center or at the lot up Doane Road from the center and take the free shuttle to the beach. At high tide the size of the beach shrinks considerably, so watch your blanket. There are showers, and lifeguards are posted between June and August. A daily charge of $10 for cars or

YEAR-ROUND ON THE CAPE

THE BEAUTY AND ABUNDANCE of our beaches, striking sunsets and blooming flora, ice cream and lobster shacks, the lush landscapes and temperate climate perfectly suited for countless outdoor activities, from biking to sailing to golf to slow strolls through town or along the harbor—the appeal of summers on Cape Cod is obvious. More than 4 million visitors flock to the Cape during the high season, from day trippers to temporary residents, and many have made a Cape trip a summer tradition, returning year after year. What might seem less obvious—at least, to those who don't live here—is what the Cape has to offer during the rest of the year.

Cape Codders and visitors alike agree that it takes a special kind of person to live on the Cape year-round: one who can endure the brutal weather and stark isolation of the winter months. In fact, among locals, there is a pecking order for those who call Cape Cod home. Those who live here full time are called residents or year-rounders; this is not to be confused with being a native Cape Codder. Having been born on the Cape holds a special distinction; if you were not, you are a "washashore," and there is no exception to this rule. The truest salt-of-the-earth natives boast generations of family born on the peninsula, and being a native who has chosen to stay and raise a family here is a point of pride; it takes a hardy person with a true love for all that nature cooks up to ride out a lifetime on these windswept shores.

It isn't always easy to live here. In addition to the rough winters, being here year-round is a financial challenge for a large portion of the Cape's 220,000 permanent residents. Many take on several jobs or work off-Cape and commute home each night to make ends meet. But to a Cape resident, life here is more than worth these difficulties. All of us, native and washashore alike, are bound by our common affection and respect for the ocean and the Cape's environment, and this sentiment runs deep, even on the darkest days of winter. Full-year residents see the beauty in every season on the Cape. Although we love summers here—for many of the same reasons that draw the tourists—we live for the off-season. Come Labor Day, the crowds disappear and traffic congestion subsides, and Cape residents eagerly reclaim our beaches and resume our quiet everyday lives. For the next nine months, until Memorial Day comes around again, we return to our seaside walks on crisp mornings, the familiar smell of low tide and the marshes on the way to work and kayaking, fishing, and sunset strolls to end the day. To us, this is the Cape's true personality—one most visitors don't see.

Tourism in the shoulder season has increased in recent years, as more people discover that the simple beauty of the Cape's natural surroundings is more serene and easily appreciated without the summer crowds; the Cape no longer rolls up its sidewalks and packs away the fun after Labor Day, and many businesses now open for the season as early as March or April. Those who come here in the few weeks before or after the high season are treated with a taste of what Cape residents love so much about their home. Before the summer crush hits, Cape Cod awakens with beauty in spring. Cheery daffodils line the streets, birds dart through the air in hypnotizing formations, bunnies hop through yards, and fishing for schoolie (baby striped bass) begins. And after Labor Day, temperatures stay mild enough to enjoy the beaches through early to mid-October. This is, for many, the ideal time to enjoy the shores—the waters have had time to warm from months of summer sun, parking restrictions are lifted, and beachgoers have all the space they need to spread out. Autumn leaves and cranberry harvests paint the area with brilliant swaths of color, creating stunning views.

But visitors still tend to shy away from the peninsula once the first hints of cold air blow in. Some are surprised to learn that average winter temperatures on the Cape are actually milder than on the mainland. Despite this, the colder months are known to bring some difficult weather conditions, but Cape locals know how to make the best of it. Fall and winter Nor'easters—powerful storms that carry in cold air from Canada—leave us in awe of the ocean's power. Most of us are content to observe these captivating scenes from indoors, but some local surfers will brave the action off the Lower Cape. These infamous storms also strengthen the sense of community here, as we check on our neighbors and help each other board up buildings and tie down our belongings. Some residents view the harsh weather as character-building, a challenge to overcome. I share my life with a Cape native who says, "I have a certain sense of satisfaction knowing that I beat the weather. When I come home from work on those days when it is 10 degrees out with 40 mph winds and I just put a cap on a roof, I feel a real sense of accomplishment."

The Atlantic surrounds us and we are at the whim of Mother Nature's brew. Yet, even living just steps from the shore, we are always trying to get closer to nature. Peek into the home of a Cape resident and you're likely to see windowsills lined with seashells, sea glass, driftwood, fish bones and pieces of mystery items that landed on our shores. You might see

mantels made of driftwood or driveways of crushed shell. We use clamshells as ashtrays, soap dishes, and coin holders. The longer you live here, the more you bring the outdoors in as close as possible. The connection to the ocean grows stronger and freeing as material needs lessen. Life simplifies, and crossing the bridge to leave for good becomes inconceivable.

— Lori A. Nolin

a season pass (by far the best bargain) for $30 grants admission to all six National Seashore swimming beaches.

Fodor'sChoice ★ **Nauset Light Beach** (✉ Off Ocean View Dr.), adjacent to Coast Guard Beach, continues the National Seashore landscape of long, sandy beach backed by tall dunes, grass, and heathland. It has showers and lifeguards in summer, but as with other National Seashore beaches, there's no food concession. Nauset charges $10 daily per car; a $30 season pass admits you here and to the other five National Seashore swimming beaches.

BIKING The **Idle Times Bike Shop** (✉ 4550 U.S. 6 and Brackett Rd. ☎ 508/255–8281) provides bikes of all sizes and types and is right near the Cape Cod Rail Trail.

The **Little Capistrano Bike Shop** (✉ Salt Pond Rd. across from Salt Pond Visitor Center ☎ 508/255–6515) has plenty of bikes and trailers available for rent and is between the Cape Cod Rail Trail and the National Seashore Bike Trail.

Nauset Trail, maintained by the Cape Cod National Seashore, stretches 1½ mi from Salt Pond Visitor Center through groves of apple and locust trees to Coast Guard Beach.

HEALTH & FITNESS CLUBS **Willy's Gym** (✉ 4730 U.S. 6, North Eastham ☎ 508/255–6370 or 508/255–6826) has four racquetball courts, two squash courts, and six indoor tennis courts; one NBA indoor basketball court; an Olympic-size, heated indoor pool; swimming lessons; aerobics and children's self-defense classes; plus Nautilus, free weights, and cardiovascular machines. You can relax in the hot tub, steam room, or sauna; you'll also find a pro shop and a restaurant. There are daily and weekly guest membership passes.

THE LOWER CAPE A TO Z

To research prices, get advice from other travelers, and book travel arrangements, visit www.fodors.com.

AIRPORTS

The town-owned **Chatham Municipal Airport** (CQX) is a public facility accessed primarily by small, private planes. Two miles northwest of Chatham, the airport has two asphalt runways with a weight limit of 30,000 pounds. Facilities and services include fuel, flight school/training, aircraft rentals, sightseeing tours, maintenance, and supplies. The CQX Café/Breakaway Café is also at the airport.

🔲 Airport **Chatham Municipal Airport** ✉ 240 George Ryder Rd., 02633 ☎ 508/945–9000.

BIKE TRAVEL

The few parking lots along the Cape Cod Rail Trail are useful for those who'd rather ride a segment of the trail than tackle all 25 mi. In Harwich there's a lot on Route 124, just off Exit 10 from U.S. 6 and directly across from the Pleasant Lake Store. In Orleans, park on West Road across from Old Colony Way. Another small parking area is on Rock Harbor Road, between Bridge Road and the U.S. 6 traffic rotary.

BOAT & FERRY TRAVEL

The Freedom Cruise Line runs express 90-minute ferries from Harwich Port to Nantucket between May 15 and October 15, allowing you to explore the rose-covered isle without having to brave the crowds of Hyannis. Parking is free for the first 24 hours; then it's $10 per day. Sightseeing and seal cruises are also offered daily. Admission is $39 round-trip, $10 extra with bicycle; $25 one-way, $5 extra with bicycle.

🚢 Boat & Ferry Line **Freedom Cruise Line** ⊠ Saquatucket Harbor, Harwich Port ☎ 508/432-8999 ⊕ www.nantucketislandferry.com.

BUS TRAVEL

The Cape Cod Regional Transit Authority operates several buses between Cape towns. The Lower Cape route, which operates year-round, begins in Hyannis and follows Route 28 all the way to Orleans, stopping in Harwich Port and Chatham; buses will stop according to passenger discretion. Rates vary.

🚌 Bus Information **Cape Cod Regional Transit Authority** ☎ 508/385-8326, 800/352-7155 in Massachusetts ⊕ www.capecodtransit.org.

CAR TRAVEL

On the north shore, the Old King's Highway, Route 6A, parallels U.S. 6 but is a scenic country road passing through equally eye-pleasing towns. When you're in no hurry, use back roads—they're less frustrating and much more rewarding. Route 28, which begins at the upper Cape in Woods Hole and continues all the way to Orleans on the south side of the Cape, is notorious for its heavy traffic and slow going. Once past Harwich Port, the route is not as frustrating, and it even becomes scenic from Chatham to Orleans, winding past the shores of Pleasant Bay. In Orleans, when you're heading east, the large rotary can create problems. Remember, when approaching a rotary, you must yield to drivers already in the circle, and once within the rotary, you should not stop your vehicle.

EMERGENCIES

For rescues at sea, call the United States Coast Guard in Chatham. The closest hospital is in Hyannis (⇨ The Mid Cape A to Z *in* Chapter 4).

🏥 Doctors & Dentists **Long Pond Medical Center** ⊠ 525 Main Long Pond Dr., Harwich ☎ 508/432-4100. **Outer Cape Health Services** ⊠ 81 Old Colony Way, Orleans ☎ 508/255-9700.

🚑 Emergency Services **Ambulance, fire, police** ☎ 911 or dial township station. **United States Coast Guard** ☎ 508/945-0164.

WHERE TO STAY

APARTMENT & HOUSE RENTALS Commonwealth Associates can assist in finding vacation rentals in the Harwiches, including waterfront properties. Great Locations Inc. specializes in vacation rentals in Brewster, Dennis, and Orleans. Vacation Cape Cod is one of many realtors with a listing of available apartments and houses on the Lower Cape.

🏠 Local Agents **Commonwealth Associates** ⊠ 551 Main St., Harwich Port 02646 ☎ 508/432-2618 🖷 508/432-1771 ⊕ www.commonwealthrealestate.com. **Great Locations Inc.** ⊠ 2660 Rte. 6A, Brewster 02631 ☎ 508/896-2090 ⊕ www.greatlocationsre.com. **Vacation Cape Cod** ⊠ Main St. Mercantile Unit 19, U.S. 6, Eastham 02642 ☎ 508/240-7600 or 800/724-1307 🖷 508/240-6943 ⊕ www.vacationcapecod.com.

BED-AND-
BREAKFASTS

B&Bs are the preferred style of accommodations for people seeking a more intimate Cape Cod experience, but the variations in size, style, and location can be mind-boggling. Bed & Breakfast Cape Cod, Inc., represents dozens of B&Bs throughout the Lower Cape and beyond.

� Reservations Services **Bed & Breakfast Cape Cod, Inc.** ◯ Box 1312, Orleans 02653 ☎ 508/255-3824 or 800/541-6226 🖷 508/245-0599 ⊕ www.bedandbreakfastcapecod. com.

CAMPING

Nickerson State Park (⇨ Brewster) is huge—almost 2,000 acres—and hugely popular. It has plenty of facilities and guest programs. Because of its immense popularity, significant advance registration is necessary if you want a site.

🔲 **Nickerson State Park** ⊠ 3488 Rte. 6A, Brewster ☎ 508/896-3491, 877/422-6762 reservations ⊕ www.state.ma.us/dem/parks/nick.htm.

TAXIS
John's Taxi & Limousine picks up only in Dennis and Harwich but will take you anywhere on the Cape.

🔲 Taxi Companies **Eldredge Taxi** ⊠ Chatham ☎ 508/945-0068. **John's Taxi & Limousine** ☎ 508/394-3209.

TOURS
The Cape Cod Museum of Natural History offers a two-hour cruise from Orleans through Nauset Marsh. Early morning cruises include breakfast in a nearby restaurant. During evening tours enjoy cocktails and appetizers on board. Tours run daily, Tuesday through Friday until Labor Day, and then weekends until Columbus Day. Guided natural history tours of Chatham's Monomoy Islands are also available through the museum.

To sightsee from the air, contact Chatham Municipal Airport.

🔲 Fees & Schedules **Cape Cod Museum of Natural History** ☎ 508/896-3867 ⊕ www. ccmnh.org. **Chatham Municipal Airport** ⊠ George Ryder Rd., West Chatham ☎ 508/ 945-9000.

VISITOR INFORMATION
Some local chambers of commerce are open only in season. The Brewster Chamber of Commerce is in the Brewster town offices building. The office includes a visitor center and the offices of the Brewster Chamber of Commerce and Board of Trade United.

🔲 Tourist Information **Brewster** ⊠ 2198 Main St. [Rte. 6A] ◯ Box 1241, 02631 ☎ 508/ 896-3500 ⊕ www.brewstercapecod.org. **Chatham** ◯ Box 793, 02633 ☎ 508/945-5199 or 800/715-5567 ⊕ www.chathamcapecod.org ⊠ visitor center ⊠ 2377 Main St., South Chatham ⊠ Information booth ⊠ 533 Main St., Chatham. **Eastham** ⊠ U.S. 6 at Fort Hill Rd. ◯ Box 1329, 02642 ☎ 508/240-7211 ⊕ www.easthamchamber.com. **Harwich** ◯ Box 34, Harwich Port 02646 ☎ 508/432-1600 or 800/441-3199 ⊕ www. harwichcc.com. **Orleans** ◯ Box 153, 02653 ☎ 508/255-1386 ⊠ Information booth ⊠ Eldredge Pkwy. off Rte. 6A ☎ 508/240-2484 ⊕ www.capecod-orleans.com.

THE OUTER CAPE

5

RIDE THROUGH THE SAND DUNES
with Art's Dune Tours ⇨*p.226*

HUNT FOR BARGAINS
at the Wellfleet Flea Market ⇨*p.199*

STEP INTO A SCENE
from an Edward Hopper painting
at Ballston Beach in Truro ⇨*p.204*

JOIN THE FESTIVE CROWD
for a late-night slice at Spiritus ⇨*p.217*

SEE ANIMALS OF AIR, WATER, AND LAND
at the Massachusetts Audubon
Wellfleet Bay Wildlife Sanctuary ⇨*p.188*

Revised by
Andrew Collins

TECHNICALLY PART OF THE LOWER CAPE, the Outer Cape is nonetheless its own entity, forming the wrist and fist of Cape Cod. There's a sense of abandon here, in the hedonistic summertime frenzy of Provincetown and out on the windswept landscape of dunes and marshes. As you drive down here, the land flattens out, vegetation gets sparser and more coniferous, and the sea feels closer as the land narrows. Much of the region is undeveloped, protected by the Cape Cod National Seashore. Long, straight, dune-backed beaches appear to go on forever; inland, trails wind through wind-stunted forests of scrub pine, beech, and oak. Wellfleet is a quiet town, with art galleries, upscale shops, and a calmly active harbor. With an expanse of high dunes, estuaries, salt marshes, pine forests, rivers, and winding back roads, Truro is the least-populated, least-developed town on the entire Cape.

The promise of solitude has long drawn artists and writers out here. Provincetown has two faces—a quiet little fishing village in winter and a magnet for throngs of pleasure seekers (including a substantial gay and lesbian community) in summer, who come for the rugged beaches, photogenic streets lined with historic homes, zany nightlife, shops selling everything from antiques to zoot suits, and the galleries, readings, and art classes that carry on Provincetown's rich history as an art colony.

Exploring the Outer Cape

Making your way around narrow Outer Cape, you really have one key option for getting around: driving along U.S. 6. There are some less congested but slower and indirect roads between the area's two least-developed communities, Wellfleet and Truro. In Wellfleet, many businesses and attractions are strung along U.S. 6, but there's also a compact downtown with art galleries, cafés, and boutiques that's ideal for strolling. Truro has just the tiniest commercial district and its few formal attractions are best reached by car, as they're somewhat far apart. In Provincetown, on the other hand, a car—especially in summer—can actually become a hinderance. This is a walkable town with two main thoroughfares, Commercial and Bradford streets. You could easily spend a full day or two just walking around downtown and checking out the dozens and dozens of shops and restaurants. Provincetown also has some excellent beaches, which are a short drive or bike ride from downtown.

Numbers in the text correspond to numbers in the margin and on the Lower and Outer Cape, Wellfleet, and Provincetown maps.

About the Restaurants

Dining on the Outer Cape means everything from humble fried-clam shacks to candlelit elegance. Most restaurants have withstood the tests of time and fashion and have developed loyal followings that keep their doors open year after year. Menus frequently highlight local seafood as a staple. In Wellfleet restaurants are known more for their creative cuisine than reasonable prices—going out with the whole family won't come cheap. Truro lacks a concentration of restaurants

Numbers in the text correspond to numbers in the margin and on the Approaching the Cape map.

Although it takes some effort to reach it, Provincetown ranks among the most visited vacation communities on the state, and with the majority of the region's restaurants and hotels, it's an excellent base for exploring the Outer Cape. That being said, many visitors to Provincetown simply pass through quieter Wellfleet and Truro on their way out here, and this is a shame, as both towns have much to offer. As you first enter **Wellfleet** ❶, make a point of stopping at historic **Marconi Station** ❷, which was the landing point for the transatlantic telegraph early in the 20th century. It's also worth walking the short but stunning White Cedar Swamp Trail. In Wellfleet, you can lose yourself among the many art galleries and distinctive shops, or plan a more outdoorsy adventure. Stroll along the sand or go for a swim in the water—Wellfleet has several beaches on both the bay and the ocean. You might also rent a canoe or kayak and tour the marshes. Bird-watchers should make a point of visiting the **Massachusetts Audubon Wellfleet Bay Wildlife Sanctuary** ❸.

Truro ❹ solidly represents the quietude of this end of the Cape, at least until you reach the seasonally bustling ▦ **Provincetown** ❼–❿, out at the tip. Catch a whale-watch boat from P-town (as Provincetown is almost universally known)— the Cape ranks fourth in the world for sighting whales. Take a trolley tour in town or bike through the National Seashore on its miles of trails. Climb the Pilgrim Monument for a spectacular view of the area—on an exceptionally clear day you can see the Boston skyline. Visit the museums and shops and art galleries, or spend the afternoon swimming and sunning on one of the beaches. To escape the crowds, walk across the breakwater to Long Point. Rent a sailboat or relax in the sand, taking in the splendid views of the bay. Then choose from an abundance of restaurants and the Cape's wildest nightlife.

(the town itself has no real center); its offerings are spread out along the byways. Provincetown opens a world of great variation to the eager diner. There are a number of elegant restaurants in town, all aglow with candles, crystal, and fine linens, but you'll find an equal number of lively and boisterous café spots. Many have outdoor seating, providing for a good view of the town's constant action. Note that a recent ruling by the Provincetown board of health bans smoking in any of the town's bars or restaurants.

In the height of the summer season, expect a long wait for a table, sometimes despite a reservation—the sheer volume of diners is to blame. To make matters worse, in the last few years Cape Cod has been experiencing a labor shortage, so good help is at a premium, leading more than a few restaurants to close their doors. Others have been forced to shorten their season.

About the Hotels

Lodging options on the Outer Cape are diverse. Wellfleet has several cozy inns and bed-and-breakfasts in the center of town, with a few larger motels on busy U.S. 6. Despite the strict building codes, there are a surprising number of large (though not so imposing) hotel complexes and cottage colonies spread out along Cape Cod Bay in North Truro. It's crowded, but it's also right on the sand, with commanding views of sunsets and the Provincetown skyline.

Provincetown lodging varies from bare-bones lodging in a tiny room in an old house to the utmost luxury in one of the many meticulously restored and grand homes. Although it seems that every other building is an inn or guest house, a place to spend the night is not so easy to come by. Provincetown fills up fast and has a longer season than its neighbors. Minimum stays of at least three nights are often the norm during the peak season and holiday times.

WHAT IT COSTS				
$$$$	$$$	$$	$	¢
RESTAURANTS over $30	$20–$30	$15–$20	$10–$15	under $10
HOTELS over $220	$140–$220	$100–$140	$80–$100	under $80

Restaurant prices are per person for a main course at dinner. Hotel prices are for a standard double room, excluding 6% sales tax (more in some counties) and 1%–4% tourist tax.

Timing

Prime time on the Outer Cape—when everything is open—is from Memorial Day to around Columbus Day. July and August are by far the most crowded times. The shoulder seasons of late May and June, and after Labor Day, have become more and more popular with childless travelers who aren't locked into a school schedule. Rates are lower during these times, and restaurants and shops are open. If the weather has been generous, swimming is still a pleasant possibility.

Wellfleet pretty much seals itself up after Columbus Day; most galleries and restaurants close, leaving just a handful of year-round businesses. But there's the entire outside world to explore, now free of thousands of others trying to do the same thing. Ocean climates keep winters milder than on the mainland. It's quiet—beautifully so—and distractions and pleasures take on a more basic flavor.

Provincetown clears out as well, but not as fully as Wellfleet. Various theme weekends throughout the year have boosted tourism in the off-season, and there are always readings, films, and places to eat. The off-season is truly a time to discover the essence of the place, see its changing natural beauty, and experience a more restful and relaxed pace.

5

Beaches

Ocean beaches on the Cape Cod National Seashore have cold water and serious surf and are backed by dunes. They're also contiguous: you can walk from Eastham to Provincetown if you've got the stamina. On the Cape Cod Bay side, you'll find warmer and more gentle waters. The tides are pivotal here: at low tide the flats expose vast, sandy expanses, and to get thoroughly wet, you'll have to trek out a ways. Bay-side beachgoers also get more time in the sun—the majestic dunes on the ocean side block the descending late-afternoon sun—and sunsets on the bay are spectacular.

Biking

The Cape Cod National Seashore maintains three bicycle trails. Head of the Meadow Trail is 2 mi of easy cycling between dunes and salt marshes from High Head Road, off Route 6A in North Truro, to the Head of the Meadow Beach parking lot. Province Lands Trail is a 5¼-mi loop off the Beech Forest parking lot on Race Point Road in Provincetown, with spurs to Herring Cove and Race Point beaches and to Bennett Pond. The paths wind up and down hills amid dunes, marshes, woods, and ponds and offer spectacular views—on an exceptionally clear day, you can see the Boston skyline. There's a picnic grove at Pilgrim Spring. South Wellfleet is the beginning (or the end, depending on how you look at it) of the Cape Cod Rail Trail, a 25-mi flat, paved route to Dennis that winds past cranberry bogs and ponds and through wooded areas. A good-size parking lot is open to cyclists just behind the South Wellfleet General Store, off LeCount Hollow Road.

Nightlife & the Arts

Many credit the unusual light and extraordinary beauty of the Outer Cape with creating its strong and vibrant artistic tradition. In Wellfleet's town center are nearly two dozen art galleries, all representing local and national artists. The works aren't limited to sea and landscapes either—you can also find abstract works and fine crafts.

Truro has fewer art galleries, but its history is rich. Painter Edward Hopper spent many years here in his modest home overlooking Cape Cod Bay; numerous recognizable scenes of Truro exist among his work. The Center for the Arts at Castle Hill has for more than 30 years held summer classes in art, writing, and crafts.

Today Provincetown remains a center for the arts. Its history is great; many world-famous artists made their homes here—some started art schools still in operation. Provincetown may have more galleries per block than any other New England town. Friday night is gallery night; stroll the streets and pop in on one of the many champagne artist receptions.

Provincetown also has an active, gay-popular nightlife, from pulsating dance clubs to pool halls, with lots of live entertainment. Drag shows, theater, comedy routines, and music concerts are held regularly throughout the summer. Wellfleet has a few more peaceful options, such as restaurant taverns that occasionally stay open late with live music performances. Truro prefers the silence, leaving the revelry to its bordering towns.

Sports & the Outdoors The waters off Provincetown are among the finest for whale-watching anywhere in the world. The Cape Cod National Seashore has nine walking trails through varied terrain. In winter, ponds and shallow flooded cranberry bogs sometimes freeze hard enough for skating—but you should check conditions with the local fire department before venturing into unfamiliar territory.

Shopping Shoppers on the Outer Cape never have to worry about the unique-ness of their purchases—all stores are individually owned and are one of a kind. Wellfleet shoppers will find a wealth of fine art and crafts to choose from as well as a couple of small, chic designer-clothing stores. On one street, you could walk away with a funky Indonesian sarong for the beach and a hand-crafted, multi-thousand-dollar gold and gem-studded ring. Out on U.S. 6, far from the sophistication of town, are a few shops specializing in $2 T-shirts, plastic lawn ornaments, and saltwater taffy. The Wellfleet Flea Market—great for bargain hunting—is held four days a week in summer.

From the most civilized and expensive art gallery to the sunglasses hut, there's a little bit of everything in Provincetown. Commercial Street, aptly named, is a tightly packed thoroughfare dominated by pedestrians ambling in and out of the shops and galleries—in recent years, steadily rising rents have pushed out some of the businesses specializing in cheap souvenirs, and higher-end art galleries and design stores have opened in their place. During fall months you can benefit from some fine sales, when shops are eager to clean out their in-ventories before winter sets in.

Wellfleet & South Wellfleet

❶ *6 mi north of Eastham, 13 mi southeast of Provincetown.*

Still famous for its world-renowned and succulent namesake oysters and, with Truro, for having been a colonial whaling and cod-fishing port, Wellfleet is today a tranquil center for artists and writers. Less than 2 mi wide, it's one of the most attractively developed Cape resort towns, with a number of fine restaurants, historic houses, art galleries, and a good old Main Street in the village proper. South Wellfleet borders North Eastham and has a wonderful Audubon sanctuary and a drive-in theater that doubles on weekends as a flea market. It has no down-town area; most businesses are set along U.S. 6.

The downtown center of Wellfleet is quite compact, so it's actually best to leave your car in one of the public parking areas and take off on foot. Historic buildings that once housed oyster and fish-drying shacks or stately residences now contain upscale art galleries, designer clothing stores, and restaurants. Wellfleet's small-town nature still somehow accom-modates the demands of a major tourist industry; the year-round pop-ulation of around 2,800 residents explodes to more than 18,000 people in July and August.

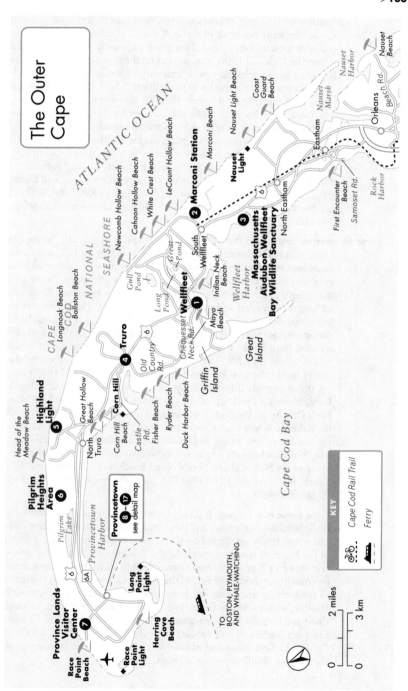

The Outer Cape

ATLANTIC OCEAN

CAPE COD NATIONAL SEASHORE

Nauset Beach

Nauset Harbor

Orleans

Coast Guard Beach

Nauset Light Beach

Nauset Light

Marconi Beach

2 Marconi Station

3 Massachusetts Audubon Wellfleet Bay Wildlife Sanctuary

Nauset Marsh

Eastham

Beach Rd.

Rock Harbor

First Encounter Beach

Samoset Rd.

North Eastham

LeCount Hollow Beach

White Crest Beach

Cahoon Hollow Beach

Newcomb Hollow Beach

South Wellfleet

Great Pond

Indian Neck Beach

Wellfleet Harbor

1 Wellfleet

Gull Pond

Long Pond

Chequesset Neck Rd.

Mayo Beach

Great Island

Griffin Island

Ballston Beach

Longnook Beach

Head of the Meadow Beach

5 Highland Light

Great Hollow Beach

Corn Hill

Corn Hill Beach

Castle Rd.

Fisher Beach

Ryder Beach

Duck Harbor Beach

4 Truro

Old Country Rd.

North Truro

Cape Cod Bay

6 Pilgrim Heights Area

Pilgrim Lake

Provincetown Harbor

8 – 17 Provincetown
see detail map

7 Province Lands Visitor Center

Race Point Beach

Race Point Light

Long Point Light

Herring Cove Beach

TO BOSTON, PLYMOUTH, AND WHALE-WATCHING

KEY

🚲 Cape Cod Rail Trail

⛴ Ferry

0 ___ 2 miles

0 ___ 3 km

Tourism isn't the only industry, though. Fishing boats still head out from the harbor daily in search of scallops, cod, and other fish. Shellfishing accounts for a major portion of the town's economy. Whaling played a role in the 18th and 19th centuries; out on the now-sunken Billingsgate Island a raucous whaling tavern once thrived. Dozens of world-traveling sea captains found their way to Wellfleet as well, the impact evident in many of the grand old houses that line the narrow streets of town. The Wellfleet Historical Society is a fine stop for those who wish to see the town as it was in its early days. Natural splendor, as well as history and sophisticated artistic culture, accounts for Wellfleet's popularity. The beaches are spectacular, with their towering sand dunes, bracing surf, and miles of unfettered expanse. Seemingly endless wooded paths in the domain of the National Seashore make for terrific walking and hiking trails, and the sheltered waters of the tidal Herring River and Wellfleet Harbor are a favorite destination for canoeists, kayakers, windsurfers, and sailors.

★ ❷ **Marconi Station,** on the Atlantic side of the Cape's forearm, is the site of the first transatlantic wireless station erected on the U.S. mainland. From here Italian radio and wireless-telegraphy pioneer Guglielmo Marconi sent the first American wireless message to Europe—"most cordial greetings and good wishes" from President Theodore Roosevelt to King Edward VII of England—on January 18, 1903. The station broadcast news for 15 years. An outdoor shelter contains a model of the original station, of which only fragments remain as a result of cliff erosion; parts of the tower bases are sometimes visible on the beach below, where they fell. The Cape Cod National Seashore's administrative headquarters is here, and though it is not an official visitor center, it can provide information at times when the centers are closed. Inside there's a mock-up of the spark-gap transmitter used by Marconi. Off the parking lot, a 1½-mi trail and boardwalk lead through the **Atlantic White Cedar Swamp,** one of the most beautiful trails on the seashore; free maps and guides are available at the trailhead. **Marconi Beach,** south of the station on Marconi Beach Road, is another of the National Seashore's ocean beaches. ⊠ *Marconi Site Rd., South Wellfleet* ☎ *508/349–3785* ⊕ *www.nps.gov/caco* ⊠ *Free* ☉ *Daily 8–4:30.*

For a **scenic loop** through a classic Cape landscape near Wellfleet's Atlantic beaches—with scrub and pines on the left, heathland meeting cliffs and ocean below on the right—take LeCount Hollow Road just north of the Marconi Station turnoff. All the beaches on this strip rest at the bottom of a tall grass-covered dune, which lends dramatic character to this outermost shore. The first of the four, **LeCount Hollow,** is restricted to residents or temporary residents in season, as is the last, **Newcomb Hollow,** with a scalloped shoreline of golden sand. In between, **White Crest** and **Cahoon Hollow** are town-managed public beaches. Cahoon has a hot restaurant and dancing spot, the Beachcomber. Backtrack to Cahoon Hollow Road and turn west for the southernmost entrance to the town of Wellfleet proper, across U.S. 6.

need a
break?

The **Blue Willow** (✉ South Wellfleet Post Office Sq., 1426 U.S. 6, ☎ 508/349–0900) is tiny, but the food is grand, transcending what you'll find in other take-out places. Shelves are lined with treats like crab cakes, crispy duck, tarragon chicken salad, and pasta dishes, all made on the premises. For breakfast, there are daily frittata and quiche specials, as well as muffins, scones, and pastries. Outside is a mini-farmers' market with fresh vegetables and flowers. Right at the Cape Cod Rail Trail, it's a good spot for a snack or the complete makings of a beach picnic or fine dinner. It's across from the chamber of commerce information booth and open daily year-round.

Wellfleet's **First Congregational Church** (✉ 200 Main St., Downtown Wellfleet ☎ 508/349–6877), a courtly 1850 Greek Revival building, is said to have the only town clock in the world to strike on ship's bells. The church's interior is lovely, with pale blue walls, a brass chandelier hanging from an enormous gilt ceiling rosette, subtly colored stained-glass windows, and pews curved to form an amphitheater facing the altar and the 738-pipe Hook and Hastings tracker-action organ, dating from 1873. To the right is a Tiffany-style window depicting a clipper ship. Concerts are given in July and August on Sunday at 8 PM.

For a glimpse into Wellfleet's past, the diminutive **Wellfleet Historical Society Museum** exhibits furniture, paintings, shipwreck salvage, needlework, navigation equipment, early photographs, Native American artifacts, and clothing. The society's Samuel Rider House is no longer open to the public. In July and August, short guided walks around the center of town are given Tuesday and Friday mornings at 10:15 for $3. *✉ 266 Main St., Downtown Wellfleet ☎ 508/349–9157 🔊 $1 ☉ Late June–mid-Sept., Wed., Thurs., and Sat. 1–4, Tues. and Fri. 10–4.*

The **Wellfleet Public Library** (✉ 55 W. Main St., Downtown Wellfleet ☎ 508/349–0310 ⊕ www.wellfleetlibrary.org) reflects the literary life of Wellfleet with readings, lectures, and exhibits by noted writers and artists in the community, and the collection of books for adults and children is impressive. Also available are videos, books on tape, and Internet access. Among the writers who have spent time here are Mary McCarthy, Edmund Wilson, Annie Dillard, and Marge Piercy.

Main Street is a good place to start if you're in the mood for shopping. **Commercial Street** has all the flavor of the fishing town that Wellfleet remains. Galleries and shops occupy small weathered-shingle houses. A good stroll around town would take in Commercial and Main streets, ending perhaps at **Uncle Tim's Bridge** (✉ Off E. Commercial St., Downtown Wellfleet). The short walk across this arching landmark—with its beautiful, much-photographed view over marshland and a tidal creek—leads to a small wooded island.

Commercial Street leads to the **Wellfleet Pier** (☎ 508/349–9818 for a fishing permit), busy with fishing boats, sailboats, yachts, charters, and party boats. At the twice-daily low tides you can fish on the tidal flats for oysters, clams, and quahogs.

RAINY DAY FUN

YOU CAN COUNT ON *plenty of wonderful things on Cape Cod: stunning beaches, fresh lobster, distinguished art galleries. Great weather, however, isn't always a sure thing. The Cape averages 3 to 4 inches of rain per month, and extended periods of inclement weather are not unheard of, no matter the season. Rain does not, however, have to put a damper on your vacation fun. If you look around a bit, you can find plenty to keep you busy in these parts, from a day at the spa to an umbrella-covered stroll along the beach.*

Here are 15 engaging activities for rainy days on the Cape:

1. **Have a bowl of chowder.** *Nothing takes the nip off a rainy day better than a steaming hot bowl of clam chowder, and the Cape has more than a few outstanding restaurants specializing in this longtime favorite. Top picks include the Lobster Pot (Provincetown), the Chatham Squire (Chatham), and Mill Way Fish and Lobster (Barnstable).*

2. **Go storm-watching.** *If it's a windy, exciting storm, grab lunch at a waterfront restaurant and enjoy watching the dramatically crashing surf outside your window. Some excellent choices for this activity include Fanizzi's by the Sea in Provincetown, Brax Landing in Harwich, and Fishmonger's Café in Woods Hole.*

3. **Visit the Cape Cod Children's Museum.** *Filled with interactive exhibits and games, plus a 30-foot play pirate ship, this Mashpee wonderland is geared mostly to kids around 8 and younger.*

4. **Curl up with a book in front of the fire.** *You may think it odd to book a room with a fireplace on Cape Cod, thinking you'll*

be out beachcombing and strolling all day long. But on those rainy days, even in summer, a fireplace can be a real treasure, and quite a few inns and vacation rentals have in-room fireplaces.

5. **Sample some fine wines.** *In East Falmouth, Cape Cod Winery produces six well-respected wines, some of which have won medals in prestigious competitions.*

6. **See a performance at the Cape Playhouse.** *This famous 26-acre compound comprises the main theater, the Cape Museum of Fine Arts, and the Cape Cinema; there's children's theater on Friday mornings in July and August.*

7. **Visit the Sandwich Glass Museum.** *On artsy Cape Cod, you can always pass time on a rainy day visiting local art galleries, but for a truly memorable art encounter, drop by this museum that traces the history of this prestigious glassmaking company. Glassblowing demonstrations are held throughout the summer.*

8. **Take a whale-watching trip.** *You're every bit as likely to see whales when it rains as when it's sunny, and two well-known Provincetown whale-watching tour operators—Dolphin Fleet and Portuguese Princess—offer these trips rain or shine, as does Hyannis's Whale Watcher Cruises. If you're prone to seasickness, however, beware of the stormy seas.*

9. **Work up a sweat at the gym.** *Willy's Gym in North Eastham and Orleans, the Mid Cape Racquet Club in South Yarmouth, and Falmouth Sports Center in Woods Hole all have indoor racquetball, squash, tennis, and basketball courts, plus indoor heated pools and all the usual workout amenities.*

10. **Head to a Christmas Tree Shop**—*you'll find them in Sagamore, Yarmouthport, Orleans, Falmouth, West Yarmouth, West Dennis, and Hyannis (the largest of the bunch). These massive, rambling shops are loaded with bargain-priced goods, from kitschy treasures to discontinued bulk items. If you're a bargain hunter, you could lose yourself in one of these shops for hours.*

11. **Book a spa treatment.** *Several Cape hotels have opened full-service spas (open to guests and nonguests) in recent years: the Crowne Pointe Inn in Provincetown, the Cape Codder Resort in Hyannis, and Dan'l Webster Inn in Sandwich. You don't have to travel far for a relaxing deep-tissue massage or algae wrap.*

12. **Go for a walk on the beach.** *Don't assume that the beach is only worth a visit when it's sunny outside—a rainy stroll can also be highly enjoyable. You won't encounter big crowds, and you may see some interesting wildlife, and once you've gotten a little wet you may forget about the showers and enjoy the brooding ocean and bay views.*

13. **Take some pictures.** *As long as you have an umbrella and proper attire in which to stow your camera and protect it from the elements, consider a day of photo-touring. Cape Cod offers plenty of intriguing photo-ops in the rain, from windswept sand dunes at Cape Cod National Seashore to dramatic street scenes in Provincetown and Dennis.*

14. **Head to the library.** *Each town on the Cape has a public library, and many of these sponsor children's programs, lectures, storytelling, art installations, and author readings.*

15. **Attend a matinee at the movies.** *The Cape is dotted with movie theaters, and although they get crowded when it rains, most theaters do offer lower-priced tickets early in the day. The famed Wellfleet Drive-In presents movies rain or shine.*

— *by Andrew Collins*

Chequessett Neck Road makes for a pretty 2½-mi drive from the harbor to the bay past Sunset Hill—a great place to catch one. At the end, on the left, is a parking lot and wooded picnic area from which nature trails lead off to **Great Island** (⊠ Off Chequessett Neck Rd., West of Downtown Wellfleet), perfect for the beachcomber and solitude seeker. The "island" is actually a peninsula connected by a sand spit built by tidal action. More than 7 mi of trails wind along the inner marshes and the water; these are the most difficult on the seashore because they're mostly in soft sand. In the 17th century, lookout towers for shore whaling as well as a tavern stood here. The residents pastured animals and engaged in oystering and cranberry harvesting. By 1800 the hardwood forest that had covered the island had been cut down for use in the building of ships and homes. The pitch pines and other growth you see here (and all over the Cape) today were introduced in the 1830s to keep the soil from washing into the sea. Cape Cod National Seashore offers occasional guided hikes on Great Island and, from February through April, seal walks. To the right of the Great Island lot, a road leads to **Griffin Island,** which has its own walking trail.

③ A trip to the Outer Cape isn't complete without a visit to the **Massachusetts Audubon Wellfleet Bay Wildlife Sanctuary,** an 1,100-acre haven for more than 250 species of birds attracted by the varied habitats found here. The jewel of the Massachusetts Audubon Society, the sanctuary is a superb place for walking, birding, and looking west over the salt marsh and bay at wondrous sunsets. The **Esther Underwood Johnson Nature Center** contains two 700-gallon aquariums that offer an up-close look at marine life common to the Cape's tidal flats and marshlands. Other rotating exhibits illustrate different facets of the area's ecology and natural history. From the center you can hike five short nature trails, including a fascinating Boardwalk Trail that leads over a salt marsh to a small beach—or you can wander through the Butterfly Garden.

Fodor'sChoice ★

The Audubon Society hosts naturalist-led wildlife tours around the Cape, including the Monomoy Islands, year-round. There are bay cruises; bird, wildlife, and insect walks; hikes; snorkeling; winter seal cruises; and birding, canoe, and kayak trips. The sanctuary also has camps for children in July and August and weeklong field schools for adults. Phone reservations are required for some programs. ⊠ Off U.S. 6 ☎ 508/349-2615 ⊕ www.wellfleetbay.org ☞ $5 ☺ Trails daily 8 AM–dusk; nature center late May–mid-Oct., daily 8:30–5; mid-Oct.–late May, Tues.–Sun. 8:30–5.

need a break? Pop inside dainty **On the Creek Cafe** (⊠ 55 Commercial St. ☎ 508/349–9841) for bracing java elixirs, hearty breakfasts, and creative lunch fare. It overlooks Duck Creek and has dining on the patio, and several galleries and B&Bs are within walking distance.

Where to Stay & Eat

★ $$–$$$$ ✕ **Aesop's Tables.** Inside this 1805 Federal-style captain's house are five dining rooms; try for a table on the porch overlooking the center of town. The signature dish is bouillabaisse with mounds of fresh-off-the-boat seafood in a hot saffron broth; the homemade sourdough bread is the perfect accompaniment. The marinated duck breast is another favorite. When it's time for dessert, you might want to tempt fate with Death by Chocolate, a heavy mousse cake. Some nights in summer there's live jazz in the tavern, where the mood and the menu are more casual; the chairs are so comfortable, you may have trouble getting up. ⊠ *316 Main St., Downtown Wellfleet* ☎ *508/349–6450* ⊟ *AE, DC, MC, V* ⊗ *Closed mid-Oct.–early May. No lunch.*

★ **$$–$$$** ✕ **Wicked Oyster.** In a rambling, gray clapboard house just off U.S. 6 on the main road into Wellfleet village, the Wicked Oyster is one of the few restaurants in Wellfleet serving truly innovative fare, and it's been a huge hit throughout the Outer Cape since it opened in early 2004. Try the rosemary-and-scallion-crusted half-rack of lamb over roasted-shallot-and-garlic potato salad, or the local mussels in tomato broth with smoky bacon, cilantro, jalapeño, and lime. Blackened-fish sandwiches and the Harry's Bar open-face burger (with caramelized onions, fresh mozzarella, and Worcestershire mayonnaise) are among the top lunch dishes. Breakfast is a favorite here—try the smoked salmon Benedict. There's also an outstanding wine list. ⊠ *50 Main St., Wellfleet* ☎ *508/ 349–3455* ⊟ *AE, D, MC, V* ⊗ *No dinner Wed.*

$–$$$ ✕ **Serena's.** One of the better values among the several restaurants lining U.S. 6, Serena's (Italian for "mermaid") offers an assortment of creative blackboard specials (such as wasabi-seared tuna) every night in addition to seafood and steaks. The Italian menu keeps with the classics, from chicken Parmesan to alfredo. Try the seafood *fra diavolo,* a bouillabaisse-like stew that can be ordered hot or extremely spicy. It's a noisy, convivial place, with outgoing servers and a crowd of both locals and visitors. ⊠ *U.S. 6, South Wellfleet* ☎ *508/349–9370* ⊟ *AE, D, DC, MC, V* ⊗ *Closed Nov.–mid-Apr. No lunch.*

$–$$ ✕ **Captain Higgins.** Fish is the obvious specialty at this popular spot at the turn of the road across from Wellfleet's town pier. Besides being close to the fishing fleet and town beach, Captain Higgins has a broad outdoor deck overlooking a golden marsh. You can watch the slender reeds sway in the breeze as you sip an icy Seabreeze and finish a plate of fresh Wellfleet oysters or a marinated calamari appetizer. This is a good place to get a big boiled lobster dinner or fresh bluefish with a sweet mustard glaze. ⊠ *250 Commercial St., across from Wellfleet Town Pier, Wellfleet Harbor* ☎ *508/349–6027* ⊟ *MC, V* ⊗ *Closed mid-Sept.–mid-June.*

$–$$ ✕ **Finely JP's.** This unassuming little roadside spot right on U.S. 6 gives
Fodor'sChoice no hint that chef John Pontius consistently turns out wonderful food full
★ of the best Mediterranean and local influences and ingredients. The dining room is small and noisy, but the fish and pasta dishes (which emphasize good olive oil and plenty of lemon) silence all. Appetizers are especially good, among them a warm spinach-and-scallop salad and a poached salmon with a tangy ginger-soy glaze. The Wellfleet paella draws raves and a steady handful of locals, but the chef is not afraid to cook down-home barbecue pork ribs, either. Be sure not to confuse this place with PJ's. ⊠ *U.S. 6, South Wellfleet* ☎ *508/349–7500* ⌲ *Reservations not accepted* ⊟ *D, MC, V* ⊗ *Closed Mon.–Wed. late Nov.–late May; Mon. and Tues. late May–mid-June and Oct.–late Nov.; Tues. early Sept.–Oct.*

$–$$ ✕ **Lighthouse Restaurant.** A line snakes out the door of this simple wood-frame house on summer mornings for a classic bacon-and-egg breakfast, or the tasty blueberry pancakes. Try a plate of steamers and a beer for lunch and perhaps chowder, cod fritters, lemon-butter scallops, and another beer for dinner. Thursday they serve Mexican fare, margaritas, and Dos Equis beer. There's a large deck, and downstairs you can order coffees, gelato, and lighter fare from the Lighthouse To-Go-Shoppe. ⊠ *Main St., Downtown Wellfleet* ☎ *508/349–3681* ⌕ *Reservations not accepted* ▭ *D, MC, V.*

¢–$$ ✕ **Moby Dick's.** A meal at this good-natured, rough-hewn fish shack with a hyper-nautical theme is an absolute Cape Cod tradition for some people. There's a giant blackboard menu (order up front and food is brought to you); a big, breezy screened-in porch in which to eat; and red-check tablecloths. Go for the Nantucket Bucket—a pound of whole-belly Monomoy steamers, a pound of native mussels, and corn on the cob served in a bucket. Also consider the rich and creamy lobster bisque or the complete lobster-in-the-rough dinner. Bring your own libations, and if you need to kill time, stop inside the bustling gift shop next door, Moby's Cargo. ⊠ *U.S. 6 near Truro border* ☎ *508/349–9795* ⌕ *Reservations not accepted* ▭ *MC, V* ☉ *Closed mid-Oct.–Apr.* ⛅ *BYOB.*

¢–$$ ✕ **PJ's Family Restaurant.** There's always a good-size but fast-moving line here, waiting for a heap of steamers or a creamy soft-serve cone. At PJ's you place your order and take a number. Food is served in utilitarian style: Styrofoam soup bowls, paper plates, plastic forks. The lobster-and-corn chowder doesn't have much lobster in it, so stick to the traditional clam chowder. Fried calamari and clam or oyster plates are generous and fresh. Try the dense, spicy stuffed clams and a pile of crispy onion rings, but avoid the veggie burger. ⊠ *U.S. 6 near Downtown Wellfleet exit* ☎ *508/349–2126* ⌕ *Reservations not accepted* ▭ *MC, V* ☉ *Closed mid-Oct.–mid-Apr.*

★ ¢–$$ ✕ **Mac's Seafood.** Right at Wellfleet Harbor, this ambitious little spot has some of the freshest seafood around. There's not a whole lot of seating here—some inside and some out on picnic tables—but when you've got a succulent mouthful of raw oyster or fried scallop in your mouth, who cares? You can always sit with your food along the pier and soak up the great water views. This place serves a vast variety of seafood, plus sushi, Mexican fare (grilled-scallop burritos), linguica sausage sandwiches and raw-bar items. There's also a selection of smoked fish, pâtés, lobster, and fish you can take home to grill yourself. You can even order a full traditional lobster clambake to go. ⊠ *Wellfleet Town Pier, Wellfleet Harbor* ☎ *508/349–0404* ▭ *MC, V* ☉ *Closed mid-Oct.–late May.*

¢ ✕ **Box Lunch.** Chances are you've seen this place before. This popular Cape franchise—the Wellfleet location is the original—serves up hot and cold roll-up sandwiches, a style it claims to have invented and perfected. A wide variety of fillings are available for breakfast, lunch, or early dinner (closing time is 7 PM in season). This tiny place gets ferociously busy in the summer season—call your order in ahead of time if you can. ⊠ *50 Briar La.* ☎ *508/349–2178* ⊕ *www.boxlunch.com* ▭ *No credit cards.* ☉ *No dinner Oct.–Apr.*

$$$$ ⊞ **Aunt Sukie's Bayside Bed & Breakfast.** Hosts Sue and Dan Hamar treat you like you're actual guests in their home, a part-contemporary, part-antique inn with three rooms and multiple decks, set on the marsh grass fronting Wellfleet Harbor and Cape Cod Bay—it's along a quiet residential stretch of road, near Power's Landing. The birds, the water, and the stunning bay views are enough to keep one content in the shade of trees with a pair of binoculars. Rooms are welcoming, with flowered quilts and private decks, and the two upstairs beds grant vistas of the water without a lift of the head. The room in the antique portion of the home has a gas fireplace, a brick patio, and a grand claw-foot tub. The owners also have a full house for rent about a mile away; it comfortably accommodates two couples or a family of four and is rented weekly from May through October. ⊠ *525 Chequessett Neck Rd., 02667* ☎ *508/349–2804 or 800/420–9999* ⊕ *www.auntsukies.com* ⇨ *2 rooms, 1 suite* ⚬ *Refrigerators, beach; no room TVs, no kids under 10, no smoking* ▤ *MC, V* ⊗ *Closed mid-Oct.–mid-May* ⦿ *CP.*

$$–$$$$ ⊞ **Surf Side Colony Cottages.** Scattered on either side of Ocean View Drive,
Fodor'sChoice accommodations range from units in a piney grove to well-equipped ocean-
★ side cottages. The cottages are a one-minute walk from Maguire's Landing town beach (Le Count Hollow), a beautiful wide strand of sand, dunes, and surf. Though the exteriors are retro-cool Floridian, with pastel shingles and flat roofs, cottage interiors are Cape-style, including knotty-pine paneling. All units have phones, wood-burning fireplaces, screened porches, kitchens, and grills. Some have roof decks with an ocean view and outdoor showers. Ocean-side cottages have dishwashers. ⊠ *Ocean View Dr.* ☍ *Box 937, South Wellfleet 02663* ☎ *508/349–3959* 🖷 *508/ 349–3959* ⊕ *www.surfsidevacation.com* ⇨ *18 cottages* ⚬ *BBQs* ⌁ *1- to 2-wk minimum in summer* ▤ *MC, V* ⊗ *Closed Nov.–Mar.*

★ **$$–$$$** ⊞ **Wellfleet Motel & Lodge.** A mile from Marconi Beach, opposite the Audubon sanctuary, is this immaculate and tasteful highway-side complex, which sits on 12 beautifully groomed wooded acres. Rooms in the single-story motel are renovated each winter; rooms in the two-story lodge are bright and spacious, with king- or queen-size beds and balconies or patios. The property offers direct access to the Cape Cod Rail Trail. ⊠ *146 U.S. 6* ☍ *Box 606, South Wellfleet 02663* ☎ *508/349–3535 or 800/ 852–2900* 🖷 *508/349–1192* ⊕ *www.wellfleetmotel.com* ⇨ *57 rooms, 8 suites* ⚬ *Restaurant, cable TV, 2 pools, hot tub, basketball, bar, meeting room* ▤ *AE, DC, MC, V* ⊗ *Closed Dec.–Mar.*

$–$$$ ⊞ **Even'tide.** Long a summer favorite, this motel is set back off the main road, surrounded by trees, and sits close to the Cape Cod Rail Trail. A central attraction is the 60-foot indoor pool (although Wellfleet's beaches are not far). Rooms are simple with clean but undistinguished modern furnishings; choose from doubles, two-room family suites, and efficiencies with kitchens. There are also cottages speckled about the property, available for stays of a week or longer. The staff is friendly and enthusiastic. ⊠ *650 U.S. 6, South Wellfleet 02663* ☎ *508/349–3410 or 800/368–0007* 🖷 *508/349–7804* ⊕ *www.eventidemotel.com* ⇨ *31 units, 10 cottages* ⚬ *BBQs, cable TV, kitchens, refrigerators, indoor pool, Ping-Pong, shuffleboard, basketball court, minigolf, playground, Internet; no smoking* ⌁ *1- or 2-wk minimum for cottages in summer* ▤ *MC, V* ⊗ *Closed Nov. and Dec.*

$–$$$ ⊞ **Southfleet Motor Inn.** Geared to active families, this carefully maintained motor inn is directly across from the entrance to the National Seashore at Marconi Station for easy access to ocean beaches. Bring your bikes to cruise the 26-mi Cape Cod Rail Trail. Rooms with an assortment of beds can sleep up to five people. The pools and game room (with a Ping-Pong table) ought to keep the kids both busy and happy. ⊠ *U.S. 6, across from Marconi Station, 02667* ☎ *508/349–3580 or 800/334–3715* ⊕ *www.southfleetmotorinn.com* ⇔ *30 rooms* ⟂ *Restaurant, refrigerators, cable TV, 2 pools (1 indoor), hot tub, video game room, lounge; no smoking* ⊟ *AE, MC, V* ⊙ *Closed mid-Oct.–mid-Apr.*

$$ ⊞ **Blue Gateways.** Not one to shun its heritage—the home was built in 1712—this inn combines the simple comfort of colonial times with a modern sense of leisure. It's a short walk from downtown Wellfleet's galleries and restaurants. The original three-sided fireplace still reigns on the ground floor, which has wide-plank pine floors and generous beams. Upstairs are three ample guest rooms with quilts, antiques, hooked rugs, and private bathrooms. Gardens, fish-filled ponds, and private sitting areas are just outside. Common areas include a chess table, plenty of reading material, a sunporch with cable TV and a VCR, and a small kitchen area with a microwave and refrigerator. ⊠ *252 Main St., 02667* ☎ *508/349–7530* ⊕ *www.bluegateways.com* ⇔ *3 rooms* ⟂ *No room phones, no room TVs, no children under 12, no smoking* ⊟ *AE, D, MC, V* ⊙ *Closed Nov.–Apr.* ❑| *CP.*

$$ ⊞ **Holbrook House.** This inn, an immaculate and crisply elegant 1818 home, is surrounded by gardens and brick patios. Antiques, sea-grass floor coverings, and artwork adorn the interior. Because there are only three rooms (plus a detached apartment available weekly), privacy is assured. The room on the first floor has a private entrance and twin beds that can be converted to a king. Upstairs, the second room has a sitting area and a large bedroom with a queen-size bed. Leave your car in the lot while in Wellfleet—the inn is close to town and to the harbor. ⊠ *223 Main St., Wellfleet 02667* ☎ *508/349–6706* ⊕ *www.holbrookwellfleet. com* ⇔ *1 room, 2 suites, 1 apartment* ⟂ *BBQs, cable TV, some in-room VCRs; no children under 12, no smoking* ⊟ *MC, V* ❑| *BP.*

$$ ⊞ **Stone Lion Inn.** B&Bs are meant to feel a bit like a home away from home—a place to feel welcome, at ease, and taken care of. Just outside the town center, yet a short walk to both the harbor and the village, is the Stone Lion Inn, a gracious mansard-roof Victorian where all of these elements meet. Rooms have queen beds, ceiling fans to encourage the breezes, hardwood floors, and antiques to reflect the 19th-century era in which the house was built. Relax amid the gardens, in the outdoor shower, or in the pretty common room. New Yorkers may recognize the subtle Brooklyn theme—nostalgic, yet happily devoid of Manhattan's frenzy. ⊠ *130 Commercial St., 02667* ☎ *508/349–9565* ⎙ *508/349–9697* ⊕ *www.stonelioncapecod.com* ⇔ *3 rooms, 1 apartment, 1 cottage* ⟂ *Internet; no room phones, no room TVs, no kids under 10, no smoking* ⊟ *MC, V* ⊙ *Closed Mar.* ❑| *BP.*

¢–$$ ⊞ **Inn at Duck Creeke.** Set on 5 wooded acres by a duck pond, a creek, and a salt marsh, this old inn consists of the circa-1815 main building and three other similar-era houses. Rooms in the main inn (except rustic third-floor rooms) and in the Saltworks house have a simple charm. Typical furnishings include claw-foot tubs, country antiques, lace curtains, chenille spreads, and rag rugs on hardwood floors. The two-room Carriage House is cabinlike, with rough barn-board and plaster walls. There's formal dining at Sweet Seasons or pub dining with entertainment at the Tavern Room. ⊠ *70 Main St.* ⌂ *Box 364, Wellfleet 02667* ☎ *508/349–9333* 🖷 *508/349–0234* ⊕ *www.innatduckcreeke. com* ❧ *25 rooms, 17 with bath* ⚄ *2 restaurants; no room phones, no room TVs* ☞ *2-night minimum weekends July and Aug.* ▭ *AE, MC, V* ⊙ *Closed mid-Oct.–late-Apr.* ⊺⊙⊺ *CP.*

$ 🛏 **Holden Inn.** If you're watching your budget and can deal with modest basics, try this old-timey place on a tree-shaded street just outside the town center but within walking distance of several galleries and restaurants. Rooms are simply decorated with Grandma's house-type wallpapers, ruffled sheer or country-style curtains, and antiques such as brass-and-white-iron or spindle beds or a marble-top table. Private baths with old porcelain sinks are available in adjacent 1840 and 1890 buildings. The lodge has shared baths, an outdoor shower, and a large screened-in porch with a lovely view of the bay and Great Island, far below. The main house has a common room and a screened front porch with rockers and a bay view through trees. ⊠ *140 Commercial St.* ⌂ *Box 816, Wellfleet 02667* ☎ *508/349–3450* ⊕ *www.theholdeninn. com* ❧ *26 rooms, 10 with bath* ⚄ *No smoking* ▭ *No credit cards* ⊙ *Closed mid-Oct.–mid-Apr.*

Nightlife & the Arts

THE ARTS **Jim Wolf, Master Storyteller** (⊠ Main St., Downtown Wellfleet ☎ 508/247–9539 information) beguiles folks of all ages with his dramatic tales of both past and present Cape Cod lore and legend. July and August show times are Wednesday–Friday at 7:30 PM at the Wellfleet United Methodist Church.

During July and August the **First Congregational Church** (⊠ 200 Main St., Downtown Wellfleet ☎ 508/349–6877) trades the serenity of worship for Sunday evening concerts. The music begins at 8 PM and has included opera, blues, jazz, and chamber music.

The drive-in movie is alive and well on Cape Cod at the **Wellfleet Drive-In Theater** (⊠ 51 U.S. 6, South Wellfleet ☎ 508/349–7176), which is right by the Eastham town line. Films start at dusk nightly in season, and there's a miniature golf course.

On Saturday evening in July and August during the **Wellfleet Gallery Crawl,** art galleries are open for cocktail receptions to celebrate show openings. You can walk from gallery to gallery meeting the featured artists and checking out their works.

★ The well-regarded **Wellfleet Harbor Actors Theater** (⊠ Kendrick St. past E. Commercial St., near Wellfleet Harbor ☎ 508/349–6835 or 866/252–9428 ⊕ www.what.org) presents world premieres of American plays, satires, farces, and black comedies in its mid-May–mid-October season. This is the place for provocative experimental theater.

NIGHTLIFE
★ Beachcomber (⊠ Ocean View Dr. off U.S. 6, by Cahoon Hollow Beach ☎ 508/349–6055) is big with the college crowd. It's right on the beach, with national touring acts most nights, weekend happy hours with live reggae, and dancing nightly in summer. Indoors or at tables by the beachfront bar, you can order appetizers, salads, burgers, seafood, and barbecue. There's also a raw bar.

A number of organizations sponsor outdoor activities at night, including the **Massachusetts Audubon Wellfleet Bay Wildlife Sanctuary**'s night hikes and lecture series.

The **Tavern Room** (⊠ 70 Main St., U.S. 6 exit to Downtown Wellfleet ☎ 508/349–7369), set in an 1800s building with a beam ceiling, a fireplace, and a bar covered in nautical charts, has live entertainment from jazz to pop to country to Latin ensembles. Munchies are served alongside the menu of traditional and Latin/Caribbean-inspired dishes.

Kick up your heels and grab a twirling partner for a long-standing Wellfleet tradition, the **Wednesday Night Square Dance.** Down at the town pier in July and August, the music and live calling by master caller Irvin "Toots" Tousignant begins at 7 and lasts as long as *you* can.

Sports & the Outdoors

State-of-the-art Skateboard Park down at **Baker's Field** (⊠ Kendrick Ave. just past Wellfleet Town Pier, near Wellfleet Harbor) was professionally designed for tricks and safety and is manned by local teens.

BEACHES
Public Beaches. Extensive storm-induced erosion has made the cliffs to most of Wellfleet's ocean beaches quite steep—so be prepared for an exerting trek up and down the dune slope.

Cahoon Hollow Beach (⊠ Ocean View Dr.) has lifeguards, rest rooms, and a restaurant and music club on the sand. This beach tends to attract younger and slightly rowdier crowds; it's a big Sunday-afternoon party place. There are daily parking fees of $10 for nonresidents in season only; parking is free for those with beach stickers.

Fodor'sChoice **Marconi Beach** (⊠ Off U.S. 6), part of the Cape Cod National Seashore, ★ charges $10 for daily parking or $30 for a season pass that provides access to all six National Seashore swimming beaches. There are lifeguards, restrooms, and outdoor showers.

Mayo Beach (⊠ Commercial St., adjacent to Wellfleet Pier) is free. But swimming here is only pleasant around high tide—once the water recedes, it's all mud and sharp shells. You can park free at the small lot by Great Island on the bay.

White Crest Beach (⊠ Ocean View Dr.) is a prime surfer hangout where the dudes often spend more time waiting for waves than actually riding them. Lifeguards are on duty. If you're up to the challenge, join in on the frequent volleyball games. There are daily parking fees of $10 for nonresidents in season only; parking is free for those with beach stickers.

Restricted Beaches. Resident or temporary resident parking stickers are required for access to Wellfleet beaches in season only, from the last week of June through Labor Day. To get a weekly ($60) or season ($250) pass, visit the Beach Sticker Booth on the town pier with your car registration in hand and a proof-of-stay form, available from rental agencies and hotels. For the rest of the year anyone can visit the beaches for free. Note that people arriving on foot or by bicycle can visit the beaches at any time; the sticker is for parking only. These parking restrictions apply to all beaches listed below.

For information about restricted beaches, call the **Wellfleet Chamber of Commerce** (☎ 508/349–2510).

Duck Harbor Beach (✉ End of Chequessett Neck Rd.) has the wonderful feeling of being nearly at the end of the world. Its shores are on the warm waters of Cape Cod Bay, and there's plenty of room to wander and find your own private space. Look out to Provincetown across the bay, but the finest view by far is the nightly sunset.

Indian Neck Beach (✉ Pilgrim Spring Rd. off U.S. 6) is on the bay side, fronting Wellfleet Harbor, and is thus affected by the tides. Low tide reveals plenty of beach but less water—walk way out before your hips get wet. It's a good spot to watch the comings and goings of fishing boats from Wellfleet Pier. It's a great beach for families: shallow and calm waters, plenty of treasure hunting at low tide, and warmer temperatures.

★ **LeCount Hollow Beach** (✉ Ocean View Dr.) is the beach closest to U.S. 6 in South Wellfleet along the meandering Ocean View Drive. Dunes are steep here, so be prepared to carry all beach belongings down (and up) the sandy slope.

Newcomb Hollow Beach (✉ Ocean View Dr.) is the northernmost beach on the Wellfleet strip, closest to Truro. If you keep your eyes on the horizon, it's not at all uncommon to see the distant spout of a passing whale. This beach is also a popular nighttime fishing spot.

The **Wellfleet Ponds,** nestled in the woods between U.S. 6 and the ocean, were formed by glaciers and are fed by underground springs. Mild temperatures and clear, clean water make swimming pleasant for the whole family, a refreshing change from the bracing salty surf of the Atlantic. They are also perfect for canoeing, sailing, or kayaking (boats are available from Jack's Boat Rentals). These fragile ecosystems have called for restricted use, and a Wellfleet beach sticker is required in season. The sticker is only for cars, however; anyone can walk or ride a bike over to the ponds. Motorized boats are not allowed.

BIKING The Cape Cod Rail Trail ends at the South Wellfleet post office. Other scenic routes for bicyclists include the winding, tree-lined Old County Road, just outside Wellfleet center at the end of West Main Street. Ambitious riders can bike all the way to Truro on this often bumpy road, but do watch for vehicular traffic around the tight curves. Ocean View Drive, on the ocean side, provides for many miles of cycling in wooded areas. There are several ponds along the route perfect for a quick dip.

The Wellfleet Chamber of Commerce publishes a pamphlet, "Bicycling in Wellfleet," with an annotated map.

Black Duck Sports Shop (⊠ U.S. 6 at LeCount Hollow Rd., South Wellfleet ☎ 508/349–9801, 508/349–2335 off-season) rents bikes.

Idle Times Bike Shop, Inc. (⊠ U.S. 6, just west of Cahoon Hollow Rd. ☎ 508/349–9161) opens Memorial Day and rents bikes, trail-a-bikes (a tandem bike with a backseat for children who are big enough to pedal), and trailer attachments for the littler passengers. The shop also handles repairs and sells parts and assorted accessories. Depending on the crowds and weather, it usually remains open until Columbus Day.

BOATING **Fun Seekers** (☎ 508/349–1429) offers windsurfing instruction and guided mountain-bike and kayak tours by appointment. Children's programs are available; the company closes in the off-season.

Jack's Boat Rental (⊠ Gull Pond, south of U.S. 6 ☎ 508/349–7553 ⊠ U.S. 6, west of Downtown Wellfleet exit ☎ 508/349–9808 long-term rentals) has canoes, kayaks, sailboards, Sunfish, pedal boats, surfboards, boogie boards, and sailboards. Guided tours are also available.

Wellfleet Marine Corp. (⊠ Wellfleet Town Pier, Wellfleet Harbor ☎ 508/349–2233) rents motorboats in various sizes and sailboats by the hour or the day.

FISHING You can climb aboard the charter boat **Jac's Mate** (⊠ Wellfleet Town Pier, Wellfleet Harbor ☎ 508/255–2978) for fishing expeditions in search of bass and blues.

Fishing trips are operated on a walk-on basis from spring through fall on the **Naviator** (⊠ Wellfleet Town Pier, Wellfleet Harbor ☎ 508/349–6003 ⊕ www.naviator.com). Rods, reels, and bait are included.

Licenses are not required for saltwater fishing, and many anglers hit the outer beaches to surf-cast for bluefish and striped bass. Rods, bait, and some advice are available at the **Black Duck Sports Shop** (⊠ U.S. 6 at LeCount Hollow Rd., South Wellfleet ☎ 508/349–9801, 508/349–2335 off-season).

GOLF & TENNIS Wellfleet maintains several tennis courts at **Baker's Field** near the Town Pier. Court time, from late June until the end of August, is $12 per hour for singles and $15 per hour for doubles; call the **Recreation Department** (☎ 508/349–0330) to reserve.

Chequessett Yacht Country Club (⊠ Chequessett Neck Rd., west of Downtown Wellfleet ☎ 508/349–3704) is a semiprivate club (public use on space-available basis) with a 9-hole golf course and five hard-surface tennis courts by the bay. Lessons are available.

Oliver's (⊠ U.S. 6, west of Downtown Wellfleet exit ☎ 508/349–3330) has one Truflex and seven clay courts, offers tennis lessons, and arranges matches.

SURFING The Atlantic-coast **Marconi** and **White Crest** beaches are the best for surfing. Surfboard rentals can be arranged at Jack's Boat Rentals.

Shopping

Blue Heron Gallery (✉ 20 Bank St., Downtown Wellfleet ☎ 508/349–6724 ⊕ www.blueheronfineart.com) is one of the Cape's best galleries, with contemporary works—including Cape scenes, jewelry, sculpture, and pottery—by regional and nationally recognized artists, among them Steve Allrich and Del Filardi.

★ **Brophy's Fine Art** (✉ 313 Main St., Downtown Wellfleet ☎ 508/349–6479 ⊕ www.brophysfineart.com), one of the few shops open year-round in Wellfleet, carries a nice selection of pottery, jewelry, and landscape paintings by several prominent New England artists as well the beautiful stained-glass works of owner Thomas Brophy.

Cove Gallery (✉ 15 Commercial St., Downtown Wellfleet ☎ 508/349–2530 ⊕ www.covegallery.com) displays the works of John Grillo, Tomi de Paola, and Leonard Baskin, among others, with Saturday-night artist receptions in July and August.

Davis Gallery (✉ 2766 U.S. 6, east of Downtown Wellfleet exit ☎ 508/349–0549 ⊕ www.thedavisgallery.com) makes its home in what was once an ugly building on the highway. The owners have turned the place into a very respectable and attractive gallery showcasing contemporary art and fine crafts. There's a pleasant outdoor sculpture gallery as well.

Jacob Fanning Gallery (✉ 25 Bank St., Downtown Wellfleet ☎ 508/349–9546 ⊕ www.jacobfanningcapecod.com) represents the art, furniture, and decorative pieces of several established local artists, including Joyce Zavorskas, Jane Lincoln, and Lynn Shaler.

Kendall Art Gallery (✉ 40 Main St., Downtown Wellfleet ☎ 508/349–2482) carries eclectic modern works, including Harry Marinsky's bronzes in the sculpture garden, photography by Walter Baron and Alan Hoelzle, watercolors by Walter Dorrell, and contemporary art by several prominent Chinese artists.

Left-Bank Gallery (✉ 25 Commercial St. ☎ 508/349–9451 ✉ 3 W. Main St., Downtown Wellfleet ☎ 508/349–7939 ⊕ www.leftbankgallery. com) has two branches. The larger one, on Commercial Street, has a display of the larger works of local and national artists and sells fine crafts in the back room facing Duck Creek. The other gallery has fine handcrafted jewelry, silk and chenille scarves, hats, and small works of original art and photography.

Nicholas Harrison Gallery (✉ 275 Main St., Downtown Wellfleet ☎ 508/349–7799) has made a name for itself in the area of lovely and unusual American crafts. Owners Mark and Laura Evangelista are also accomplished potters, so you'll see their vibrant ceramic works.

Sandpiper Gallery (✉ 95 Commercial St., Downtown Wellfleet ☎ 508/349–9500), an impressive and relatively new space, carries a wide range of oils, watercolors, photography, etchings, and jewelry by both regional and national talents.

Wellfleet Crafts Gallery (✉ 313 Main St., Downtown Wellfleet ☎ 508/349–6123 ⊕ www.wellfleetglassworks.com) is a bright storefront space packed to the rafters with innovative housewares and decorative arts—jewelry, candles, arty postcards and stationary, windchimes, and other small treasures.

Wellfleet Glassworks (⊠ 15 Bank St., Downtown Wellfleet ☎ 508/349–0200 ⊕ www.wellfleetglassworks.com) carries a wide assortment of contemporary glassware, sculpture, and jewelry created by owners Jason and Erin Robicheau; you can come in to watch glassblowing demonstrations throughout the day.

SPECIALTY STORES **Abiyoyo** (⊠ 286 Main St., Downtown Wellfleet ☎ 508/349–3422) has a full line of Wellfleet T-shirts and sweatshirts, along with shoes, children's clothing, and bath and beauty products. The store, open April–December, shares its phone number with its older Main Street sibling, Abiyoyo Toys.

Eccentricity (⊠ 361 Main St., Downtown Wellfleet ☎ 508/349–7554) keeps the corner of Main and Briar offbeat. One of the most interesting stores on the Cape, it sells gorgeous kimonos, ethnic-inspired cotton clothing, African carved-wood sculptures, barbershop paintings, odd Mexican items, and trinkets.

★ **Herridge Books** (⊠ 11 E. Main St., between U.S. 6 and town center, Downtown Wellfleet ☎ 508/349–1323) is a perfect store for a town that has hosted so many writers. Its dignified literary fiction, art and architecture, literary biography and letters, mystery, Americana, sports, and other sections are full of used books in very nice condition. Herridge also carries new editions on the Cape and its history.

Jules Besch Stationers (⊠ 15 Bank St., Downtown Wellfleet ☎ 508/349–1231) has extraordinary cards, fine stationery, journals, papers, and pens. Proprietor Michael Tuck's warm and welcoming nature is as beautiful as his products. He also offers full calligraphy services.

Karol Richardson (⊠ 11 W. Main St., Downtown Wellfleet ☎ 508/349–6378) fashions women's wear in luxurious fabrics and sells interesting shoes, hats, and jewelry.

Kite Gallery (⊠ 75 Commercial St., Downtown Wellfleet ☎ 508/349–7387) overlooks a salt marsh and stocks not only kites but all kinds of colorful beach toys, windsocks, flags, and garden goodies.

Off Center (⊠ Off Main St., Downtown Wellfleet, diagonally across from Eccentricity ☎ 508/349–3634), another of the Eccentricity owners' enterprises, sells mainstream yet stylish women's clothing.

Pickle and Puppy (⊠ 355 Main St., Downtown Wellfleet ☎ 508/349–0606) has a bit of everything: housewares, T-shirts, fanciful foodstuffs, ceramics, luxury bath and beauty-parlor items, and a selection of unusual children's toys, games, and puzzles.

Secret Garden (⊠ Main St., Downtown Wellfleet ☎ 508/349–1444) doesn't waste any precious space—from floor to ceiling are whimsical folk art pieces, handbags, clothing, decorative accessories, and good buys on sterling silver jewelry.

FLEA MARKET
Fodor'sChoice
★
The giant **Wellfleet Flea Market** (✉ 51 U.S. 6, South Wellfleet ☎ 508/ 349–2520) sets up shop in the parking lot of the Wellfleet Drive-In Theater mid-April–June and September and October, weekends and Monday holidays 8–4; July and August, Monday holidays, Wednesday and Thursday, and weekends 8–4. You'll find antiques, sweat socks, old advertising posters, books, Beanie Babies, Guatemalan sweaters, plants, trinkets, and plenty more. On Monday and Tuesday in July and August the vendors make way for large arts-and-crafts shows. A snack bar and playground keep fatigue at bay.

en route
If you're in the mood for a quiet, lovely ride winding through what the Cape might have looked like before Europeans arrived, follow **Old County Road** from Wellfleet to Truro on the bay side. It's bumpy and beautiful, with a stream or two to pass. So cycle on it, or drive slowly, or just stop and walk to take in the nature around you.

Truro

❹ *2 mi north of Wellfleet; 7 mi southeast of Provincetown.*

Settled in 1697, Truro has had several names. It was originally called Pamet after the local Indians, but in 1705 the name was changed to Dangerfield in response to all the sailing mishaps off its shores. "Truroe" was the final choice, and Truro became the namesake of a Cornish town that homesick settlers thought it resembled. The town relied on the sea for its income—whaling, shipbuilding, and cod fishing were the main industries. Today a town of high dunes, estuaries, and rivers fringed by grasses, rolling moors, and houses sheltered in tiny valleys, Truro is a popular retreat of artists, writers, politicos, and numerous vacationing psychoanalysts. Edward Hopper summered here from 1930 to 1967, finding the Cape light ideal for his austere brand of realism. One of the largest towns on the Cape in land area—almost 43 square mi—it's also the smallest in population, with about 1,400 year-round residents. If you thought neighboring Wellfleet's downtown was small, wait until you see— or don't see—Truro's. It's a post office, a town hall, a shop or two. You'll know it by the sign that says DOWNTOWN TRURO at a little plaza entrance. Truro also has a library, a firehouse, and a police station, but that's about all. It's the Cape's narrowest town, and from a high perch you can see the Atlantic Ocean on one side and Cape Cod Bay on the other.

☾ For a few hours of exploring, take the children to **Pamet Harbor** (✉ Depot Rd.). At low tide you can walk out on the flats and discover the creatures of the salt marsh. A nearby plaque identifies the plants and animals and describes the area's ecological importance.

On **Corn Hill** (✉ Off Corn Hill Rd.), near the beach area of the same name, a tablet commemorates the finding of a buried cache of corn by Myles Standish and the *Mayflower* crew. They took it to Plymouth and used it as seed, returning later to pay the Native Americans for the corn they'd taken.

CloseUp

TRURO'S EDWARD HOPPER

THE OUTER CAPE has inspired thousands of acclaimed artists, but perhaps none is more closely associated with its serene yet dramatic landscape than Edward Hopper, the esteemed realist painter who lived in Truro for most of the last four decades of his life. Quiet Truro, with its peaceful, sandy lanes, suited the introspective Hopper perfectly.

Hopper, born in Nyack, New York in 1882, enjoyed little commercial or critical success before middle age. Early in his career, he worked as a commercial illustrator to support himself while living in New York City's Greenwich Village. At age 43 he married fellow painter Josephine Nivison. It was during the 1920s, following his marriage, that Hopper achieved marked success as both an oil painter and watercolorist and became known for his starkly realistic scenes, often depicting public places filled with people, such as his most iconic work, Nighthawks.

Edward and Josephine first summered in Truro in 1930. A few years later they designed their own Truro home. Much of Hopper's work conveyed the emptiness and alienation of big-city life, and although his Cape paintings were similar in their simplicity, they nevertheless offered a slightly more hopeful vision, if for no other reason than their tendency to focus more on the region's sensuous luminosity than strictly on lonely or bored people.

Most famously, his Truro work captured the undulating auburn hills along Pamet Road in Corn Hill Truro Cape Cod. Other notable paintings that portray the Outer Cape include Cape Cod Evening (1939), Route 6 Eastham (1941), Martha McKeen of Wellfleet (1944), and Cape Cod Morning (1950).

— by Andrew Collins

The **Truro Center for the Arts at Castle Hill,** in a converted 19th-century barn, has summer arts-and-crafts workshops for children, as well as courses and single classes in art, crafts, photography, and writing for adults. Teachers have included notable New York- and Provincetown-based artists. ⊠ *10 Meetinghouse Rd.* ☎ *508/349–7511* ⊕ *www.castlehill.org.*

> **need a break?**

Jams (⊠ 14 Truro Center Rd., off U.S. 6 in Truro Center ☎ 508/349–1616) has fixings for a great picnic lunch: sandwiches, fresh produce, a bottle of wine or Evian, or a sweet treat. Unless you like getting your knees knocked, don't bother sitting at the bench outside—the best part of the Cape awaits just outside the door, anyway.

Built at the turn of the 20th century as a summer hotel, the **Truro Historical Museum** has 17th-century firearms, mementos of shipwrecks, early fishing and whaling gear, ship models, a pirate's chest, and scrimshaw. One room exhibits wood carvings, paintings, blown glass, and ship models by Courtney Allen, artist and founder of Truro's historical society. The museum also hosts local art and artifact shows each year. ⊠ *6 Lighthouse Rd., off S. Highland Rd., North Truro* ☎ *508/487–3397* ⊠ *$3* ⊙ *Late May–Sept., daily 10–4:30.*

❺ Truly a breathtaking sight, **Highland Light,** also called Cape Cod Light, is the Cape's oldest lighthouse. It was the last to have become automated, in 1986. The first light on this site, powered by 24 whale-oil lamps, began warning ships of Truro's treacherous sandbars in 1798—the dreaded Peaked Hills Bars alone, to the north, have claimed hundreds of ships. The current light, a white-painted 66-foot tower built in 1857, is powered by two 1,000-watt bulbs reflected by a huge Fresnel lens. Its beacon is visible for 20 mi.

One of four active lighthouses on the Outer Cape, Highland Light has the distinction of being listed in the National Register of Historic Places. Thoreau used it as a stopover in his travels across the Cape's backside, as the Atlantic side of the Outer Cape is called. Erosion threatened to cut this lighthouse from the 117-foot cliff on which it stood and drop it into the sea; thanks to a concerted effort by local citizens and lighthouse lovers, the necessary funds were raised, and the lighthouse has since been moved back 450 feet to safety. It's still surrounded by the Highland Links golf course, however. Twenty-five-minute tours of the lighthouse are given daily in summer. Children must be at least 51 inches tall to climb the tower. ⊠ *Off S. Highland Rd.* ☎ *508/487–1121* ☞ *$3* ☉ *Mid-June–Sept., daily 10–5:30.*

The gardens of **A Touch of Heaven** are a beautiful place and, unlike most other gardens, are meant to be picked. The lawns are set with benches and birdbaths. The flowers are so abundant you don't feel guilty gathering a bunch to take home. ⊠ *Pond Village Heights, North Truro* ☎ *No phone* ☞ *Free* ☉ *Daily dawn–dusk.*

❻ At the **Pilgrim Heights Area** (⊠ Off U.S. 6) of the Cape Cod National Seashore, a short trail leads to the spring where members of a Pilgrim exploring party stopped to refill their casks, tasting their first New England water in the process. Walking through this still-wild area of oak, pitch pine, bayberry, blueberry, beach plum, and azalea gives you a taste of what it was like for these voyagers in search of a new home. "Being thus passed the vast ocean . . ." William Bradford wrote in *Of Plimoth Plantation,* "they had no friends to welcome them, no inns to entertain them or refresh their weather-beaten bodies; no houses, or much less towns to repair to, to seek for succour."

From an overlook you can see the bluffs of High Head, where glaciers pushed a mass of earth before melting and receding. Another path leads to a swamp, and a bike trail leads to Head of the Meadow Beach, often a less crowded alternative to others in the area.

Where to Stay & Eat

$$–$$$ ✕ **Adrian's.** Adrian Cyr's restaurant crowns a high bluff overlooking Pilgrim Lake and all of Provincetown; his cooking also hits the heights. Grilled swordfish with ginger-lime butter is one of the well-prepared dishes here. Tuscan salad is also a hit, with tomatoes, olives, fresh basil, plenty of garlic, and balsamic vinegar. Pizzas, too, are standouts, especially one made with cornmeal dough and topped with shrimp and artichokes. The outdoor deck bursts at the popular breakfasts and brunches, served every day in season—try the Brie and shallot omelet. ⊠ *Outer Reach Hotel,*

535 U.S. 6, North Truro ☎ *508/487–4360* ⚘ *Reservations not accepted* 🖃 *AE, MC, V* ☾ *Closed mid-Oct.–late May. No lunch.*

★ **$$–$$$**   ✕ **Blacksmith Shop.** Here's where Truro locals like to linger at the bar, gossiping about what's going on in town while choosing from an eclectic menu with everything from seafood to Mexican items. The restaurant looks like it might have once been a place to bring your horse for a shoeing, but these days it's a nice out-of-the-way spot for company. There are excellent steaks as well as an oven-baked pistachio-crusted salmon with pistachio oil, chicken marsala, and a pan-roasted rack of lamb with cranberry-port reduction. Local shellfishermen deliver excellent quahogs and oysters, then hang around for the gossip. ⊠ *17 Truro Center Rd., off Rte. 6A, Truro Center* ☎ *508/349–6554* 🖃 *AE, MC, V* ☾ *Closed weekdays Nov.–May.*

$$–$$$ ✕ **Montano's.** This friendly, cavernous Italian restaurant with vaulted ceilings and hanging plants sits along U.S. 6. Old harpoons, fish barrels, and lobster-pot "chandeliers" add the requisite nautical touch. Built to handle a tour-bus crowd, Montano's serves comfortable, predictable Italian-American fare with a leaning toward seafood and a solid selection of steaks. You can't go wrong with classics such as linguine and mussels in a red or white sauce or a simple thick, center-cut filet mignon with roasted garlic butter. The 14-inch pizzas are made on fresh dough, and you can taste the difference; try the white-clam pie. ⊠ *481 U.S. 6* ☎ *508/487–2026* 🖃 *AE, MC, V* ☾ *No lunch.*

$$–$$$ ✕ **Terra Luna.** An insider's favorite for a special breakfast, Terra Luna has also become a wonderful choice for dinner. The dining room seems cramped rather than intimate, but the food is stylish, with surprising sauces for both fish and meat dishes. The striped bass is grilled perfectly, and spicy stuffed lamb chops are an excellent alternative to the usual fish. ⊠ *104 Shore Rd. (Rte. 6A), North Truro* ☎ *508/487–1019* 🖃 *AE, MC, V* ☾ *Closed late Oct.–May.*

$$–$$$ ✕ **Whitman House.** What began as a modest pancake house has been transformed by the Rice family into a vast—if touristy—restaurant, but pewter plates, candlelight, and rustic wood accents make the place feel comfortably tavernlike. Seafood, steaks, and chicken (Chicken à la Whitman, topped with asparagus and cheese, is a time-honored favorite) keep the menu uncomplicated. Lunch is served daily in the Bass Tavern; dinner begins at 5. If you have to wait for a table, browse in the adjacent Amish quilt shop. ⊠ *Off U.S. 6* ☎ *508/487–1740* 🖃 *AE, D, DC, MC, V.*

$–$$$ ✕ **Paparazzi.** Practically on the sands of Cape Cod Bay, this family favorite has changed little during the last two decades. Blackboard specials entice those looking for a big meal at a good value, with the added benefits of the well-stocked soup-and-salad bar. Giant cuts of prime rib are a perennial favorite, as are the Italian specialties that pay homage to the owners' heritage. Fill up on ribs, fried calamari, or pizza, or choose from a host of fresh seafood. It's a small and festive place—not unlike a big family reunion—with lots of good food, lively conversation, and the swift efficiency of a seasoned waitstaff. ⊠ *Shore Rd. (Rte. 6A)* ☎ *508/487–7272* ⚘ *Reservations not accepted* 🖃 *AE, MC, V* ☾ *Closed late Nov.–early Apr.*

¢–$$ ╳ **Highland Restaurant & Catering.** Reasonably priced, casual, and very family oriented, this little place does a brisk business with breakfast, lunch, and dinner. It has the feel of a small-town diner, and its menu reflects that with the likes of good, honest burgers, omelets, corned beef hash, hot chicken Parmesan subs, roasted chicken, and even meat loaf. Seafood (including lobster in summer), local shellfish, steaks, and pasta add to the mix, and parents will be pleased with the kids' menu. If you're looking for a substantial beach picnic, all menu items are available for takeout, as well as a selection of sandwich meats and salads from the adjacent deli. ⊠ *8 Highland Rd.* ☎ *508/487–4744* ⌕ *Reservations not accepted* ▭ *MC, V* ⊗ *Closed Mon. late Oct.–May.*

$$–$$$ ▦ **Moorlands Inn.** The creative works of innkeepers Bill and Skipper Evaul—artists and musicians—fill the walls and rooms of this towering Queen Anne Victorian beauty. Antiques adorn the bright rooms in the main house; the spacious penthouse has a full kitchen, two bedrooms, and a deck. Those staying in the Carriage House have their own outdoor whirlpool, while others can use the communal hot tub out back. ⊠ *11 Hughes Rd., North Truro 02652* ☎ *508/487–0663* ⊕ *www.themoorlands.com* ⤳ *5 rooms, 1 apartment, 3 cottages* ⌂ *Some kitchens, cable TV, some in-room VCRs, outdoor hot tubs, croquet; no a/c in some rooms* ▭ *MC, V* ⎸◎⎸ *BP.*

$$ ▦ **Shoreline Motel.** Although this pleasant clapboard motel won't win any awards for beauty, it's perched right on the sands of Cape Cod Bay, with views of daily sunsets and the glimmering lights of Provincetown beyond. There are standard motel rooms, suites, and a few efficiencies from which to choose; all come with stunning water views and have plenty of room to spread out. Efficiencies have full kitchens, and suites have kitchenettes. Upstairs rooms have private balconies from which to contemplate the tides. ⊠ *Rte. 6A* ⊡ *Box 761, North Truro 02652* ☎ *508/487–9109* ⊕ *www.capecodtravel.com/shoreline* ⤳ *24 rooms* ⌂ *Some kitchens, some kitchenettes, refrigerators, cable TV, beach* ▭ *AE, MC, V* ⊗ *Closed mid-Oct.–mid-Apr.*

★ $–$$ ▦ **East Harbour.** This meticulously maintained complex outside Provincetown has simple Cape-style cottages and motel units ringing a manicured lawn and separated from the bay beach by low grasses. The two-bedroom cottages have paneled walls, colonial-style furnishings, and full kitchens. Motel rooms have large picture windows, mini-refrigerators and coffeemakers, light paneling, and 1960s furnishings. A contemporary apartment is all white and bright, with skylights, Shaker-reproduction furnishings, a modern kitchen, and second-floor views of the harbor from a private deck. ⊠ *618 Shore Rd. (Rte. 6A)* ⊡ *Box 183, North Truro 02652* ☎ *508/487–0505* 🖷 *508/487–6693* ⊕ *www.eastharbour.com* ⤳ *7 cottages, 9 rooms, 1 apartment* ⌂ *Picnic area, some kitchens, microwaves, cable TV, beach, laundry facilities* ⌲ *In season, 1-wk minimum for cottages and apartment, 2-night minimum for rooms* ▭ *AE, D, MC, V* ⊗ *Closed Nov.–Mar.*

¢–$$ ▦ **Cape View Motel.** The real beauty of this roadside motel is its noble perch on the westward bluff, looking out to sunsets over Cape Cod Bay and the distant lights of Provincetown. Deluxe rooms have private balconies, as well as fully equipped kitchenettes and a king bed or two doubles. Inside, the style doesn't at all try to compete with the outside vistas, but rooms are clean, simple, reasonably priced, and a 10-minute drive to Provincetown. ⊠ *Junction of U.S. 6 and Rte. 6A, 02652* ☎ *508/ 487–0363 or 800/224–3232* ⊕ *www.capeviewmotel.com* ⤳ *32 rooms* ⚘ *Some kitchenettes, refrigerators, cable TV, pool* ⊟ *AE, MC, V* ☉ *Closed mid-Oct.–mid-May.*

¢–$$ 🖼 **Sea Gull Motel.** This motel's location, right on the beach, is the real draw. Lodging is in standard motel rooms, motel studios, and beach apartments—the latter two are rented weekly, but you can rent rooms by the night. Because it's been family run for decades, you may feel like you're spending time in someone's summer house. Most rooms have splendid water views. ⊠ *Rte. 6A* ⬦ *Box 126, North Truro 02652* ☎ *508/487– 9070* ⊕ *www.capecodtravel.com/seagullmotel* ⤳ *26 rooms* ⚘ *Refrigerators, cable TV* ⊟ *AE, D, MC, V* ☉ *Closed mid-Oct.–Apr.*

¢ 🖼 **Hostelling International–Truro.** In a former Coast Guard station right on the dunes, this handsome, well-placed hostel has kitchen facilities, a common area, and naturalist-led programs. It's also right by the ½-mi-long Cranberry Bog Trail, which takes you by a refurbished cranberry bog and an old bog house. ⊠ *N. Pamet Rd.* ⬦ *Box 402, Truro 02666* ☎ *508/349–3889* ⊕ *www.hihostels.com* ⤳ *42 beds* ⊟ *MC, V* ☉ *Closed early Sept.–mid-June.*

Sports & the Outdoors

BEACHES Parking at a number of Truro's **town beaches** is reserved for residents and renters in season, although anyone can walk or bicycle in. Ask at the **town hall** (☎ 508/349–3635) about a seasonal sticker.

Corn Hill Beach (⊠ Corn Hill Rd.), on the bay, has beautiful views of Provincetown. The waters are generally calm and warm, typical of bay beaches. There are restrooms on-site as well. Parking requires a Truro beach sticker or a $10 daily fee.

Truro has several other accessible beaches stretched along Cape Cod Bay. All are beautiful and ideal for long, lazy days of watching the boats go by, with views of Provincetown in the distance.

Cold Storage Beach (⊠ Pond Rd. off Rte. 6A [Shore Rd.]) is just as popular with anglers looking for passing blues and stripers as it is with sunseekers and swimmers. A Truro beach sticker is required for parking.

Just off one of Truro's backcountry roads, **Fisher Road Beach** (⊠ Fisher Rd.) is usually quiet, due to its smaller parking capacity. A Truro beach sticker is required for parking.

To get to **Great Hollow Beach** (⊠ Great Hollow Rd. off U.S. 6) you must be ready to scale some moderate stairs from the parking lot to the sands below. A Truro beach sticker is required for parking.

Ryder Beach (⊠ Ryder Beach Rd. off Old County Rd.) rests just below a rise in the small dunes. A Truro beach sticker is required for parking.

On the ocean side, three spectacular beaches are marked by massive dunes and bracing surf.

★ **Ballston Beach** (⊠ Pamet Rd.) lies at the end of the winding and residential Pamet Road and is backed by the golden hills that artist Edward Hopper made famous in his Truro paintings. Parking is reserved for residents and renters in season, although anyone can walk or bicycle in.

Fodor'sChoice
★ **Coast Guard Beach** (⊠ Coast Guard Rd.) sits just down the road from Highland Light. Parking is for residents and renters with stickers only, although anyone can walk or bicycle in. Keep in mind that the parking area is small and tends to fill quickly.

Head of the Meadow Beach (⊠ Head of the Meadow Rd. off U.S. 6) in North Truro, part of Cape Cod National Seashore, is often less crowded than other beaches in the area. Since the bathhouse burned down, it has only temporary restroom facilities available in summer and no showers. The daily parking fee is $10 in season, or the beach can be accessed with the purchase of a season pass ($30) good for all National Seashore locations.

A not-so-secret favorite of nude sunbathers, **Longnook Beach** (⊠ Long Nook Rd.) shares the senses of wildness and isolation synonymous with Truro's outer reaches. Truro beach stickers are required for parking.

BIKING The **Head of the Meadow Trail** provides 2 mi of easy cycling between dunes and salt marshes from High Head Road, off Route 6A in North Truro, to the Head of the Meadow Beach parking lot. Bird-watchers also love the area.

Bayside Bikes (⊠ 102 Rte. 6A, North Truro ☎ 508/487–5735) rents bicycles by the hour, day, or week, with easy access to the Head of the Meadow Trail.

Cape Outback Adventures (☎ 508/349–1617 or 800/864–0070 ⊕ www.capeoutback.com) has friendly instruction and guided tours for kayakers, mountain bikers, and beginning surfers. Times and location are arranged by phone, and owner Richard Miller and staff provide equipment. Kayak trips explore areas in both Wellfleet and Truro, while off-road mountain-biking excursions take place in the vast wooded areas within the National Seashore. Surfing instruction is available by the hour. These trips are designed for those of all ages and skill levels.

GOLF The **Highland Golf Links** (⊠ Lighthouse Rd., North Truro ☎ 508/487–
★ 9201), a 9-hole, par-36 course on a cliff overlooking the Atlantic and Highland Light, is unique for its resemblance to Scottish links rather than the well-manicured courses that are more typically found in the United States.

SURFING **Longnook Beach** (⊠ End of Long Nook Rd., off U.S. 6) is good for surfing.

Shopping

Atlantic Spice Co. (⊠ U.S. 6 at Rte. 6A, North Truro ☎ 508/487–6100 ⊕ www.atlanticspice.com) has spices, teas, and potpourris, as well as herbs, dried flowers, soaps, sauces, and kitchenware items.

Whitman House Quilt Shop (⊠ County Rd. just off U.S. 6, North Truro ☎ 508/487–3204 ⊕ www.whitmanhouse.com) sells Amish quilts and other country items.

Provincetown

 7 mi northwest of Truro; 27 mi north of Orleans; 62 mi from Sagamore Bridge.

The Cape's smallest town in area and the second smallest in year-round population, Provincetown is a place of liberating creativity, startling originality, and significant diversity. In the busy downtown, Portuguese-American fishermen mix with painters, poets, writers, whale-watching families, cruise-ship passengers on brief stopovers, and gay and lesbian residents and visitors. In summer Commercial Street is packed with sightseers and shoppers hunting for treasures in the overwhelming number of galleries and crafts shops. At night raucous music and people spill out of bars, drag shows, and sing-along lounges galore. It's a fun, crazy place, with the extra dimension of the fishing fleet unloading their catch at MacMillan Wharf, in the center of the action.

The town's 8 square mi are also rich in history. The curled fist at the very tip of the Cape, Provincetown has shores that curve protectively around a natural harbor, perfect for sailors from any epoch to anchor. Historical records suggest that Thorvald, brother of Viking Leif Erikson, came ashore here in AD 1004 to repair the keel of his boat and consequently named the area Kjalarness, or Cape of the Keel. Bartholomew Gosnold came to Provincetown in 1602 and named the area Cape Cod after the abundant codfish he found in the local waters.

The Pilgrims remain Provincetown's most famous visitors. On Monday, November 21, 1620, the *Mayflower* dropped anchor in Provincetown Harbor after a difficult 63-day voyage from England; while in the harbor they signed the Mayflower Compact, the first document to declare a democratic form of government in America. One of the first things the ever-practical Pilgrims did was to come ashore to wash their clothes, thus beginning the ages-old New England tradition of Monday wash day. They lingered for five weeks before moving on to Plymouth. Plaques and parks commemorate the landing throughout town.

During the American Revolution, Provincetown Harbor was controlled by the British, who used it as a port from which to sail to Boston and launch attacks on colonial and French vessels. In November 1778 the 64-gun British frigate *Somerset* ran aground and was wrecked off Provincetown's Race Point. Every 60 years or so, the shifting sands uncover its remains.

Incorporated as a town in 1727, Provincetown was for many decades a bustling seaport, with fishing and whaling as its major industries. In the late 19th century, groups of Portuguese fishermen and whalers began to settle here, lending their expertise and culture to an already cosmopolitan town. Fishing is still an important source of income for many Provincetown locals, but now the town ranks among the world's leading whale-watching, rather than whale-hunting, outposts.

Artists began coming here in the late 1890s to take advantage of the unusual Cape Cod light—in fact, Provincetown is the nation's oldest

PROVINCETOWN: AMERICA'S GAY SUMMER PLAYGROUND

AMERICA'S ORIGINAL GAY RESORT, Provincetown developed as an artists' colony at the turn of the 20th century. In 1899, a young artist and entrepreneur named Charles Hawthorne founded the Cape Cod School of Art. Within 20 years, a half-dozen art schools opened, the Provincetown Art Association had staged its first exhibitions, and the Provincetown Players, a small band of modernist theater folk began to produce plays on a small wharf in the town's East End.

After a year in Provincetown the players moved to New York City's Greenwich Village, where gay culture was already thriving. This kinship helped spur Provincetown's early flourish as a gay community. Tourism became a significant revenue source, and local homes began letting rooms to the hundreds of writers, painters, and other creative spirits drawn to the town's thriving arts community.

Over the next few decades, many innovative writers and artists spent time in Provincetown, including such openly gay luminaries as Truman Capote and Tennessee Williams. The town became identified increasingly for its willingness to flout convention and by the 1960s it was a haven for anyone whose artistic leaning, political platform, or sexual persuasion was subject to persecution elsewhere in America. This hotbed of counterculture, naturally nurtured one of the country's most significant gay communities.

Today Provincetown is as appealing to artists as it is to gay and lesbian—as well as straight—tourists. The awareness brought by the AIDS crisis and, most recently, Massachusetts's becoming the first state to legalize same-sex marriage, has turned the town into the most visibly gay vacation community in America.

— by Andrew Collins

continuous art colony. Poets, writers, and actors have also been part of the art scene. Eugene O'Neill's first plays were written and produced here, and the Fine Arts Work Center continues to have in its ranks some of the most important writers working today.

During the early 1900s, Provincetown became known as Greenwich Village North. Artists from New York and Europe discovered the town's unspoiled beauty, special light, lively community, and colorful Portuguese flavor. By 1916, with five art schools flourishing here, painters' easels were nearly as common as shells on the beach. This bohemian community, along with the availability of inexpensive summer lodgings, attracted young rebels and writers as well, including John Reed (*Ten Days That Shook the World*) and Mary Heaton Vorse (*Footnote to Folly*), who in 1915 began the Cape's first significant theater group, the Provincetown Players. The young, then unknown Eugene O'Neill joined them in 1916, when his *Bound East for Cardiff* premiered in a tiny wharfside East End fish house. After 1916 the Players moved on to New York. Their theater, at present-day 571 Commercial Street, is long since gone, but a model of it and of the old Lewis Wharf on which it stood is on display at the Pilgrim Monument museum.

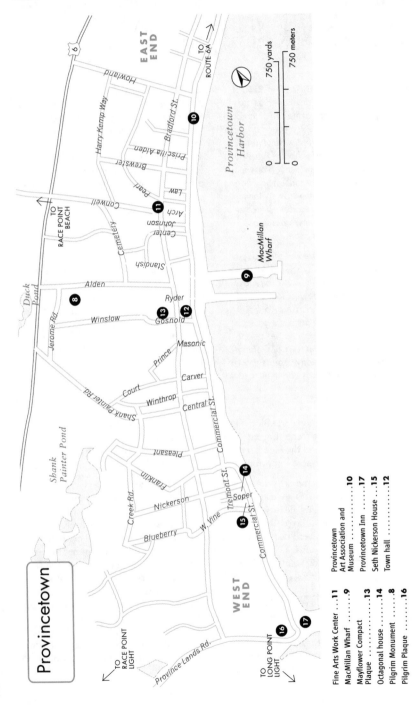

Provincetown

EAST END

TO ROUTE 6A

Howland

Harry Kemp Way

Priscilla Alden

Brewster

Pearl

Law

Cornwell

Arch

Johnson

Center

Standish

Cemetery

Alden

Ryder

Winslow

Gosnold

Masonic

Prince

Carver

Court

Winthrop

Central St.

Shank Painter Rd.

Pleasant

Commercial St.

Franklin

Nickerson

Tremont St.

Soper

W. Vine

Blueberry

Commercial St.

WEST END

TO RACE POINT LIGHT

Province Lands Rd.

TO LONG POINT LIGHT

Jerome Rd.

Creek Rd.

Duck Pond

Shank Painter Pond

TO RACE POINT BEACH

Provincetown Harbor

MacMillan Wharf

6

750 yards

750 meters

0

0

8 **9** **10** **11** **12** **13** **14** **15** **16** **17**

Near the Provincetown border, **massive dunes** actually meet the road in places, turning U.S. 6 into a sand-swept highway. Scattered among the dunes are primitive cottages called dune shacks, built from flotsam and other found materials, that have provided atmospheric as well as cheap lodgings to a number of famous artists and writers over the years—among them poet Harry Kemp, Eugene O'Neill, e. e. cummings, Jack Kerouac, and Norman Mailer. The few surviving shacks are privately leased from the Cape Cod National Seashore, whose proposal to demolish the shacks was halted by their inclusion on the National Register of Historic Places in 1988. The dunes are fragile and should not be walked on, but paths lead through them to the ocean. You can see some of the shacks by van on Art's Dune Tours.

The **Province Lands** begin at High Head in Truro and stretch to the tip of Provincetown. The area is scattered with ponds, cranberry bogs, and scrub; unfortunately, this terrain provides optimal conditions for the deer tick, which can cause Lyme disease, so use extra caution. Bike and walking trails lace through forests of stunted pines, beech, and oak and across desertlike expanses of rolling dunes. Protected against development, the Province Lands are the "wilds" of the Cape.

A beautiful spot to stop for lunch before biking to the beach, the **Beech Forest picnic area** (⊠ Race Point Rd., east of U.S. 6) in the National Seashore borders a small pond covered with water lilies. The adjacent bike trails lead to Herring Cove and Race Point beaches, both part of the National Seashore.

❼ Inside the **Province Lands Visitor Center** in the Cape Cod National Seashore you'll find literature and nature-related gifts, frequent short films on local geology, and exhibits on the life of the dunes and the shore. You can also pick up information on guided walks, birding trips, lectures, bonfires, and other current programs throughout the seashore, as well as on the Province Lands' own beaches, Race Point and Herring Cove, and the walking, biking, and horse trails. Don't miss the wonderful 360-degree view of the dunes and the surrounding ocean from the observation deck. ⊠ *Race Point Rd., east of U.S. 6* ☎ *508/487–1256* ⊕ *www.nps. gov/caco* ☜ *Free* ☉ *May–Oct., daily 9–5.*

Not far from the present Coast Guard station is the **Old Harbor Station,** a U.S. Life Saving Service building towed here by barge from Chatham in 1977 to rescue it from an eroding beach. It's reached by a boardwalk across the sand, and plaques along the way tell about the lifesaving service and the whales seen offshore. Inside are displays of such equipment as Lyle guns, which shot rescue lines out to ships in distress when seas were too violent to launch a surfboat, and breeches buoys, in which passengers were hauled across those lines to safety. At 6:30 on Thursday night in summer there are reenactments of this old-fashioned lifesaving procedure. ⊠ *Race Point Beach, end of Race Point Rd.* ☎ *No phone* ☜ *Donations accepted; Thurs. night $3* ☉ *July and Aug., daily 10–4.*

★ Provincetown's main downtown thoroughfare, **Commercial Street,** is 3 mi from end to end. In season, driving from one end of the main street to the other could take forever, so wear comfortable shoes and get ready to walk; even walking can be slow because of the crowds. You can see signs for parking lots as you head into town. A casual stroll will allow you to see the many architectural styles (Greek Revival, Victorian, Second Empire, and Gothic, to name a few) used in the design of the impressive houses for wealthy sea captains and merchants. Be on the lookout for blue plaques fastened to housefronts explaining their historical significance—practically the entire town has been designated part of the Provincetown Historic District. The Historical Society puts out a series of walking-tour pamphlets, available for about $1 each at many shops in town, with maps and information on the history of many buildings and the more or less famous folk who have occupied them. You may also want to pick up a free Provincetown gallery guide.

The center of town is where the crowds and most of the touristy shops are. The quiet East End is mostly residential, with an increasing number of nationally renowned galleries, and the similarly quiet West End has a number of small inns with neat lawns and elaborate gardens.

need a break? The **Provincetown Portuguese Bakery** (⊠ 299 Commercial St., Downtown center ☎ 508/487–1803) makes fresh Portuguese breads and pastries and serves breakfast and lunch all day from March to October. While it may be difficult to choose among the sweet splendor, favorite pastries include *malassadas*, a sweet fried dough; lemon custard; sponge cake with Bavarian creme; and the more unusual *trutas*, with rich, sweet potato filling. It's open until 11 PM in summer.

★ ❽ The first thing you'll see in Provincetown is the **Pilgrim Monument.** This grandiose edifice, which seems somewhat out of proportion to the rest of the low-rise town, commemorates the Pilgrims' first landing in the New World and their signing of the Mayflower Compact (the first colonial-American rules of self-governance) before they set off from Provincetown Harbor to explore the mainland. Climb the 116 steps and 60 short ramps of the 252-foot-high tower for a panoramic view—dunes on one side, harbor on the other, and the entire bay side of Cape Cod beyond. On an exceptionally clear day you can see the Boston skyline. At the tower's base is a museum of Lower Cape and Provincetown history, with exhibits on whaling, shipwrecks, and scrimshaw; a diorama of the *Mayflower*; and another of a glass factory.

The tower was erected of granite shipped from Maine, according to a design modeled on a tower in Siena, Italy. President Theodore Roosevelt laid the cornerstone in 1907, and President Taft attended the 1910 dedication. On Thanksgiving Eve, in a ceremony that includes a museum tour and open house, 5,000 white and gold lights that drape the tower are illuminated—a display that can be seen as far away as the Cape Cod Canal. They are lighted nightly into the New Year. ⊠ *High Pole Hill Rd.* ☎ *508/487–1310* ⊕ *www.pilgrim-monument.org* ☎ *$7* ⊗ *Apr.–June and Sept.–Nov., daily 9–4:15; July and Aug., daily 9–6:15.*

❾ **MacMillan Wharf,** with its large municipal parking facility, is a sensible place to start a tour of town. It's one of the remaining 5 of the 54 wharves that once jutted into the bay. The wharf serves as the base for P-town whale-watch boats, fishing charters, and party boats. The **Chamber of Commerce** is also here, with all kinds of information and events schedules. Kiosks at the wharf have restroom and parking-lot locations, bus schedules, and other information for visitors.

The former Provincetown Marina building, on MacMillan Wharf, holds the **Expedition Whydah Sea Lab and Learning Center,** a home for artifacts recovered from the pirate ship *Whydah,* which sank off the coast of Wellfleet in 1717. The *Whydah* is the only pirate shipwreck ever authenticated anywhere in the world, and the museum, though tiny, is entertaining and educational, with one display on the restoration and conservation processes and another on the untold story of the 18th-century pirating life. The curators hope to collect all the recovered pieces eventually; some are on loan to other museums across the country. ⊠ *16 MacMillan Wharf, Downtown Center* ☎ *508/487–8899 or 800/949–3241* ⊕ *www.whydah.com* ⌨ *$8* ⊙ *May and early Sept.–Oct., daily 10–4; June–early Sept., daily 10–7; Nov. and Dec., weekends 10–4.*

Founded in 1914 to collect and show the works of artists with Provincetown connections, the **Provincetown Art Association and Museum** (PAAM) has a 1,650-piece permanent collection, displayed in changing exhibits that mix up-and-comers with established 20th-century figures. Some of the work hung in the four bright galleries is for sale. The museum store carries books of local interest, including works by or about area artists and authors, as well as posters, crafts, cards, and gift items. PAAM-sponsored year-round courses (one day and longer) offer the opportunity to study under such talents as Sal Del Deo, Carol Whorf Westcott, and Tony Vevers. Late in 2003, PAAM began a major renovation and expansion, which will eventually see the addition of a huge exhibition wing. Work is slated to continue through at least 2005, and the museum is expected to remain open during most of this time; still, it's prudent to call ahead first to double-check hours and access. ⊠ *460 Commercial St., East End* ☎ *508/487–1750* ⊕ *www.paam.org* ⌨ *$3 donation suggested* ⊙ *Apr.–late May, weekends noon–5; late May–early July and Sept., daily noon–5, also Fri. and Sat. 8 PM–10 PM; early July–Aug., daily noon–5 and 8 PM–10 PM; Oct.–Mar., weekends noon–4.*

To see or hear the work of up-and-coming artists, visit the gallery or attend a reading at the **Fine Arts Work Center** (FAWC). A nonprofit organization founded in 1968, the FAWC sponsors 10 writers and 10 artists from October through May each year with a place to live and work, a stipend on which to live, and access to artists and teachers. A summer program has open-enrollment workshops in both writing and the visual arts. The buildings in the complex around the center, which it owns, were formerly part of Day's Lumber Yard Studios, built above a lumberyard by a patron of the arts to provide poor artists with cheap accommodations. Robert Motherwell, Hans Hoffmann, and Helen Frankenthaler have been among the studios' roster of residents over the years. ⊠ *24 Pearl St., East End* ☎ *508/487–9960* ⊕ *www.fawc. org* ⊙ *Weekdays 9–5.*

CloseUp
CAPE COD'S MADAME BUTTERFLY

*MID THE GENTLY SWAYING DUNE
GRASSES and beneath the waves
of the Atlantic waft the whispers
of a legend. It's a classic tale with
all the ingredients—true love, pirate
treasure, and a storm-wrought tragedy—
and for nearly three centuries it has
inspired fanciful embellishments and lustful
searchings. Though she was wrecked in a
treacherous storm back in April of 1717,
the pirate ship Whydah still captivates.*

*As with any great legend, that of the
Whydah has several versions, some
conflicting. Many say the story began with
an innocent love, when a dark, ambitious
sailor named Sam Bellamy met the
beautiful Maria Hallett in Wellfleet. From
their brief acquaintance blossomed love,
grand promises, and a child (the latter
unknown to the wayward Bellamy), and
the sailor gave his word that he would
return, armed with riches.*

*He set off for England in hopes of finding
fortune in shipping, but he soon realized
that piracy was far more lucrative. Black
Sam Bellamy, as he became known, and
his men were wildly successful, taking
over many dozens of ships. On a pirating
jaunt in the Caribbean, Bellamy and his
men captured a beauty—a slave ship
loaded with gold and silver. Wealthy
beyond their dreams, the men headed
north with Bellamy at the helm of this
exciting vessel, called the Whydah.*

*While the sailors grew rich and famous,
young Maria Hallett was banished by her
family because of her pregnancy. She fled
to a small cabin in Eastham, awaiting the
birth of her child and the return of her
lover. She had a son, but he died in
infancy, and the discovery of the dead
child landed Maria in jail. Reputations
were made swiftly in those days: it wasn't
long before the townspeople decided
Maria was a witch who had made an*

*unholy pact with the devil. She suffered in
isolation as Bellamy made his way back to
Wellfleet.*

*Mariners have long feared the dangerous
shoals, sand bars, and temperamental
weather of the waters off Cape Cod. On
the night of April 26, 1717, a sudden
fierce storm interrupted Bellamy's
homecoming, and the once sleek and swift
Whydah was no match for the fury of the
sea. Blasted by wave and wind, she met
her demise in the form of a sturdy
sandbar—nearly all hands were lost, and
the ship lay broken, exposed to the tides.*

*At this point the legend sways wildly. The
Whydah lay a mere 200 yards off the
beach, within easy reach of eager
treasure hunters. Historical records show
that an officer, sent by the king to gather
the spoils of the pirate ship, left the scene
empty-handed, so the location of the gold,
silver, and gems remains a mystery.
Perhaps they were hidden by 18th-century
scavengers; perhaps they still await
discovery in the depths.*

*In 1984 modern-day pirate Barry Clifford
and his crew uncovered some of the
Whydah's remains, but the promise of
grand treasure has yet to be fulfilled. In
Provincetown, at the Expedition Whydah
museum, you can see some artifacts from
this ship and other historic wrecks.*

*And what of poor Maria? Some say her
ghost still wanders among the dunes,
wailing and cursing all sailors. Listen
closely on a foggy and ominous evening,
and decide for yourself.*

— by Laura V. Scheel

⑫ The **town hall** was used by the Provincetown Art Association as its first exhibit space and still displays paintings donated to the town over the years, including Provincetown scenes by Charles Hawthorne and WPA-era murals by Ross Moffett. ⊠ *260 Commercial St., Downtown Center* ☎ *508/487–7000* ⊙ *Weekdays 8–5.*

⑬ In a little park behind the town hall is the **Mayflower Compact Plaque** (⊠ Bradford St., Downtown Center), carved in bas-relief by sculptor Cyrus Dalin and depicting the historic signing.

need a break? The **Provincetown Fudge Factory** (⊠ 210 Commercial St., Downtown Center ☎ 508/487–2850), across from the post office, makes silky peanut-butter cups, chocolates, saltwater taffy, yard-long licorice whips, custom-flavor frozen yogurt, and the creamiest fudge on the Cape—and will ship such sweet goodies to you, too.

⑭ An **octagonal house** (⊠ 74 Commercial St., West End) built in 1850 is an interesting piece of Provincetown architecture in the West End. The house is not open to the public.

⑮ The oldest building in town, dating from 1746, is the small Cape-style **Seth Nickerson House** (⊠ 72 Commercial St., West End), still a private home. It was built by a ship's carpenter, with massive pegged, hand-hewn oak beams and wide-board floors. Modern renovations have somewhat replaced the glimpse into centuries past that it once had, but it's still impressive.

⑯ The bronze **Pilgrim Plaque** (⊠ West end of Commercial St., Downtown Center), set into a boulder at the center of a little park, commemorates the first footfall of the Pilgrims onto Cape soil—Provincetown's humble equivalent of the Plymouth Rock.

⑰ In the **Provincetown Inn** (⊠ 1 Commercial St., West End ☎ 508/487–9500) you can see a series of 19 murals, painted in the 1930s from old postcards, depicting life in the 19th-century town. The inn still operates as a hotel; the murals are in the lobby and hallways.

Where to Stay & Eat

★ **$$$–$$$$** ✕ **Chester.** Named for a pet terrier, this single-room restaurant in a Greek Revival sea captain's house serves beautifully presented meals from a small, contemporary menu that changes regularly. In addition to locally procured meats and seafood, the chef collects tomatoes, herbs, and lettuces from a garden behind the restaurant. Try duck prosciutto and arugula salad with Vermont chevre, toasted pine nuts and balsamic vinaigrette, before moving on to grilled French pork chop with fig, walnut, and blue cheese stuffing, fig sauce, and roasted potatoes. The carefully crafted wine list has 160 selections. An outdoor, upper terrace patio has great views of Provincetown Harbor. ⊠ *404 Commercial St.* ☎ *508/487–8200* ⊕ *www.chesterrestaurant.com* ⊲ *Reservations essential* ☐ *AE, MC, V* ⊙ *Closed parts of Dec.–Mar.*

$$–$$$$ ✕ **Martin House.** It's a relief to find this sanctuary of calm and creative
Fodor'sChoice contemporary fare right on bustling Commercial Street. Original 18th-
★ century woodwork lends a touch of history, and Provincetown paint-

ings grace the walls. The menu leans toward regional fare with a sophisticated touch, including unusually flavorful chutneys, risotto, and wild game. Some of the more interesting dishes include Oysters Claudia, which matches native Wellfleets-on-the-half-shell with an Asian dipping sauce, wasabi, and pickled ginger; New England seafood paella with lobster, littlenecks, chorizo, corn, peas, and blood orange–tomato nage on saffron rice; and pan-roasted medium rare duck breast and smoked leg with ginger-orange-quince coulis and corn pudding. ☒ 157 Commercial St. ☎ 508/487-1327 ▭ AE, D, DC, MC, V ☉ Closed Jan. and Mon.–Wed. Feb.–Apr.

★ **$$$** ╳ **Front Street.** Front Street is so good, so consistent, and so romantic that many locals consistently rate it the best restaurant in P-town. Classic Italian cooking is linked to offerings from Greece, southern France, and even North Africa. There's a nightly char-grilled fish special: match salmon, swordfish, or tuna with a Latin, berber, or Cajun spice rub; lemon-caper butter; or a ginger-soy-wasabi glaze. Tuscan beef barciola with spinach, fresh mozzarella, and prosciutto is essentially a simple dish, but its vibrant flavors show off these traditional ingredients in a new light. The wine list is also a winner. Call well ahead for a reservation, even during the shoulder seasons, when the menu is purely Italian. ☒ 230 Commercial St., Downtown Center ☎ 508/487-9715 ⌣ Reservations essential ▭ AE, D, MC, V ☉ Closed Jan.–mid-May.

$$–$$$ ╳ **Bubala's by the Bay.** Look for the bright yellow building adorned on top with campy carved birds. The kitchen rarely stops, serving breakfast, lunch, and dinner; it's strong on seafood bought directly off local boats. Lobster salad, duck foie gras crostini, seafood cassoulet with white beans and chorizo, and grilled venison rack with currant, sage, and shiitake demi-glaze are wonderfully fresh and tasty. The wine list is priced practically at retail, and the U-shape bar picks up into the evening. Outdoor seating is a social focal point, while quieter indoor seating reaches right down to the bay. It's one of the few Commercial Street restaurants with its own parking lot. ☒ 183 Commercial St. ☎ 508/487-0773 ▭ AE, D, MC, V ☉ Closed late Oct.–late Apr.

$$–$$$ ╳ **Ciro & Sal's.** Tucked inside a cozy house down an alley behind Commercial Street, this long-time local favorite offers a low-key, romantic alternative to some of the town's busier restaurants. The most memorable tables are inside a cozy brick wine cellar; the rest fill a pair of art-filled dining rooms, one of them warmed by a huge fireplace. You can also relax with a cocktail on the garden patio. The restaurant is justly known for its fresh pastas and bountiful salads. Favorite entrées include calamari sautéed with anchovies, lemon, garlic, and cream; and chicken livers sautéed with prosciutto, marsala wine, and sage. ☒ 4 Kiley Ct., Downtown Center ☎ 508/487-6444 ▭ AE, D, MC, V.

$$–$$$ ╳ **Jackson's at the Flagship.** An atmospheric, dark-wood space set on stilts over Cape Cod Bay, this relatively new restaurant serves innovative regional American fare and has an outstanding wine list. The barbecue oysters with slab bacon and blue cheese make for an addictive starter. Tops among the main courses are grilled swordfish with roasted shallot tapenade and lobster-mashed potatoes; and grilled pork tenderloin with a relish of smoked corn, poblano peppers, and black-eyed peas alongside fingerling potatoes. ☒ *463 Commercial St.* ☏ *508/487–2813* ☐ *AE, D, MC, V* ☉ *Closed Jan.–Apr.*

★ **$$–$$$** ✕ **Lorraine's.** Having moved recently into a cozy cottage toward the West End, Lorraine's has a more intimate feel, but the nouvelle Mexican-inspired menu is as good as ever. An appetizer of three large shrimp stuffed with cheese and fresh jalapeños packs a punch, and the enchiladas with fresh crab, cheese, green peppers, tomatoes, capers, and green olives with sauce picante is a revelation. Also wonderful is a mesquite-grilled rack of lamb with roasted-garlic chipotle demi-glaze. The bar draws a loyal, lively crowd and is famous for its long list of premium tequilas. ☒ *133 Commercial St.* ☏ *508/487–6074* ☐ *MC, V* ☉ *Closed 2 wks late Mar.–early Apr. and Mon. and Wed. Apr. and May. No lunch.*

★ **$$–$$$** ✕ **L'Uva.** Something of a hidden gem, L'Uva—which occupies an 1840s cottage—ranks among Provincetown's most sophisticated and memorable small restaurants. The menu works off a novel premise: it's divided into four distinct culinary categories—Italian, French, Spanish, and American, and everything is prepared with artful, innovative flair. For instance, the Frenched pork chops come with lavender-honey sauce, the cod is wrapped in flaky phyllo dough and paired with a feathery spinach-cream sauce, and the filet mignon comes with a tamarind and chipotle demi-glaze. For dessert, the vodka panna cotta with jicama chips in pear-cilantro sauce is a must. ☒ *133 Bradford St.* ☏ *508/487–2010* ☐ *MC, V.*

$$–$$$ ✕ **Napi's.** A steady favorite for its lively ambience and dependable Mediterranean fare, Napi's presents a long and varied menu. The food and the interior share a penchant for unusual, striking juxtapositions—a classical sculpture in front of an abstract canvas, for instance. On the gustatory front, look for sharp combinations such as shrimp Santa Fe, sautéed with tequila, fresh lime juice, cilantro, garlic, roasted chipotle peppers, and black beans with a zippy gazpacho garnish. A cashew vegetable stir-fry with baby bok choy, onions, mushrooms, tomatoes, and broccoli is just one of several very nice vegetarian dishes. ☒ *7 Freeman St., Downtown Center* ☏ *508/487–1145* ⬧ *Reservations essential* ☐ *AE, D, DC, MC, V* ☉ *No lunch May–Sept.*

$$–$$$ ✕ **Ross' Grill.** Likening itself to a French bistro with American tastes, the kitchen here is modest but busy, preparing everything from scratch, including its signature hand-cut, double-dipped French fries. Local fish and shellfish dominate the menu; a favorite is the sautéed local sea scallops with leeks, garlic, and pear tomatoes over linguine. Portions are generous—you'll get eight meaty racks of baby New Zealand lamb—and prices are reasonable. Choose from 75 wines by the glass. The location is grand: up on the second floor of the Whaler's Wharf complex, views of Provincetown Harbor are unlimited. It's a popular place, so expect to wait. ☒ *237 Commercial St., Downtown Center* ☏ *508/ 487–8878* ⬧ *Reservations not accepted* ☐ *AE, MC, V* ☉ *Closed Tues. and Wed. Jan.–Apr.*

$$–$$$ ✕ **Sal's Place.** Tucked away in the peaceful West End, this little waterfront place dishes up massive portions of southern Italian specialties. Calamari and linguine, *vongole* (tiny clams) over pasta, and vegetarian spinach lasagna are all longtime favorites. Carnivores will want to tackle the steak *pizzaiola*—a 25-ounce rib-eye steak served with marinara sauce. The back dining room overlooks the harbor. ⊠ *99 Commercial St., West End* ☎ *508/487–1279* ▭ *MC, V* ☉ *Closed Nov.–Apr. and Mon.–Thurs. early Oct.–mid-June. No lunch.*

$$–$$$ ✕ **Way Downtown.** This snazzy, late-night spot in the center of Commercial Street's action is a noteworthy spot for consistently good Mediterranean-influenced contemporary fare, such as an organic beet salad with frisee, goat cheese, and walnuts. Also try seared tuna loin Niçoise with caper berries, radicchio, haricot vert, egg, and tomato coulis; and pan-roasted pork tenderloin with pancetta and sweet-potato succotash. There's an extensive dessert and cognac list. Way Downtown offers excellent live jazz most nights. There's also a café serving coffees and lighter, less expensive fare. ⊠ *265 Commercial St., Downtown Center* ☎ *508/ 487–8800* ▭ *AE, D, MC, V.*

$–$$$ ✕ **Bayside Betsy's.** Named for the feisty chef and co-owner, this spot has a curious mix of feel-good meals like blackened swordfish and teriyaki pork medallions with splashes of classic French and Italian flavors. Nightly specials often reflect the luck of local fishermen. You might try pan-seared scallops with chorizo and tossed with fettuccine. You can expect reliable food for breakfast, lunch, and dinner year-round, but the real draws are the colorful people-watching and the views of Provincetown Harbor. ⊠ *177 Commercial St.* ☎ *508/487–6566* ⊕ *www.baysidebetsys.com* ▭ *AE, D, MC, V* ☉ *Closed Mon.–Wed. Nov.–May.*

$–$$$ ✕ **Fanizzi's by the Sea.** A dependable, year-round East Ender that sits directly over the bay and offers fine water views, Fanizzi's presents a varied menu heavy on comfort food, but often with a few creative twists. The baked cod is served with a tangy coating of almonds and mustard, and the hearty roasted half-chicken is glazed with fresh garlic, lemon juice, rosemary, and thyme. You can order burgers and substantive dinner salads, including a fine salmon Caesar. The dining room, lined with large windows, is softly lighted and casual. ⊠ *539 Commercial St., East End* ☎ *508/487–1964* ▭ *AE, D, DC, MC, V.*

$–$$$ ✕ **Lobster Pot.** Provincetown's Lobster Pot is fit to do battle with all the lobster shanties anywhere (and everywhere) on the Cape. This hard-working kitchen turns out classic New England cooking: lobsters, generous and filling seafood platters (try the linguine tossed with shrimp, scallops, lobster and Newburg sauce), and some of the best chowder around. The upstairs deck overlooks the comings and goings of the harbor and is a great spot for lunch. There's also a take-out lobster market and bakery on the premises. You'll have to wait in line, but you'll be in the center of town, ideal for people-watching. ⊠ *321 Commercial St., Downtown Center* ☎ *508/487–0842* ⌒ *Reservations not accepted* ▭ *AE, D, DC, MC, V* ☉ *Closed Jan.*

$–$$$ ✕ **The Mews.** This perennial favorite focuses on seafood with a cross-cultural flair. Some popular entrées include roasted vegetable and polenta lasagna with a tomato-olive sauce; and an 8-ounce flatiron steak and scallops with chile butter and a savory bread pudding of applewood-smoked bacon and mushrooms. Downstairs, the main dining room opens onto magnificent harbor views. A piano bar upstairs serves lunch (weekdays in summer) and dinner from a light café menu (burgers, tarragon chicken pot pie). The view of the bay from the bar is near perfect, and the gentle lighting makes this a romantic spot for a drink. Brunch is also served daily in season. The restaurant claims its vodka bar is New England's largest. ⊠ *429 Commercial St.* ☎ *508/487–1500* ⚱ *Reservations not accepted* ▤ *AE, D, DC, MC, V* ☉ *Closed Jan. No lunch weekdays off-season or Sat. mid-Oct.–late May.*

¢–$$ ✕ **Clem & Ursie's.** It's worth the short drive or long walk from downtown to sample the tantalizing seafood prepared at this colorful café, market, and bakery. The mammoth menu touches on just about every kind of food from the ocean: tuna steaks, crab claws, squid stew, Japanese baby octopus salad, hot lobster rolls, lobster scampi—even sushi. A nice range of nonfishy items are offered, too, from pulled pork barbecue to bacon cheeseburgers. You order and pay at the counter and grab a seat inside the decidedly casual dining room; they bring your chow out to you. ⊠ *85 Shank Painter Rd.* ☎ *508/487–2333* ▤ *MC, V* ☉ *Closed Jan.–early Apr.*

Fodor'sChoice ★

¢–$$ ✕ **Post Office Cafe.** A dapper yet casual bistro beneath Provincetown's favorite cabaret bar, the Post Office serves food most nights until 1 AM, making it one of the area's best options for late-evening snacking. The kitchen turns out a mix of substantial but straightforward American entrées, such as chicken piccata over fettuccine, and lighter pub favorites. Sandwiches are a specialty; consider the grilled yellowfin tuna and greens over focaccia, or the grilled portobello mushroom with artichoke, sundried tomatoes, roasted red peppers, feta cheese, and mixed greens on a pita. The place becomes increasingly festive—if even a little raucous—the later it gets. ⊠ *303 Commercial St.* ☎ *508/487–3892* ▤ *AE, D, MC, V.*

¢–$ ✕ **Lagniappe Cafe.** In Creole, "lagniappe" means "that little something extra"—and that's what you'll get at this cozy little joint near Provincetown's movie theater. The café brings the colorful flavors of New Orleans to Provincetown, serving tasty Cajun and Creole dishes alongside traditional Southern comfort foods for breakfast and lunch (or early dinner—they're open until 5). Sample great biscuits and gravy in the morning, or a nice tofu scramble; at lunch dig into Black Angus hot dogs, Cajun chicken, baked mac-and-cheese, or the zesty jambalaya. ⊠ *214 Commercial St.* ☎ *508/487–1200* ▤ *No credit cards.* ☉ *No dinner.*

¢–$ ✕ **Spiritus.** The local bars close at 1 AM, at which point this pizza joint–coffee stand becomes the town's epicenter. It's the ultimate place to see and be seen, pizza slice in hand and witty banter at the ready. In the morning, the same counter serves up restorative coffee and croissants as well as ice cream. ⊠*190 Commercial St.* ☎*508/487–2808* ▤*No credit cards* ☉ *Closed Nov.–Apr.*

¢–$ ✕ **Tofu A Go-Go.** This popular spot for light snacks and quick meals serves consistently fresh vegetarian and vegan fare to a wildly devoted cadre of regulars. It's open for three meals daily. Try tofu breakfast burritos in the morning or gazpacho and the hummus-and-tabouli platter at lunch. Enticing dinner specialties include seasonal veggies sautéed

Fodor'sChoice ★

with spicy Indonesian peanut sauce over brown rice or fettuccine, and the tofu-scallion bowl with tamari-ginger dressing. There's a casual dining area upstairs and more seating out on a front patio. ⊠ *336 Commercial St.* ☎ *508/487–6237* ▭ *No credit cards* ⊘ *No dinner early Sept.–May.*

$$$$ ✕▥ **Red Inn.** A rambling red 1915 house that once hosted Franklin and Eleanor Roosevelt, this small and luxurious inn has been completely refurbished after several years of decline. Most of the airy rooms afford bay views, and all are fitted with big plush beds with high-thread-count linens, goosedown comforters, and pillow-top mattresses. Other luxe amenities include radio–CD players, phones with voice mail, and high-speed Internet. The Cape Light Room contains a decorative fireplace with an ornate hand-painted fresco, and the secluded Chauffer's Cottage has a living room with a soaring vaulted ceilings and a sundeck with far-reaching water views. The low-key, intimate restaurant ($$$–$$$$) serves superb contemporary fare. Start off with the sweet and chunky lobster-corn chowder, before moving on to pepper-crusted filet mignon with truffle-mashed potatoes and onion-garlic-butter sauce. The fresh salmon wrapped with rice paper and sesame seeds and served with ginger dressing, cucumber salad, and sticky rice is also excellent. ⊠ *15 Commercial St., 02657* ☎ *508/487–7334 or 866/473–3466* ▤ *508/487–5115* ⊕ *www.theredinn.com* ↶ *4 rooms, 2 suites, 2 cottages* ⚎ *Restaurant, room service, refrigerators, in-room data ports, cable TV, in-room VCRs, in-room hot tubs, massage, free parking; no kids under 18, no smoking* ▭ *AE, MC, V* ¦○¦ *CP.*

$$–$$$ ✕▥ **The Commons.** Built as an inn in the 1860s, this combination guesthouse and bistro run by Carl Draper and Chuck Rigg has tasteful rooms with wide-board floors, antique furnishings, Oriental carpets, and marble-tile baths. Most rooms can claim a view of the bay; some have balconies. All have TVs and air-conditioning. The bistro ($–$$$) presents an innovative, ever-changing continental menu that lists dishes such as Moroccan barbecue leg of lamb with harissa and apricot chutney, minted couscous, and sautéed greens, plus several inventive wood-fired pizzas. They have an outstanding brunch. You can relax in the garden or at the deck bar that overlooks the bay. ⊠ *386 Commercial St., 02657* ☎ *508/ 487–7800 or 800/487–0784* ▤ *508/487–0358* ⊕ *www.commonsghb. com* ↶ *14 rooms* ⚎ *Restaurant, bar, cable TV* ▭ *AE, MC, V* ⊘ *Restaurant closed Jan.–mid-Feb., guesthouse closed Dec.–Apr.* ¦○¦ *CP.*

$$$$ ▥ **Esther's.** Named most affectionately for the late Ms. Chamberlain, a former owner, this inn captures all the glamour and ritzy sophistication that embodies her reputation. Many believe that Esther has never actually left the place—in spirit, anyway. Rooms are serene and cleanly elegant, with custom-designed, Italian-built blond-wood furniture, butterscotch imported marble in all bathrooms, and such luxuries as water views, high-thread-count sheets, hot tubs or large soaking tubs— there's even a four-head European shower in one room. Also on hand is a fine dining restaurant with both indoor and outdoor seating, as well as a downstairs, art deco–style piano bar. It's said that Esther's spirit is most pleased. ⊠ *186 Commercial St., 02657* ☎ *508/487–7555 or 888/873–5001* ▤ *508/487–6611* ⊕ *www.estherlives.com* ↶ *5* *rooms* ⚒ *Restaurant, in-room data ports, refrigerators, cable TV, in-room VCRs, piano bar, free parking; no smoking* ▤ *AE, MC, V* ⊘ *Closed early Jan.–Apr.* |◯| *CP.*

$$$–$$$$ ⊡ **Benchmark Inn & Central.** Made up of two separate buildings on a quiet, narrow street just a block from downtown, this is an inn of simple, refined luxury. Rooms are painted in soothing neutral tones, floors are bare wood, and fresh flowers are placed atop every stainless-steel wet bar. Most rooms have private entrances and fireplaces; some have skylights and private balconies with rooftop and water views. When you're ready to turn in, indulge in the nightly turndown service. There are also three very large and cushy penthouse suites. ✉ *6 & 8 Dyer St., 02657* ☎ *508/487–7440 or 888/487–7440* 🖷 *508/487–3446* ⊕ *www.benchmarkinn.com* ⇄ *11 rooms, 3 suites* ⚒ *Minibars, refrigerators, cable TV, in-room VCRs, pool, 2 hot tubs, sauna, laundry service, concierge, airport shuttle, free parking; no smoking* ▤ *AE, MC, V* ⊘ *Closed Jan.–late Feb.*

★ **$$$–$$$$** ⊡ **Brass Key.** One of Provincetown's most luxurious resorts, the Brass Key comprises a beautifully restored main house—originally an 1828 sea captain's home—and several other carefully groomed buildings and cottages. Rooms mix antiques with such modern amenities as Bose stereos and TV–VCRs. Deluxe rooms also come with gas fireplaces and whirlpool baths or French doors opening out to wrought-iron balconies. A widow's-walk sundeck has a panoramic view of Cape Cod Bay. Complimentary cocktails are served in the courtyard; in winter, wine is served before a roaring fire in the common room. As is true of many of Provincetown's smaller hotels, the Brass Key draws a largely gay clientele, especially in summer, but the owners and staff make everyone feel welcome and pampered. ✉ *67 Bradford St., 02657* ☎ *508/487–9005 or 800/842–9858* 🖷 *508/487–9020* ⊕ *www.brasskey.com* ⇄ *36 rooms* ⚒ *In-room safes, some in-room hot tubs, cable TV, in-room VCRs, hot tubs, pool; no children under 16, no smoking* ▤ *AE, D, MC, V* ⊘ *Closed late Nov.–mid-Apr. except for New Year's week* |◯| *CP.*

$$$–$$$$ ⊡ **Crown & Anchor.** If you're looking to eat, sleep, and live amid the pulsing entertainment center of Provincetown, then this is just the place. Upstairs from the daily clamor of drag shows and discos are 18 pleasant rooms adorned with Oriental rugs and deep cranberry hues, calm cover from the ongoing festivities below. Deluxe rooms have whirlpool tubs, fireplaces, and private balconies facing Provincetown Harbor, while all rooms have the choice of a king or two full-size beds. In addition, two rooms are fully ADA compliant. Complimentary continental breakfast is served, but why not take advantage of the complete room service and simply stay in bed? ✉ *247 Commercial St., 02657* ☎ *508/487–1430* 🖷 *508/487–3237* ⊕ *www.onlyatthecrown.com* ⇄ *18 rooms* ⚒ *2 restaurants, in-room data ports, some in-room hot tubs, minibars, microwaves, refrigerators, cable TV, pool, beach, 5 bars, lounge, cabaret, dance club, business services* ▤ *AE, D, MC, V* |◯| *CP.*

$$$–$$$$ ⊡ **Crowne Pointe Historic Inn.** Meticulously created from four different
Fodor'sChoice buildings, this inn has not left a single detail unattended. Owners Tom
★ Walter and David Sanford skillfully mix luxury and comfort. Period fur-

niture and antiques fill the common areas and rooms; a queen-size bed is the smallest you'll find, dressed in 250-thread-count linens, with treats on the pillow for nightly turndown service. Many rooms have fireplaces: in one room, view the flames from your bed or the whirlpool tub. Penthouse suites have two floors of living space with a full kitchen; and many rooms have private balconies with water or town views. The grounds are accented with brick pathways, flowers, and trees. All rooms are equipped with high-speed DSL. A stunning new day spa was added in 2004. Start the day with a full, hot breakfast and graze freshly baked treats and wine and cheese in the afternoon. ⊠ *82 Bradford St., 02657* ☎ *508/487–6767 or 877–276–9631* 🖷 *508/487–5554* ⊕ *www. crownepointe.com* 🛏 *37 rooms, 3 suites* ⚲ *In-room data ports, some in-room hot tubs, some kitchens, some microwaves, refrigerators, cable TV, in-room VCRs, spa, pool, 2 outdoor hot tubs, laundry service, concierge, business services, airport shuttle, free parking; no smoking* 🖃 *AE, D, MC, V* 🍽 *BP.*

$$$–$$$$ 🏨 **Watermark Inn.** A modern all-suites inn facing the bay at the very east end of Commercial Street, the Watermark has enormous accommodations with separate living/dining rooms, making it a favorite for longer stays (weekly or daily rates are available in summer; rates are daily the rest of the year). Although these airy suites with tall windows feel more like rental condos than hotel rooms, they do come with fine linens and daily maid service. It's a very private setup, and guests enjoy plenty of independence. Four suites on the top level have private sundecks and panoramic water views; two less-expensive ground-floor units overlook a courtyard. ⊠ *603 Commercial St., 02657* ☎ *508/487–0165* 🖷 *508/ 487–2383* ⊕ *www.watermark-inn.com* 🛏 *10 suites* ⚲ *Kitchens or kitchenettes, cable TV; no smoking* 🖃 *MC, V.*

★ $$–$$$$ 🏨 **Bayshore and Chandler House.** This beautifully kept apartment complex on the water, ½ mi from the town center, is a great option for longer stays. Many of the units have decks, fireplaces, and large water-view windows; all have full kitchens, modern baths, and phones. Number 8 is like a light, bright beach house on the water, with three glass walls, cathedral ceilings, private deck, dining table, and chairs. Number 20 has a fireplace and a home-style kitchen. Rental is mostly by the week in season; there's a two-night minimum off-season. ⊠ *493 Commercial St., 02657* ☎ *508/487–9133* 🖷 *508/487–0520* ⊕ *www.bayshorechandler. com* 🛏 *27 apartments* ⚲ *Kitchens, cable TV, some in-room VCRs, beach, some pets allowed* 🖃 *AE, MC, V.*

$$–$$$$ 🏨 **Beaconlight Guesthouse.** The English country interior includes designer wallpaper, freshly painted walls, antiques, and extra pillows on your bed; modern conveniences include VCRs, CD radios, and phones with voice mail. Outside, three decks provide varied, stunning views of the entire town and the harbor, and an outdoor hot tub invites soaks under the night skies. The guesthouse is between busy Commercial and Bradford streets, so it's close to everything but still relatively quiet. The owners also run the Oxford guesthouse, a short walk away in the West End; it's similarly well-decorated and has six rooms and one suite. ⊠ *12 Winthrop St., 02657* ☎ *508/487–9603 or 800/696–9603* ⊕ *www. beaconlightguesthouse.com* 🛏 *8 rooms, 2 suites* ⚲ *In-room data ports,* *refrigerators, cable TV, in-room VCRs, outdoor hot tub* ⊟ *AE, D, DC, MC, V* ⵋ⃝| *CP.*

$$-$$$$ ⊡ **Fairbanks Inn.** This meticulously restored colonial inn a block from Commercial Street includes the 1776 main house and auxiliary buildings. Guest rooms have four-poster or canopy beds, Oriental rugs on wide-board floors, and antique furnishings; some have fireplaces or kitchens. Many original touches remain here, from the 18th-century wallpaper to artifacts from the inn's first residents. The baths are on the small side, but they help preserve the colonial integrity of the home. The wicker-filled sunporch and the garden are good places for afternoon cocktails. ⊠ *90 Bradford St., 02657* ☎ *508/487–0386 or 800/324–7265* ⊕ *www.fairbanksinn.com* ⇆ *13 rooms, 1 efficiency* ⚇ *Some kitchens, cable TV, some in-room VCRs, free parking* ⊟ *AE, MC, V* ⵋ⃝| *CP.*

$$-$$$$ ⊡ **Officer's Quarters.** Built in 1887 for a sea captain, this stately mansard-roof Victorian (formerly called Captain and His Ship) is only a short walk from the center of town and is across the street from Provincetown bay. New owners bought the property in 2003 and have done a wonderful job adding their own touches and maintaining this B&B's outstanding reputation. Room 3, done in vibrant reds, has a four-poster bed, a gas fireplace, and private access to the garden. Most rooms have water views; some have private decks. ⊠ *164 Commercial St., 02657* ☎ *508/487–1850 or 800/400–2278* ⊕ *www.officersquarters.org* ⇆ *6 rooms* ⚇ *Refrigerators, cable TV, in-room VCRs; no smoking* ⊟ *MC, V* ⊘ *Closed Nov.–Apr.* ⵋ⃝| *CP.*

★ $$-$$$$ ⊡ **Somerset House Inn.** The owner of this delightful retreat worked in San Francisco for the swanky Kimpton Group boutique hotel chain, and his experience shows in the hip, whimsical decor and superb personal service. From the outside, it looks like a classic 1830s Provincetown house, but inside is a cozy den of mod sofas and cool colors. A communal computer is equipped with high-speed wireless, and you'll find reams of magazines throughout the common areas. Rooms are compact but charming with eclectic themes—safari, Asia, modern. The third-floor units, with pitched ceilings, are especially romantic. Somerset House serves one of the best breakfasts in town and also has an extensive afternoon wine-and-cheese social. ⊠ *378 Commercial St., east of Downtown Center, 02657* ☎ *508/487–0383 or 800/575–1850* ⊟ *508/487–4237* ⊕ *www. somersethouseinn.com* ⇆ *12 rooms* ⚇ *Refrigerators, some in-room hot tubs, cable TV, Internet* ⊟ *AE, D, MC, V* ⵋ⃝| *BP.*

$-$$$$ ⊡ **The Masthead.** Hidden away in the quiet west end of Commercial Street, the Masthead is a charming cluster of shingle houses that overlooks a lush lawn, a 450-foot-long boardwalk, and a private beach. Accommodations include spacious rooms (with microwaves and refrigerators), efficiencies (with kitchenettes), and apartments and cottages (with kitchens); some have verandas facing the water. The cottages, which sleep four to seven, are an ideal choice for families or larger groups and for longer stays (kids under 12 stay free). All units have phones with direct incoming and outgoing calls. The deepwater and in-shore moorings on the property are convenient if you're boating into town. It's one of the few West End properties popular with families. ⊠ *31–41 Commercial St.* ⵘ *Box 577, 02657* ☎ *508/487–0523 or 800/395–5095* ⊟ *508/487–*

9251 ⊕ *www.themasthead.com* ⟿ *7 apartments, 4 cottages, 2 efficiencies, 9 rooms* ♿ *BBQs, some kitchens, some refrigerators, some microwaves, cable TV, some in-room VCRs, beach, dock; no TV in some rooms, parking* ⊟ *AE, D, DC, MC, V.*

$$$ ⊞ **Best Western Chateau Motor Inn.** This may be part of a chain, but the personal attention of owners Charlotte and Bill Gordon, whose family has run the place for decades, shows in the landscaped grounds and in the well-maintained modern rooms with wall-to-wall carpeting and tile baths. Atop a hill with expansive views from picture windows of marsh, dunes, and sea, the motel is a longish walk to the center of town but is relatively close to beaches. ⊠ *105 Bradford St. Ext.* ⬚ *Box 558, 02657* ☎ *508/487–1286 or 800/528–1234* 🖷 *508/487–3557* ⊕ *www. bestwestern.com/chateaumotorinn* ⟿ *54 rooms* ♿ *In-room data ports, refrigerators, cable TV, pool; no smoking* ⊟ *AE, D, DC, MC, V* ⊘ *Closed Nov.–Apr.* ⦿ *CP.*

$$$ ⊞ **Snug Cottage.** Noted for its extensive floral gardens and its enviable perch atop one of the larger bluffs in town, this inn decked in smashing English country antiques and fabrics delights anglophiles. The oversize accommodations have distinctly British names (Victoria Suite, Royal Scott); most are full suites with sitting areas, and many have woodburning fireplaces and private outdoor entrances. The Churchill Suite has 10 big windows overlooking the flowers and bushes outside, and the York Suite has a partial view of Cape Cod Bay. All rooms have phones with voice mail and high-speed Internet, plus clock radios with CD players. Nightly turndown service and plush robes in each room lend a touch of elegance. ⊠ *178 Bradford St., east of Downtown Center, 02657* ☎ *508/487–1616 or 800/432–2334* 🖷 *508/ 487–5123* ⊕ *www.snugcottage.com* ⟿ *3 rooms, 5 suites* ♿ *Some kitchenettes, in-room data ports, cable TV, in-room VCRs; no smoking* ⊟ *AE, D, MC, V* ⦿ *BP.*

$–$$$
⊞ **Christopher's by the Bay.** The rooms in this elegant but reasonably priced art-inspired inn are named after the greats—Rembrandt, Picasso, Monet, van Gogh—and are elegantly appointed with brass beds and rich fabrics. Many have great views of the bay. The building is a graceful old Victorian and is surrounded by carefully maintained gardens and brick patios. Rooms on the upper floors share bathrooms. Set back from the bustle, it's still a quick walk from the center of town. Young and friendly new owners Jason and Ash took over the property in 2003. ⊠ *8 Johnson St., east of Downtown Center, 02657* ☎ *508/487–9263* ☎ *877/ 487–9263* ⊕ *www.christophersbythebay.com* ⟿ *9 rooms, 5 with bath* ♿ *In-room data ports, refrigerators, cable TV, in-room VCRs* ⊟ *AE, MC, V* ⦿ *BP.*

Nightlife & the Arts

THE ARTS   **Provincetown Inn** (⊠ 1 Commercial St., West End ☎ 508/487–9500) hosts several unusual theater productions in summer. Look for shows performed by C.A.P.E. Inc. Theatre and those offered during the Provincetown Fringe Festival in August. There are also nights of live music.

The annual **Provincetown International Film Festival** (☎ 508/487–3456 ⊕ www.ptownfilmfest.com) has become so popular that most of the screenings sell out. Aside from a full schedule of independent films, there are guest appearances by such notables as director John Waters, Lily Tomlin, and Christine Vachon. The festival hits town in mid-June.

Established in 2004 as the new home base for both the Provincetown Repertory Theatre and the Provincetown Theatre Company, the **Provincetown Theater** (✉ 238 Bradford St., Downtown Center ☎ 508/487–7487 or 800/791–7487 ⊕ www.provincetowntheater.org) hosts a wide variety of performances throughout the year, but especially during the summer high season. The Provincetown Repertory Theatre has a summer lineup of classic and modern drama with Equity actors and local talent. The Provincetown Theatre Company presents classics, modern drama, and works by local authors, as well as staged readings and playwriting workshops.

NIGHTLIFE **Atlantic House** (✉ 4 Masonic Pl., Downtown Center ☎ 508/487–3821),
★ the grandfather of the gay night scene, is the only gay bar open year-round. It has several lounge areas and an outdoor patio.

Boatslip Beach Club (✉ 161 Commercial St., Downtown Center, toward West End ☎ 508/487–1669) holds a gay and lesbian tea dance daily in summer and on weekends in spring and fall from 4 to 7 on the outdoor pool deck. The club has indoor and outdoor dance floors. There's ballroom dancing here as well, in addition to two-stepping Thursday through Sunday nights.

The **Cape Cod National Seashore** schedules summer evening programs, such as slide shows, sunset beach walks, concerts (local groups, military bands), and sing-alongs, at its **Province Lands Visitor Center** (✉ Race Point Rd., east of U.S. 6 ☎ 508/487–1256), and sunset campfire talks on the beaches in Provincetown.

Club Euro (✉ 258 Commercial St., Downtown Center ☎ 508/487–2505) has weekend concerts by big names in world music, including African music, Jamaican reggae, Chicago blues, and Louisiana zydeco. The venue, an 1843 Congregational church that later housed a movie theater, is an eerie ocean dreamscape with sea-green walls with a half-submerged three-dimensional mermaid spouting fish, and a black ceiling high above. Pool tables and a late-night menu are available.

The gay-oriented **Crown & Anchor Complex** (✉ 247 Commercial St., Downtown Center ☎ 508/487–1430) has plenty of action—in fact, the most in town—with a video bar, several stages, and a giant disco. Seven nightly shows in summer range from cabaret to comedy.

Governor Bradford Restaurant (✉ 312 Commercial St., Downtown Center ☎ 508/487–9618) is perhaps better known as a sometimes-rowdy pool and dance hall. In the afternoon you can play chess or backgammon at the tables by the window. After 8 PM, the place revs up with live music or a DJ spinning everything from hip-hop to disco.

Pied Piper (✉ 193A Commercial St., Downtown Center, toward West End ☎ 508/487–1527) draws hordes of gay men to its post-tea dance gathering at 6:30 every evening in July and August and weekends during the shoulder seasons. Later in the evening, the crowd is mostly (though not exclusively) women. The club has a deck overlooking the harbor, a small dance floor with a good sound system, and two bars.

The **Post Office Cabaret** (⊠ 303 Commercial St., Downtown Center ☎ 508/487–3892) has long been a dishy and lively spot for piano cabaret. The upstairs lounge draws some of the top talents in the region, and downstairs an excellent restaurant serves dependable American bistro fare until 1 AM most nights.

The **Squealing Pig** (⊠ 335 Commercial St., Downtown Center, toward East End ☎ 508/487–5804) has DJs presenting rock, hip-hop, reggae, and house; they also show late-night movies on Monday. There's never a cover charge.

Vixen (⊠ 336 Commercial St., Downtown Center ☎ 508/487–6424), a lively women's club, gets packed with dancers. On most nights, before the dance crowd sets in, there are both national and local women entertainers. Look for live music and comedy. There are also a couple of pool tables in the front room.

Whalers' Wharf (⊠ 237–241 Commercial St., Downtown Center) resembles an old European marketplace, with a brick pathway that leads straight to the beach and a rotunda theater alive with street performers and entertainment. The first floor of the building holds shops; upstairs are artists' studios and a museum dedicated to the town's history. Off-season, moviegoers can view the latest in independent films, classics, and most types of movies you won't find in the usual megaplex.

Sports & the Outdoors

BEACHES The entire stretch of Commercial Street is backed by the waters of Provincetown Harbor, and most hotels have private beaches. Farther into town there are plenty of places to settle on the sand and take a refreshing dip. Just be mindful of the busy boat traffic.

Herring Cove Beach is relatively calm and warm for a National Seashore beach, but is not as pretty as some since its parking lot isn't hidden behind dunes. However, the lot to the right of the bathhouse is a great place to watch the sunset. There's a hot dog stand, showers, and restrooms. Lifeguards are on duty in season. From mid-June through Labor Day, parking costs $10 per day, or $30 for a yearly pass to all National Seashore beaches.

For a day of fairly private beachcombing and great views, you can walk across the stone jetty at low tide to **Long Point,** a sand spit south of town with two lighthouses and two Civil War bunkers, called Fort Useless and Fort Ridiculous because they were hardly needed. It's a 2-mi walk across soft sand—beware of poison ivy and deer ticks if you detour from the path—or hire a boat at **Flyer's** (☎ 508/487–0898) to drop you off and pick you up; the cost is $8 one-way, $12 round-trip.

FodorsChoice **Race Point Beach** (⊠ Race Point Rd., east of U.S. 6), one of the Cape Cod
★ National Seashore beaches in Provincetown, has a wide swath of sand stretching far off into the distance around the point and Coast Guard

station. Behind the beach is pure duneland, and bike trails lead off the parking lot. Because of its position on a point facing north, the beach gets sun all day long, whereas the east coast beaches get fullest sun early in the day. Parking is available, there are showers and restrooms, and lifeguards are stationed in season. From mid-June through Labor Day, parking costs $10 per day, or $30 for a yearly pass good at all National Seashore beaches.

BIKING   **Arnold's** (✉ 329 Commercial St., Downtown Center ☎ 508/487–0844) rents all types of bikes, children's included.

The **Beech Forest bike trail** (✉ Off Race Point Rd., east of Rte. 6) in the National Seashore offers an especially nice ride through a shady forest to Bennett Pond.

Gale Force Bikes (✉ 144 Bradford St. Ext. ☎ 508/487–4849) stocks a wide variety of bikes for sale and for rent; it's a good source for parts and repairs, too.

Nelson's Bicycle Shop (✉ 43 Race Point Rd., east of U.S. 6 ☎ 508/487– 8849), across from the Beech Forest bike trail, rents bikes of all sizes and types, including trailers, and has a deli with picnic-ready food; parking is free.

The **Province Lands Trail** is a 5¼-mi loop off the Beech Forest parking lot on Race Point Road, with spurs to Herring Cove and Race Point beaches and to Bennett Pond. The paths wind up and down hills amid dunes, marshes, woods, and ponds, affording spectacular views. More than 8 mi of bike trails lace through the dunes, cranberry bogs, and scrub pine of the National Seashore, with many access points, including Herring Cove and Race Point.

Ptown Bikes (✉ 42 Bradford St., east of Downtown Center ☎ 508/487– 8735) has Trek and Mongoose mountain bikes at good rates. The shop also provides free locks and maps.

BOATING   **Bay Lady II Excursion Schooner** (✉ MacMillan Wharf, Downtown Center ☎ 508/487–9308), a beautiful 73-foot sailing vessel, heads out for two-hour cruises three times daily. You're welcome to bring your own spirits and snacks for this scenic and peaceful sail.

Flyer's Boat Rental (✉ 131A Commercial St., West End ☎ 508/487–0898) has kayaks, surfbikes, Sunfish, Hobies, Force 5s, Lightnings, powerboats, and rowboats. Flyer's will also shuttle you to Long Point.

FISHING   You can go for fluke, bluefish, and striped bass on a walk-on basis from spring through fall with **Cap'n Bill & Cee Jay** (✉ MacMillan Wharf, Downtown Center ☎ 508/487–4330).

HORSEBACK   **Bayberry Hollow Farm** (✉ 27 W. Vine St. Ext., West End ☎ 508/487–
RIDING   6584) has pony rides year-round.

The **Province Lands Horse Trails** lead to the beaches through or past dunes, cranberry bogs, forests, and ponds.

TENNIS **Bissell's Tennis Courts** (✉ 21 Bradford St. Ext., east of Downtown Center ☎ 508/487–9512) has five clay courts and offers lessons. It's open from late May to September.

Provincetown Tennis Club (✉ 286 Bradford St. Ext., east of Downtown Center ☎ 508/487–9574) has five clay and two hard courts open to non-members; you can also take lessons with the resident tennis pro.

TOURS **Art's Dune Tours** (✉ Commercial and Standish Sts., Downtown Center
Fodor'sChoice ☎ 508/487–1950 or 800/894–1951 ⊕ www.artsdunetours.com) has been
★ taking eager passengers into the dunes of Province Lands for more than 50 years. Bumpy but controlled rides transport you through sometimes surreal sandy vistas peppered with beach grass and along shoreline patrolled by seagulls and sandpipers. Tours are filled with lively tales, including the fascinating history of the exclusive (and reclusive) dune shacks (18 still stand today). These 1- to 1½-hour tours are offered several times daily; especially intriguing are the sunset and moonlight tours. The rides coupled with clambakes or barbecues are popular; call for availability and pricing.

Harbor Tours on the Viking Princess (✉ MacMillan Wharf, Downtown Center ☎ 508/487–7323) are given in mornings throughout the summer. These narrated harbor excursions tell stories of shipwrecks and pirate raids and pass by Civil War forts and the Long Point Lighthouse.

WHALE- One of the joys of Cape Cod is spotting whales while they're swimming
WATCHING in and around the feeding grounds at Stellwagen Bank, about 6 mi off the tip of Provincetown. On a sunny day the boat ride out into open ocean is part of the pleasure, but the thrill, of course, is in seeing these great creatures. You might spot minke whales; humpbacks (who put on the best show when they breach); finbacks; or perhaps the most endangered great whale species, the right whale. Dolphins are a welcome sight as well; they play in the boat's bow waves. Many people also come aboard for birding, especially during spring and fall migration. You can see gannets, shearwaters, and storm petrels, among many others. Several boats take you out to sea (and bring you back) with morning, afternoon, or sunset trips lasting from three to four hours. All boats have food service, but remember to take sunscreen and a sweater or jacket—the breeze makes it chilly. Some boats stock seasickness pills, but if you're susceptible, come prepared.

The municipal parking area by the harbor in Provincetown fills up by noon in summer. Consider taking a morning boat to avoid crowds and the hottest sun. And although April may be cold, it's one of the better months for spotting whales, who at that time have just migrated north after mating and are very hungry. Good food is, after all, what brings the whales to this part of the Atlantic.

Dolphin Fleet tours are accompanied by scientists from the Center for Coastal Studies in Provincetown who provide commentary while collecting data on the whale population they've been monitoring for years. They know many of the whales by name and will tell you about their habits and histories. Reservations are required. ✉ *Ticket office: Cham-*

DUNE SHACKS

PROVINCETOWN'S rich artistic legacy continues to manifest itself in the dozens of galleries along Commercial Street and through the countless resident writers and painters. But out along the seashore, along a 3-mi stretch of sand extending from about Race Point to High Head (in Truro), you can see a more unusual remnant of the town's artistic past—the dune shacks.

Originally, in the 19th century, these small, austere structures were built by the Life Saving Service to house seamen. But in more recent times, they've been occupied by artists seeking solitude in the magnificent scenery. The terrain that holds these 18 shacks remains about as wild and untamed today as it was 150 years ago.

Sometime around the 1920s, long after the dune shacks stopped housing life-saving personnel, many of the community's creative or eccentric spirits began using them as retreats and hideaways. Probably the most famous of these was playwright Eugene O'Neill, who purchased one and spent many summers there with his wife, Agnes Boulton. O'Neill penned Anna Christie (1920) and The Hairy Ape (1921) while living in his shack, and in doing so gave the whole collection of dune shacks something of an arty cachet.

Other Provincetown artists soon followed O'Neill, including the self-proclaimed "poet of the dunes," Harry Kemp, who wrote many a verse about the seashore's stark, desolate splendor. Author Hazel Hawthorne-Werner wrote The Salt House, a memoir tracing her time amid the dunes, in 1929. It's said that this book helped get the shacks, along with the entire dunes district, onto the National Register of Historic Places, helping to preserve them for years to come. In later years, Jack Kerouac, e. e. cummings, Norman Mailer, and Jackson Pollack have lived at different times in these primitive structures.

The generally primitive structures haven't been modernized much—none have electricity, running water, or toilets. You stay in them for a chance to be with nature and perhaps commune with the artistic spirits of the many who have gone before you. Many of the people fortunate enough to have a chance to stay in a dune shack these days find their experiences to be highly inspirational.

The dune shacks are now all set along part of the Cape Cod National Seashore known as the Province Lands. The park owns most of the Provincetown dune shacks, though a few are managed by nonprofit groups aimed at preserving them and their legacy; some of these organizations, such as the Peaked Hills Bars Trust and the Provincetown Community Compact, allow visitors to stay in the dune shacks through a variety of arrangements. Both groups run an artist-in-residence program—artists can apply for short stays in some of the shacks during the summer season. Only a handful of applicants are admitted each year.

If you're not an artist, you can enter a lottery for the opportunity to lease one of the shacks for a week in spring or fall. If you're interested in applying to spend time in a dune shack or joining one of the nonprofit organizations that sponsors them, contact **Dune Shacks** (Box 1705, Provincetown, 02657, 508/487–3635).

If you're simply interested in exploring the terrain and seeing the shacks, you can either book a tour with **Art's Dune Tours** (508/487–1950 or 800/894–1951 or www.artsdunetours.com), or park behind the Cape Inn, on Snail Road just off U.S. 6, where a 3-mi trail leads through the dunes and by many of the dune shacks.

— by Andrew Collins

ber of Commerce building at MacMillan Wharf, Downtown Center ☎ *508/240–3636 or 800/826–9300* ⊕ *www.whalewatch.com* 🎫 *$24* 🕐 *Tours Apr.–Oct.*

The **Portuguese Princess** sails with a naturalist on board to narrate. The snack bar sells Portuguese specialties. *Tickets* ✉ *70 Shank Painter Rd., ticket office, east of Downtown Center* ✉ *Whale Watchers General Store, 309 Commercial St., Downtown Center* ☎ *508/487–2651 or 800/442–3188* ⊕ *www.princesswhalewatch.com* 🎫 *$24* 🕐 *Tours May–Oct.*

Shopping

ART GALLERIES **Albert Merola Gallery** (✉ 424 Commercial St., Downtown Center, toward East End ☎ 508/487–4424) focuses on 20th-century and contemporary master prints and Picasso ceramics, and showcases artists from in and around Provincetown, Boston, and New York, including James Balla and Richard Baker.

Bangs Street Gallery (✉ 432 Commercial St., Downtown Center, toward East End ☎ 508/487–0743) represents contemporary artists as well as those from the 1970s.

Berta Walker Gallery (✉ 208 Bradford St., east of Downtown Center, toward East End ☎ 508/487–6411) specializes in Provincetown-affiliated artists, including Selina Trieff, Nancy Whorf, and many of the artists who migrated here from the now-defunct Long Point Gallery.

The **DNA Gallery** (✉ 288 Bradford St., east of Downtown Center, toward East End ☎ 508/487–7700) represents artists working in various media, including many emerging talents. The gallery also hosts readings, films, and concerts.

Hilda Neily Art Gallery (✉ 432 Commercial St., Downtown Center, towards East End ☎ 508/487–6300) is named for its featured artist, who was once a student of impressionist painter Henry Hensche. Her oil paintings follow the same tradition of magical light and color.

Julie Heller Gallery (✉ 2 Gosnold St., Downtown Center ☎ 508/487–2169) has contemporary artists as well as some Provincetown icons. The gallery has works from the Sol Wilson and Milton Avery estates, as well as those from such greats as Robert Motherwell and Blanche Lazzell.

Rice/Polak Gallery (✉ 430 Commercial St., Downtown Center, toward East End ☎ 508/487–1052) stocks a remarkably comprehensive and eclectic variety of contemporary works, from paintings and pastels to photography and sculpture. More than 50 prominent artists regularly exhibit here.

★ The **Schoolhouse Center** (✉ 494 Commercial St., Downtown Center, toward East End ☎ 508/487–4800) houses Driskel, Silas Kenyon, and Paula Horn Kotis galleries. It has changing exhibitions of antiques as well as the works of local and national artists and photographers. A schedule of performing- and visual-arts classes is available year-round, and the center has a Summer Reading Series on Thursday evening at 8. The center is open Thursday–Monday. Upstairs are the offices and studios for Provincetown's famed WOMR radio station.

Simie Maryles Gallery (✉ 435 Commercial St., Downtown Center, toward East End ☎ 508/487–7878) represents about 10 contemporary artists, most of them working in traditional styles. Oil paintings, glasswork, ceramics, and metal sculpture are among the strong suits here.

The **William-Scott Gallery** (✉ 439 Commercial St., Downtown Center, toward East End ☎ 508/487–4040) primarily shows contemporary works such as John Dowd's reflective, realistic Cape 'scapes.

SPECIALTY STORES **Far Side of the Wind** (✉ 389 Commercial St., Downtown Center, toward East End ☎ 508/487–3963) stocks new age paraphernalia, including some intriguing Native American jewelry and artifacts, gifts, books, and music. Psychic readings are also available.

Giardelli Antonelli (✉ 417 Commercial St., Downtown Center, toward East End ☎ 508/487–3016) sells quality handmade clothing by local designers. Hand-knit sweaters are especially popular.

Angel Foods (✉ 467 Commercial St., Downtown Center, toward East End ☎ 508/487–6666) offers a great selection of gourmet and organic foods—juices, breads, ethnic specialty groceries, free-range meats, fine cheeses. It's a great resource if you're renting a place in town or stocking up for a picnic by the beach.

Impulse (✉ 188 Commercial St., Downtown Center, toward West End ☎ 508/487–1154) has contemporary American crafts, including jewelry and an extraordinary kaleidoscope collection. The Autograph Gallery exhibits framed photographs, letters, and documents signed by celebrities.

Kidstuff (✉ 381 Commercial St., Downtown Center, toward East End ☎ 508/487–0714) carries unusual, colorful children's wear.

★ **Marine Specialties, Inc.** (✉ 235 Commercial St., Downtown Center ☎ 508/487–1730) is full of treasures, knickknacks, and clothing. Here you can purchase some very reasonably priced casual and military-style clothing, as well as seashells, marine supplies, stained-glass lamps, candles, rubber sharks (you get the idea), and prints of old advertisements.

Moda Fina (✉ 349 Commercial St., Downtown Center ☎ 508/487–6632) displays an eclectic selection of women's fashions, shoes, and jewelry—everything from flowing linen or silk night wear to funky and casual pieces. Unique Mexican crafts are also for sale.

Provincetown Antique Market (✉ 131 Commercial St., Downtown Center, toward West End ☎ 508/487–1115) has one of the town's better selections of vintage lighting, jewelry, Bakelite, costumes, toys, textiles, and furnishings.

Remembrances of Things Past (✉ 376 Commercial St., Downtown Center, toward East End ☎ 508/487–9443) deals with articles from the 1920s to the 1960s, including Bakelite and other jewelry, telephones, neon items, ephemera, and autographed celebrity photographs.

Silk & Feathers (✉ 377 Commercial St., Downtown center, toward East End ☎ 508/487–2057) carries an assortment of fine lingerie, women's clothing, and jewelry.

Tim's Used Books (✉ 242 Commercial St., Downtown Center ☎ 508/487–0005) has volumes of volumes—rooms of used-but-in-good-shape books, including some rare and out-of-print texts. It's a great place to browse for that perfect book to read on vacation.

Wa (✉ 184 Commercial St., Downtown Center, toward West End ☎ 508/487–6355) is an oasis of peace and Zenlike tranquillity. Unusual and Japanese-inspired items include fountains, home accent pieces, and framed (and sometimes frightening) tropical insects.

West End Antiques (✉ 146 Commercial St., Downtown Center, toward West End ☎ 508/487–6723) sells everything from $4 postcards to a $3,000 model ship. Handmade dolls and high-quality glassware—Steuben, Orrefors, and Hawkes—are also available.

THE OUTER CAPE A TO Z

To research prices, get advice from other travelers, and book travel arrangements, visit www.fodors.com.

AIR TRAVEL

CARRIERS Cape Air/Nantucket Airlines flies direct from Boston to Hyannis and Provincetown year-round and from New Bedford to Martha's Vineyard and Nantucket. There's also seasonal (midsummer–early Sept.) service between Provincetown and Nantucket. Cape Air has joint baggage agreements with eight major U.S. airlines and with KLM.

🛪 Airline & Contact : **Cape Air/Nantucket Airlines** ☎ 508/771–6944 or 800/352–0714 ⊕ www.flycapeair.com.

AIRPORTS

Cape Air serves Boston year-round from Provincetown Municipal Airport (PVC).

🛪 Airport Information **Provincetown Municipal Airport** ✉ Race Point Rd. ☎ 508/487–0241.

BIKE TRAVEL

Despite the heavy summertime traffic, the Outer Cape is quite blessed with bike trails. *See* Biking *in* Pleasures and Pastimes, *above.* Off-road, the sandy, pine needle–covered trails of miles of fire roads traverse the National Seashore on the ocean side, from Wellfleet all the way on up to Truro. Bikers with thick wheels, stamina, and ambition will find hours of uninterrupted time with which to ride these trails, coming upon little other life than squirrels, birds, and the occasional deer. Provincetown is very bike-friendly, as cycling is a far better way to get around than driving in summer. There are several stunning trails within the grounds of the Province Lands that will take riders through dunes and forest and alongside salt marshes.

Black Duck Sports Shop rents several kinds of bikes. Gale Force Bikes stocks a wide variety of bikes for sale and for rent; it's a good source for parts and repairs, too. Bayside Bikes rents bicycles by the hour, day, or week, with easy access to the Head of the Meadow Trail. Cape Outback Adventures, in Truro, has friendly instruction and guided tours for kayakers, mountain bikers, and beginning surfers. These trips are designed for those of all ages and skill levels. Arnold's rents all types of bikes, children's included. Nelson's Bike Shop and Rentals, across from the Beech Forest bike trail, rents bikes of all sizes and types, including trailers, and has a deli with picnic-ready food; parking is free. Ptown Bikes has Trek and Mongoose mountain bikes at good rates; the shop also provide free locks and maps.

🚲 Bike Rentals **Arnold's** ✉ 329 Commercial St., Downtown Center ☎ 508/487-0844. **Bayside Bikes** ✉ 102 Rte. 6A, North Truro ☎ 508/487-5735. **Black Duck Sports Shop** ✉ U.S. 6 at LeCount Hollow Rd., South Wellfleet ☎ 508/349-9801. **Cape Outback Adventures** ☎ 508/349-1617 or 800/864-0070 ⊕ www.capeoutback.com. **Gale Force Bikes** ✉ 144 Bradford St. Ext. ☎ 508/487-4849. **Nelson's Bicycle Shop** ✉ 43 Race Point Rd., east of U.S. 6 ☎ 508/487-8849. **Ptown Bikes** ✉ 42 Bradford St., east of Downtown Center ☎ 508/487-8735.

BOAT & FERRY TRAVEL

Bay State Cruise Company offers both standard and high-speed ferry service between Commonwealth Pier in Boston and MacMillan Wharf in Provincetown. High-speed service runs daily from late May through late September and costs $58 round-trip; the ride takes 90 minutes. Standard service runs Friday through Sunday from mid-June through early September and costs $29 round-trip; the ride costs three hours. On either ferry, the round-trip charge for bikes is $10.

Capt. John Boats' passenger ferry makes the 1½- to 2-hour trip between Plymouth's State Pier and Provincetown from Memorial Day to mid-June, weekends; mid-June to Labor Day, daily. Schedules allow for day excursions. Fares are $30 round-trip, and bicycles are an additional $3.

🚢 Boat & Ferry Lines **Bay State Cruise Company** ☎ 617/748-1428 in Boston, 508/487-9284 in Provincetown ⊕ www.baystatecruisecompany.com. **Capt. John Boats'** ☎ 508/747-2400 or 800/242-2469 ⊕ www.provincetownferry.com.

BUS TRAVEL

Plymouth & Brockton Street Railway provides bus service to Provincetown from downtown Boston and Logan Airport, with stops en route. The Logan Direct airport express service bypasses downtown Boston and makes stops in Plymouth, Sagamore, Barnstable, and Hyannis. The company also has service between Boston and Provincetown, with stops at many towns in between, including Wellfleet center, Truro, and Provincetown. Round-trip fares from the Outer Cape range from $39 to $45 to Boston, and $48 to $54 to Logan.

The Shuttle, run by the Cape Cod Regional Transit Authority, provides a much-needed transportation boost. The shuttle begins its route at Dutra's Market in Truro and continues to Provincetown along Route 6A; it stops wherever a passenger or roadside flagger dictates. Once in Provincetown, the shuttle continues up Bradford Street, with alternating trips to Herring Cove Beach and Pilgrim Park as well as summertime service up to Provincetown Airport and Race Point Beach. It runs every 20 minutes and is outfitted to carry bicycles. The service is popular and reasonably priced ($1 for a single fare, $3 for a day pass), and the only trouble seems to be finding parking on the Truro end. Plans are in the works to find alternative areas for parking. The shuttle runs from late May until mid-October, with more limited service during the spring and fall.

There are no bus stations or depots, per se, in the Outer Cape, though there are designated stops within each town: in Provincetown, in front of the Chamber of Commerce office on Commercial Street; in Truro, Dutra's Market–Route 6A (Shore Road); in North Truro, Depot Road, near the Truro Post Office and Jams store; in Wellfleet, D&D Market, U.S. 6, in South Wellfleet, in front of Town Hall, Main Street, and Wellfleet Village.

⑪ Bus Lines Plymouth & Brockton Street Railway ☎ 508/746-0378 ⊕ www.p-b.com. **Shuttle** ☎ 800/352-7155 ⊕ www.capecodtransit.org.

CAR TRAVEL
From the Bourne Bridge to Provincetown, expect to be in your car for a good hour and a half—and that's when traffic is light. During peak driving times (Friday afternoon and Saturday), expect lengthy delays on U.S. 6 at Exit 9 and then again just before the Wellfleet town line—here U.S. 6 narrows to one lane. For a more pleasant drive that will avoid aggravating delays (but won't get you there faster), detour on historic Route 6A. From the bridge to Orleans the road ambles alongside some beautiful old sea captains' homes and dozens of shops.

Driving to Provincetown from other points on the Cape is mostly a scenic adventure. The wooded surrounds of Truro break into a breathtaking expanse of open water and sand dunes, with the skyline of Provincetown beyond. The busiest time is early morning—especially on days when the sun is reluctant to shine—when it seems that everyone on Cape Cod is determined to make it to Provincetown. Traffic is heaviest around Wellfleet, and since the road is just one lane until North Truro, it can be slow going. Except during the traffic-heavy season, you'll find the drive from Wellfleet to Provincetown beautiful and only 25 minutes in duration.

PARKING Parking in Wellfleet is fairly simple: designated lots throughout town are free, though most have time restrictions (two hours). Parking at local inns is not a problem if you are a guest, and if you're staying in town, there's little need to take your car to any in-town sites. Most restaurants have parking. There really is no town center in Truro, so parking is typically available throughout town.

In Provincetown, parking is not so simple. There are a few public parking lots, in which cars pay by the hour (usually about $2 an hour). Also spread around the downtown area are private parking areas, where a set price is designated for parking for the day, usually about $10 per day. Parking on Commercial Street and on side streets is extremely limited. A few lots have meters, which take quarters and are usually limited to about two hours. Know that tow trucks are eager to remove illegally parked cars, and their retrieval is an expensive and tedious process. Tickets for parking illegally, or in a time-expired zone, cost about $15–$25 per violation. Most accommodations in Provincetown have some parking, but you should always check first if you're bringing a car during busy periods.

TRAFFIC   Weekend traffic is unpleasant, especially Friday evening, Saturday (general turn-around day for weekly rentals), and Sunday afternoon and evening. Traffic during the week can be heavy in July and August; especially on rainy days, when it seems that everyone on Cape Cod is heading for Provincetown. There's basically one road on the Outer Cape, U.S. 6, so there's little to alleviate the trek to Provincetown from Wellfleet.

CHILDREN IN THE OUTER CAPE

Wellfleet is the best Outer Cape community for folks traveling with kids, as Truro has little organized for children and Provincetown is more adult-oriented. The playground at Wellfleet's Baker's Field, near the Skateboard park and tennis courts and Mayo Beach, has all kinds of slides, tunnels, and places to climb, though may be too rowdy for the under-3 set. In Provincetown—on the corner of Nickerson and Bradford streets—there's a playground with both baby swings and regular swings, and separate climbing structures for toddlers and bigger kids. On rainy days, the Wellfleet Library is a hopping spot for children. Temporary borrowing cards are available, and there are two story hours—one for older kids and one for toddlers. Conveniently, public restrooms are accessible from the library's parking lot, and there's a changing table in the women's room.

🔖 Local Information : **Baker's Field** ⊠ Kendrick Ave. just past Wellfleet Town Pier, near Wellfleet Harbor. **Wellfleet Public Library** ⊠ 55 W. Main St. ☎ 508/349-0310.

DISABILITIES & ACCESSIBILITY

Many inns (especially the more modern ones) have handicapped-accessible rooms and facilities. Those with disabilities may have more trouble with inns that are historic in nature; the very architecture and structure makes for narrow passages and stairways. National Seashore beaches are handicapped-accessible; some of the smaller local beaches are not. As for parking, there are many handicapped spaces that are free from meter fees and close to shops, restaurants, and attractions. The Cape Cod Disability Access Directory has information on accessible ATM machines, beaches, lodging, health care, and theater destinations, as well as other pertinent information; try the Web site, ⊕ www.capecoddisability.org.

EMERGENCIES

The closest hospital is in Hyannis (⇨ The Mid Cape A to Z *in* Chapter 4). For rescues at sea call the Coast Guard in Provincetown. Boaters should use Channel 16 on their radios.

Adams Pharmacy is open until 10 PM. A&P Pharmacy offers prescription service until 8 PM.

🔳 Doctors & Dentists **Outer Cape Health Services** ✉ 3130 U.S. 6, Wellfleet ☎ 508/349-3131 ✉ 49 Harry Kemp Way, Provincetown ☎ 508/487-9395. **Provincetown Dental Associates** ✉ 86 Harry Kemp Way ☎ 508/487-9936.

🔳 Emergency Services **Ambulance, fire, police** ☎ 911 or dial township station. **Coast Guard** ☎ 508/487-0070.

🔳 Late-Night Pharmacies **Adams Pharmacy** ✉ 254 Commercial St., Provincetown ☎ 508/487-0069. **A&P Pharmacy** ✉ 28 Shank Painter Rd., Provincetown ☎ 508/487-3738.

LODGING

HOUSE RENTALS Cape Cod Realty lists rentals for Wellfleet, and Atlantic Bay Real Estate specializes in Provincetown rentals but covers all of the Outer Cape. Ruth Gilbert Real Estate also lists Provincetown vacation rentals. Kinlin Grover Vacation Rentals lists available apartments and houses on the Outer Cape.

🔳 Local Agents **Atlantic Bay Real Estate** ✉ 168 Commercial St., Provincetown 02657 ☎ 508/487-2430 ⊕ www.atlanticbayre.com. **Cape Cod Realty** ✉ At U.S. 6 and Old County Rd., Wellfleet 02667 ☎ 508/349-2245 ⊕ www.capecodrealty.net. **Ruth Gilbert Real Estate** ✉ 167 Commercial St., Provincetown 02657 ☎ 508/487-2004 ⊕ www.ruthgilbertrealestate.com. **Kinlin Grover Vacation Rentals** ✉ 2548 U.S. 6, Wellfleet 02657 ☎ 508/349-9000 or 800/444-6756 ⊕ www.vacationcapecod.com.

BED-AND-BREAKFASTS In summer, lodgings should be booked as far in advance as possible—several months for the most popular cottages and B&Bs. Assistance with last-minute reservations is available at the Cape Cod Chamber of Commerce information booths. Off-season rates are much reduced, and service may be more personalized. Most lodging establishments require a minimum stay of three days during peak season and holiday times, and some even command a seven-night minimum.

CAMPING Coastal Acres Camping Court, Inc., in Provincetown, is within walking distance of the town center. There are numerous tent and RV sites, with showers, restrooms, and a small general store for supplies. It's open until November. The only camping permitted on the Cape Cod National Seashore itself is in nonrented, self-contained RVs at Provincetown's Race Point Beach.

🔳 **Coastal Acres Camping Court, Inc.** ✉ W. Vine St. Ext. ☎ 508/487-1700 ⊕ www.coastalacres.com. **Race Point Beach** ✉ Provincetown ☎ 508/349-3785.

MEDIA

The major national New York and Boston newspapers are readily available at most newsstands. The *Cape Codder* focuses on the towns from Harwich to Provincetown, with local news and entertainment. The *Provincetown Banner* covers politics, entertainment, and the arts. *Provincetown Arts* is an annual magazine, published midsummer, on the town's arts scene.

RADIO   The best community station in Provincetown—and throughout the entire Outer Cape—is 92.1, WOMR, on the FM dial, with everything from local-interest talk shows to history to old country, swing, and alternative music.

TAXIS

The companies below provide cab service throughout the Outer Cape. Mercedes Cab Co. offers local and long-distance service in vintage Mercedes sedans.

🚕 Taxi Companies **Cape Cab** ⊠ Provincetown ☎ 508/487-2222. **Mercedes Cab Co.** ⊠ Provincetown ☎ 508/487-3333. **Provincetown Taxi** ⊠ North Truro ☎ 508/487-8294.

TOURS

The gaff-rigged schooner *Bay Lady II* makes two-hour sails, including a sunset cruise, across Provincetown Harbor into Cape Cod Bay; fares are $12 to $18. Private charters are also available. The Provincetown Trolley leaves from the town hall on the hour from 10 to 7 and on the half hour from 10:30 to 3:30; you can also hop on and off at the Provincetown Inn, Province Lands Visitor Center, and Provincetown Art Association. Points of interest on the 40-minute narrated tours include the downtown area and the Cape Cod National Seashore. Tours are available between May and October for $9. For other tours, including whale-watching trips, *see* Outdoor Activities and Sports *in* Provincetown, *above.*

🎟 Fees & Schedules *Bay Lady II* ⊠ MacMillan Wharf, Provincetown ☎ 508/487-9308 ⊕ www.sailcapecod.com. **Provincetown Trolley** ☎ 508/487-9483 ⊕ www.provincetowntrolley.com.

VISITOR INFORMATION

The Provincetown Chamber of Commerce is open from March until New Year's Day. The Provincetown Business Guild specializes in gay tourism, and the office is open year-round. The Truro Chamber of Commerce is open weekends only in June and September, daily in July and August. The Wellfleet Chamber is open from mid-May through Columbus Day.

🏛 Tourist Information : **Provincetown** ⊠ 307 Commercial St. ⌂ Box 1017, 02657 ☎ 508/487-3424 ⊕ www.ptownchamber.com. **Provincetown Business Guild** ⊠ 3 Fremont St., No. 2 ⌂ Box 421-94, 02657 ☎ 508/487-2313 or 800/637-8696 ⊕ www.ptown.com. **Truro** ⊠ U.S. 6 at Head of the Meadow Rd. ⌂ Box 26, North Truro 02652 ☎ 508/487-1288 ⊕ www.trurochamberofcommerce.com. **Wellfleet** ⌂ Box 571, 02667 ☎ 508/349-2510 ⊠ Information center off U.S. 6 in South Wellfleet ⊕ www.wellfleetchamber.com.

UNDERSTANDING CAPE COD

CAPE COD AT A GLANCE

Fast Facts

Type of government: Cape Cod falls within the Barnstable County district, established in 1685 and made up of 15 towns. Nantucket Island belongs to Nantucket County and has just one town, also called Nantucket. Martha's Vineyard is part of Duke's County, made up of the six towns on the Vineyard as well as the town of Gosnold, on Cuttyhunk, which is part of the Elizabeth Islands. The majority of Cape towns still run local government in its most basic form, holding annual town meetings where the registered voters of the community conduct town business and vote major issues.

Capital: The County Seat is in Barnstable Village along Route 6A, also known as the Old King's Highway. Dukes County Seat is in Edgartown. Nantucket County Seat is in Nantucket.

Administrative divisions: Cape Cod has 15 coastal towns, a representative from each town is elected to the county Assembly of Delegates for a term of two years. Nantucket and two small islands Tuckernuck and Muskeget make up Nantucket town. There are just two villages within the town.

Founded: The Vikings explored the Cape as early as 1000 AD. Native Americans have inhabited Cape Cod for more than 10,000 years. Cape Cod's historical European roots began when Bartholomew Gosnold encountered the sandy peninsula surrounded by codfish in 1602, thus dubbing it Cape Cod. In 1620 the Pilgrims arrived in Provincetown Harbor and camped on the Outer Cape before crossing the bay to Plymouth in search of more suitable land. Barnstable County was formed on June 2, 1685, when Plymouth Colony was divided into three counties

Population: Barnstable County: 222,230; Nantucket County: 9,938; Duke's County: 15, 402

Population growth since 1990: Barnstable County: 19.1%; Nantucket County: 58.3%; Duke's County: 28.8%

Language: English

Ethnic groups: Caucasian 94.2%; African-American 1.8%; Native American .6%; Asian .6%; other 2.8%. Portuguese Americans continue to have a strong presence on the Cape. Immigrants forming ethnic conclaves in recent years include the Irish, Brazilians, and those from the former Soviet Republics.

The seashore is a sort of neutral ground, a most advantageous point from which to contemplate this world.
Henry David Thoreau, 1961

Inventions: In 1901 Guglielmo Marconi (1874–1937) sent the first wireless signal across the Atlantic from Wellfleet. Stan Gibbs (1915–2004) changed fishing for saltwater surfcasters trying to nab striped bass with the invention of Stan Gibbs Lures. They are still sold today. The handmade wooden lures invented in 1948 had a weighted center to make long casts easier.

Geography

Cape Cod land area: 395.56 square mi
Natural Resources: Beaches, oceans, lakes, ponds, salt marshes
Cape Cod coastline: 560 mi
Number of ponds and lakes: 350

Terrain: Retreating glaciers formed Cape Cod between 15,000 and 20,000 years ago at the end of the Ice Age. The resulting landscape is low-relief land surface near sea level in most places.

The land is made of sandy soil with clay and gravel beneath. The highest point is 311 feet on Martha's Vineyard followed by 306 feet in Bourne.

Islands: Since the construction of the Cape Cod Canal in 1914, Cape Cod itself is technically a man-made island. The two largest and most visited islands off its coast are Martha's Vineyard and Nantucket. Nantucket has two small islands off its shores—Tuckernuck and Muskeget. The Elizabeth Islands (Nashawena, Pasque, Gosnold, Penikeseare, and Cuttyhunk) are off the coast of New Bedford and primarily privately owned. Cuttyhunk Island is the last in the chain and open to the public. Monomoy Island is a barrier island and coastal wildlife refuge off the coast of Chatham. The barren and scenic Lieutenant's's and Great Islands are off the shores of Wellfleet. Dozens of smaller islands, primarily small barrier islands or sandbars, dot the Cape.

Natural hazards: Severe winter storms called nor'easters

There is a sumptuous variety about the New England weather that compels the stranger's admiration— and regret. The weather is always doing something there; always attending strictly to business; always getting up new designs and trying them on people to see how they will go. But it gets through more business in Spring than in any other season. In the Spring I have counted one hundred and thirty-six different kinds of weather inside of twenty-four hours.

Mark Twain, 1876

Economy

The once-thriving fishing industry has been in severe decline in the past decade. The Cape economy now relies heavily on tourism. Each year, the Cape is becoming more of a year-round vacation destination, boosting its economy.

Median household income: $45,933

Persons below poverty level: 15,021
Major industry: Tourism: 23.1%
Annual visitor trips: 4.7 million
Summer labor force: 130,220
Winter labor force: 96,839
Number of businesses: 8,554
Agricultural products: Cranberries, fish, and shellfish

Environment

Flora: Cape Cod's thousands of species of flora include pine, beech, chestnut, sassafras, sheep laurel, buttonbush, cedar, large cranberries, willows, hickory, holly, and maple.

Fauna: On the land Cape Cod is home to bats, chipmunks, woodchucks, squirrels, mice, meadow vole, muskrat, coyote, red fox, raccoon, mink, river otter, white-tailed deer, and dozens of frogs, snakes, and turtles. Off the coast the Cape hosts harbor and gray seals, four types of baleen whales, two varieties of toothed whales, 15 saltwater fish, and 10 freshwater fish.

Environmental issues: Erosion, water and air pollution, rapid build-out and increased population density.

Land area developed: 44%
Land area protected: 39%
Number of visits to Cape Cod National Seashore: 4.5 million

Did You Know?

- Vehicles cross the Cape Cod Canal more than 99,700 times a year.

- Nantucket County has only one traffic light.

- Scrod, a popular option on Cape dinner menus, is not a specific fish but any white fish catch of the day.

- Route 6 is the longest highway in the United States, beginning on Cape Cod and ending in California.

- The town of Gosnold on Cuttyhunk has the smallest population in Massachusetts: 86.

- Wellfleet is famous for its oysters; neighboring Eastham is renowned for its turnips.

- Nantucket is the only place in America that is an island, a county, and a town with the same name for all.

- The oldest house on Cape Cod is called the Hoxie House, built in Sandwich in 1637.

- Cape Cod anglers harvest bluefin tuna offshore and sell it primarily to Japan for sashimi.

- Both bridges leading to the Cape are closed down in hurricanes if the winds reach 74 mph.

- The biggest lobster ever caught was trapped off the Cape Cod coast in 1974 and weighed 37.4 pounds.

- Barnstable's Sturgis Library is the oldest library in the United States, built in 1644.

THE CAPE'S SIX SEASONS

SO MUCH HAS BEEN MADE of the difference between "the season" and "the off-season" that you might think a magic switch flicks Cape Cod on and off. The truth is something more complicated. Far from having only two seasons, much less the traditional four, the Cape really has six identifiable seasons, each distinct and dramatic.

From early April until Memorial Day, it's spring—a season that can be beautiful, bursting with wildflowers and green grass. Locals shake out the kinks and get ready. In the old days you could smell tar and pitch as fishermen prepared their nets for another season at sea. Now, you're likelier to smell paint as bed-and-breakfast owners put on a fresh coat. Provincetown's exotic little gardens, nurturing unusual plants brought home from seaports around the world, are in their glory. And it's a great time to enjoy bird walks, nature hikes, and country drives, along with lower prices and a lack of crowds.

"The season" is generally thought to start on Memorial Day, but, in fact, the holiday is a quick and busy harbinger, nothing more. After the long weekend a lull sets in that lasts until the end of June, when schools finally let out. The weather is still iffy—balmy one minute, freezing the next—but everything is open, and not too many summer people have arrived yet. It's the calm before the rush—more anticipation than real hustle.

Then, all at once, comes the high tide of visitors—from late June through early September, with surges on July 4 and Labor Day. Inns, restaurants, beaches, and roads can be packed; everything is open and bustling, and the weather can be warm and beautiful. It's not a time for people who don't enjoy being in a crowd at least occasionally, although it's always possible to walk a bit farther on the beach and escape everyone.

Some people find the spell between Labor Day and Columbus Day the most intriguing time on the Cape. School's back in session, so families are gone. Yet summer often sticks around. And the ocean, not nearly as fickle as the air, holds on to its warmth. Many people not tied to summer vacations have discovered this so-called shoulder season.

Columbus Day to New Year's becomes a time of slow retraction. Under crisp blue skies in the clear autumn light, the Lower Cape's cover of heather, gorse, cranberry, bayberry, box berry, and beach plum resembles, in Thoreau's words, "the richest rug imaginable spread over an uneven surface." Oaks and swamp maples burnish into beautiful, subtle tones, and fields of marsh grass that were green just a few weeks ago become tawny, like a miniature African savanna. Thanksgiving is a particularly evocative moment, when the Cape's Pilgrim history comes to the fore.

And then—winter. The mainland generally gets more snow than the Cape, but nonetheless, it's a stark, tough time. The landscape has a desolate, moorish quality, which makes the inns and restaurants that do remain open all the more inviting. Many museums and shops close, although a year-round economy has emerged, especially around Hyannis, Falmouth, and Orleans. The Cape's community-theater network continues throughout the year, and many golf courses remain open, except when it snows (some open their courses to cross-country skiers). Intimate B&Bs and inns make romantic retreats after a day of ice fishing or pond skating.

Still, the farther toward the fringes you get, the quieter life becomes. If you believe that less can be more, this is the time to discover what others never could have found during the hectic high-season months.

Many towns on the Cape celebrate Christmas in an old-fashioned way, with wandering carolers and bands, theatrical performances, crafts sales, and holiday house tours. The Cape's holiday season extends from Thanksgiving to New Year's, with celebratory activities including First Night celebrations in many towns.

—Seth Rolbein

A BRIEF HISTORY OF THE CAPE

THE FORTUNES OF CAPE COD have always been linked to the sea. For centuries fishermen in search of a livelihood, explorers in search of new worlds, and pilgrims of one sort or another in search of a new life—down to the beach-bound tourists of today—all have turned to the waters around this narrow peninsula arcing into the Atlantic to fulfill their needs and ambitions.

Although some maintain that Iceland Viking Thorvald broke his keel on the shoals here in 1004, European exploration of Cape Cod most likely dates from 1602, when Bartholomew Gosnold sailed from Falmouth, England, to investigate the American coast for trade opportunities. He first anchored off what is now Provincetown and named the cape for the great quantities of cod his crew managed to catch. He then moved on to Cuttyhunk, in the Elizabeth Islands (which he named for the queen); on leaving after a few weeks, he noted the crew was "much fatter and in better health than when we went out of England." Samuel de Champlain, explorer and geographer for the king of France, visited in 1605 and 1606; his encounter with the resident Wampanoag tribe in the Chatham area resulted in deaths on both sides.

None of these visits, however, led to settlement; that began only with the chance landing of the Pilgrims, some of whom were Separatists rebelling from enforced membership in the Church of England, others merchants looking for economic opportunity. On September 16, 1620, the *Mayflower*, with 101 passengers, set out from Plymouth, England, for an area of land granted them by the Virginia Company (Jamestown had been settled in 1607). After more than two months at sea in the crowded boat, they saw land; it was far north of their intended destination, but after the stormy passage and in light of the approach of winter, they put in at Provincetown Harbor on November 21. Before going ashore they drew up the Mayflower Compact, America's first document establishing self-governance, because they were in an area under no official jurisdiction, and dissension had already begun to surface.

Setting off in a small boat, a party led by Captain Myles Standish made a number of expeditions over several weeks, seeking a suitable site for a settlement in the wilderness of woods and scrub. Finally they chose Plymouth and there established the colony, governed by William Bradford, that is today re-created at Plimoth Plantation.

Over the next 20 years settlers spread north and south from Plymouth. The first parts of Cape Cod to be settled were the bay-side sections of Sandwich, Barnstable, and Yarmouth (all incorporated in 1639), along an old Indian trail that is now Route 6A. Most of the newcomers hunted, farmed, and fished; salt hay from the marshes was used to feed cattle and roof houses.

The first homes built by the English settlers on Cape Cod were wigwams built of twigs, bark, hides, cornstalks, and grasses, which they copied from those of the local Wampanoag people who had lived here for thousands of years before the Europeans arrived. Eventually, the settlers stripped the land of its forests to make farmland, graze sheep, and build more European-style homes, though with a new-world look all their own. The steep-roof saltbox and the Cape Cod cottage—still the most popular style of house on the Cape and copied all over the country—were designed to accommodate growing families.

A newly married couple might begin by building a one- or two-room half-Cape, a rather lopsided 1½-story building with a door on one side of the facade and two windows on the other; a single chimney rose up on the wall behind the door. As the family grew, an addition might be built on the other side of the door large enough for a single window, turning the half-Cape into a three-quarter-Cape; a two-window addition would make it a symmetrical full Cape. Additions built onto the sides and back were called warts. An interesting feature of some Cape houses is the graceful bow roof, slightly curved like the bottom of a boat (not surprising, since ships' carpenters did much of the house building as well). More noticeable, often in the older houses, is a profusion of small, irregularly shaped and located windows in the gable ends; Thoreau wrote of one such house that it looked as if each of the various occupants "had punched a hole where his necessities required it." Many ancient houses have been turned into historical museums. In some, docents take you on a tour of the times as you pass from the keeping room—the heart of the house, where meals were cooked at a great hearth before which the family gathered for warmth—to the nearby borning room, in whose warmth babies were born and the sick were tended, to the relatively showy front parlors, where company was entertained. Summer and winter kitchens, backyard pumps, beehive ovens, elaborate raised-wall paneling, wide-board pine flooring, wainscoting, a doll made of corn husks, a spinning wheel, a stereopticon, a hand-stitched sampler or glove—each of these historic remnants gives a glimpse into the daily life of another age.

The Wampanoags taught the settlers what they knew of the land and how to live off it. Early on they showed them how to strip and process blubber from whales that became stranded on the beaches. To coax more whales onto the beach, men would sometimes surround them in small boats and make a commotion in the water with their oars until the whales swam to their doom in the only direction left open

to them. By the mid-18th century, as the supply of near-shore whales thinned out, the hunt for the far-flung sperm whale began, growing into a major New England industry and making many a sea captain's fortune. Wellfleet, Truro, and Provincetown were the only ports on the Cape that could support deepwater distance whaling (and these were overtaken by Nantucket and New Bedford), but ports along the bay conducted active trade with packet ships carrying goods and passengers to and from Boston. Cape seamen were in great demand for ships sailing from Boston, New York, and other deepwater ports. In the mid-19th century the Cape saw its most prosperous days, thanks largely to the whaling industry.

The decline in whaling hit the economy hard, and the Cape began cultivating tourism in the 19th century. Whereas previously people traveled from Boston to and along the Cape only by stagecoach or packet boat, in 1848 the first train service from Boston began, reaching to Sandwich; by 1873 it had been extended little by little to Provincetown. In the 1890s President Grover Cleveland made his Bourne residence (now gone) the Cape's first "summer White House" (to be followed in the 1960s by John F. Kennedy). Grand seaside resorts grew up for summering families, and Cape Cod began to court visitors actively.

Artists were drawn to Provincetown starting in the early part of the 20th century. In 1899 Charles W. Hawthorne opened the Cape Cod School of Art and taught the Impressionist *en plein air* (outdoors) style on the beach. It was the first of several art schools established over the next few years that promoted Provincetown as an art colony. Writers (including John Reed and the young Eugene O'Neill) started the Provincetown Players, which would be the germ of Cape community theater and professional summer-stock companies. The Barnstable Comedy Club, founded in 1922 and still going strong, is the most notable of the area's many amateur groups; novelist Kurt Vonnegut acted in its productions in the 1950s and 1960s and had some of his early plays produced by the group. Professional summer stock began with the still-healthy Cape Playhouse in Dennis in 1927, and its early years featured Bette Davis (who was first an usher), Henry Fonda, Ruth Gordon, Humphrey Bogart, and Gertrude Lawrence. In 1928 the University Players Guild (which later became the Falmouth Playhouse, and subsequently closed) opened in Falmouth, attracting the likes of James Cagney, Orson Welles, Josh Logan, Tallulah Bankhead, and Jimmy Stewart (who, while on summer vacation from Princeton, had his first bit part during Falmouth's first season).

The idea of a Cape Cod canal, linking the bay to the sound, was studied as early as the 17th century, but not until 1914 did the privately built canal merge the waters of the two bays. It was not, however, a thunderous success; too narrow and winding, the canal allowed only one-way traffic and created dangerous currents. The federal government bought it in 1928 and had the U.S. Army Corps of Engineers rebuild it. In the 1930s three bridges—two traffic and one railroad—went up, and the rest is the latter-day history of tourism on Cape Cod.

The building of the Mid Cape Highway (U.S. 6) in the 1950s marked the great boom in the Cape's growth, and the presidency of John F. Kennedy, who summered in Hyannis Port, certainly added to the area's allure. In 1961 President Kennedy signed the legislation that established Cape Cod National Seashore. Today the Cape's summer population is more than 500,000, 2½ times the year-round population.

Though tourism, construction, and light industry are the mainstays of the Cape's economy these days, the earliest inhabitants' occupations have not disappeared. There are still more than 40 farms on the Cape, and the fishing industry—including lobstering, scalloping, and oyster aquaculture, as well as the fruits of fishing fleets such as those in Provincetown and Chatham—is still thriving.

Visitors are still drawn here by the sea: scientists come to delve into the mysteries of the deep, artists come for the light, and everyone comes for the charm of the beach towns, the beauty of the white sand, the softness of the breezes, and the roaring of the surf.

EATING AND DRINKING IN PROVINCETOWN

PROVINCETOWN IS, OF COURSE, part of New England, a region of hard-knobbed hills and low mountains rising up from a cold ocean amenable only to crustaceans, squids, and some of the hardier, less glamorous finned fish; cods and blues, flounder and bass; fish that tend toward practical shapes, the torpedo or the platter; fish with powerful jaws and blunt, businesslike heads and sleek strong bodies of gunmetal, pewter, or muddy brown. The soil around there produces almost nothing delicate—no fragile or thin-skinned fruits, no tentative greens that would expire in a cold snap, hardly anything that can reasonably be eaten raw. Cranberries and pumpkins do well; bivalves flourish in the chill waters. It is most agreeable to that which has developed thick rinds or shells. If New England has been, from its inception, home to preternaturally determined human settlers, to those who equate hardship with virtue, its Puritan and Calvinist roots are apparent in its diet, which runs not only, of necessity, to that which must have the toughness boiled out of it before it can be served but which tends to eschew, by choice, any spices more flamboyant than slat and pepper. When a friend of mine moved from New Orleans to Boston, she said one night in exasperation, after another bland and sensible meal, "You notice they didn't call it New *France*. You notice they didn't call it New *Italy*."

Fresh fish is Provincetown's most prominent glory, and most fabulous among its fish, to me, are the clams and oysters that come from the tidal flats of Wellfleet, two towns away. A Wellfleet oyster, especially in the colder months, is supernal: firm and immaculately saline, a little mouthful of the Atlantic itself. One autumn several years ago when I was staying for a few days with a friend, she came home in the afternoon with a bucket each of clams and oysters she had dug from the flats in Wellfleet, bearded with bright brown seaweed, and a huge bouquet of wild irises, dark as bruises, with tight, cogent little blossoms so unlike the paler, more ephemeral irises sold in flower shops it was hard to believe they were the same flower at all. It is possible to stride out into the landscape and return not only with dinner but with flowers for for the table as well.

Fresh local fish is not, however, as abundant in the restaurants of Provincetown as you might expect it to be. A century or more of excess has depleted the surrounding ocean, and much of what can still be coaxed from the water is bedded in ice and shipped elsewhere. There are only two or three raw bars in town, where you can actually procure shellfish forked out of the sand nearby. Fried clams are easier to find, and while a proper clam roll—crisply fried clams with briny, gelatinous bellies served on a grilled hot dog bun—is a marvelous thing, the precise origins and even the pristine freshness of the clams in question are not matters of great concern. Squid and scallops, among the less endangered inhabitants of these waters, are mysteriously hard to find in restaurants in town, and you're at least as likely to be offered fresh cod in New York or Philadelphia as you are in Provincetown.

To whatever extent a discernible local cuisine exists, it is Portuguese. The Portuguese food most common in New England runs to soups and stews, whatever can be simmered until its fibrousness or bitterness begins to yield. Kale soup studded with circles of linguiça, a Portuguese sausage, is a staple, as are dark, tomato-based squid stews and salt cod in various forms. Some of the local Portuguese families still dry cod in their yards, either laid out flat on the ground or hung from the limbs of trees. But Portuguese food, too, is increasingly hard to find, at least in part because the restaurants of Provincetown have, for some time now, aspired to a certain pan-American sophistication that tends to involve the same pasta and chicken, the same tuna and salmon and beef, that you can get just about anywhere. Generally speaking, you are best advised while in Provincetown to forget any protracted search for indigenous foods and just eat and drink whatever most appeals to you. You need not seek out the rare or quintessential; no one back home will be disappointed if you've failed to taste something famous that's made in a seaside cavern and aged ten years in kelp, or that's been retrieved by specially trained ferrets from the upper branches of particular trees, or that secretes a deadly venom unless harvested at the apogee of the full moon. You are free.

— by Michael Cunningham

HOME, SWEET RENTAL HOME

ONE OF THE JOYS of a Cape Cod vacation can be renting a furnished house—one with plenty of space to accommodate extended families or groups of friends, a backyard or deck where you can kick back with a cool drink, and a kitchen where you can boil up some lobsters. If a house rental is in your plans, you must act early. Cape realtors report it's not unusual to get bookings a year in advance, and by January in some years, the summer pickings in many prime beachfront areas may already be getting slim.

Most Cape Cod house rentals run weekly, from Saturday to Saturday—you can move in on Saturday afternoon, and you must be out the following Saturday morning. There may be some flexibility outside the peak summer season of July 4 through Labor Day, but otherwise you'll have to cross the bridges with the rest of the week-to-week renters. Two-week minimums for some choicer properties are not uncommon. Note that summer rental prices can vary, even from week to week, depending on the most popular times; early to mid-June and mid- to late-September prices may be a bit lower.

If you're planning a summer rental, here are some tips on making arrangements:

Decide where you'd like to be. Most Cape realtors deal with a particular town or area, so narrow your search before you start asking about houses. Do you want to be on Cape Cod Bay or Nantucket Sound, or close to the beaches of the Cape Cod National Seashore? Will you stay put, or do you want a central location that lets you explore the Cape easily? The towns on the Cape have different personalities, and that will be part of your decision making.

Know what you'll need. How many bedrooms (with how many beds) and how many bathrooms? Is there a washer and dryer? Is there a telephone? How about a television? What about a yard or a deck? How close to the beach? Is a water view important? Or a quiet street where the children can play? Do you want to be close to a supermarket and other stores, or are you willing to drive a bit?

Ask what's included. Most Cape rentals do not include linens, so you'll need to bring your own sheets and towels. Many do provide a cleaning service before you arrive and after you leave, but ask whether you're responsible for taking trash to the dump or for handling other cleanup tasks. Check ahead of time about any recycling regulations. Inquire about using the phone; some owners restrict their tenants to local calls, while others ask for a deposit to cover your phone bill. If you want anything special—a crib, bicycles, a barbecue grill, air-conditioning—be sure to ask.

Use the Internet. Many realtors post property listings—with photos—on their Web sites, and a growing number of property owners handle their own rentals via the Internet. If you can't visit properties in person, be sure to ask the realtor or owner for pictures of the house, either by post or by e-mail. What is described as cozy may turn out to be cramped, and old-fashioned may sometimes be run-down; photos will help avoid misunderstandings.

Don't forget the beach permits. Before you head for the Cape, ask your realtor or the local chamber of commerce about beach stickers. Many towns with resident-only beaches or ponds will sell you a weekly beach permit if you present a copy of your lease at the town hall or the town recreation department.

Then pack up the family, pick up some lobsters, and relax in that lawn chair. At least for the week, you're home.

— Carolyn Heller

FURTHER READING

Authors and artists cross the Cape Cod Canal and quickly find themselves inspired to create work to salute the area's beauty. Cape natives are also compelled to share their sacred place with the rest of the world. The result is a vast number of books, from hard-to-find, locally published autobiographical reminiscences to handsomely illustrated coffee-table books from national publishers. You can explore some of these before your trip at your local library, bookstore, or online bookseller, but try to make time to visit some of the many excellent bookstores on the Cape. You may well make a special discovery that will illuminate your stay or inspire your own creation. For information about local newspapers and magazines, *see* Media *in* Smart Travel Tips A to Z.

General

The classic works on Cape Cod are Henry David Thoreau's readable and often entertaining *Cape Cod,* an account of his walking tours in the mid-1800s, and Henry Beston's 1928 *The Outermost House,* which chronicles the seasons during a solitary year in a cabin at ocean's edge. Both reveal the character of Cape Codders and are rich in tales and local lore, as well as observations of nature and its processes. *Cape Cod Pilot,* by Josef Berger (alias Jeremiah Digges), is a Works Progress Administration guidebook from 1937 that is filled with "whacking good yarns" about everything from religion to fishing, as well as a lot of still-useful information. *A Place Apart: A Cape Cod Reader* (1993), edited by Robert Finch, includes stories about the Cape from dozens of writers, from Herman Melville to Adam Gopnik. Harry Kemp's Provincetown classic *Poet of the Dunes* peeks into the bohemian lifestyle of the famed Kemp with writings composed in his dune shack.

History

Cape Cod, Its People & Their History, by Henry C. Kittredge (first published in 1930), is the standard history of the area,

told with anecdotes and style as well as scholarship. *Becoming Cape Cod: Creating a Seaside Resort* (2003) by James O'Connell accounts the evolution of the tourist industry on Cape Cod illustrated with the author's collection of rare historical postcards. Now out of print, *Sand in Their Shoes,* compiled by Edith and Frank Shay, is a compendium of writings on Cape Cod life throughout history. *Of Plimoth Plantation* is Governor William Bradford's 17th-century description of the Pilgrims' voyage to, and early years in, the New World. Nathaniel Philbrick's *In the Heart of the Sea, The tragedy of the Whaleship Essex* (2002) recounts one of the greatest maritime disasters in history, the story which inspired *Moby Dick,* based on written accounts of the few who survived. *Art in Narrow Streets,* by Ross Moffett; *Figures in a Landscape,* by Josephine Del Deo; *Provincetown as a Stage,* by Leona Rust Egan; and *Time and the Town: A Provincetown Chronicle,* by Provincetown Playhouse founder Mary Heaton Vorse, paint the social landscape of Provincetown in the first half of the 20th century, concentrating on the lives and contributions of the many writers, artists, and actors who flocked to the town. Paul Schneider's book, *The Enduring Shore: A History of Cape Cod, Martha's Vineyard, and Nantucket,* chronicles the region's past. P-town's enduring history is explored by Pulitzer Prize–winning author Michael Cunningham in *Land's End: A Walk Through Provincetown.* Also worthy is Peter Manso's *Ptown: Art, Sex, and Money on the Outer Cape.* The controversial *Invisible Eden: A Story of Love and Murder on Cape Cod* (2003) by Maria Flook is an intriguing beach read of "literary nonfiction" that chronicles the 2002 murder of a famed fashion writer in her Truro home. An illustrated history for children, *Cape Cod Light: The Lighthouse at Dangerfield* (2002) by Paul Giambarba recalls the lost profession of lighthouse keeping at the

Cape's oldest lighthouse. *In the Footsteps of Thoreau: 25 Historic and Nature Walks on Cape Cod,* by Adam Gamble, is a useful guide for naturalists and Thoreau admirers. For baseball fans, Christopher Price's *Baseball by the Beach: A History of America's National Pastime on Cape Cod* provides a portrait of the Cape Cod Baseball League and the Cape's version of summer on the sandlots. *The Cape Cod Canal,* by Robert Farson, traces the history of the Cape Cod Canal. *America's Landfall: the Historic Lighthouses of Cape Cod, Nantucket & Martha's Vineyard* by Donald W. Davidson is a comprehensive history of the area's beloved beacons.

Fiction

Herman Melville's *Moby-Dick,* set on a 19th-century Nantucket whaling ship, captures the spirit of the whaling era. *Cape Cod,* by William Martin, is a historical novel and mystery following two families from the *Mayflower* voyage to the present, with lots of Cape history and flavor along the way. Norman Mailer's *Tough Guys Don't Dance* is a murder mystery set in Provincetown and Truro, and several other novels use Provincetown as a setting, including *Resuscitation of a Hanged Man,* by Denis Johnson, and Anne LeClaire's *Grace Point.* Other writers who have set books on the Cape are Margot Arnold, Rick Boyer, Philip A. Craig, Virginia Rich, Marie Lee, Alice Hoffman, Jane Langton, David Osborn, and Phoebe Atwood Taylor. *Cape Cod Stories,* edited by John Miller, is a collection of Cape-related short fiction by such luminaries as Edgar Allen Poe, John Cheever, and Sylvia Plath. *Cape Discovery,* edited by Bruce Smith and Catherine Gammon, an anthology of poetry and fiction by former fellows of the Fine Arts Work Center in Provincetown, includes the work of noted contemporary American writers such as Louise Glück, Michael Cunningham, Dean Albarelli, and Maria Flook. Many of the poems in *Passing Through,* Pulitzer Prize–winning poet Stanley Kunitz's collection, evoke the natural beauty of the Cape, and several refer to his garden on Commercial Street in Provincetown.

Memoirs

In *Heaven's Coast,* Mark Doty, a Provincetown writer, recounts the death of his lover, Wally Roberts, from complications caused by AIDS. In a similar vein, David Gessner's *A Wild, Rank Place: One Year on Cape Cod* combines insights about the Cape with reminiscence about battling cancer and confronting his father's death. In *The Salt House: A Summer on the Dunes of Cape Cod,* Cynthia Huntington describes a summer during the first year of her marriage spent in a tiny Outer Cape beach shack called Euphoria, while Gladys Taber chronicles her life on the Cape at Still Cove in *My Own Cape Cod.* Journalist Alec Wilkinson portrays a different side of Cape life in *Midnights: A Year with the Wellfleet Police.* In *House on Nauset Marsh,* Wyman Richardson observes life on the Cape in the 1940s and 1950s. *Once Upon Cape Cod* and *Cape Cod Lucky: In Another Time* are collections of essays about 13th-generation Cape Codder Dana Eldridge's boyhood on Cape Cod. In *Haunted Cape Cod & the Islands,* Mark Jasper interviews local property owners who recall ghostly experiences at their inns, homes, shops, and restaurants.

Natural History

Robert Finch, editor of *A Place Apart,* has also written four lyrical books about natural history: *The Cape Itself, Outlands: Journeys to the Outer Edges of Cape Cod, Common Ground: A Naturalist's Cape Cod,* and *The Primal Place,* a meditation about life on the Cape, especially its natural rhythms and history. Finch is also the author of *Death of a Hornet and Other Cape Cod Essays* and the attractively illustrated *Cape Cod: Its Natural and Cultural History,* a National Park Service handbook about the National Seashore and the Cape and *Special Places on Cape Cod and the Islands* with 24 essays about the Cape's delicate areas owned and managed by town conservation commissions or private trusts. *In the Company of Light* traces John Hay's journey from Maine to Cape Cod, recounting his observations of light and luminescence—in nature and as revelation. Hay is a wonderful nature writer; his other titles include *The Run,* about the life cycle of alewives, and *Great Beach. A Guide to Nature on Cape Cod and the Islands,* edited by Greg O'Brien, has sections by a variety of experts on the area's flora and fauna.

Outdoors

In *Adventure Kayaking: Trips on Cape Cod: Includes Cape Cod National Seashore,* David Weintraub outlines routes suitable for beginners to experts interested in kayaking Cape Cod's waterways. *Paddling Cape Cod: A Coastal Explorer's Guide* by Shirley and Fred Bull takes you on 35 trips to the nooks and crannies of the Cape's waterways to experience wildlife. Ned Friary and Glenda Bendure's *Walk & Rambles on Cape Cod and the Islands: A Naturalist's Hiking Guide* leads you to the areas best sights to stroll. Gene

Bourque's *Fishing New England: A Cape Cod Shore Guide* is published by local fishing experts at *On the Water* publications. If you want to snag a prized striped bass, Bill Quinn's *Striped Bass & Other Cape Cod Fishing: A Fisherman's Guide to Cape Cod Bay and the National Seashore* offers the tips to improve your chances.

Photography

Cape Cod and the National Seashore (2003) and *Provincetown and the National Seashore* (2002), both by Charles Fields, take you on a photographic journey through the Cape's seasons on the stark Outer Cape. Fields captures serene, unblemished sites with the aid of the Cape's ethereal lighting and fog-laden skies. *A Summer's Day* (winner of the 1985 Ansel Adams Award for Best Photography Book) and *Cape Light* present color landscapes, still lifes, and portraits by Provincetown-associated photographer Joel Meyerowitz. *Cape Cod: Gardens and Houses* is a collection of photographs by Gred Hadley and Taylor Lewis with accompanying text by Catherine Fallin.

INDEX

NOTES

NOTES

NOTES

NOTES

NOTES

NOTES

NOTES

FODOR'S KEY TO THE GUIDES

America's guidebook leader publishes guides for every kind of traveler.
Check out our many series and find your perfect match.

FODOR'S GOLD GUIDES
America's favorite travel-guide series
offers the most detailed insider reviews
of hotels, restaurants, and attractions in
all price ranges, plus great background
information, smart tips, and useful maps.

COMPASS AMERICAN GUIDES
Stunning guides from top local writers
and photographers, with gorgeous
photos, literary excerpts, and colorful
anecdotes. A must-have for culture
mavens, history buffs, and new residents.

FODOR'S CITYPACKS
Concise city coverage in a guide plus a
foldout map. The right choice for urban
travelers who want everything under
one cover.

FODOR'S EXPLORING GUIDES
Hundreds of color photos bring your
destination to life. Lively stories lend
insight into the culture, history, and
people.

FODOR'S TRAVEL HISTORIC AMERICA
For travelers who want to experience
history firsthand, this series gives in-
depth coverage of historic sights, plus
nearby restaurants and hotels. Themes
include the Thirteen Colonies, the Old
West, and the Lewis and Clark Trail.

FODOR'S POCKET GUIDES
For travelers who need only the
essentials. The best of Fodor's in pocket-
size packages for just $9.95.

FODOR'S FLASHMAPS
Every resident's map guide, with dozens
of easy-to-follow maps of
public transit, restaurants, shopping,
museums, and more.

FODOR'S CITYGUIDES
Sourcebooks for living in the city:
thousands of in-the-know listings for
restaurants, shops, sports, nightlife,
and other city resources.

FODOR'S AROUND THE CITY WITH KIDS
Up to 68 great ideas for family days,
recommended by resident parents.
Perfect for exploring in your own
backyard or on the road.

FODOR'S HOW TO GUIDES
Get tips from the pros on planning the
perfect trip. Learn how to pack, fly
hassle-free, plan a honeymoon or cruise,
stay healthy on the road, and travel with
your baby.

FODOR'S LANGUAGES FOR TRAVELERS
Practice the local language before you
hit the road. Available in phrase books,
cassette sets, and CD sets.

KAREN BROWN'S GUIDES
Engaging guides—many with easy-to-
follow inn-to-inn itineraries—to the
most charming inns and B&Bs in the
U.S.A. and Europe.

SEE IT GUIDES
Illustrated guidebooks that include the
practical information travelers need,
in gorgeous full color. Thousands of
photos, hundreds of restaurant and
hotel reviews, prices, and ratings for
attractions all in one indispensable
package. Perfect for travelers who want
the best value packed in a fresh, easy-
to-use, colorful layout.

OTHER GREAT TITLES FROM FODOR'S
Baseball Vacations, The Complete
Guide to the National Parks, Family
Vacations, Golf Digest's Places to Play,
Great American Drives of the East,
Great American Drives of the West,
Great American Vacations, Healthy
Escapes, National Parks of the West,
Skiing USA.